lonely planet

Copenhagen

Glenda Bendure
Ned Friary

LONELY PLANET PUBLICATIONS
Melbourne • Oakland • London • Paris

Copenhagen
1st edition – June 2001

Published by
Lonely Planet Publications Pty Ltd ABN 36 005 607 983
90 Maribyrnong St, Footscray, Victoria 3011, Australia

Lonely Planet Offices
Australia Locked Bag 1, Footscray, Victoria 3011
USA 150 Linden St, Oakland, CA 94607
UK 10a Spring Place, London NW5 3BH
France 1 rue du Dahomey, 75011 Paris

Photographs
All of the images in this guide are available for licensing from
Lonely Planet Images.
email: lpi@lonelyplanet.com.au

Front cover photograph
Oi! Who's that bloke standing behind the Royal Palace Guardsman?
Copenhagen (Jon Davison)

ISBN 1 86450 203 7

Printed by SNP SPrint (M) Sdn Bhd
Printed in Malaysia

Contents – Text

Contents – Maps

The Authors

Glenda Bendure & Ned Friary

Glenda grew up in California's Mojave Desert and first travelled overseas as a high school AFS exchange student to India. Ned grew up near Boston and studied Social Thought and Political Economy at the University of Massachusetts in Amherst.

After meeting in Santa Cruz, California, where Glenda was finishing up her university studies, they took to the road and spent several years travelling throughout Asia and the Pacific, including stints in Japan where Ned taught English and Glenda edited a monthly magazine. They eventually came back to the States, settled down on Cape Cod in Massachusetts and began to write for Lonely Planet.

In addition to this Copenhagen book, Ned and Glenda are the authors of Lonely Planet's guides to *Denmark, Hawaii, Oahu* and *Bermuda* and they write the Denmark and Norway chapters of Lonely Planet's *Scandinavian & Baltic Europe* guide.

FROM THE AUTHORS

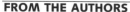

We'd like to thank Lillian Hess of the Danish Tourist Board in New York, Henrik Thierlein of Wonderful Copenhagen and Merethe Andersen at Use It. Thanks also to Irene Greve of the Copenhagen Jazz Festival, Susanne Hartz of the Louisiana modern art museum, Christian Dorow and Malene Simonsen of Hvidovre Kommune, Svend Ravnkilde of the Dansk Musik Informations Center, Charlotte Christiansen of the Traffic Information Center, and Tove and Knud Bøjland in North Zealand.

This Book

From the Publisher

The coordinating editor of this 1st edition was Craig MacKenzie. He was assisted by Carolyn Bain and Elizabeth Swan. The coordinating designer was Cris Gibcus. He was assisted by Csanád Csutoros, Ray Thomson, Mark Griffiths and Paul Clifton. Thanks also to Barbara Dombrowski from Lonely Planet Images. Jamieson Gross produced the cover, Matt King supervised the illustrative content, Emma Koch did likewise with the Language chapter and Mark Germanchis supervised layout.

Foreword

ABOUT LONELY PLANET GUIDEBOOKS

The story begins with a classic travel adventure: Tony and Maureen Wheeler's 1972 journey across Europe and Asia to Australia. Useful information about the overland trail did not exist at that time, so Tony and Maureen published the first Lonely Planet guidebook to meet a growing need.

From a kitchen table, then from a tiny office in Melbourne (Australia), Lonely Planet has become the largest independent travel publisher in the world, an international company with offices in Melbourne, Oakland (USA), London (UK) and Paris (France).

Today Lonely Planet guidebooks cover the globe. There is an ever-growing list of books and there's information in a variety of forms and media. Some things haven't changed. The main aim is still to help make it possible for adventurous travellers to get out there – to explore and better understand the world.

At Lonely Planet we believe travellers can make a positive contribution to the countries they visit – if they respect their host communities and spend their money wisely. Since 1986 a percentage of the income from each book has been donated to aid projects and human rights campaigns.

Updates Lonely Planet thoroughly updates each guidebook as often as possible. This usually means there are around two years between editions, although for more unusual or more stable destinations the gap can be longer. Check the imprint page (following the colour map at the beginning of the book) for publication dates.

Between editions up-to-date information is available in two free newsletters – the paper *Planet Talk* and email *Comet* (to subscribe, contact any Lonely Planet office) – and on our Web site at www.lonelyplanet.com. The *Upgrades* section of the Web site covers a number of important and volatile destinations and is regularly updated by Lonely Planet authors. *Scoop* covers news and current affairs relevant to travellers. And, lastly, the *Thorn Tree* bulletin board and *Postcards* section of the site carry unverified, but fascinating, reports from travellers.

Correspondence The process of creating new editions begins with the letters, postcards and emails received from travellers. This correspondence often includes suggestions, criticisms and comments about the current editions. Interesting excerpts are immediately passed on via newsletters and the Web site, and everything goes to our authors to be verified when they're researching on the road. We're keen to get more feedback from organisations or individuals who represent communities visited by travellers.

Lonely Planet gathers information for everyone who's curious about the planet – and especially for those who explore it first-hand. Through guidebooks, phrasebooks, activity guides, maps, literature, newsletters, image library, TV series and Web site we act as an information exchange for a worldwide community of travellers.

Research Authors aim to gather sufficient practical information to enable travellers to make informed choices and to make the mechanics of a journey run smoothly. They also research historical and cultural background to help enrich the travel experience and allow travellers to understand and respond appropriately to cultural and environmental issues.

Authors don't stay in every hotel because that would mean spending a couple of months in each medium-sized city and, no, they don't eat at every restaurant because that would mean stretching belts beyond capacity. They do visit hotels and restaurants to check standards and prices, but feedback based on readers' direct experiences can be very helpful.

Many of our authors work undercover, others aren't so secretive. None of them accept freebies in exchange for positive write-ups. And none of our guidebooks contain any advertising.

Production Authors submit their raw manuscripts and maps to offices in Australia, USA, UK or France. Editors and cartographers – all experienced travellers themselves – then begin the process of assembling the pieces. When the book finally hits the shops, some things are already out of date, we start getting feedback from readers and the process begins again ...

WARNING & REQUEST

Things change – prices go up, schedules change, good places go bad and bad places go bankrupt – nothing stays the same. So, if you find things better or worse, recently opened or long since closed, please tell us and help make the next edition even more accurate and useful. We genuinely value all the feedback we receive. A well travelled team reads and acknowledges every letter, postcard and email and ensures that every morsel of information finds its way to the appropriate authors, editors and cartographers for verification.

Everyone who writes to us will find their name in the next edition of the appropriate guidebook. They will also receive the latest issue of *Planet Talk*, our quarterly printed newsletter, or *Comet*, our monthly email newsletter. Subscriptions to both newsletters are free. The very best contributions will be rewarded with a free guidebook.

Excerpts from your correspondence may appear in new editions of Lonely Planet guidebooks, the Lonely Planet Web site, *Planet Talk* or *Comet*, so please let us know if you *don't* want your letter published or your name acknowledged.

Send all correspondence to the Lonely Planet office closest to you:

Australia: Locked Bag 1, Footscray, Victoria 3011
USA: 150 Linden St, Oakland, CA 94607
UK: 10A Spring Place, London NW5 3BH
France: 1 rue du Dahomey, 75011 Paris

Or email us at: talk2us@lonelyplanet.com.au

For news, views and updates see our Web site: www.lonelyplanet.com

HOW TO USE A LONELY PLANET GUIDEBOOK

The best way to use a Lonely Planet guidebook is any way you choose. At Lonely Planet we believe the most memorable travel experiences are often those that are unexpected, and the finest discoveries are those you make yourself. Guidebooks are not intended to be used as if they provide a detailed set of infallible instructions!

Contents All Lonely Planet guidebooks follow roughly the same format. The Facts about the Destination chapters or sections give background information ranging from history to weather. Facts for the Visitor gives practical information on issues like visas and health. Getting There & Away gives a brief starting point for researching travel to and from the destination. Getting Around gives an overview of the transport options when you arrive.

The peculiar demands of each destination determine how subsequent chapters are broken up, but some things remain constant. We always start with background, then proceed to sights, places to stay, places to eat, entertainment, getting there and away, and getting around information – in that order.

Heading Hierarchy Lonely Planet headings are used in a strict hierarchical structure that can be visualised as a set of Russian dolls. Each heading (and its following text) is encompassed by any preceding heading that is higher on the hierarchical ladder.

Entry Points We do not assume guidebooks will be read from beginning to end, but that people will dip into them. The traditional entry points are the list of contents and the index. In addition, however, some books have a complete list of maps and an index map illustrating map coverage.

There may also be a colour map that shows highlights. These highlights are dealt with in greater detail in the Facts for the Visitor chapter, along with planning questions and suggested itineraries. Each chapter covering a geographical region usually begins with a locator map and another list of highlights. Once you find something of interest in a list of highlights, turn to the index.

Maps Maps play a crucial role in Lonely Planet guidebooks and include a huge amount of information. A legend is printed on the back page. We seek to have complete consistency between maps and text, and to have every important place in the text captured on a map. Map key numbers usually start in the top left corner. Map and grid references are indicated where appropriate throughout the text.

Although inclusion in a guidebook usually implies a recommendation we cannot list every good place. Exclusion does not necessarily imply criticism. In fact there are a number of reasons why we might exclude a place – sometimes it is simply inappropriate to encourage an influx of travellers.

Introduction

Copenhagen (København), Scandinavia's largest and liveliest city, is home to a quarter of all Danes. It's an appealing and still largely low-rise city comprised of block after block of period six-storey buildings. Church steeples add a nice punctuation to the skyline and only a couple of modern buildings burst up to mar the scene.

Capital of Denmark since the early 15th century, Copenhagen grew by gradually radiating out from its centre; consequently most of the city's foremost historical and cultural sites remain concentrated in a relatively small area. Parks, gardens, water fountains, squares and green areas lace the city centre. Along the waterfront you'll find the scenic rowhouses that line Nyhavn, the famed statue of the Little Mermaid and the canal-cut district of Christianshavn.

Copenhagen has a lot to offer, no matter what your interest. Historic or modern, gay or straight, sleek shops or cosy cafes – it's all right in the heart of the city.

A cosmopolitan city, Copenhagen boasts a plethora of sightseeing and entertainment possibilities. For music lovers and other revellers, there's an active nightlife that buzzes into the early hours of the morning, and for sightseers the city has a treasure-trove of old churches, museums and castles to explore.

As for Danes themselves, they've come a long way since those ruthless Viking days, Denmark having become the epitome of civilised society with its progressive policies, widespread tolerance and liberal social welfare system.

Copenhageners of all persuasions tend to be fun-loving and you can get a sense of that throughout the city. You'll find the pedestrianised street Strøget teeming with the music of street performers, the nearby Latin Quarter peppered with spirited clubs and the venerable Tivoli park offering family-oriented amusements – all within minutes of each other. You can hop on a canal boat and tour the waterfront, admire the world's finest collection of Viking relics, lunch on *smørrebrød* sandwiches and Danish beer at outdoor cafes and dance till the sun rises at trendy clubs.

For a big city, Copenhagen is surprisingly easy to get around. It's a particularly pleasant place for walking, as many of the sightseeing areas and shopping districts in the city centre are reserved for pedestrians. For those who prefer to move at a faster pace, there are bicycle lanes on Copenhagen's main roads and a unique system of free bikes, as well as an excellent metropolitan bus and train system.

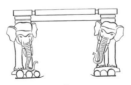

Facts about Copenhagen

HISTORY
Founding of Copenhagen

Until the mid-12th century Copenhagen was a lightly settled trading hamlet surrounded by salt marsh. King Valdemar I, wanting to put an end to the free movement of marauding Wends who were staging frequent raids along the East Zealand coast, turned the area over to his close friend Bishop Absalon of Roskilde. Absalon, who was from one of Zealand's most prominent families, was not only a religious leader but also a successful military commander.

The city of Copenhagen dates its founding to 1167, when Absalon constructed a fortress on Slotsholmen Island, fortifying the previously unprotected harbourside village with ramparts and a moat. Under the guidance of Absalon, a series of successful crusades into eastern Germany were launched against the Wends.

In the years that followed, the harbourside village expanded and took on the name Kømandshavn (Merchant's Port), which over time was condensed to København. The port did much of its trade in salted herring, which was in high demand, in part due to the religious restrictions against eating meat during Catholic holy days, such as Lent.

Perched on the edge of the Baltic Sea and just across the sound from Sweden, Copenhagen grew in importance as a regional trade centre. Its success made it a target of the powerful Hanseatic League, the northern German traders who dominated Baltic commerce. The league attacked Copenhagen several times, and in a particularly fierce battle in 1369, Absalon's fortress was destroyed. To stop the raids the Danish Crown agreed to pay an annual ransom and give the league a voice in Danish affairs.

In 1376 construction began on a new Slotsholmen fortification, Copenhagen Castle. In the years that followed the Crown wrested control of the city from the church. In 1416 King Erik of Pomerania took up residence at the castle, marking the beginning of Copenhagen's role as the capital of Denmark. He also moved the headquarters of his navy and army to Copenhagen.

During this era the Danish Crown convinced Norway and Sweden to join Denmark in an alliance known as the Kalmar Union. A primary objective of the union was to counter the influence of the powerful Hanseatic League. The Danish monarchy, which by marriage had intertwined royal ties with the other two countries, headed the union. In essence the union made Copenhagen not only capital of Denmark but of the tri-country Kalmar Union as well.

As it turned out, Erik of Pomerania had a penchant for appointing Danes to public offices in Sweden and Norway, which soured native aristocrats in those countries and in 1438 the Swedish council withdrew from the union, whereupon the Danish nobility deposed Erik.

Erik's successor, the Danish king Christopher III, made amends and was accepted as king by both Norway and Sweden. The union continued to be a rocky one, however, marred by Swedish rebellions and a few fully fledged wars between Denmark and Sweden. In 1523 the Swedes elected their own king, Gustav Vasa, and the Kalmar Union was permanently dissolved. Norway, however, remained under Danish rule for another three centuries.

Reformation & Civil War

A pivotal power struggle involving the monarchy and the Catholic Church was played out during the Danish Reformation. Frederik I ascended the throne in 1523, promising to fight heresy against Catholicism, but in an attempt to weaken the influence of Danish bishops he switched course and instead invited Lutheran preachers to Denmark. Their fiery messages against the corrupt power of the Catholic Church, which over the centuries had accumulated an ungodly amount of property and wealth, found a ready ear among the disenchanted.

The king governed in consultation with the Rigsråd, a powerful national council comprised of nobles and bishops. After Frederik I died in 1533, the Catholic majority in the Rigsråd postponed the election of a new king, afraid that heir-apparent Prince Christian, Frederik's eldest son and a declared Lutheran, would favour the further spread of Lutheranism. Instead they attempted to position Christian's younger brother Hans as a candidate for the throne.

The country, already strained by social unrest, erupted into civil war in 1534. Mercenaries from the Hanseatic city of Lübeck, which hoped to gain control of Baltic trade by allying with Danish merchants against the Danish nobility, took advantage of the situation and invaded Denmark. By and large the Lübeckers were welcomed as liberators by peasants and members of the middle class.

Alarmed by the revolt against the nobility, the Rigsråd now threw its support behind Prince Christian and his skilful general, Johan Rantzau. Even the Catholic bishops, who realised the coronation of Christian would signal the end of the Catholic Church in Denmark, felt compelled to add their support rather than face the consequences of a peasant uprising. In 1534 the prince was crowned King Christian III.

The rebellion raged strongest in the countryside, where manor houses were set ablaze and the peasants made advances against the armies of the aristocracy. Rantzau took control and quickly secured Denmark's southern border by cutting Lübeck off from the sea. He then swept north through the countryside, smashing the peasant bands in brutal fighting.

Copenhagen, where merchants supported the uprising and the idea of becoming a Hanseatic stronghold, was besieged by Rantzau's troops for more than a year. Totally cut off from the outside world, Copenhagen's citizens suffered widespread starvation and epidemics before finally surrendering in the summer of 1536, marking the end of the civil war.

With the war's end, Christian III took advantage of the opportunity to consolidate his power. He took a surprisingly lenient approach to the Copenhagen merchants and burghers who had revolted, and in turn they now pledged their allegiance to the Crown, seeing opportunities for themselves in a stabilised Denmark. On the other hand, the Catholic bishops were arrested and monasteries, churches and other ecclesiastical estates became the property of the Crown.

The Danish Lutheran Church was established as the only state-sanctioned denomination and was placed under the direct control of the king. For all practical purposes the church officials, appointed at the whim of the king, now became civil servants – reliant upon the government for approval of their actions and for financial support.

Sharing power only with the nobility, the monarchy emerged from the civil war stronger than ever, buoyed by a treasury that was greatly enriched by the confiscated church properties.

Copenhagen Comes of Age

It was during the reign of Christian IV (1588–1648) that Copenhagen was endowed with much of its splendour – so much so that the king is sometimes referred to as the second founder of the city.

Christian IV ascended the throne at the age of 10 and ruled for more than 50 years. When he took power, Denmark held a firm grip on Baltic trade, providing strong export markets for Danish agricultural products and reaping handsome profits for landowners and merchants. With a robust economy and a seemingly boundless treasury at hand, the ambitious king established trading companies and a stock exchange, using this wealth to build new Renaissance cities, castles and fortresses throughout his kingdom.

Many of Copenhagen's most lavish buildings were erected during Christian IV's reign. The king also extended the city significantly, developing the district of Christianshavn, which he skilfully modelled on Amsterdam. Among the many grand buildings that have survived through the centuries are: Børsen, the ornately embellished stock exchange building; Rosenborg Slot (Map 7, A5), the

Don't Pillage the Village

In the early 1600s, Christian IV, intent on protecting his growing capital from outside siege, started work on a ring fortress consisting of earthen ramparts, moats and bastions. This ring fortress, also referred to as the city wall, extended some 10km in circumference and defined Copenhagen's boundaries. For two centuries it proved effective in warding off sieges, but with the devastating British naval attack of 1807, launched with cannon volleys from the harbour, it was clear that the ramparts offered little protection against the powerful new weapons of the day.

In addition to losing their military value, the ramparts restricted the growth of the city, resulting in crowded, unsanitary conditions. During the 1850s work began on demolishing the ramparts and the city quickly expanded its boundaries beyond the old fortifications.

Today the ramparts remain intact only at Kastellet (Map 4, F9), the citadel at the northern side of the city centre, and along the outer canal of Christianshavn.

Remnants of the western portion of the ramparts have been incorporated into a curving arc of public parks: Østre Anlæg, Botanisk Have and Ørstedsparken. The lakes found in these parks were once part of the moat system.

---

king's Dutch Renaissance summer home; and the Rundetårn (Map 8, B5), Europe's oldest astronomical observatory.

Unfortunately, the king's foreign policies weren't nearly as brilliant as his domestic undertakings. When the Swedes began to vie for greater influence in the Baltic, Christian IV, hoping to neutralise Swedish expansion, dragged Denmark into a protracted struggle known as the Thirty Years' War.

The war drained Danish resources and resulted in substantial territorial losses for Denmark. The king himself, always anxious to be in the midst of the action, lost an eye to shrapnel when his flagship was attacked in battle. In a treaty in 1645, signed after a Swedish invasion of Denmark, the Baltic island of Gotland and two Norwegian provinces were handed over to the Swedes, while a second treaty signed in 1648 relinquished Denmark's southern territories.

In 1655 the Swedish king invaded Poland and, although the victory was swift, the Swedes found themselves bogged down trying to secure that vast country. Word of the Swedish troubles ignited nationalistic fervour throughout a Denmark that was seething for revenge.

In 1657, Christian IV's successor, Frederik III, hoping to take advantage of the Polish situation, once again declared war on the Swedes. For the Danish government, itself ill-prepared for battle, it was a tremendous miscalculation.

Sweden's King Gustave, looking for an honourable way out of war-ravaged Poland, which had already been pillaged to the limit, gladly withdrew and readied his forces for an invasion of Denmark. He led his troops through Germany and into Denmark's Jutland peninsula, plundering his way north.

In the winter of 1657–58 – the most severe winter in Danish history – King Gustave marched his soldiers across the frozen seas of the Lille Bælt between Jutland and the island of Funen. His uncanny success unnerved the Danes and he proceeded without serious resistance across the similarly frozen Store Bælt to the islands of Lolland and Falster.

The Swedish king had barely made it across the frozen waters of the Storstrømmen to Zealand when the thawing ice broke behind him, separating Gustave and his advance detachment from the main body of his forces.

However, the Danes, who had amassed most of their troops in Zealand to protect Copenhagen, were in such a state of panic that they failed to recognise their sudden military advantage and, instead of capturing the Swedish king, they sued for peace and agreed to yet another disastrous treaty.

On 26 February 1658 the Treaty of Roskilde, the most lamented treaty in Denmark's history, was signed. The territorial losses were staggering, with Denmark's borders shrinking by a third.

Fires Ravage the City

In spite of all the military setbacks, international trade continued to flourish and Copenhagen became homeport to one of the largest merchant fleets in Europe. The ships, which travelled far and wide, not only returned with great wealth for Copenhagen's trading companies, but unavoidably served as carriers for pestilence as well. In 1711 an outbreak of the bubonic plague hit the city, reducing Copenhagen's population by a third.

In 1728 a sweeping fire razed most of Copenhagen's medieval buildings, levelling one-third of the city, including the centre of government, Copenhagen Castle. A new and grander edifice, Christianborg Slot, was built to replace it, and the city began to rebuild. Then in 1795, a second fire ravaged the city's remaining timber buildings, destroying the final remnants of Absalon's medieval town and the new Christianborg Slot as well.

Copenhagen recovered from this fire only to find itself getting caught up in international strife. Britain, which dominated the seas, was not altogether keen on the growth of Denmark's foreign trade. In 1800, trying to counter potential threats posed by the British, Denmark signed a pact of armed neutrality with Sweden, Prussia and Russia. Britain regarded the act as hostile and in 1801 sent a naval expedition to attack Copenhagen, inflicting heavy damage on the Danish fleet and forcing Denmark to withdraw from the pact.

Denmark managed to avoid further conflicts and Copenhagen merchants actually profited from war trade until 1807, when a new treaty between France and Russia once again drew the Danes closer to the conflict. The British, weary of Napoleon's growing

Christian Threw Johan to the Lions

One of the more curious political players of the 18th century was not a Danish king but a German doctor named Johan Struensee. In 1768 Struensee was appointed court physician to King Christian VII, who suffered from bouts of insanity. The doctor managed to win favour both with the ailing king, who granted Struensee broad powers of state, and with the 18-year-old queen, Caroline Matilda, who became Struensee's lover.

Emboldened by his assumed powers, the 34-year-old physician dismissed the prime minister and, over the next 16 months, succeeded in proclaiming some 2000 decrees in the name of the monarch. Contemptuous of the aristocracy, Struensee applied the same laws for all citizens across class lines. The exploitation of peasants for the benefit of landlords was restricted and ill treatment in prisons, orphanages and poorhouses was outlawed. Trade barriers were lifted and money from the king's treasury was transferred to public sources for the support of new social endeavours.

Unfortunately for Struensee, he was ahead of his time – the French Revolution that would stir similar passions was still some 20 years away. Instead of broad support, Struensee elicited widespread resentment that was inflamed by unfounded rumours of his ill treatment of the ailing king. In actuality, however, it seems that the mad king had taken some comfort in being relieved of both his stately and marital duties.

In January 1772 a coup d'etat was instigated at a palace ball and the conspirators, led by the queen mother, forced the king to sign a statement against Struensee, who was being arrested elsewhere in the palace. Unable to prove that Struensee had forcibly taken control of the government, or even that he had been corrupt, the court instead condemned him to death for his illicit relations with the young queen, which it ruled to be lese-majesty.

The queen, incidentally, had her marriage dissolved by a special court and was subsequently taken by a British frigate to England to live on the estate of her brother, King George III. Forbidden to take her young daughter (who was deemed Christian VII's heir although fathered by Struensee) with her to England, Caroline Matilda died a broken woman at the age of 24.

influence in the Baltic, feared, without solid grounds, that the Danes might soon be convinced to place their fleet at the disposal of the French.

In September 1807, without attempting diplomacy, a British fleet under the command of admiral Horatio Nelson unleashed a brutal bombardment upon neutral Copenhagen. The attack targeted the heart of the city, inflicting numerous civilian casualties and setting hundreds of homes, churches and public buildings ablaze.

The British then proceeded to confiscate the entire Danish fleet, sailing away with nearly 170 gunboats, frigates, transports and sloops. Ironically, the only ship left standing in Copenhagen harbour was a private yacht that the king of England had bestowed upon his nephew, Denmark's crown prince Frederik, two decades earlier.

In October 1807 the Danes, incensed by the assault, joined the continental alliance against Britain. In turn, Britain blockaded Danish waters, crippling its economy. When Napoleon fell in 1814 the Swedes, by then allied with Britain, successfully demanded that Denmark cede Norway to them.

The Golden Age

Although the 19th century started out dismal and lean, by the 1830s Copenhagen had awakened to a cultural revolution in the arts, philosophy and literature. The times gave rise to such prominent figures as philosopher Søren Kierkegaard, theologian Nikolaj Frederik Severin Grundtvig and writer Hans Christian Andersen. It was the 'Golden Age' of the arts, with sculptor Bertel Thorvaldsen bestowing his grand neoclassical statues on Copenhagen while painter Christoffer Wilhelm Eckersberg introduced a new art movement to the city.

Spurred on by new ideas and the rising expectations of a growing middle class, the absolute rule of the Crown was challenged by an unprecedented interest in democratic principles. The powers of the monarchy were already on the wane when revolution swept across the continent from Paris to Germany in the spring of 1848. In its wake Denmark adopted its first democratic constitution. Enacted on 5 June 1849, it established a parliament with two chambers, Folketing and Landsting, whose members were elected by popular vote.

Although the king retained a limited voice, legislative powers shifted to the parliament. An independent judiciary was established and citizens were guaranteed the rights of free speech, religion and assembly. Denmark changed overnight from a virtual dictatorship to one of the most democratic countries in Europe.

At the same time Copenhagen, which had previously been under royal administration, was granted the right to form a municipal council. Industry flourished in the last half of the 19th century, bringing a wave of new workers from the countryside into Copenhagen. A labour movement developed and by the 1870s many of the city's workplaces had begun to unionise. Copenhagen's boundaries were extended into the districts of Østerbro, Vesterbro and Nørrebro to accommodate the city's growth and the new working class.

20th-Century Advances

The growth of industrialisation had a major impact on national politics, with old power bases losing ground to new urban movements. In 1901 Denmark's conservative landowners, who had long held a stranglehold on national government, were ousted by the Left Reform Party.

The party completed a number of broadminded reforms, most notably applying the progressive principles of NFS Grundtvig to the educational system and amending the constitution in 1915 to extend voting rights to women. The city of Copenhagen had already, in 1908, granted female taxpayers the right to vote in municipal elections but the new national amendment now extended the vote to all, regardless of economic status.

With universal suffrage, the political landscape changed dramatically. The union movement and the growing mass of industrial workers organised themselves politically and formed the Social Democratic Party, which quickly became Denmark's largest party and leading political force.

Denmark remained neutral during WWI and in the period between the two world wars, under the leadership of the Social Democratic Party, the government passed landmark legislation that not only softened the effects of the Great Depression but also laid the foundations for a welfare state.

WWII

Denmark again declared its neutrality at the outbreak of WWII but, with the growing Allied presence in Norway, Germany became intent on acquiring advance coastal bases in northern Jutland.

In the early hours of 9 April 1940 the Germans crossed the frontier in southern Jutland and simultaneously landed troops at strategic points throughout Denmark. A military airfield in Copenhagen was attacked and commandoes landed in the city, promptly taking Kastellet, the citadel that served as a headquarters for the Danish military.

The German troops proceeded to the royal family's residence, Amalienborg Slot, where they met resistance from the royal guards. In the meantime the German envoy delivered an ultimatum, warning that if the Danes resisted Copenhagen would be bombed.

With German warplanes flying overhead, Christian X and parliamentary heads hastily met at Amalienborg and decided to yield, under protest, to the Germans. The Danish government gained assurances from the Nazis that Denmark would be allowed to retain a degree of internal autonomy.

The Danes, with only nominal military forces, had no capacity to ward off a German attack and little alternative but to submit. In all, the lightning blow lasted only a matter of hours, and before nightfall Denmark was an occupied country.

For three years the Danes managed to tread a thin line, basically running their own domestic affairs but doing so under Nazi supervision, until August 1943 when the Germans took outright control. The Danish Resistance movement quickly mushroomed. In October 1943, as the Nazis were preparing to round up Jewish Danes, the Resistance, using night-running fishing boats, quickly smuggled 7000 Jews, some 95% of

those remaining in Denmark, from Zealand into neutral Sweden.

Despite the occupation, Copenhagen and the rest of Denmark emerged from WWII relatively unscathed.

Modern-Day Issues

Under the leadership of the Social Democrats a comprehensive social-welfare state was established in postwar Denmark.

During the war and in the economic depression that had preceded it, many Copenhagen neighbourhoods had deteriorated into slums. In 1948 an ambitious urban renewal policy called the 'Finger Plan' was adopted that redeveloped much of the city, creating new housing projects interspaced with green areas of parks and recreational facilities that spread out like fingers from the city centre.

On a national level the cradle-to-grave securities that guarantee medical care, education and public assistance were expanded. As the economy grew and the labour market increased, women entered the work force in unprecedented numbers and household incomes reached lofty new heights.

In the 1960s a rebellion by young people, who were disillusioned with growing materialism, the nuclear arms race and an authoritarian educational system, took hold in Copenhagen. Student protests broke out on the university campus and squatters began to occupy vacant buildings around the city. The movement came to a head in 1971 when protesters tore down the fence of an abandoned military camp at the east side of Christianshavn and began an occupation of the 41 hectare site.

The squatters declared the area the 'free state of Christiania', based on the concept of communal living, and outside the realm of Danish laws. As word of the new community spread, all sorts of people – hippies, the homeless, back-to-the-earth folks who wanted to live off the land, and idealists attracted by the idea of turning a military base into a peaceful utopian community – began to flock to Christiania.

Because of the size of the movement, police attempts to remove people from the site were largely futile, and Christiania became a controversial issue in the Danish parliament, which after much debate reluctantly allowed the community to continue as a 'social experiment'.

The occupants of Christiania quickly grew to around 1000 people who set up their own system of rule, organised social activities and started progressive businesses. Most controversial was the establishment of Pusherstreet, a market where vendors could sell hashish and marijuana.

In the late 1970s, heroin became a problem in Copenhagen and some users and dealers saw Christiania as a safe haven. This made the community a target for police raids and in 1980 Christiania itself outlawed hard drugs and demanded that junkies either go into rehabilitation programs or face banishment from the community.

After three decades, self-governing Christiania continues to serve as a bastion for alternative lifestyles. Its population has settled to around 800; Pusherstreet still has its hashish market; and most politicians remain lukewarm at best in their acceptance of Christiania.

One of the most controversial issues of recent times has been Denmark's role in the European Union (EU). Denmark joined the European Community, the predecessor of the EU, in 1973, but Danes have been hesitant to support expansion of the EU's powers. Indeed when the Maastricht Treaty, which established the terms of a European economic and political union, came up for ratification in 1992, Danish voters rejected it by a margin of 51% to 49%. After being granted exemptions from the Maastricht Treaty's

A Thoroughly Modern Monarchy

Denmark's current monarch, Queen Margrethe II, was born on 16 April 1940, the eldest daughter of Frederik IX (1899-1972), who had no sons. As a result of a 1953 referendum that amended the sex-bias of the Danish constitution to allow women to succeed to the throne, Margrethe was proclaimed queen on 15 January 1972, the first female monarch of Denmark since the 14th century.

Margrethe II is a popular queen who has been credited with giving a fresh perspective to the Danish monarchy and minimising the privilege that has traditionally separated royalty from commoners.

In addition to performing her ceremonial roles as head of state, the queen is an accomplished artist. She has illustrated a number of books, including Tolkien's *Lord of the Rings*, and has also designed Christmas seals for Unicef and stamps for the Danish postal service. The queen has been active in the theatre as well, designing costumes for a production of Hans Christian Andersen's *The Shepherdess and the Chimney Sweep* and creating both the settings and costumes for the Royal Theatre's ballet *Et Folkesage* (The Legend). Together with her French-born husband, Prince Henrik, the queen translated Simone de Beauvoir's novel *Tous les hommes sont mortels* (All Men Are Mortal) from its original French into Danish.

Queen Margrethe and Prince Henrik have two sons. Crown prince Frederik was born in 1968 and, like his mother, is a graduate of Århus University, where he studied politics and law. Prince Joachim was born in 1969 and attended a smaller Danish college. Both princes did stints in the armed services following their graduation and also have undertaken work internships overseas, Joachim on a farm in Australia and Frederik at a California winery.

Frederik, who is hands-down Copenhagen's most eligible bachelor, is a world traveller whose journeys have taken him far and wide. In 2000, the crown prince, along with five companions, completed a 110-day Arctic journey by dogsled across the frozen tundra of northern Greenland.

CLINT CURÉ

common defence and monetary provisions, the Danes, by a narrow majority, voted to accept the treaty in a second referendum held in 1993.

In September 2000 the Danes signalled a deeper discontent with European integration when they rejected adopting the euro, the EU's common currency. Denmark, the first EU country to put that decision in the hands of the people, saw a remarkable 87% voter turnout. Despite a passionate campaign to win support for the euro by Danish Prime Minister Poul Nyrup Rasmussen and the business community, the euro was rejected by a 6% margin. Protesters in Copenhagen and other cities had been effective in convincing Danes they had more to lose than gain, arguing that local control over Danish issues would be ceded to a European bureaucracy dominated by stronger nations and that Denmark's generous welfare state securities would also be endangered by the provision.

GEOGRAPHY

Copenhagen is on the eastern coast of Zealand (Sjælland), the largest of Denmark's 406 islands. A harbour city, Copenhagen borders the Baltic Sea and is separated from Sweden by the 16km-wide Øresund sound. Copenhagen municipality covers 88.3 sq km and consists of 15 small districts radiating out in an arc shape about 7km from Copenhagen harbour.

The greater Copenhagen urban area, also sometimes referred to as the Copenhagen Region or the Capital Region, covers a much broader swath that includes North Zealand and extends west to Roskilde and south to Køge. It encompasses many small cities and towns and covers an area of 2866 sq km.

CLIMATE

Copenhagen is at a latitude of 55°41', approximately the same as Moscow, central Scotland and southern Alaska. Considering its northerly location the climate is relatively mild.

In the coldest winter months of January and February, the average daily temperature hovers around freezing point – and while that

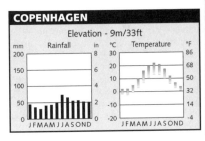

COPENHAGEN
Elevation - 9m/33ft

may be cold, it's nearly 10°C above average for this latitude. Winter, however, also has the highest relative humidity (90%) and the cloudiest weather (with greater than 80% cloud cover on an average of 17 days a month), both of which can make it feel much colder than the actual mercury reading.

From May to September, there are about nine cloudy days a month and the humidity drops to a comfortable level of around 70% at noon.

Expect to see rain and grey skies. Measurable rain falls on average from 11 days in June (the month with the fewest rainy days) to 18 days in November, with the greatest amount of precipitation from July to December – although, when all's said and done, rain is fairly evenly spread over the year. During the most popular months to visit of May, June, July and August, there's an average of 42mm, 52mm, 68mm and 64mm of rain, respectively.

The normal mean temperature for Copenhagen is 2.5°C in March, 11.4°C in May, 17.3°C in July, 16.7°C in August, 9.1°C in October and 1.7°C in December.

You can get a five-day weather forecast in English from the Danish Meteorological Office at its Web site at www.dmi.dk or by calling ☎ 38 38 36 63.

ECOLOGY & ENVIRONMENT

Overall, Copenhageners have a high degree of awareness of environmental issues and have made significant efforts to address environmental concerns on both personal and political levels. Far more people commute to work by public transport than by private vehicle and thousands of commuters better that still by hopping on a bicycle rather than a bus.

Relative to other cities of its size, Copenhagen's air quality is good and pollution levels have decreased dramatically in recent years. Since 1993, when Danish businesses were first required to pay a tax based on their pollution emissions, Copenhagen's levels of sulphur dioxide have decreased by 80%, carbon monoxide has been cut in half and nitrogen dioxide and soot have fallen by about a third.

Recycling is extensive, with more than 80% of all paper produced from used paper and nearly 60% of all of Copenhagen's waste recycled. All industries, including tourism, are expected to contribute to efforts to reduce unnecessary waste and energy expenditures.

In the late 1990s the Danes introduced a system called the 'Green Key' in which hotels can display a special environmental-friendly logo if they enact a series of conservation efforts.

These include using biodegradable cleaning products and energy-efficient lightbulbs, refitting baths with low-flow shower heads and low-flush toilets, and offering breakfast items grown without chemical pesticides and fertilisers.

In 1971 Denmark created a cabinet-level ministry to deal specifically with environmental matters, becoming the first industrialised country to do so. The EU has placed its European Environment Agency in Copenhagen and the Danes have taken an active role in promoting international efforts to reduce pollution.

FLORA & FAUNA
Flora
A great place for plant lovers to visit is Botanisk Have, the city's botanical garden, where a wide range of both native and exotic flora is on display.

In the summer, many other Copenhagen gardens also bloom with a colourful mix of temperate-climate flowers. Kongens Have, the park surrounding Rosenborg Slot, is noted for its fragrant rose garden. The national flower is the marguerite, a white daisy with a yellow centre, which can be seen growing wild in many areas around Zealand.

Natural woodlands, such as those at the northern side of Copenhagen, are largely deciduous with a prevalence of beech and oak trees. Other common trees found in woodlands are hazel, maple, pine, birch, aspen, lime (linden) and horse chestnut.

Elm trees are also common, but an outbreak of Dutch elm disease 1993 has devastated these stately trees in many areas. In central Copenhagen, virtually all of the city's estimated 10,000 elm trees contracted the disease and most have been cut down.

Fauna
About 160 bird species breed in Denmark. Some of the more commonly seen birds in the Copenhagen area include the magpie, crow, sparrow, pigeon, coot, goose and duck.

The national bird, the swan, is found in ponds in Copenhagen and elsewhere on the island of Zealand. A picturesque place to see swans is at the moat at Rosenborg Slot and a great park for birding overall is Frederiksberg Have, at the west side of the city.

The largest wild animal species found in Denmark is the red deer, which can weigh over 200kg. A fun place to find grazing deer is at Dyrehaven, a former royal hunting ground that's now a public park in Klampenborg in the northern part of the city.

GOVERNMENT & POLITICS
Copenhagen is the seat of both municipal and national government. Within walking distance of each other in the city centre are the Rådhus (Map 7, D4; city hall), where local government is administered; Folketing (parliament), where national legislation is enacted; and Amalienborg Slot, home to the monarchy.

National Government
Denmark is a constitutional monarchy with a single-chamber parliamentary system. The parliament, called Folketing, is responsible for enacting legislation. The prime minister leads the government with the assistance of cabinet ministers who head the various government departments. Queen Margrethe II, who has been on the throne since 1972, has a largely ceremonial role

but her signature is required on the enactment of new legislation.

The minimum voting age is 18; parliamentary elections are held at least once every four years. There are close to a dozen parties represented in the 179 seat parliament. The two largest parties are Socialdemokratiet (Social Democrats), which received 36% of the vote in the last election, and Venstre (Liberals – a right-of-centre party), which received 24%. Despite the domination of these two parties, any party that wins 2% of the vote gains representation in parliament.

Heated parliamentary debates are uncommon and consultation and consensus building across party lines are the norm, with most legislation passed by large majorities. The major parties are quite moderate and most parliamentary members linger near the centre; however, one noteworthy change in the political landscape is the emergence of the far-right Dansk Folkeparti (Danish People's Party) which, in the last election, captured 13 seats on an anti-immigration, anti-EU platform. In a bit of a counterbalance, the other right-leaning party, Fremskridtspartiet (Progress Party), saw its representation drop from 11 delegates to just four during that election.

Socialdemokratiet, the largest party, is a moderate socialist party. It's founded on the belief in the right of guaranteed security to all in the form of extensive social-welfare programs that are funded by high taxes. Socialdemokratiet first came to power in 1924 and has been in power, either alone or as part of a coalition government, for most of the time since then. Since 1993 Poul Nyrup Rasmussen, the leader of Socialdemokratiet, has led the government under various left-centre coalitions.

Local Government

In 1998 the city adopted a new system of government intended to provide greater accessibility to citizens. Copenhagen's municipal government now consists of a city council and a system of committees. The city council, which has 55 elected members, establishes overall policy but it's the committees that are now charged with enacting the details of these policies.

There are seven committees, each with its own area of responsibility and its own mayor. This system gives the city seven mayors, though not all mayors are equal – one is designated the Lord Mayor.

The most important of the committees is the purse-controlling Finance Committee, which is headed by the Lord Mayor along with six elected councillors and the six mayors of the other committees. The remaining six committees, which each have 11 members, cover the areas of: culture, libraries and sport; education and youth; health; family and labour; building and construction; and energy, water and the environment.

ECONOMY

Denmark has the highest per-capita gross national product (GNP) in the EU and its citizens enjoy a high standard of living. Relative to other European countries the Danish economy remains strong, despite the fact that the government impounds almost half of its GNP for social services and transfer payments to the disadvantaged.

Almost all government funding is derived from taxes: over 50% comes from taxes on personal income and about one-third comes from value-added tax (VAT) and taxes on petrol, alcohol and other dutiable items.

Copenhagen's position as the country's centre of government and commerce is reflected in its employment market, with almost 30% of Copenhageners working in finance and business services, 11% in public service and 15% in social and health services.

Copenhagen has one of the most gender-equitable workplaces in Europe with 51% of the labour force comprised of males and 49% of females. However, there's still some wage disparity, with male workers earning an average of 204kr per hour versus 160kr for female workers.

Many of Denmark's leading industrial exports, which include beer, home electronics, furniture, silverware and porcelain, are produced in the Copenhagen area or elsewhere on the island of Zealand.

POPULATION & PEOPLE

The population of greater Copenhagen is 1,785,000, of which 491,000 people live in the central districts that form the core of Copenhagen municipality. Slightly more than 25% of the entire population of Denmark lives within the greater Copenhagen area.

The vast majority of Copenhageners are ethnic Danes, people of the Teutonic ancestry common to Scandinavia. Foreign nationals account for 11.7% of Copenhagen's population, an increase from 7.2% a decade ago. Approximately 12% of all foreign nationals come from Nordic countries, 43% from other parts of Europe, 25% from Asia, 12% from Africa and 5% from the Americas.

What's in a Name?

Of the five-million-plus Danes on the planet today, two-thirds have a surname ending in 'sen'. The three most common – Jensen, Nielsen and Hansen – account for 23% of all Danish surnames. Next, in order of frequency, are Pedersen, Andersen, Christensen, Larsen and Sørensen.

You may notice a trend here. The most common Danish surnames are derived from the most common *given* names with 'sen' suffixed on. This is because up until the mid-19th century most folks did not have a permanent family name but simply added 'sen', meaning 'son', onto their father's first name. Thus if your father was Peder Hansen and your name was Eric, you would be known as Eric Pedersen.

CLINT CURÉ

A relaxation of immigration policies during the economic expansion of the 1960s attracted 'guest workers', many of whom established a permanent niche, and there are now sizable Turkish and Pakistani communities in the city. More recent humanitarian policies, introduced in response to famine and war crises, have resulted in small Somalian and Ethiopian immigrant communities and a significant number of refugees from the former Yugoslavia.

EDUCATION

Education is free and nine years of schooling starting at the age of seven is compulsory. Preschool and kindergarten are optional; about two-thirds of children aged five and six attend.

About half of all Danish students who graduate from secondary school continue on to higher education. Slightly more than half of these graduates enrol in vocational programs providing training in business, nursing, maritime studies and other career-specific fields. Most others attend one of Denmark's five state-supported universities. The most elite of these institutions is Copenhagen University, which was founded in 1479, and has campuses in the Latin Quarter of central Copenhagen and in Amagar at the southern side of the city. With a student body of 35,000, Copenhagen University is Denmark's largest institution of research and learning and is divided into six faculties: Law, Health, Humanities, Science, Theology and Social Sciences.

SCIENCE & PHILOSOPHY

The great Danish astronomer Tycho Brahe (1546–1601) paved the way for later astronomers by inventing precision astronomical instruments and challenging previously held beliefs. He was such a leading figure of his day that Frederik II presented him with his own island in the sound north of Copenhagen from which to conduct his research, and at one point provided Brahe with funding equivalent to 1% of all Crown revenues.

Brahe rejected most earlier astronomical observations and in essence began surveying

Great Danes

In addition to Niels Bohr and his son Aage Bohr, 10 other Danes have received a Nobel Prize since 1901, the year the prizes were first awarded. They are as follows:

1903 – Physiology/Medicine: Niels R Finsen, who introduced light-radiation treatment for diseases such as lupus

1908 – Peace: Fredrik Bajer, a peace activist and writer

1917 – Literature: Karl A Gjellerup, for poetry inspired by lofty ideals, and Henrik Pontoppidan, for his insightful descriptions of everyday life in Denmark

1920 – Physiology/Medicine: Auguste Krogh, for discovering the capillary motor-regulating mechanism

1926 – Physiology/Medicine: cancer researcher Johannes AG Fibiger, for his discovery of the Spiroptera carcinoma

1943 – Physiology/Medicine: Henrik CP Dam (with Edward Doisy of the USA), for the discovery of Vitamin K

1944 – Literature: Johannes V Jensen, for the strength of his poetic imagination

1984 – Physiology/Medicine: Niels K Jerne (with Georges JF Koehler of Germany and Cesar Milstien of the UK), for theories on the development and control of the immune system and the discovery of the principle of monoclonal antibody production

1997 – Chemistry: Jens C Skou (with John Walker of the UK and Paul Boyer of the USA), for discovering aspects of how the body's cells store and use energy

the sky anew. In 1577 he demonstrated that comets were not atmospheric phenomenon, but rather heavenly bodies. He went on to catalogue more than a thousand fixed stars and to explain the movements of the moon.

In 1597, after a quarrel with Christian IV, Brahe gathered up his equipment and left for Vienna. Nonetheless, his influence continued, with one of Brahe's students, Christen Sørensen Longomontanus, playing a role in creating Copenhagen's Round Tower, the oldest astronomical observatory in Europe.

Niels Bohr, born in Copenhagen in 1885, was one of the foremost scientists of the 20th century. He won the Nobel Prize in Physics in 1922 for his investigation into radiation and the structure of atoms. After this he began work on the formation of general quantum mechanics and in the 1930s developed a theory on the fission process of uranium. Because of his prominence in the field, he maintained ties with scientists in both Germany and the West. In the winter of 1939, during a stay at Princeton University, he revealed to US authorities that German scientists had succeeded in splitting

the uranium atom, and in so doing set off the race to develop the first atomic bomb.

In 1943, Bohr escaped Nazi-occupied Denmark, returned to the USA and played a crucial role in the creation of the atomic bomb. In the 1950s, concerned with the consequence of atomic weapons, Bohr became a leading critic of the nuclear arms race and a peace activist. After his death in 1962, Copenhagen University renamed its world-renowned theoretical physics department – which Bohr had once directed – the Niels Bohr Institute.

Aage Bohr, Niels' son, also won a Nobel Prize in Physics. He received his award in 1975 (shared with Ben Mottelson and James Rainwater) for the discovery of the link between collective motion and particle motion in atomic nuclei and the development of the theory of the structure of the atomic nucleus.

Denmark's most famous philosopher was the 18th-century Copenhagener Søren Kierkegaard, whose works expounded upon tenets of existentialism (see the boxed text 'Sage Søren').

Sage Søren

Denmark's most famous philosopher, Søren Kierkegaard, was born into a prosperous Copenhagen family on 5 May 1813. When he was in his early 20s, his father died and left Søren with an inheritance that freed him from the need to work. He studied theology and philosophy at Copenhagen University and devoted his entire life to studying and writing.

Kierkegaard was vehemently opposed to the philosophy of Georg Wilhelm Friedrich Hegel, which was prevalent in 19th-century Europe and embraced by the Danish Lutheran Church. In contrast, Kierkegaard's writings challenged the individual to make choices entirely of his or her own among the alternatives that life offered. In his first great work, *Either/Or*, published in 1843, the alternative was between aesthetic pleasures or an ethical life. This work, like many that followed, was in part inspired by Kierkegaard's lifelong pain over breaking off an engagement to a young woman named Regine Olsen. He continued to wrestle with the implications of his broken engagement in subsequent writings, including *Fear and Trembling* (1843), which compares the biblical tale of Abraham's sacrifice of Isaac to Kierkegaard's own sacrifice.

Kierkegaard's greatest attack on Hegelianism, and his most philosophically important work, was *Concluding Unscientific Postscript to the Philosophical Fragments* (1846), which passionately expounded the tenets of existentialism.

Kierkegaard was considered by many members of the Copenhagen establishment to be a fanatic and his friends were few, even in the literary world. His works remained virtually unknown outside Denmark until the 20th century.

The last years of Kierkegaard's life were dominated by an acrimonious battle with the established church. The toll was so great that it slowly drained his health and he died of exhaustion in a Copenhagen hospital in 1855 at the age of 42. At the time of his death, Kierkegaard felt his works had largely fallen upon deaf ears, but his writings posthumously have become the vanguard for existentialist philosophers worldwide.

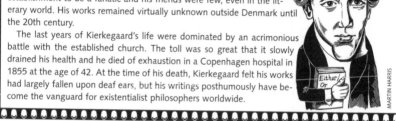

MARTIN HARRIS

ARTS
Fine Arts

Prior to the 19th century, Danish art tended to revolve around formal portraits of the bourgeoisie, the aristocracy and the royal family. One of the most highly regarded portrait painters was Jens Juel (1745–1802).

Denmark's 'Golden Age' of the arts (1800–50) produced the Copenhagen artist Christoffer Wilhelm Eckersberg (1783–1853), who depicted more universal scenes of everyday Danish life, and Eckersberg's student Christen Købke (1810–48), who was little known in his time but is now regarded as one of the most important painters of the era. Exceptional collections of 'Golden Age' works can be found at the city's Statens Museum for Kunst (Map 7, A5) and the nearby Den Hirschsprungske Samling (Map 4, F7).

The leading Danish sculptor of the day was Bertel Thorvaldsen (1770–1844), who re-created classical sculptures during a long sojourn in Rome and returned to Copenhagen to establish his own museum. The works of Thorvaldsen can be seen at Copenhagen's cathedral Vor Frue Kirke and at the Thorvaldsen Museum on Slotsholmen.

The COBRA (COpenhagen-BRussels-Amsterdam) movement, partially centred in Copenhagen, was formed in 1948 with the aim of exploiting the free artistic expression of the unconscious. One of its founders, Danish artist Asger Jorn (1914–73), achieved an international following for his abstract paintings, many of which evoke imagery from Nordic mythology. The Louisiana modern art museum north of Copenhagen has a fine collection of COBRA works.

Literature

The literary arts began to flourish in Copenhagen during the first half of the 19th century, which has been characterised as the 'Golden Age' of Danish literature. The foremost writers of that period included Adam Oehlenschläger (1779–1850), a romantic lyric poet who also wrote short stories and plays; Hans Christian Andersen (1805–75), whose fairy tales have been translated into more languages than any other book except the Bible; and philosopher Søren Kierkegaard (1813–55), who is considered the father of existentialism.

Around 1870 a trend towards realism emerged, focusing on contemporary issues of the day. A writer of this genre, novelist Henrik Pontoppidan, won the Nobel Prize for Literature in 1917 shortly after publishing the epic *The Realm of the Dead*, which attacked materialism. Another Dane who won the Nobel Prize for Literature was Johannes Vilhelm Jensen (1873–1950), who wrote the six volume novel *The Long Journey*, and *The Fall of the King*, a story about Danes in Renaissance times.

The most famous Danish writer of the 20th century, Karen Blixen (1885–1962), started her career with *Seven Gothic Tales*, which was published in New York under the pen name Isak Dinesen. She is best known for *Out of Africa*, the memoirs of her farm life in Kenya, which she wrote in 1937. Other works include *Winter's Tales* (1942), *The Angelic Avengers* (1944), *Last Tales* (1957), *Anecdotes of Destiny* (1958) and *Shadows on the Grass* (1960). Her family home in Rungsted, north of Copenhagen,

Once Upon a Time ...

Born on 2 April 1805 in Odense, Hans Christian Andersen was the son of a poor cobbler. At the age of 14 he ran away to Copenhagen 'to become famous' and the following year entered the Royal Danish Theatre as a student of dance and music. In 1822, on the recommendation of the theatre board, he was sent to a preparatory school in Helsingør, and in 1828 he passed his university entrance exams.

The following year Andersen self-published his first book, *A Walk From Holmen's Canal to the Eastern Tip of Amager*. In 1831, after being jilted in a love affair, Andersen travelled to Germany and wrote the first of a number of stories about his travels abroad.

In 1835 he finally made a name for himself with the successful novel *The Improvisators*. He followed that with his first volume of fairy tales, *Tales, Told for Children*, which included such classics as 'The Tinderbox' and 'The Princess and the Pea'. Over the next few decades, he continued writing novels and accounts of his travels, but it was his fairy tales that brought him worldwide fame.

Andersen had a superb talent for humanising animals, plants and innate objects without compromising their original character.

In his stories the villains are not evil characters such as witches or trolls, but rather human weaknesses such as indifference and vanity, and his tales are imbued with moral realism instead of wishful fantasy. Some of his most famous fairy tales are 'The Little Mermaid,' 'The Ugly Duckling', 'The Snow Queen', 'The Constant Tin Soldier', 'The Nightingale' and the satirical 'The Emperor's New Clothes'.

Besides his fairy tales and poems, Andersen wrote six novels, numerous travel books, many dramatic works and two autobiographies, of which the most highly regarded is *The Fairy Tale of My Life*. All in all, he published 156 stories and other works.

Andersen had a penchant for travel and over his lifetime made 29 journeys abroad, several of them lasting many months. On 4 August 1875, at the age of 70, he died of liver cancer at a villa outside Copenhagen. His grave is in the city's Assistens cemetery.

MARTIN HARRIS

has been turned into a museum detailing her life and works.

Denmark's foremost contemporary novelist is Peter Høeg, who in 1992 wrote the international bestseller *Miss Smilla's Feeling For Snow* (published in the USA as *Smilla's Sense of Snow*), a suspense mystery set largely in Copenhagen's Christianshavn district, which touches upon Danish colonialism and the struggle for Greenlandic cultural identity. Since then, three other Høeg novels have been published in English: *The History of Danish Dreams*, a narrative that sweeps through many generations of a Danish family; *Borderliners*, which deals with social issues surrounding private schooling in Denmark; and *The Woman and the Ape*, the main character of which saves a rare primate from the clutches of scientists. All of Høeg's works focus on nonconformist characters on the margins of Danish society.

Theatre & Dance

Det Kongelige Teater (Map 8, D10; The Royal Theatre) at Kongens Nytorv first opened in 1748 as a court theatre, performing the plays of Denmark's most famous playwright, Ludvig Holberg (1684–1754). Today, its repertoire encompasses international works, including Shakespearian plays as well as classical and contemporary Danish plays.

In the mid-19th century, Den Kongelige Ballet (The Royal Danish Ballet), which also performs at Det Kongelige Teater, took its present form under the leadership of the choreographer and ballet master August Bournonville (1805–79). Today, Den Kongelige Ballet, which has a troupe of nearly 100 dancers, still performs a number of Bournonville's romantic ballets, such as *La Sylphide* and *Napoli*, along with more contemporary works.

Also based in Det Kongelige Teater is Den Kongelige Opera (The Royal Danish Opera), which has an ensemble of 32 singers and a renowned 60 member opera chorus. It performs about 16 operas each season.

Det Kongelige Kapel (The Royal Danish Orchestra) was founded in 1448, giving it claim to be the oldest orchestra in the world; it accompanies the ballet and opera performances at Det Kongelige Teater.

In terms of modern dance, Copenhagen was a bit of a late starter. In the 1960s, after visits to Copenhagen by the American modern dance luminary Martha Graham, local dance initiatives began to emerge. Today, the leading modern dance group is Nyt Dansk Danseteater (the New Danish Dance Theatre), which was formed in 1980.

Music

Virtually all forms of music are alive and well in Copenhagen.

Jazz came to Denmark in the 1920s and developed a loyal following among Copenhageners that continues to this day. The Copenhagen Jazzhouse, in the city centre, is the venue for top Danish and international performers and a focal point for the summertime Copenhagen Jazz Festival, one of Europe's foremost jazz events. Among the leading local jazz performers to look for are bass players Niels-Henning Ørsted Pedersen and Mads Vinding, saxophonist Christina Nielsen, drummer Jonas Johansen, trumpeter Thomas Fryland and popular vocalist Cæcilie Norby.

Danish folk and rock have been strongly influenced over the decades by American and British trends. One folk music idol is Bob Dylan, who has performed in Denmark on numerous occasions, and whose influence in both music and lyrical style continues to resonate in contemporary Danish folk music. In the field of rock, Copenhageners party to it all: hard rock, punk, pop, new wave, hip hop, grunge and fusion. A couple of Danish rock bands have been able to attract international audiences, including Aqua, Kashmir and D-A-D, who sing in English.

Denmark's best-known classical composer is Carl Nielsen (1865–1931). In 1888 he wrote his first orchestral work, *Suite for Strings*, for a performance at Copenhagen's Tivoli concert hall. It received critical acclaim and since then has become a regular piece in the Danish concert repertory. Nielsen's music includes six symphonies, several operas, and many hymn tunes and popular songs, often with patriotic themes.

Cinema

The best-known Danish director of the early 20th century was Carl Theodor Dreyer (1889–1968), who directed numerous films including the 1928 French masterpiece *La Passion de Jeanne d'Arc*, which was acclaimed for its rich visual textures and innovative use of close-ups. In the midst of WWII, Dreyer boldly filmed *Vredens Dag* (Day of Wrath), which made so many allusions to the tyranny of Nazi occupation that he was forced to flee to Sweden.

Since 1972 most Danish films have been produced with the support of government-funded subsidies. These days the funding comes via the Danish Film Institute, which generally provides at least 40% of a film's production costs. Despite the fact that only about 20 feature-length Danish films are made annually, Danish film makers have managed to attract an international audience and win some notable awards.

In 1988 *Babette's Feast*, directed by Gabriel Axel, won the Academy Award for Best Foreign Film. *Babette's Feast* was an adaptation of a story written by Karen Blixen, whose novel *Out of Africa* had been turned into an Oscar-winning Hollywood movie just three years earlier.

In 1989 Danish director Bille August won the Academy Award for Best Foreign Film as well as the Cannes Film Festival's Palme d'Or award for *Pelle the Conqueror*, a film adapted from Martin Andersen Nexø's book about the harsh reality of life as an immigrant in 19th-century Denmark. August also directed *Smilla's Sense of Snow* (1997), based on the bestseller by Peter Høeg, which starred Julia Ormond and Gabriel Byrne, and *Les Misérables* (1998), an accessible adaptation of Victor Hugo's classic tale of good and evil, starring Liam Neeson and Geoffrey Rush.

The leading director of the new millennium is Lars von Trier, whose better-known films include the melodrama *Breaking the Waves* (1996), featuring Emily Watson, which took the Cannes Film Festival's Grand Prix award, and *Dancer in the Dark* (2000), a musical starring Icelandic pop singer Björk and Catherine Deneuve.

Dancer in the Dark won the Cannes Film Festival's Palme d'Or in 2000.

Another up-and-coming Danish director is Thomas Vinterberg, whose film *Festen* (The Celebration) won the jury prize at the 1998 Cannes Film Festival.

Both Vinterberg and von Trier were instrumental in developing Dogme 95, sometimes dubbed the 'vow of chastity'. This artistic manifesto pledges the use of a minimalist approach, which involves using only hand-held cameras, shooting on location with natural light and refraining from the use of special effects and pre-recorded music.

Lars von Trier's production company, Zentropa, along with most other Danish film companies, maintain their studios at the site of a converted military base at Avedøre, 20 minutes south of central Copenhagen.

Two Danish actresses who have jumped into the international film scene are Connie Nielsen, who co-starred in the Roman Empire epic *Gladiator* (2000) with Russell Crowe, and Copenhagen native Iben Hjejle, who made her Hollywood debut as the lead actress in the quirky romantic comedy *High Fidelity* (2000).

Architecture

Copenhagen has a low skyline with only a few high-rise buildings. The city centre is predominantly historic, but it does have blocks of mundane office buildings as well as some sleek modern structures.

Over the years, Copenhagen has been struck by a number of fires, and architectural styles are often the consequence of whatever was fashionable at the time of rebuilding. For example, around Strøget and the Latin Quarter, there are numerous neoclassical buildings that were erected following devastating 18th-century blazes. Some of the grander neoclassical buildings of the period are the cathedral Vor Frue Kirke in the Latin Quarter and the city courthouse Domhuset on Nytorv.

Pre-eminent among the city's rococo structures are Amalienborg Slot's four nearly identical mansions, which were designed by architect Nicolai Eigtved at the end of the 18th century. The buildings are the residence of the royal family, but one of them is accessible to the public as a museum.

The ornate baroque style was a popular design for public building in the 17th century and two splendid buildings representative of the style are the church Vor Frelsers Kirke in Christianshavn and Charlottenborg at Kongens Nytorv, a former palace that now houses an art gallery.

The city's leading architect of the late 19th century was Vilhelm Dahlerup, who borrowed from a broad spectrum of European Renaissance influences. His most spectacular works include Ny Carlsberg Glyptotek, the nearby Peacock Theatre at Tivoli and the richly ornate Royal Theatre.

In terms of modern design, the pride of the city is the new Royal Library, which incorporates a slanting cube shape so that no two exterior walls are parallel. Canalside on the edge of historic Slotsholmen, the multistorey building – dubbed the 'Black Diamond' – has a striking facade of black granite and smoked glass and a brilliant use of internal space.

Danish Design

The cool, clean lines of industrial design are evident in Danish silver and porcelain, both of which merge aesthetics and function. Danish silverworks are highly regarded both in Denmark and abroad, with the company named after the late silversmith Georg Jensen the most renowned. You can view some of his works at the museum in the Georg Jensen shop (Map 8, D7) on Strøget.

One of the world's most famous sets of porcelain is the Royal Porcelain Manufactory's Flora Danica dinner service. No two pieces of this 1800-piece set are alike, each hand-painted with a different native Danish wildflower or other plant, and then rimmed with gold. Some of the pieces have trompe l'oeil applications, such as cup handles that appear as flower stems. Commissioned in 1790 by crown prince Frederik, the original set took 13 years to complete, and is still part of the Danish royal collection today. Pieces of the set are on display at Copenhagen's Rosenborg Slot.

NICKY CAVEN

Modern Danish furniture focuses on the functional refinement of style, and the principle that design should be tailored for the comfort of the user. In 1948, Hans Wegner designed the Round Chair, whose smooth curving lines made it an instant classic and a model for many furniture designers to follow (pictured above) – so popular was the chair at the time that it appeared on the cover of many international interior design magazines. A decade later Arne Jacobsen produced the Ant, a form chair designed to be mass produced, which became the model for the stacking chairs found in schools and cafeterias worldwide. You can see chairs by both designers in Copenhagen at the Dansk Design Center (Map 7, D4) and at Kunstindustrimuseet, the Museum of Decorative Art.

SOCIETY & CONDUCT

Copenhageners pride themselves on being thoroughly modern, and the wearing of folk costumes, the celebration of traditional festivals and the tendency to cling to old-fashioned customs is much less prevalent here than in most other European countries. There are, of course, traditional aspects of the Danish lifestyle that aren't apparent at first glance.

Perhaps nothing captures the Danish perspective more than the concept of *hygge* which, roughly translated, means cosy and snug. It implies shutting out the turmoil and troubles of the outside world and striving instead for a warm intimate mood. Hygge affects how Danes approach many aspects of their personal lives, from the design of their homes to their fondness for small cafes and pubs. There's no greater compliment that a Dane can give their host than to thank them for a cosy evening.

Social changes since the 1960s have had a dramatic effect on Copenhagen families. There are better career opportunities for women, easier access to abortions and a growth in childcare institutions.

About 20% of all couples living together these days aren't married and the average age for those who do opt to tie the knot has risen to 35 years. Family size has dropped dramatically, with Danish women averaging 1.8 children.

Women are often well established in their careers by the time they have their first child, and generous leave schemes make it easy to take a temporary pause from the workplace. The role of homemaker, in which a woman stays home to care for children, has all but disappeared in Denmark. Fewer than 5% of Danish women are still at home after the end of their maternity leave, which typically lasts 24 weeks but can be extended up to another year with paid parental leave.

From infancy, Copenhagen children spend a significant amount of time away from home – daycare centres and nursery schools are a normal part of daily life for the vast majority of preschoolers.

Danes of childbearing age, those in their 30s today, were the first generation to be raised with so much time spent outside the family. Perhaps as a result of being around many different people at an early age, they are notably tolerant and have a high degree of social responsibility. Danes also tend to be involved in club activities and organisations at a rate that surpasses most other societies.

More than 80% of all Danish women are in the workplace, nearly twice as many as in 1970. The law prevents job discrimination between the sexes but opportunities at the highest echelons have opened slowly. A third of the members of parliament are now women, but women hold fewer than 10% of the top management positions in the private sector.

Visitors will find Copenhageners to be relaxed, casual and not given to extremes. Danes like to think of themselves as a classless society and there are seldom any hints of chauvinism, sexism or any other ism.

Copenhageners are very open-minded on lifestyle issues. In 1989, Denmark became the first European country to legalise same-sex marriages and to offer gay partners most of the same rights as heterosexual couples. In 1999 a further step in recognising a broader definition of the family was taken when the decade-old Registered Partnership Act was amended to allow married gays to legally adopt the children of their partners.

Dos & Don'ts

Nothing out of the ordinary is expected of visitors, but there are a couple of potential pitfalls to avoid. Copenhageners generally queue by a number system; when you go to the post office, a bakery, the tourist office – just about any place there can be a queue – there's invariably a machine dispensing numbered tickets. Grab one as you enter and always wait until your number is called.

Danes love to joke about a lot of things, but can be sensitive to criticism. They have a high degree of respect for the queen and any flippant remark about the royal family is apt to offend most people.

Casual dress is perfectly fine. Simply put, you don't have to dress snazzy to do most anything in Copenhagen other than for the fanciest of fine dining. Nonetheless, Copenhageners themselves are often very stylish dressers. If you want to blend in and hit the club scene, black clothing is the trend.

RELIGION

More than 90% of all Danes officially belong to Folkekirken (Danish People's Church), the state-supported national church, an Evangelical Lutheran denomination. However, fewer than 5% of Danes are regular churchgoers.

Although Folkekirken is connected with the state, Danes enjoy freedom of religion and Copenhagen has places of worship for several other Christian denominations as well as Buddhists, Hindus, Moslems and Jews.

A listing of the city's churches, temples and mosques, with addresses and service times, can be found in the free tourist publication *Copenhagen This Week*.

LANGUAGE

The national language is Danish, which belongs to the northern branch of the Germanic language group. Most Danes speak at least basic English, however, and it is easy for English-language speakers to get around without a workable knowledge of Danish. German is also widely spoken.

For more information on Danish, including a guide to pronunciation and a list of useful words and phrases, see the Language chapter at the back of this book.

For a more comprehensive guide to the language, as well as those of the surrounding countries and Iceland, make sure to get a copy of Lonely Planet's *Scandinavian Europe phrasebook*.

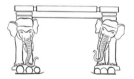

Facts for the Visitor

WHEN TO GO

Considering its northern latitude, Copenhagen has a relatively mild climate year-round. And, of course, as Scandinavia's leading city there's always plenty of action.

Still, the winter months – cold and with short daylight hours – are certainly the least hospitable. Many tourist attractions have shorter opening hours and a few are outright mothballed in the winter and don't come alive until April, when the weather begins to warm up and daylight hours start to increase.

In May and June the weather is generally warm and comfortable, and you'll beat the rush of tourists. Autumn can also be pleasant.

Nonetheless, July/August is the peak season and the time for open-air concerts and music festivals, lots of street activity and longer hours at sightseeing attractions. Of course you won't be the only tourist during summer, as many Europeans travel during their summer holidays and celebrate midsummer with gusto. The school year is back into swing by mid-August, so the last half of August can be a particularly attractive time to travel, as it still has summer weather but far fewer crowds.

Before planning a trip, see also Climate in the Facts about Copenhagen chapter.

ORIENTATION

Copenhagen is an easy city to get around. It has a reasonably compact centre and the entire metro area is served by an excellent public transit system of trains and buses.

The main train station, Central Station (also called Hovedbanegården or København H), is flanked on the west by the main hotel zone and on the east by the city's famous Tivoli amusement park. Opposite the northern corner of Tivoli is Rådhuspladsen, the central city square and the main terminus for buses around the city.

The world's longest pedestrian street, Strøget, runs from Rådhuspladsen through the city's commercial centre to Kongens Nytorv, a large square at the head of the scenic Nyhavn canal. Pedestrian streets run north from Strøget to the Latin Quarter, a haunt for students.

MAPS

The tourist office produces a free, four-colour map of Copenhagen with a street index and keys for hotels and major attractions. It covers the entire greater Copenhagen area and includes a detailed blow-up of the city centre. You can pick one up at the airport information desk, at the tourist office and at the front desk of many hotels.

Although there's not much that the free tourist map doesn't show, you can also buy commercial maps at bookshops that are larger and have more complete indexes; one of the best is *Kraks citykort over København* (1:15.000).

There are also detailed atlases with a similar scale that cover the entire Copenhagen region and list virtually every street and alley throughout North Zealand. The best among them is *Politikens Kortborg*, a weighty 425-page atlas sold at all Copenhagen bookshops.

TOURIST OFFICES
Local Tourist Offices

The city tourist office (☎ 70 22 24 42, fax 70 22 24 52, ⒠ touristinfo@woco.dk), Bernstorffsgade 1, is just north of Central Station. It has a well-stocked information desk and helpful staff. Here you can get the useful booklet *Copenhagen This Week*, free city maps and sightseeing brochures for both Copenhagen and destinations throughout Denmark. There's also a room and hotel booking service on site (see the Places to Stay chapter). The office is open 9 am (10 am on Sunday) to 8 pm daily from 1 May to 31 August; the rest of the year it's open 9 am to 4.30 pm weekdays, to 1.30 pm Saturday.

Use It (Map 8, G4; ☎ 33 73 06 20, ⒠ useit@ui.dk), Rådhusstræde 13, is a fine alternative information centre catering to young budget travellers but open to all. It books rooms, stores luggage, holds mail, provides information on everything from hitching to nightlife, and puts out a useful general guide called *Playtime* – all free of charge. It's open 9 am to 7 pm daily from mid-June to mid-September, and 11 am to 4 pm weekdays (to 2 pm on Friday) at other times.

Tourist Offices Abroad
Danish tourist offices abroad include:

Finland (☎ 9-586 0330, ✉ tanska@dt.dk),
  Tanskan Matkailutoimisto, Salomonsgatan 17
  A 6 vån, 00100 Helsinki
France (☎ 01 53 43 26 26, ✉ paris@dt.dk)
  Conseil du Tourisme de Danemark,
  18 boulevard Malesherbes, 75008 Paris
Germany (☎ 40-32 02 10, ✉ daninfo@dt.dk)
  Dänisches Fremdenverkehrsamt,
  Glockengiesserwall 2, 20095 Hamburg
Italy (☎ 2-87 48 03, ✉ info.dk@dt.dk) Ente
  Danese per il Turismo, Via Cappuccio 11,
  20123 Milano
Netherlands (☎ 0900-202 52 80,
  ✉ denemarken@dt.dk) Deens Verkeersburo
  Benelux, Postbus 266, 2300 AG Leiden
Norway (☎ 22 00 76 46, ✉ danmark@dt.dk)
  Danmarks Turistkontor, Tollbugaten 27,
  Postboks 406 Sentrum, 0103 Oslo
Sweden (☎ 08-611 7222, ✉ info@dtab.se)
  Danmarks Turistråd, Box 5524, 114 85
  Stockholm
UK (☎ 020-7259 5959, ✉ dtb.london@dt.dk)
  Danish Tourist Board, 55 Sloane St, London
  SW1X 9SY
USA (☎ 212-885 9700, ✉ info@goscandinavia
  .com) Danish Tourist Board, PO Box 4649,
  Grand Central Station, New York, NY 10163

DOCUMENTS
Visas
Citizens of the USA, Canada, Australia and New Zealand need a valid passport to enter Denmark, but they don't need a visa for tourist stays of less than three months. In addition, no entry visa is needed by citizens of EU and Scandinavian countries.

Citizens of many African, South American, Asian and former Soviet bloc countries do require a visa. The Danish Immigration Service publishes a list of countries whose citizens require a visa at its Web site at www.udlst.dk/sjle1/visacountries.html.

If you're in Copenhagen and have questions on visa extensions or visas in general, contact the Danish Immigration Service: Udlændingestyrelsen (☎ 35 36 66 00) at Ryesgade 53.

Work Visas Citizens of EU countries are allowed to stay in Denmark for up to three months searching for a job and it's generally straightforward to get a residency permit if work is found. The main stipulation is that the job provides enough income to adequately cover living expenses. EU citizens in Copenhagen can apply for the residency permit at Københavns Overpræsidium (☎ 33 12 23 80), Hammerensgade 1.

Citizens of other countries are required to get a work permit before entering Denmark. This means first securing a job offer then applying for a work and residency permit from a Danish embassy or consulate while still in your home country. You can enter Denmark only after the permit has been granted and they are usually limited to people with specialised skills that are in high demand.

Travel Insurance
A travel agent can sell you a travel insurance policy to cover losses you might incur should you unexpectedly have to cancel your trip or change your itinerary. Keep in mind that many airlines and package tours have hefty penalties for cancellations or changes, and some are totally nonrefundable.

A good travel insurance policy also provides coverage for lost luggage and medical emergencies. There are a wide variety of policies available, so check the fine print. Check also to see if the policy covers an emergency flight home in the case of a medical crisis.

It's a good idea to purchase travel insurance as early as possible. If you buy it the week before you leave, you might find, for instance, that you're not covered for delays to your departure caused by strikes or other industrial action that may have been in force before you took out the insurance.

Paying for your ticket with a credit card often provides limited travel accident insurance, and you may also be able to reclaim the payment if the operator doesn't deliver. Ask your credit card company what it will cover.

Driving Licence & Permits

Bring your home driving licence, as Denmark accepts many foreign driving licences without restriction, including those issued in the USA, Canada, the UK and other EU countries.

If you don't hold a European driving licence and plan to drive outside Denmark, it's a good idea to obtain an International Driving Permit (IDP) from your local automobile association before you leave. You'll need a passport photo and a valid licence. IDPs are usually inexpensive and valid for one year only.

Hostel Cards

There are several Hostelling International (HI) hostels in the Copenhagen area. If you have an international hostel card be sure to bring it. If you don't have an international card you can buy one in Denmark at the first hostel you stay at for 160kr.

Even if you're not planning to stay at hostels on this trip, but happen to have a card, bring it along, as it'll get you discounts at some museums and sightseeing spots.

Student & Youth Cards

The most useful is the International Student Identity Card (ISIC), an ID-style card with your photograph, with discounts on many forms of transport and reduced admission to some museums and sights.

There is a worldwide industry in fake student cards, and some places now stipulate a maximum age for student discounts or, more simply, they've substituted a 'youth discount' for a 'student discount'. If you're aged 25 or younger but not a student, you can apply for the Federation of International Youth Travel Organisations (FIYTO) card, called GO25, which gives much the same discounts as an ISIC.

Both types of card are issued by student unions, hostelling organisations or student travel agencies. They don't automatically entitle you to discounts, but you won't find out until you flash the card.

Other Documents

In many countries, local camping federations issue a Camping Card International (CCI), which is basically a camping ground ID. These passes incorporate third-party insurance for any damage you may cause. In Denmark your home-country CCI will be accepted if it has the current year's stamp. If you arrive in the country without a CCI, you can purchase a Danish carnet (45kr for an individual or 75kr for a family) at the first camping ground you visit or from tourist offices.

Copies

Before you leave home, you should photocopy all important documents (passport data page, credit cards, travel insurance policy, air tickets, driving licence etc). Leave one copy with someone at home and keep another with you, separate from the originals.

It's wise to store details of your vital travel documents in Lonely Planet's free online Travel Vault in case you lose the photocopies or can't be bothered with them. Your password-protected Travel Vault is accessible online anywhere in the world – create it at www.ekno.lonelyplanet.com.

EMBASSIES & CONSULATES
Danish Embassies & Consulates

Danish missions overseas include those listed below.

Australia (☎ 02-6273 2195) 15 Hunter St, Yarralumla, ACT 2600
Canada (☎ 613-562 1811) 47 Clarence St, Suite 450, Ottawa, Ontario K1N 9K1
Finland (☎ 9-684 1050) Centralgatan 1A, 00101 Helsinki
France (☎ 01 44 31 21 21) 77 Avenue Marceau, 75116 Paris
Germany (☎ 5050 2000) Rauchstrasse 1, 10787 Berlin
Iceland (☎ 56 21 230) Hverfisgata 29, 121 Reykjavík
Ireland (☎ 1-475 6404) 121 St Stephen's Green, Dublin 2
Netherlands (☎ 70-302 5959) Koninginnegracht 30 (Postbus 85654), 2508 CJ Den Haag
New Zealand Contact the embassy in Australia
Norway (☎ 22 54 08 00) Olav Kyrres Gate 7, 0244 Oslo

Sweden (☎ 08-406 7500) Jakobs Torg 1, 11186 Stockholm
UK (☎ 020-7333 0200) 55 Sloane St, London SW1X 9SR
USA (☎ 202-234 4300) 3200 Whitehaven St NW, Washington DC 20008

Embassies & Consulates in Copenhagen

It's important to realise what your own embassy can and can't do.

Generally, it won't be much help in emergencies if the trouble you're in is your own fault. Remember you are bound by the laws of the country you are in. In most cases, your embassy is not likely to be terribly sympathetic if you are jailed after committing a crime locally, even if such actions are legal in your own country. Some embassies do send representatives to visit citizens arrested abroad, so don't hesitate to contact them.

In genuine emergencies you might get assistance, but only if other channels have been exhausted. If you need to get home urgently, a free ticket home is exceedingly unlikely as the embassy would expect you to have insurance. If you have all your money and documents stolen, its assistance will likely be limited to getting you a new passport.

These foreign diplomatic representatives to Denmark are in the Copenhagen area:

Australia (Map 4, B8; ☎ 70 26 36 76) Strandboulevarden 122, Copenhagen (the embassy expects to move to a new location in 2001 but the phone number won't change so ring ahead)
Canada (Map 8, D8; ☎ 33 48 32 00) Kristen Bernikows Gade 1, Copenhagen
Finland (Map 7, B7; ☎ 33 13 42 14) Sankt Annæ Plads 24, Copenhagen
France (Map 8, B10; ☎ 33 15 51 22) Kongens Nytorv 4, Copenhagen
Germany (Map 4, F8; ☎ 35 45 99 00), Stockholmsgade 57, Copenhagen
Iceland (Map 7, E4; ☎ 33 15 96 04) Dantes Plads 3, Copenhagen
Ireland (Map 4, E9; ☎ 35 42 32 33) Østbanegade 21, Copenhagen
New Zealand Contact the British embassy
Netherlands (Map 7, B7; ☎ 33 70 72 02) Toldbodgade 33, Copenhagen
Norway (Map 7, A8; ☎ 33 14 01 24) Amaliegade 39, Copenhagen

Poland (Map 3, D4; ☎ 39 62 72 45) Richelieus Allé 12, Hellerup
Russia (Map 4, E8; ☎ 35 42 55 85) Kristianiagade 5, Copenhagen
Sweden (Map 7, B7; ☎ 33 36 03 70) Sankt Annæ Plads 15A, Copenhagen
UK (Map 4, E8; ☎ 35 44 52 00) Kastelsvej 40, Copenhagen
USA (Map 4, E7; ☎ 35 55 31 44) Dag Hammarskjölds Allé 24, Copenhagen

CUSTOMS

One litre of spirits and 200 cigarettes can be brought into Denmark duty free if you're coming from outside the EU. Those coming from an EU country are allowed to bring in 300 cigarettes and 1.5L of spirits.

When you arrive in Denmark, there will be two customs channels. You must use the red channel if you're bringing in more than the usual allowance of duty-free goods or any restricted items (guns, drugs etc). Use the green channel – which is generally a quick exit – if you have nothing to declare.

MONEY
Currency

The Danish *krone* is most often written DKK in international money markets, Dkr in northern Europe and kr within Denmark.

The krone is divided into 100 øre. There are 25 øre, 50 øre, one krone, two kroner, five kroner, 10 kroner and 20-kroner coins. Notes come in 50, 100, 200, 500 and 1000-kroner denominations.

Exchange Rates

The following currencies convert at these approximate rates:

country	unit		kroner
Australia	A$1	=	4.55kr
Canada	C$1	=	5.48kr
euro	€1	=	7.46kr
France	1FF	=	1.14kr
Germany	DM1	=	3.81kr
Japan	¥100	=	7.41kr
New Zealand	NZ$1	=	3.60kr
Norway	1 Nkr	=	0.92kr
Sweden	1 Skr	=	0.86kr
UK	UK£1	=	12.25kr
USA	US$1	=	8.34kr

The scenic waterfront quarter of Nyhavn

Panoramic view of the city

Slotsholmen, seat of Denmark's national government

Vor Frelsers Kirke's 95m-high spiral tower

Swanky pub interior

Spectacular stage foyer at Det Kongelige Teater

Exchanging Money

If you arrive by air, the bank at Copenhagen airport is open 6.30 am to 10 pm daily, which covers virtually all flights. If you're on an international ferry to Denmark, you'll typically be able to exchange US dollars and local currencies to Danish kroner on board.

The US dollar is generally the handiest foreign currency to bring. However, Danish banks will convert a wide range of other currencies as well, including the Australian dollar, Austrian schilling, British pound, Canadian dollar, Dutch guilder, Finnish markka, French franc, German mark, Italian lira, Japanese yen, kroner from Norway and Sweden, and the Swiss franc. Foreign coins are seldom accepted by banks, so try to unload those before arriving in Denmark.

Banks can be found on nearly every second corner in central Copenhagen. Most are open 9.30 am to 4 pm weekdays (to 6 pm on Thursday). The best place to go for longer hours is Central Station, which has a Den Danske Bank that's open 8 am to 8 pm daily, although higher commissions are charged outside normal banking hours.

Central Station also has a Forex exchange office open 8 am to 9 pm daily offering lower commissions than the banks. There are two other Forex offices in Copenhagen, one opposite Tivoli at Vesterbrogade 2B (Map 7, D3) open 10 am to 6 pm weekdays and the other at Nørre Voldgade 90 (Map 7, B4) in the Nørreport area open 9 am to 7 pm weekdays and 9 am to 3 pm Saturday.

Exchange Fees It's best to bring travellers cheques in higher denominations as bank fees for changing money are a hefty 20kr per cheque with a 40kr minimum. Cash transactions are usually charged a 25kr fee for any size transaction; travellers cheques command about a 1% better exchange rate.

The Forex exchange offices attract customers by charging only 10kr per travellers cheque, with no minimum, and 20kr on cash transactions.

Post offices also exchange foreign currency at rates comparable to the banks – the main benefit for travellers being Saturday morning opening hours.

Travellers Cheques All common travellers cheques are accepted at major banks in Denmark. The main benefit of travellers cheques is to provide protection from theft. Large companies such as American Express (AmEx) and Thomas Cook generally offer efficient replacement policies.

Keeping a record of the cheque numbers and those you have used is vital when it comes to replacing lost cheques. You should keep this information separate from the cheques themselves.

Eurocheques Guaranteed personal cheques are another way of carrying money or obtaining cash. The most popular of these is the Eurocheque, which requires having a European bank account.

Throughout Europe, when paying for something in a shop or withdrawing cash from a bank or post office, you write out a Eurocheque and show the accompanying guarantee card with your signature and registration number. The card can double as an ATM card, and should obviously be kept separate from the cheques for safety.

ATMs Plastic cards are ideal travelling companions – they eliminate the need to carry a wad of cash, allowing you instead to withdraw money as you need it from banks and automatic teller machines (ATMs).

Cards issued by your home bank to withdraw money directly from your bank account have become increasingly linked internationally. Both the Cirrus and Plus networks are now used at ATMs throughout Denmark. However, seek advice from your home bank before you travel as some accounts can be accessed internationally, while others can't. Remember that to use a credit card with an ATM you'll need to have established a personal identification number (PIN) – do that before you travel.

Most banks in Copenhagen have ATMs, many of them accessible 24 hours a day. In addition to regular ATMs, there are specialised 24-hour cash-exchange machines that change major foreign currencies (bills only) into Danish kroner at a number of locations, including Den Danske Bank in

Central Station, Unibank on Axeltorv and Jyske Bank at Vesterbrogade 9 near the Grand Hotel.

Credit Cards Credit cards like Visa and MasterCard (also known as Access or Euro-card) are widely accepted in Denmark. Charge cards like AmEx and Diners Club are also accepted, but not as often. On the plus side, charge cards have a reputation for quick replacement, often within 24 hours of reporting the card lost.

Lost or Stolen Cards If a card is lost or stolen, inform the issuing company as soon as possible. Here are Copenhagen numbers for cancelling your cards:

AmEx	☎ 80 01 00 21
Diners Club	☎ 36 73 73 73
MasterCard, Access, Eurocard	☎ 80 01 60 98
Visa	☎ 80 01 85 88

You can also call ☎ 44 89 25 00, which handles lost Danish-issued credit cards, for 24-hour advice if you're unable to get through on any of the credit card reporting numbers listed above.

International Transfers Transferring money from your home bank will be easier if you've authorised someone back home to access your account. Specify the city, the bank and the branch to which you want your money directed, or ask your home bank to tell you where there's a suitable one, and make sure you get the details right. If you have the choice, find a large bank and ask for the international division.

Security

Whichever way you decide to carry your money, it makes sense to keep most of it out of easy reach of thieves in a moneybelt or something similar. It also makes sense to keep something like 500kr apart from the rest of your cash for use in an emergency.

Take particular care in crowded places such as Central Station and never leave wallets sticking out of trouser pockets or day-packs.

Costs

By anything other than Scandinavian standards, Copenhagen is an expensive city. Part of the credit lies with the 25% value-added tax (VAT), called *moms* in Danish, which is included in every price from hotel rooms and restaurant meals to car rentals and shop purchases.

Still, your costs will depend on how you travel and it's possible to visit Copenhagen without spending a fortune. If you're travelling on a budget, one way to cut down on expenses is to take advantage of camping grounds and hostels.

In terms of basic expenses, if you camp or stay in hostels and prepare your own meals you might get by on 200kr a day. If you stay in modest hotels and eat at inexpensive restaurants, you can expect to spend about 450kr a day if you're doubling up, 600kr if you're travelling alone. Interestingly, 1st-class hotels, which commonly have discounted specials, often cost only about 30% more than mid-range hotels.

On top of these amounts you'll need to budget for local transport, admission fees to museums and other sights, entertainment etc, although deals like the Copenhagen Card and transportation passes can save you money.

If you're touring by car, it's going to be more expensive. Petrol is around 9kr a litre, and if you opt to rent a car in Copenhagen the costs range from high to exorbitant. Expect to pay about 700kr per day for car rental, although the daily rate on week-long rentals can average about half that – in either case this is for the cheapest economy car.

Tipping & Bargaining

Restaurant bills and taxi fares include service charges in the quoted prices. Further tipping is unnecessary, although rounding up the bill is not uncommon when the service has been particularly good. Bargaining is not a common practice in Denmark.

Taxes & Refunds

Foreign visitors from countries outside the EU who buy goods in Denmark can get a refund of the 25% VAT, less a handling fee, if they spend at least 300kr at any retail outlet that participates in the 'Tax Free Shopping Global Refund' plan. This includes most shops catering to tourists. The 300kr can be a single item or several items, as long as they're purchased from the same shop.

Be sure to obtain the 'Global Refund cheque' from the store when you make the purchase; it should include the date, both the buyer's and seller's name and address, the number and type of goods, the selling price and the VAT amount.

Contact the Global Refund office at your point of departure from Denmark to get the refund, and allow extra time in case there's a queue at the booth. At Copenhagen airport, you'll find a booth in the international departure hall; if you depart by ship, inquire at the port as you board. If you have any questions about these VAT refunds call ☎ 32 52 55 66, or pick up a brochure on the program from participating shops.

POST & COMMUNICATIONS
Post

The main post office (Map 7, E3) on Tietgensgade, just south-east of Central Station, is open 11 am to 6 pm weekdays and 10 am to 1 pm on Saturday. If you're having poste restante mail sent to Copenhagen, it can be picked up here; have letters addressed to: addressee, Poste Restante, Main Post Office, Tietgensgade 37, 1500 Copenhagen V.

If you're not using the poste restante service, the post office in Central Station will generally prove more convenient. It's open 8 am to 10 pm weekdays, 9 am to 4 pm Saturday and 10 am to 5 pm Sunday.

In addition, there are numerous neighbourhood branch post offices throughout Copenhagen. Hours vary but these neighbourhood post offices are generally open at least 10 am to 5 pm weekdays and some also have limited Saturday hours.

Postal Rates It costs 4.50kr to airmail a postcard or letter weighing up to 20g to Scandinavia or Western Europe, 5.50kr to other countries. Heavier letters weighing up to 50g cost 5.25kr within Denmark, 6.75kr to other Scandinavian countries, 9.75kr to Western Europe and 12.25kr to other countries. Inter-

national mail sent from Copenhagen is generally out of the country within 24 hours.

Telephone

Denmark has an efficient phone system and pay phones abound in busy public places such as train stations and shopping arcades.

You have a choice of using either cardphones or coin phones. Coin phones take all Danish coins in denominations of 1kr to 20kr, but they won't return change from larger coins, so it's generally best to use the smaller denominations.

If you're going to be making many calls, consider using a cardphone, which operates with a debit phonecard *(telekort)*, sold in denominations of 30kr, 50kr and 100kr. These cards can be used for making both local and international calls and are more convenient than pumping in coins. Cards can be bought at post offices and many kiosks, especially those at train stations.

Cardphones work out slightly cheaper than coin phones because you pay for the exact amount of time you speak; an LCD screen keeps you posted on how much time is left on the card.

It's possible to replace an expiring card with a new card without breaking the call. Cardphones are posted with information in English detailing their use as well as the location of the nearest place that sells phonecards.

Domestic Calls All telephone numbers in Denmark have eight numbers. There are no area codes and all eight numbers must be dialled, even when making calls within the same city.

It generally costs a minimum of 2kr to make a local call at coin phones. Local calls are timed and you get twice as much calling time for your money on domestic calls made between 7.30 pm and 8 am.

International Calls to Denmark The country code for Denmark is 45. To call Denmark from another country, dial the international access code for the country you're in, followed by 45 and the local eight digit number.

International Calls from Denmark The international access code in Denmark is 00. To make direct international calls from Denmark dial 00 followed by the country code for the country you're calling, the area code, then the local number.

For assistance, including information on rates for international calls, dial toll free ☎ 80 60 40 55. If you want to make a collect or reverse-charge call, dial ☎ 80 60 40 50.

Lonely Planet's eKno global communication service provides low-cost international calls – for local calls you're usually better off with a local phonecard. eKno also offers free messaging services, email, travel information and an online travel vault, where you can securely store all your important documents. Join online at www .ekno.lonelyplanet.com, where you will find the local-access numbers for the 24-hour customer-service centre, then always check the eKno Web site for updated access numbers for each country and new features.

Fax

Faxes can be sent from larger post offices. The charge for sending within Europe is 35kr for the first page and 20kr for each additional page. If you're sending to a number outside Europe the charge is 50/30kr for the first/additional pages.

Email & Internet Access

Travelling with a portable computer is a great way to stay in touch with home but, unless you know what you're doing, it's fraught with potential problems. If the power supply voltage in Denmark varies from that at home, bring a universal AC adapter, which will enable you to plug it in without frying the innards. You may also need a plug adapter, which is often easiest to buy before you leave home.

Also, your PC-card modem may not work once you leave your home country – but you won't know for sure until you try. The safest option is to buy a 'global' modem before you leave home. Keep in mind that the telephone socket may be different from that at home as well, so ensure that you have at least a US RJ-11 telephone

adapter that works with your modem. You can almost always find an adapter that will convert from RJ-11 to the local variety. For more information on travelling with a portable computer, visit the Web sites www.teleadapt.com and www.warrior.com.

Major Internet service providers (ISPs), such as AOL (www.aol.com), have dial-in nodes in Denmark and throughout Europe; it's best to download a list of the dial-in numbers before you leave home. If you access your Internet email at home through a smaller ISP, your best option is either to open an account with a global ISP, or to rely on public access points to collect your mail.

To use public access points to get your email, you'll need to know your incoming (POP or IMAP) mail server name, your account name and your password. A final option for collecting mail through public access points is to open a free Web-based email account such as HotMail (www.hotmail.com) or Yahoo! Mail (mail.yahoo.com). You can then access your mail from anywhere in the world from any Internet-connected machine running a standard Web browser.

A growing number of hotels in Denmark are adding modem hookups in guest rooms, so if you intend to use your own computer, you should inquire when making reservations.

Public libraries in the Copenhagen area, and elsewhere in Denmark, have computers with Internet access, though access policies vary and you may need to book in advance.

As most families in Denmark have their own computers, cybercafes are not terribly abundant and tend to be short-lived.

Diablo Net Café (Map 7, E1; ☎ 33 31 50 70, ⓔ dnc@diablo.dk), Værnedamsvej 5A, in Vesterbro on a side street a few minutes east of Københavns Bymuseum, charges 10kr per 15 minutes to surf the Net and is open noon to midnight daily.

Other options include Babel (Map 7, A3; ☎ 33 33 93 38, ⓔ postmaster@babel.dk), Copenhagen's oldest cybercafe at Frederiksborggade 33, which is open 2 to 11 pm weekdays and 2 to 6 pm Saturday, and the more central Netpoint (☎ 33 42 60 00, ⓔ netpoint.dk), which is in the SAS Royal

Hotel (Map 7, D3) on the corner of Bernstorffsgade and Vesterbrogade, and is open 9 am to 10 pm weekdays and noon to 10 pm at weekends. Both places have Internet access for 30kr an hour.

The main public library in the Latin Quarter at Krystalgade 15 has computers with Internet access that can be used free of charge for up to 30 minutes, but the queuing time can easily exceed an hour.

If you just want to check your email, a better bet is to drop by Kongelige Bibliotek (Royal Library), a public research library at the southern side of Slotsholmen, where more than 100 online computers fill the hallways and visitors can make a quick online run as long as no-one else is waiting to use the computer. Another free option is Use It, the youth information centre at Rådhusstræde 13, which offers Internet access but has only three computers available, so online time is limited and there can be a lengthy queue.

INTERNET RESOURCES

The World Wide Web is a rich resource for travellers. You can research your trip, hunt down bargain air fares, book hotels, check weather conditions or chat with locals and other travellers about the best places to visit (or avoid!).

There's no better place to start your Web explorations than the Lonely Planet Web site (www.lonelyplanet.com). Here you'll find succinct summaries on travelling to most places on earth, postcards from other travellers and the Thorn Tree bulletin board, where you can ask questions before you go or dispense advice when you get back. You can also find travel news and updates to many of our most popular guidebooks, and the subWWWay section links you to the most useful travel resources elsewhere on the Web.

Denmark has lots of Web sites related to travel. Many attractions, hotels and tourist-related services have their own sites, and we've listed these in the book when they would be of particular use to travellers.

One of the best general Web sites is the Danish foreign ministry site located at www.denmark.org, which has a wealth of information, including updated weather and exchange rates, and links to many other Danish sites, such as the tourist office.

BOOKS

Most books are published in different editions by different publishers in different countries. So a book might be a hardcover rarity in one country but readily available in paperback in another. Fortunately, bookshops and libraries can search by title or author, so your local bookshop or library is best placed to advise you on availability.

Lonely Planet

If your travels will take you beyond the Copenhagen area, Lonely Planet's *Denmark* guide comprehensively covers the entire country.

Should other Scandinavian or Baltic countries beckon, you'll find these destinations covered in Lonely Planet's *Scandinavian & Baltic Europe* guide. A good companion to help you communicate with people along the way is Lonely Planet's *Scandinavian Europe phrasebook*.

General

The hardback *Denmark: A Modern History*, by W Glyn Jones, is one of the more comprehensive and insightful accounts of contemporary Danish society.

Women in Denmark, Yesterday and Today, by Inga Dahlsgård, traces Danish history from a woman's perspective.

Copenhagen – The Queen's City, by Gitte Olsen & Robert Trojaborg, is a softcover souvenir book with attractive photos and some accompanying background text.

Copenhagen Architecture Guide, by Olaf Lind & Annemarie Lund, is a substantial softcover book covering more than 300 noteworthy buildings in Copenhagen, with interesting descriptions and colour photos.

Louisiana: The Collection and Buildings, produced by the modern art museum in Humlebæk, is a handsome 376-page oversized softcover book with photos and descriptions of this landmark museum and its collection.

Copenhagen is a thought-provoking drama by Michael Frayn, which speculates what may have transpired during the September 1941 meeting in Copenhagen of Danish physicist Niels Bohr and German scientist Werner Heisenberg. These two former colleagues went on to play pivotal roles in the development of atomic weapons, Bohr for the Allies and Heisenberg for the Nazis.

Copenhagen philosopher Søren Kierkegaard produced volumes of works, including *The Concept of Dread* (1844), which is considered by many to be the first work of depth psychology ever written, and *Concluding Unscientific Postscript to the Philosophical Fragments* (1846), in which Kierkegaard passionately expounded the tenets of the school of thought that would become existentialism. *A Kierkegaard Anthology*, by Robert Bretall, comprises a broad cross section of his major works.

There's an avalanche of books by and about Hans Christian Andersen as well as numerous biographies of the author, including the definitive *Hans Christian Andersen* by Elias Bredsdorff. *Thomas Gray in Copenhagen: In Which the Philosopher Cat Meets the Ghost of Hans Christian Andersen* by Philip J Davis, is a witty blend of fact and fiction.

NEWSPAPERS & MAGAZINES

Copenhagen's leading daily newspaper is *Politiken*. There are scores of smaller papers too. All of the dailies are in Danish only.

English readers can pick up the *Copenhagen Post*, a weekly newspaper that publishes an interesting mix of Danish news, events and entertainment information every Thursday. You can also read this English-language paper online at www.cphpost.dk.

Copenhagen This Week – despite its name, a monthly publication – is a pocket-sized English-language magazine loaded with tourist-related information, from event and entertainment schedules to listings of restaurants and escort services. It's free at the tourist office and many hotels.

Tourist in Copenhagen, updated annually, is a 100-plus-page, four-colour publication with detailed sightseeing information and museum descriptions. It's available free at the tourist office and some museums.

Copenhagen Living is a sleek, new, English-language magazine focusing on fashion, design and contemporary cuisine, is published a couple of times a year. It costs 59kr and is available at Copenhagen bookshops and newsstands. Subscription information is online at www.cphliving.dk.

English-language magazines and newspapers are readily available at the Interkiosk newsstand in Central Station, at the newspaper kiosk on Rådhuspladsen and in the lobbies of larger hotels. The 7-Eleven convenience stores also sell international papers, but may not have as wide a selection.

Among more common English-language newspapers sold in Copenhagen are the *International Herald Tribune*, *USA Today*, *Wall Street Journal*, the *European* and the *Guardian*. In addition, numerous British and US magazines on various topics, from computers to gardening to news, can be found at Interkiosk in Central Station and at bookshops throughout Copenhagen.

RADIO & TV

You can hear a five-minute news brief in English at 8.40 and 11 am and 5.10 and 10 pm weekdays on Radio Danmark International at 1062MHz. The BBC World Service is broadcast on short wave at 6195kHz and 9410kHz.

British and US network programs are common on Danish TV and are often presented in English with Danish subtitles. Many hotels have live CNN news, BBC World Service and other English-language cable and satellite TV programing.

VIDEO SYSTEMS

If you buy videos in Denmark, make sure they're compatible with your home system. Denmark uses PAL, which is incompatible with the North American NTSC system.

PHOTOGRAPHY & VIDEO

Both print and slide film is readily available in Copenhagen. A 24 exposure roll of Kodacolor Gold 100 will cost about 40kr to buy and 100kr to develop and print. A 36 exposure roll of Kodak slide film costs about 65kr.

There are numerous photo centres (including Japan Photo at Råhusarkaden on Vesterbrogade near city hall) which offer a range of photo-processing options. The cost to develop and print a roll of 24 exposure film is around 125kr for one-hour photo processing, 100kr for same-day service and 65kr for three day service.

Video

Properly used, a video camera can give a fascinating record of your holiday. As well as videoing the obvious things – sunsets, landmark buildings – remember to record some of the ordinary everyday details of life in the city. Video cameras these days have amazingly sensitive microphones, and you might be surprised how much sound will be picked up. This can also be a problem if there is a lot of ambient noise – filming by the side of a busy road might seem OK when you do it, but viewing it back home might simply give you a deafening cacophony of traffic noise.

One good rule to follow for beginners is to try to film in long takes, and don't move the camera around too much. Otherwise, your video could well make your viewers seasick! If your camera has a stabiliser, you can use it to obtain good footage while travelling on various means of transport, even on bumpy roads. And remember, you're on holiday – don't let the video turn your entire trip into a Cecil B de Mille production.

Make sure you keep the batteries charged and have the necessary charger, plugs and transformer for Denmark. Copenhagen photo stores sell P-5 videotape; a 90-minute tape costs around 80kr.

TIME

Time in Denmark is normally one hour ahead of GMT/UTC, the same as in neighbouring European countries. When it's noon in Copenhagen, it's 11 am in London, 6 am in New York and Toronto, 3 am in San Francisco, 9 pm in Sydney and 11 pm in Auckland.

Clocks are moved forward one hour for daylight-saving time from the last Sunday in March to the last Sunday in October. Denmark uses the 24-hour clock system and all timetables and business hours are posted accordingly. Klokken, which means o'clock, is abbreviated kl (kl 19.30 is 7.30 pm).

Dates are written with the day followed by the month, thus 3/6 means 3 June and 6/3 means 6 March.

ELECTRICITY
Voltages & Cycles

Denmark, like most of Europe, runs on 220V (volts), 50Hz (cycles) AC.

Check the voltage and cycle (usually 50Hz) used in your home country. Most appliances that are set up for 240V (such as those used in the UK) will handle 220V without modifications and vice versa. It's always preferable to adjust your appliance to the exact voltage if you can – a few items, such as some electric razors and radios, will do this automatically. If your appliance doesn't have a built-in transformer, don't plug a 110/125V appliance (the kind used in the USA and Canada) into a Danish outlet without using a separate transformer.

Plugs & Sockets

Denmark uses the 'europlug' with two round pins. Many europlugs and some sockets don't have provision for earth wiring because most local home appliances are double-insulated; when provided, earth usually consists of two contact points along the edge.

If your plugs are of a different design, you'll need an adapter. These are usually available in shops specialising in travel needs. Make sure to get one before you leave, because most adapters available in Copenhagen are intended for Danes travelling to a country that doesn't use the europlug.

WEIGHTS & MEASURES

Denmark uses the metric system. Petrol and beverages are sold by the litre, meats and vegetables are weighed in kilograms,

FACTS FOR THE VISITOR

Daylight Delight

Throughout the summer, visitors to Copenhagen can enjoy long lingering hours of daylight. The longest days are in late June, when the sun rises around 4.30 am and sets around 10 pm, providing nearly 17½ daylight hours.

month	sunrise	sunset
1 January	8.40 am	3.48 pm
1 February	8.08 am	4.39 pm
1 March	7.06 am	5.40 pm
1 April	6.36 am	7.51 pm
1 May	5.29 am	8.46 pm
1 June	4.36 am	9.40 pm
1 July	4.33 am	9.54 pm
1 August	5.17 am	9.23 pm
1 September	6.16 am	8.02 pm
1 October	7.14 am	6.43 pm
1 November	7.15 am	4.31 pm
1 December	8.23 am	3.37 pm

distance is measured either in kilometres or metres and speed limits are posted in kilometres per hour (km/h).

Fruit is often sold by the piece *(stykke)*, abbreviated 'stk'. Decimals are indicated by commas and thousands by points.

For those unaccustomed to the metric system, there's a conversion chart on the inside back cover of this book.

LAUNDRY
Coin laundries (look for the word *møntvask*) are not hard to find around the city.

There's one at Holbergsgade 9 near Nyhavn (Map 7, C7); one in the Vesterbro hotel district at Istedgade 45 (Map 7, F2) near its intersection with Absalonsgade; and another in the Nørreport area at Vindersgade 13. Hostels and camping grounds usually have coin-operated machines as well. The cost to wash and dry a load of clothes depends on the drying time, but generally comes to around 50kr.

TOILETS & SHOWERS
Toilets in Denmark are western-style. Public ones, which can be used free of charge,

are easy to find in Copenhagen at such places as train stations, public squares and shopping centres.

Copenhagen has public showers as well. At Central Station, the showers are adjacent to the underground toilets, open 5 am to 2 am, and cost 15kr. At Rådhuspladsen, they're underground at the eastern side of the bus information office, open 8.30 am to 11.30 pm, and cost 10kr.

LEFT LUGGAGE
Central Station has both coin-operated lockers and a left-luggage room *(bagageudlevering)* on the ground level near the Reventlowsgade exit. The lockers cost 25kr (35kr for large) per 24 hours and can be used for a maximum of 72 hours. The left luggage room (☎ 33 69 21 15) at the same site will hold small items for 30kr and large items for 40kr, per 24 hours, with no time limit.

There are also a few large lockers at Rådhuspladsen beneath the bus information office; the cost is 20kr per 24 hours.

Outside of the city centre you can find storage lockers at the Copenhagen airport and at larger train stations such as those in Helsingør, Hillerød and Roskilde.

HEALTH
Denmark is a healthy place and travellers shouldn't need to take any unusual health precautions. Sanitation standards are high and tap water is safe to drink.

Visitors whose countries have reciprocal agreements with Denmark are covered by the Danish national health-insurance program. For citizens of EU countries, in most cases you'll need to present EU form E-111; inquire at your national health service or travel agent before leaving home. In some situations you may have to pay pharmacies and doctors directly and then obtain a refund from the nearest health insurance office. Travel insurance may still be advisable because of the flexibility it offers, as well as covering expenses for an emergency flight home.

All visitors, regardless of where they are from, receive free hospital treatment in the event of an accident or a sudden illness, provided the patient has not come to Denmark for the purpose of obtaining the treatment and is too ill to return home.

Controlled medicine is only available from a pharmacy with a prescription that is issued by a Danish or other Scandinavian doctor.

Pharmacies *(apotek)* are plentiful. Most have the same opening hours as other shops, but there are some 24-hour pharmacies. The most conveniently located is Steno Apotek (Map 7, D3; ☎ 33 14 82 66) at Vesterbrogade 6, just north of Central Station.

Frederiksberg Hospital (Map 6, A2; ☎ 38 16 38 16), west of the city centre at Nordre Fasanvej 57, has a 24-hour emergency ward. Private doctor visits (☎ 33 93 63 00 for referrals) usually cost around 350kr.

In medical emergencies, dial ☎ 112; the call can be made without coins from public phones.

Predeparture Planning

Ensure that you have adequate health insurance. Before leaving home, ask your insurance company what your coverage is when you're abroad and consider buying additional travel insurance if it's not sufficient.

Make sure you're healthy before you start travelling. Pharmacies in Denmark stock all of the items you likely to need, but it's a good idea to carry a basic medical kit (see the Medical Kit Check List on the following page). Pseudoephedrine hydrochloride (Sudafed) may be useful if flying with a cold to avoid ear damage.

If you require a particular prescription medication take an adequate supply to cover your entire trip. Also take part of the packaging showing the generic name of the drug, rather than the brand, which will make getting replacements easier. It's always a good idea to have a legible prescription or letter from your doctor to show that you legally use the medication in order to avoid any problems.

Immunisations

Jabs are generally not necessary for Denmark or elsewhere in Europe; however, a yellow fever vaccination may be a requirement if you're coming from an affected area.

Everyday Health

Normal body temperature is up to 37°C or 98.6°F; more than 2°C (4°F) higher indicates a high fever. The normal adult pulse rate is 60 to 100 per minute (children 80 to 100, babies 100 to 140). As a general rule the pulse increases about 20 beats per minute for each °C (2°F) rise in fever.

Respiration (breathing) rate is also an indicator of illness. Count the number of breaths per minute: between 12 and 20 is normal for adults and older children (up to 30 for younger children, 40 for babies). People with a high fever or serious respiratory illness breathe more quickly than normal. More than 40 shallow breaths a minute may indicate pneumonia.

Motion Sickness

Eating lightly before and during a trip will reduce the chances of motion sickness. If prone to motion sickness, try to find a place that minimises movement – near the wing on aircraft, close to midships on boats, near the centre on buses.

Fresh air usually helps; reading and cigarette smoke don't.

Commercial motion-sickness preparations, which can cause drowsiness, have to be taken before the trip commences. Ginger (available in capsule form) and peppermint (including mint-flavoured sweets) are natural preventatives.

Jet Lag

When we travel long distances rapidly, our bodies take time to adjust to the 'new time' of our destination, and we may experience fatigue, disorientation, insomnia, anxiety, impaired concentration and loss of appetite. These effects will usually be gone within three days of arrival, but there are ways of minimising the impact of jet lag:

- Rest for a couple of days prior to departure; try to avoid late nights and last-minute dashes for travellers cheques and the like.
- Try to select flight schedules that minimise sleep deprivation; arriving late in the day means you can go to sleep soon after you arrive. For very long flights, try to organise a stopover.

Medical Kit Check List

Following is a list of items you should consider including in your medical kit – consult your pharmacist for brands available in your country.

☐ **Aspirin or paracetamol (acetaminophen in the USA)** – for pain or fever

☐ **Antihistamine** – for allergies, eg, hay fever; to ease the itch from insect bites or stings; and to prevent motion sickness

☐ **Cold and flu tablets, throat lozenges and nasal decongestant**

☐ **Multivitamins** – consider for long trips, when dietary vitamin intake may be inadequate

☐ **Antibiotics** – consider including these if you're travelling well off the beaten track; see your doctor, as they must be prescribed, and carry the prescription with you

☐ **Loperamide or diphenoxylate** – 'blockers' for diarrhoea

☐ **Prochlorperazine or metaclopramide** – for nausea and vomiting

☐ **Rehydration mixture** – to prevent dehydration, which may occur, for example, during bouts of diarrhoea; particularly important when travelling with children

☐ **Insect repellent, sunscreen, lip balm and eye drops**

☐ **Calamine lotion, sting relief spray or aloe vera** – to ease irritation from sunburn and insect bites or stings

☐ **Antifungal cream or powder** – for fungal skin infections and thrush

☐ **Antiseptic (such as povidone-iodine)** – for cuts and grazes

☐ **Bandages, Band-Aids (plasters) and other wound dressings**

☐ **Water purification tablets or iodine**

☐ **Scissors, tweezers and a thermometer** – note that mercury thermometers are prohibited by airlines

☐ **Sterile kit** – in case you need injections in a country with medical hygiene problems; discuss with your doctor

• Avoid excessive eating (which bloats the stomach) and alcohol (which causes dehydration) during the flight. Instead, drink plenty of non-carbonated, nonalcoholic drinks such as fruit juice or water.

• Make yourself comfortable by wearing loose-fitting clothes and perhaps bringing an eye mask and earplugs to help you sleep.

And if all else fails, and you find yourself newly arrived in Copenhagen and wide awake at 2 am, take advantage of the situation and hit the town! This is a night-owl city and many clubs are still in their prime at this time.

HIV & AIDS

Infection with the human immunodeficiency virus (HIV) may lead to acquired immune deficiency syndrome (AIDS). Any exposure to blood, blood products or body fluids may put the individual at risk. The disease is often transmitted through sexual contact or via dirty needles – vaccinations, acupuncture, tattooing and body piercing can be potentially as dangerous as intravenous drug use.

If you have any questions regarding AIDS while in Denmark, there's an AIDS Hotline (☎ 33 91 11 19) in Copenhagen, open 9 am to 11 pm daily.

WOMEN TRAVELLERS

Although women travellers are less likely to encounter problems in Copenhagen than in most other capital cities, the usual commonsense precautions apply when it comes to potentially dangerous situations such as hitchhiking and walking alone at night.

KVINFO, Center for Information om Kvinde-og Kønsforskning (Danish Centre for Information on Women and Gender; ☎ 33 13 50 88, e kvinfo@kvinfo.dk), Christians Brygge 3, Copenhagen, is a good place to get involved in local feminist issues.

Kvindehuset (☎ 33 14 28 04), Gothersgade 37, Copenhagen, is a help centre and meeting place for women.

If you think you might be pregnant, pregnancy tests are available at pharmacies. Foreningen Sex og Samfund (☎ 33 13 19 13), a clinic at Skindergade 28, can provide information on the morning-after pill and other pregnancy-related issues.

Dial ☎ 112 for rape crisis assistance or in other emergencies.

GAY & LESBIAN TRAVELLERS

Copenhagen is a popular destination for gay and lesbian travellers. It has an active gay community and lots of nightlife options. The main gay and lesbian festival of the year is the Mermaid Pride parade, a big Mardi Gras-like bash that occurs on a Saturday in early August.

There's also the Copenhagen Gay & Lesbian Film Festival, held each year in October. For more information on activities and nightlife, see Gay & Lesbian Venues in the Entertainment chapter.

Danes have a high degree of tolerance for alternative lifestyles of all sorts, and gays are as free as anyone to express themselves. In 1989, Denmark became the first country in Europe to legalise same-sex marriages and to offer gay partners most of the same legal rights as heterosexual couples.

Landsforeningen for Bøsser og Lesbiske (Map 8, D1; LBL; ☎ 33 13 19 48, ✉ lbl@lbl.dk), the national organisation for gay men and lesbians, is at Teglgårdstræde 13. It has a library, bookshop, cafe, various gay and lesbian support groups, religious services and counselling. There's also a telephone information line (☎ 33 36 00 86) that operates from 8 to 11 pm on Monday, Thursday and Sunday.

LBL is also behind the main gay magazine in Denmark, *PAN bladet*, which covers gay-related issues, upcoming events and entertainment. There's an annual English-language version published each June. For more information contact PAN Bladet (☎ 33 36 00 82, ✉ lbl-panblad@lbl.dk), Postboks 1023, 1007 Copenhagen K.

Copenhagen Gay Life is a network of gay and gay-friendly businesses in Copenhagen. The Web site, which includes useful tourist information and listings in English, as well as links to LBL and other gay organisations, is at www.copenhagen-gay-life.dk.

A fun general book if you're looking for something to read before coming to Denmark is *Are You Two ... Together? A Gay and Lesbian Travel Guide to Europe*, by Lindsy Van Gelder & Pamela Robin Brandt, which has a particularly enjoyable chapter on Copenhagen.

Do You Eric, Take Hans ...

In October 1989, the Danish Law of Registered Partnership took effect, allowing people of the same sex to tie the knot. Since that time some 5000 couples have taken advantage of the law and registered their partnership with city hall.

During the early years of the new law approximately one-third of the partnerships were lesbian women, while two-thirds were gay men, but since 1997 the majority of same-sex marriages have been between women and the overall numbers have evened out.

If you're interested in learning more about the struggles leading up to the 1989 law, visit the Internet at users.cybercity.dk/~dko12530, a Web site produced by Axel and Eigil Axgil, the first same-sex couple to be married in Denmark.

For information on gay-friendly hotels, see Hotel Jørgensen and Hotel Windsor in the Places to Stay chapter.

DISABLED TRAVELLERS

If you have a physical disability, get in touch with your national support organisation (preferably the 'travel officer' if there is one).

They often have libraries devoted to travel and can put you in touch with travel agents who specialise in tours for disabled travellers.

For instance, the UK-based Royal Association for Disability & Rehabilitation (RADAR) publishes a useful guide called *Holidays and Travel Abroad: A Guide for Disabled People*, which gives a good overview of the facilities available in Europe. The book is available by post (UK£6) from RADAR (☎ 7250 3222), Unit 12, City Forum, 250 City Rd, London EC1V 8AF.

Copenhagen tries to be a handicapped-friendly city, but facilities do vary greatly with the establishment. The main hotel district has a lot of older hotels that were not erected with wheelchair patrons in mind, and many of these are not accessible. Newer hotels, such as the Cab Inn Scandinavia and the Hotel Imperial, are the best bets for up-to-date handicapped facilities.

Most Danish tourist literature (the Danish Tourist Board's hotel guide, the camping association listings and the hostel booklet) indicate which places have rooms and facilities accessible to people in wheelchairs.

Dansk Handicap Forbund, the national association for the handicapped, puts out a free booklet called *København og Frederiksberg ... uden besvær?* listing hotels, restaurants, museums, churches and entertainment venues that are handicapped accessible in the greater Copenhagen area.

It's in Danish only, but is fairly straightforward to use as it employs international symbols to indicate facilities such as handicapped parking, elevators and accessible toilets. It can be picked up free at the Copenhagen tourist office.

In addition the Danish Tourist Board has in years past produced a useful English-language publication, *Access in Denmark – a Travel Guide for the Disabled*, which contains similar types of information. The latest edition is out of date but it's worth inquiring about as an update may be available in the future.

Once in Copenhagen, disabled travellers with specific questions can contact Dansk Handicap Forbund (☎ 39 29 35 55), Kollektivhuset, Hans Knudsens Plads 1A, 2100 Copenhagen Ø.

SENIOR TRAVELLERS

Many discounts are available to senior citizens for things such as public transport and museum admission fees, with proof of age. The minimum qualifying age is generally between 60 and 65. One example is the discount system on the Danish State Railways (DSB), which offers reductions of 25% to 50% to seniors aged 65 and older for travel on most days.

The basic rule is to always inquire about the availability of senior discounts whenever you're visiting a museum or sightseeing attraction or when you're booking transport. Although it's not as common, hotels also occasionally offer promotions geared to seniors.

In your home country, there may be a lower age entitling you to special travel packages and discounts (on car hire, for instance) through organisations and travel agencies that cater to senior travellers.

COPENHAGEN FOR CHILDREN

How can you go wrong in a city that has a century-old amusement park at its heart? Quite simply, there's plenty for kids to do in Copenhagen – beginning at Tivoli, which has a variety of games and rides that can be a blast for kids of all ages.

There are other outright fun places as well, such as the science-oriented Experimentarium (Map 3, G3), with its vast and varied collection of hands-on installations ranging from water wheels and weird mirrors geared to preschoolers to computer games and logic puzzles that will challenge teens. Bakken (Map 1, B4), the Copenhagen area's second and more casual amusement park, has loads of rides and family-oriented activities. At the edge of Bakken is Dyrehaven, where a walk or horse-drawn carriage ride in the woods will reward children with a view of grazing deer.

Some of Copenhagen's leading museums have special features of interest just for kids. Statens Museum for Kunst (Map 7, A5), the state art museum, added a new children's gallery when it was renovated in the late 1990s. The stalwart Nationalmuseet (Map 7, D4) has, in addition to stuffy mummies and millennium-old archaeological finds, a fun hands-on section just for kids, as well as an antique toy collection. Louisiana, the splendid modern art museum in Humlebæk, boasts a special children's section where young budding artists can let the paint hit the canvas.

Younger children will enjoy the free marionette theatre performed on summer afternoons in Kongens Have, the city's oldest public park; and as long as you're there the kids might want to cross the swan-filled moat and visit the Rosenborg Slot, where kings and queens once lived. If flowers dazzle, the adjacent botanical gardens have an abundance of them, including a huge greenhouse with brilliant tropicals.

And of course there are the more conventional sites. Copenhagen's substantial zoo, Zoologisk Have (Map 6, E2), has elephants, lions and other awesome beasts as well as a children's zoo with more approachable creatures. The Danmarks Akvarium (Map 3, A4), at the northern side of the city, has lots of colourful tropical fish, sea turtles and small sharks. Last and perhaps least – for kids who enjoy oddities, the city centre has a Ripley's Believe It or Not Museum (Map 8, G2), a Guinness World of Records Museum (Map 8, C9) and a Louis Tussaud's Wax Museum (Map 7, D4).

Keep in mind that successful travel with young children requires planning and effort. When you plot out your day, try not to overdo things. Include children in the planning progress; if they've helped to work out where you're going, they'll be much more interested when they get there. A good book to pick up is Lonely Planet's *Travel with Children* by Maureen Wheeler, which is loaded with tips and information.

USEFUL ORGANISATIONS
Danish Cultural Institute
The government-sponsored Danish Cultural Institute (Det Danske Kulturinstitut; ☎ 33 13 54 48, fax 33 15 10 91, e dancult@cultur.dk), Kultorvet 2, 1175 Copenhagen K, arranges cultural events and exchanges, sponsors Danish language classes and distributes information on various aspects of Danish culture. Its Web site is at www.dancult.demon.co.uk. It has branches in the following countries:

Belgium
Deens Cultureel Instituut/Institut Culturel Danois (☎ 02-230 7326, fax 02-230 5565, e d-k-i@innet.be or e d-k-i@club.innet.be) rue du Comet/Hoomstraat 22, 1040 Brussels

Estonia
Taani Kultuuriinstituut (☎/fax 6-466 373, e dki@uninet.ee) Vene 14, 0001 Tallinn

Germany
Dänisches Kulturinstitut (☎ 511-6965 005, fax 511-6965 008, e d-k-i@t-online.de) Pelikanstrasse 7, 30177 Hannover

Latvia
Danijas Kulturas Instituts (☎/fax 7-289 994, e d-k-i@mail.bkc.lv) Marijas iela 13, k3, 2sal, 1050 Riga

Lithuania
Danijos Kulturos Institutas (☎ 2-222 607, fax 2-222 412, e d-k-i@post.omnitel.net) Vilniaus 39/6, Room 208, 2001 Vilnius

Poland
Dunski Instytut Kultury (☎ 58-661 5553, fax 58-661 5469, e d-k-i@rubikon.net.pl) ul Kilinskiego 16, 81 393 Gdynia

UK
Danish Cultural Institute (☎ 131-225 7189, fax 131-220 6162, e dci.dancult@dancult.demon.co.uk) 3 Doune Terrace, Edinburgh EH3 6DY

American-Scandinavian Foundation
In the USA, the American-Scandinavian Foundation (☎ 212-879 9779, fax 212-686 1157), 58 Park Ave, New York, NY 10016, arranges cultural exchanges, publishes an English-language magazine and also presents a wide range of cultural programs. It covers not only Denmark but all of Scandinavia. In addition, its members are entitled to discounted air fares between the USA and Scandinavia, which sometimes work out to be good deals. The American-Scandinavian Foundation's Web site is at www.amscan.org.

LIBRARIES
Hovedbiblioteket (Map 8, C4), the central public library at Krystalgade 15 in the Latin Quarter, has international newspapers in English, including the *Financial Times* and the *International Herald Tribune* which visitors are free to browse, and other services including online computers. It's open 10 am to 7 pm weekdays and 10 am to 2 pm Saturday.

Kongelige Bibliotek (Royal Library), at the southern side of Slotsholmen, is primarily a research library, but it's also open to the public and has a collection of foreign newspapers and computers with online access. It's open 10 am to 7 pm Monday to

Saturday and is entered at the waterfront on Christians Brygge.

DANGERS & ANNOYANCES

Denmark is by and large a very safe country and travelling presents no unusual dangers. Travellers should nevertheless be careful with their belongings, particularly in busy places such as Copenhagen's Central Station.

You'll need to quickly become accustomed to the busy cycle lanes that run beside roads between the vehicle lanes and the pedestrian pavement, as these cycle lanes (and fast-moving cyclists) are easy to veer into accidentally.

Call ☎ 112 for emergency police, fire or ambulance services.

Theft

As a traveller you're often fairly vulnerable and when you do lose things it can be a real hassle. The most important things to guard are your passport, important papers, tickets and money. It's best to always carry these next to your skin or in a sturdy leather pouch on your belt.

Be careful even in hotels; don't leave valuables lying around in your room. Those planning to stay in hostels should bring a padlock to secure their belongings in the hostel lockers.

Never leave your valuables unattended in parked cars. If you must leave your luggage in a vehicle, be sure that your car has a covered area that keeps bags out of sight and carry the most important items with you in a day-pack. Remove all luggage overnight, even if the car is left in a garage.

If you're unlucky enough to have something stolen, immediately report it to the nearest police station. If your credit cards or travellers cheques have been taken, notify your bank or the relevant company immediately (see Lost or Stolen Cards under Money earlier in this chapter for phone numbers in Copenhagen).

Lost Property

Every day hundreds of items are left on the city's trains and buses. Fortunately, many

of them are returned and find their way to lost property offices.

If you've lost something on a train, contact the DSB Hittegodskontor (☎ 33 16 21 10) in Central Station. If you've lost something on a bus, call ☎ 36 13 14 15 and they'll let you know where to go, depending on what bus you left it on.

EMERGENCIES

Dial ☎ 112 for emergency police, ambulance and fire services; the call can be made without coins from public phones.

There's a small police office (☎ 33 15 38 01) in Central Station and another at Copenhagen airport (☎ 32 45 14 48).

Larger police stations in the city include Politigården (Map 7, E4; ☎ 33 14 14 48), the police headquarters at Polititorvet, a couple of blocks east of the main post office; Station 1 (☎ 33 25 14 48) at Halmtorvet 20, in Vesterbro at the south-west section of the main hotel district; and Station 2 (Map 7, A7; ☎ 33 93 14 48) at Store Kongensgade 100, a couple of blocks north-west of Amalienborg Slot.

Frederiksberg Hospital has a 24-hour emergency ward (see Health earlier in this chapter). Farther from the city centre are Bispebjerg Hospital (Map 4, A1; ☎ 35 31 23 73), Tuborgvej 7, at the northern side of the city, and Amager Hospital (☎ 32 34 35 00), Kastrupvej 63, south of the centre in Amager; both also have casualty wards open day and night.

There's a 24-hour pharmacy, Steno Apotek, opposite the northern side of Central Station (see Health earlier in this chapter).

Emergency dental treatment is available from Tandlægevagten (☎ 35 38 02 51), Oslo Plads 14.

LEGAL MATTERS

The drinking age in Denmark is 18 years of age. Don't drink and drive, as even a couple of drinks can put you over the legal limit. The authorities are very strict about drink-driving.

It's illegal to drive with a blood-alcohol concentration of 0.05% or greater. Drivers under the influence of alcohol are liable to receive stiff penalties and a possible prison sentence.

Always treat drugs with a great deal of caution. There is a fair bit of marijuana and hashish available in the region, sometimes quite openly, but note that in Denmark (unlike in the Netherlands) all forms of cannabis are officially illegal.

If you are arrested for any punishable offence in Denmark, you can be held for up to 24 hours before appearing in court. You have a right to know the charges against you and a right to a lawyer, and you are not obliged to answer police questions before speaking to the lawyer. If you don't know of a lawyer, the police will provide a list.

You can get free legal advice on your rights from EU Legal Aid (☎ 33 14 41 40) or Emergency Legal Aid (☎ 35 37 68 13).

BUSINESS HOURS

Office hours are generally from 9 am to 4 pm weekdays. Most banks are open 9.30 am to 4 pm weekdays (to 6 pm on Thursday), though banks at the airport and at Central Station are open longer hours and at weekends.

Most stores are open 9.30 am to 5.30 pm weekdays and to 2 pm Saturday, although the trend is towards longer hours.

PUBLIC HOLIDAYS & SPECIAL EVENTS

Summer holidays for schoolchildren begin around 20 June and end around 10 August. Schools also take a break for a week in mid-October and during the Christmas and New Year period. Many Danes take their main work holiday during the first three weeks of July.

Banks and most businesses are closed on public holidays, and transport schedules are commonly reduced as well. Public holidays observed in Denmark are:

New Year's Day (Nytårsdag) – 1 January
Maundy Thursday (Skærtorsdag) – the Thursday before Easter
Good Friday (Langfredag) – the Friday before Easter
Easter Day (Påskedag) – a Sunday in March or April

Easter Monday (2.påskedag) – the day after Easter
Common Prayer Day (Stor Bededag) – the fourth Friday after Easter
Ascension Day (Kristi Himmelfartsdag) – the sixth Thursday after Easter
Whitsunday (Pinsedag) – the seventh Sunday after Easter
Whitmonday (2.pinsedag) – the eighth Monday after Easter
Constitution Day (Grundlovsdag) – 5 June
Christmas Eve – 24 December (from noon)
Christmas Day (Juledag) – 25 December
Boxing Day (2.juledag) – 26 December

Following is a list of some of the larger Copenhagen-area annual events. Since the dates and venues can change a bit from year to year, check with the tourist office for current schedule information.

January
New Year concerts They are performed at various venues in the greater Copenhagen area.

February & March
The arts Despite the paucity of major festivals during the winter, there are concerts by local musicians, changing museum exhibitions and full programs by both the royal ballet and opera companies.
Night Film Festival This is held at various Copenhagen cinemas and features more than a hundred films by Danish and international directors, shown in their original languages, over a 10-day period in early March.
Bakken (Map 1, B4) This amusement park in Klampenborg opens for the season at the end of March with celebrations kicked off by a parade of some 5000 motorcyclists.
Copenhagen Fashion & Design Festival Held at the end of March, it focuses on Danish design and the latest in fashions. There are special displays in many shops and exhibits at Nikolaj Kirke on Strøget.

April
Queen Margrethe II's birthday This is on 16 April and is celebrated at Amalienborg Slot with the royal guards in full ceremonial dress and the queen waving from the palace balcony at noon.
Tivoli and Legoland Copenhagen's venerable amusement park Tivoli and Denmark's world-famous Legoland theme park in Billund both open for the season in April.

May

Labour Day Celebrated on 1 May, this is not officially a public holiday. Try telling that to thousands of people who take the day off, many ending up in Fælledparken, where there's often a big bash.

Copenhagen Marathon This 42km race through the streets of Copenhagen is held on a Sunday in mid-May and is open to both amateur and professional runners.

Copenhagen Carnival This three-day event in the heart of the capital takes place on Whitsunday weekend (usually late May or early June). Highlights include an offbeat parade, samba dancing in the streets and various carnival activities. During the day there are special events for children.

Swingin' Copenhagen This jazz festival in late May, features traditional style jazz played in squares and clubs throughout the city.

5-øren A series of outdoor beachside rock and pop concerts is held at Amager Strandpark on Saturdays throughout the month.

June

Midsummer Eve Held on 23 June and also called Sankt Hans eve, this is a time for evening bonfires at beaches all around Denmark. Copenhagen's Fælledparken is the site of a big bonfire, and there are special activities at Tivoli and Bakken.

Danish Derby Denmark's most important horse race is held in late June at Klampenborg.

Round Zealand Boat Race This large yacht race circles the island of Zealand and is held over three days in late June, starting and ending in Helsingør.

Roskilde Festival Northern Europe's largest rock music festival is held in Roskilde on the last weekend in June. Some 150 bands, including big-name international performers, attract 80,000 concertgoers.

Viking Festival Held in Frederikssund this event is spread over a two-week period in late June and early July. Costumed Vikings present an open-air drama, followed by a banquet with Viking food and entertainment.

5-øren A series of outdoor beachside rock and pop concerts is held at Amager Strandpark on Saturdays throughout the month.

July

Copenhagen Jazz Festival Held for 10 days in early July this is one of the world's major jazz festivals, with indoor and outdoor concerts all around the city, featuring local and big-name artists.

5-øren A series of outdoor beachside rock and pop concerts, is held at Amager Strandpark on Saturdays throughout the month.

Klokkespilskoncerter i Vor Frelsers Kirke Features free carillon recitals each Saturday during July at the atmospheric Vor Frelsers Kirke in Christianshavn.

August

Copenhagen International Ballet Festival Held for 14 days in August it features top solo dancers from the Royal Danish Ballet as well as visiting performers from international ballet companies.

Sommerkoncerter i Vor Frue Kirke Features free classical music performances throughout the month at Vor Frue Kirke, the city's theatre-like cathedral.

Copenhagen Guitar Festival Held during the first two weeks of August at the Rundetårn in the Latin Quarter.

Mermaid Pride Parade Held on the first or second Saturday in August, this festive gay pride parade marches with Carnival-like extravagance through the city to Slotsholmen.

CIEF (Copenhagen International Experimental Music Festival) This highlights performances by up-and-coming experimental musicians at Huset over 10 days in mid-August.

Copenhagen Fashion Fair Held over four days in mid-August with activities at the Bella Center in Amager.

Golden Days in Copenhagen Held over two weeks in late August and early September, it features art exhibits, poetry readings, theatre, ballet and concerts that focus on Denmark's 'Golden Age' (1800–50).

Danish Trotting Derby Denmark's major trotting event is held in late August at the Charlottenlund Travbane.

September

Amager Musikfestival Held from the middle of September to early October, it features music performances by Danish and international soloists and ensembles at several churches in Amager, all with free admission.

Copenhagen Film Festival Highlighting Danish and international film, it is held during the third week in September.

October

Cultural Night in Copenhagen Held on the first night of the autumn school holidays (typically the second Friday in October) when museums, theatres, galleries and even the Rosenborg Slot throw open their doors for free from 6 pm to midnight to those who purchase a 50kr culture badge. Free buses transport visitors between the various sites.

Autumn school holidays During the week-long autumn school holidays in mid-October, numerous museums and attractions in the city extend their hours and add special activities for children.

Copenhagen Gay & Lesbian Film Festival Spread over a week in late October, it shows contemporary gay and lesbian films from around the world.

Flea market Denmark's largest flea market takes place at the Bella Center in Amager on the last weekend of October.

November

Copenhagen Irish Festival Features traditional Irish folk music at various venues in the city for three days in early November.

Copenhagen Autumn Jazz Produced by the Copenhagen Jazz Festival folks, it features top jazz musicians performing at clubs around the city for four days in early November.

Copenhagen Bluegrass Festival Held for two days in mid-August at Amager Kulturpunkt in Amager.

Great Christmas Parade Held on the last Saturday in November. 'Father Christmas' parades through the city followed by jazz musicians, costumed fairy-tale characters and scores of children, lighting Christmas trees in public squares and ending in Rådhuspladsen to light up the city's largest tree.

December

Tivoli It reopens its gates from mid-November to a few days before Christmas with a holiday

market and fair. There's ice skating on the pond and some Tivoli restaurants offer menus with hot mulled wine and traditional holiday meals.

Christmas fairs Held throughout December and featuring food booths, arts and crafts stalls, and sometimes parades. Check the tourist office for the latest venues.

DOING BUSINESS

Copenhagen is the commercial and financial centre of Denmark and home to the country's main transportation and shipping facilities.

Scandinavia's busiest commercial airport, which serves as a hub for much of the region, is just a 10-minute train ride from central Copenhagen.

Many international companies have their regional headquarters based in Copenhagen and the city is a major host of international conferences.

Several 1st class hotels provide business facilities ranging from secretarial services to conference rooms.

In addition, new top-end hotels, such as First Hotel Copenhagen, are now equipping guestrooms with business-friendly amenities like voicemail, ISDN outlets and Internet access.

There's no locally published English-language business newspaper, but the British newspaper *Financial Times* includes coverage of business issues in Denmark and it's readily available in Copenhagen.

FACTS FOR THE VISITOR

Jul-tide Celebrations

By far the most eagerly awaited holiday in Copenhagen is *jul*, or Christmas. Celebrations begin on 1 December with the lighting of candles, the placing of wreaths in windows and the opening of advent calendars. Every day from 1 December to 23 December children unwrap a small gift. A couple of weeks before the holiday a Christmas tree is brought in and decorated with candles, heart-shaped ornaments and strings of miniature Danish flags.

The main celebration takes place on 24 December, when Danes have their traditional Christmas dinner. This typically features apple-stuffed roast goose or duck, sweet and sour red cabbage, liver pâté, caramelised potatoes and an abundance of sweets, including *brune kager* (gingerbread), *klejner* (fried knotted dough) and *pebernødder* (spiced cookies). After the meal, the family joins hands and circles around the tree, singing traditional Christmas songs, followed by the unwrapping of presents. On 25 December, most Danes have a Christmas lunch featuring a hearty cold table with plenty of leftovers from the day before.

Useful sources of information for business travellers include:

Confederation of Danish Industries (☎ 33 77 33 77, fax 33 77 33 00) Dansk Industri, HC Andersens Blvd 18, 1787 Copenhagen K

Danish Bankers Association (☎ 33 12 02 00, fax 33 93 02 60) Amaliegade 7, 1256 Copenhagen K

Danish Confederation of Trade Unions (☎ 35 24 60 00, fax 35 24 63 00) Rosenørns Allé, 1634 Copenhagen V

Danish Employers Confederation (☎ 33 38 90 00, fax 33 12 29 76) Vester Voldgade 113, 1552 Copenhagen V

Danish Ministry of Foreign Affairs (☎ 35 24 60 00, fax 35 24 63 00) Asiatisk Plads 2, 1448 Copenhagen V

European Environment Agency (☎ 33 36 72 00, fax 33 36 71 99) Kongens Nytorv 6, 1050 Copenhagen K

Wonderful Copenhagen (☎ 33 25 74 00, fax 33 25 74 10) Gammel Kongevej 1, 1610 Copenhagen V

Secretarial services include Copenhagen City Business Centre (☎ 33 33 88 33, fax 33 33 98 20), Købmagergade 2, 1150 Copenhagen K; and the AAA Servicebureau (☎ 33 11 64 40, fax 33 11 41 18), Nørregade 15, 1165 Copenhagen K.

Translation service is available as well, including from Bay & Co Translation (☎ 40 25 58 58, fax 33 91 06 86), Nyhavn 43C, 1051 Copenhagen K; and the Translatør Centret (☎ 33 25 01 44, fax 33 25 01 65), Vesterbrogade 48, 1620 Copenhagen V.

Meeting facilities and conference services include:

Bella Center (Map 1, F4; ☎ 32 52 88 11, fax 32 51 96 36) Center Blvd, 2300 Copenhagen S

DIS Congress Service Copenhagen (☎ 44 92 44 92, fax 44 92 50 50) Herlev Ringvej 2C, 2730 Herlev

DSB Group & Conference Services (☎ 33 37 89 00, fax 33 37 89 99) Store Kongensgade 128, 1264 Copenhagen K

JDS Meeting & Conference Services (☎ 33 33 01 71, fax 33 33 01 91) Vandkunsten 6, 1467 Copenhagen K

WORK

Denmark has a significant level of unemployment and the job situation is not particularly promising for those who are not Danes, doubly so for those who don't speak Danish.

In terms of qualifying to work in Denmark, foreigners are generally divided into three categories: Scandinavian citizens, citizens of EU countries and other foreigners. Essentially, Scandinavian citizens have the easiest go of it, as they can generally reside and work in Denmark without restrictions (see Work Visas under Documents earlier in this chapter).

If you do decide to look for work in Copenhagen, the AF Arbejdsformidling (☎ 33 55 10 20), a public job centre at Kultorvet 17, 1019 Copenhagen K, helps link up the unemployed with employers looking for workers. The newspapers with the best jobs-wanted columns are the Sunday issues of *Politiken* and *Berlingske Tidende*. If you don't mind being a waiter, kitchen helper or cleaning person, restaurants and hotels are two types of businesses that are more likely to offer jobs to foreigners, so you might try inquiring directly.

There are, of course, less formal ways to pick up spare change. Copenhageners are generous to street performers who can put on a good show. Individuals or groups with a maximum of three people, are allowed to perform live acoustic music at a few places in the city centre. The main rule is that you don't upset traffic or neighbours and that you perform within certain hours only. Currently along Strøget, the city's central pedestrianised street, performances are allowed from 4 to 8 pm weekdays, 10 am to 5 pm Saturday and noon to 5 pm Sunday. Rådhuspladsen, the square in front of city hall, allows buskers from 7 am to 10 pm daily.

Copenhagen Jazz Festival

The Copenhagen Jazz Festival is the biggest entertainment event of the year, with 10 days of music beginning on the first Friday in July. It's a cornucopia of hundreds of indoor and outdoor concerts, with music wafting out of practically every public square, park, club and cafe throughout the city.

It's a fun scene that brings everyone in the city out to party. Most of the open-air events are free. Those held in the cafes are either free or have small cover charges and it's only the largest big-name events that have significant ticket prices.

Note that events and venues can change a bit from year to year so what follows is intended as a general guide. For the latest in schedules, contact Copenhagen Jazz Festival (☎ 33 93 20 13, fax 33 93 20 24, ✉ info@jazzfestival.dk), Nytorv 3, 1450 Copenhagen K, or check its Web site at www.jazzfestival.dk.

History

Jazz first arrived in Copenhagen in the 1920s and Danes quickly took to it, producing some fine local jazz musicians and band leaders of their own. Jazz reached its height of popularity in Copenhagen during the Nazi occupation of WWII, when it dominated the music scene in virtually every club and cafe in the city. Musical tastes began to change after the war. Jazz slipped in popularity and many of the old jazz musicians found it tough to eke out a living.

Spurred on in the 1960s by new innovations and a major revival, jazz musicians came back on the scene in force. Curiously, at about the same time that jazz was making a strong resurgence in Copenhagen, it was facing dwindling audiences back in the USA, where the music has its roots.

During the 1970s a number of accomplished US jazz musicians began to tour Europe for their main gigs and some ended up settling in jazz-friendly cities like Copenhagen, Paris and Amsterdam. Among those who selected Copenhagen were saxophonist Ernie Wilkins, pianist Butch Lacy and Ella Fitzgerald's former drummer Ed Thigpen. Ella Fitzgerald herself lived in Copenhagen briefly.

With jazz securely footed in the Copenhagen music scene, in 1978 the city kicked off the first Copenhagen Jazz Festival, a citywide event that featured Denmark's top jazz musicians and many international names.

Since that time the Copenhagen Jazz Festival has mushroomed into one of Europe's leading jazz events. Over the years, performers have included such renowned names as Dizzy Gillespie, Miles Davis, Sonny Rollins, Oscar Peterson, Ray Charles and Wynton Marsalis. In 1998 the Woody Herman Orchestra and Tony Bennett highlighted; in 1999 Keith Jarrett and Gary Peacock were lead acts; and in 2000 there was a large international representation that included Canadian Diana Krall, the Australian Art Orchestra, Ian Bellamy from the UK, Cæcilie Norby from Denmark, and Americans Natalie Cole and David Sanborn.

Previous page: The Festival's beat begins – with all that jazz! (Photo by Martin Moos)

Music Venues

At last count the Copenhagen Jazz Festival had grown to nearly 500 events held at more than 50 venues throughout the city. The music is virtually nonstop, with events beginning in the morning and going throughout the day and night. Many of the biggest name musicians perform at the Cirkus Bygningen concert hall and at Tivoli; both places are just minutes from Central Station.

But literally the whole city is a venue. The rest of the musical performances occur in Copenhagen's numerous clubs and small cafes, in the city's public squares and alongside the canals. And there are also plenty of street parades and special events such as midnight concerts at Nationalmuseet and daily children's jazz programs at Kongens Have.

Among the top venues are the venerable *Copenhagen Jazz House* (☎ 33 15 26 00, *Niels Hemmingsensgade 10*), the city's leading jazz spot, and Copenhagen's three other foremost jazz venues: *La Fontaine* (☎ 33 11 60 98, *Kompagnistræde 11*), *JazzHuset Vognporten* (☎ 33 15 20 02, *Rådhusstræde 13*) and *Mojo* (☎ 33 11 64 53, *Løngangstræde 21*). All four places are in the heart of the city.

Clubs & Cafes

Other music clubs and cafes that give themselves over to jazz during the festival include:

ABC Café (☎ 33 23 58 28, *Frederiksberg Allé 98*)
Bartof Café (*Nordre Fasanvej 46*)
Café Blågårds Apotek (☎ 35 37 24 42, *Blågårdsgade 20*)
Café Chips (☎ 35 38 47 91, *Øster Farimagsgade 53*)
Café Cire (☎ 36 30 45 67, *Valby Langgade 58*)
Café Cobra (☎ 33 91 91 88, *Landgreven 3*)
Café Grock (☎ 38 21 19 00, *Allégade 5*)
Café Sommersko (☎ 33 14 81 89, *Kronprinsensgade 6*)
Café Svejk (☎ 38 86 25 60, *Smallegade 31*)
Café Victor (☎ 33 13 36 13, *Ny Østergade 8*)
Christianshavns Bådudlejning og Café (☎ 32 96 53 53, *Overgaden neden Vandet 29*)
Cirkus Bygningen (☎ 70 16 65 65, *Jernbanegade 8*)
Den Blå Hund (☎ 38 87 46 88, *Godthåbsvej 28*)
Diamanten (☎ 33 93 55 45, *Gammel Strand 50*)
Drop Inn (☎ 33 11 24 04, *Kompagnistræde 34*)
Finn Zieglers Hjørne (☎ 33 24 54 54, *Vodroffsvej 24*)
Huset (☎ 33 32 40 77, *Rådhusstræde 13*)
Kruts Karport Café (☎ 35 26 86 38, *Øster Farimagsgade 12*)
Kul-Kaféen (☎ 33 32 17 77, *Teglgårdsstræde 5*)
Long John (☎ 33 11 79 97, *Købmagergade 48*)
MG Petersens Familiehave (☎ 36 16 11 33, *Pile Allé 16*)
Park Café (☎ 35 42 62 48, *Østerbrogade 79*)
Peder Oxe (☎ 33 11 00 77, *Gråbrødre Torv 11*)
Pumpehuset (☎ 33 93 14 32, *Studiestræde 52*)
Pussy Galore's Flying Circus (☎ 35 24 53 00, *Sankt Hans Torv*)
Rust (☎ 35 24 52 00, *Guldbergsgade 8*)
Sabines Cafeteria (☎ 33 14 09 44, *Teglgårdsstræde 4*)

JAZZ FESTIVAL MAP

1 Bartof Café
2 Den Blå Hund
3 Blågårds Plads
4 Café Blågårds Apotek
5 Stengade 30
6 Rust
7 Pussy Galore's Flying Circus
8 Kruts Karport Café
9 Café Chips
10 Langelinie Promenaden
11 Rosenborg Slot; Kongens Have
12 Café Cobra
13 Charlottenborg
14 Café Victor
15 Café Sommersko
16 Filmhusets Cinematek
17 Studenterhuset/Long John

19 Kultorvet
20 Musikhistorisk Museum
21 Sticks 'N' Sushi
22 Sabines Cafeteria
23 Kul-Caféen
24 Pumpehuset
25 Finn Zieglers Hjørne
26 ABC Café
27 Café Grock
28 Café Svejk

29 Frederiksberg Have
30 Café Cire
31 MG Petersens Familiehave
32 Vega
33 Øksnehallen
34 DGI-byen
35 Tivoli
36 Tivoli Billetcenter
37 Axeltorv
38 Cirkus Bygningen
39 Vor Frue Plads
40 Gråbrødretorv
41 Peder Oxe
42 Copenhagen Jazz House

43 Højbro Plads
44 Diamanten
45 La Fontaine
46 Drop Inn
47 Højskolernes Hus
48 Nytorv; Copenhagen Jazz Festival Office
49 JazzHuset Vognporten; Huset
50 Mojo
51 Sabor Latino
52 Nationalmuseet
53 Det Kongelige Bibliotek
54 Christians Kirke
55 Christianshavns Bådudlejning og Café

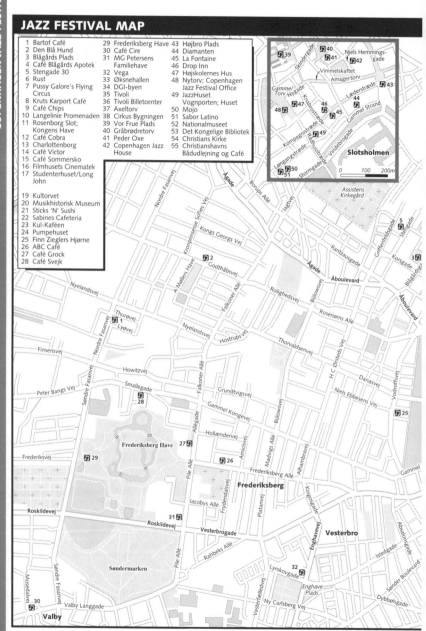

JAZZ FESTIVAL MAP

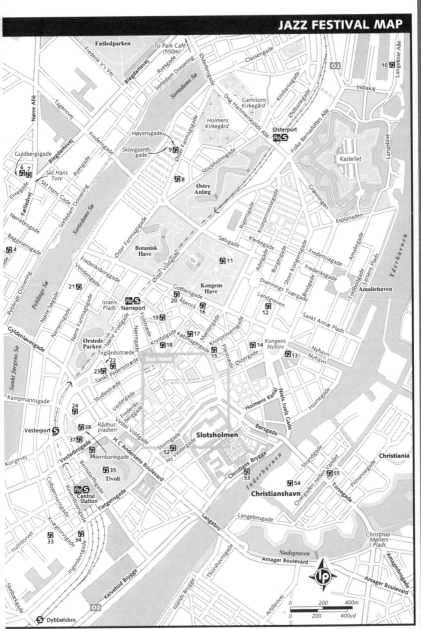

Sabor Latino (☎ 33 11 97 66, Vester Voldgade 85)
Stengade 30 (☎ 35 36 09 38, Stengade 18)
Sticks 'N' Sushi (☎ 33 11 14 07, Nansensgade 59)
Studenterhuset (☎ 35 32 38 61, Købmagergade 52)
Vega (☎ 33 25 70 11, Enghavevej 40)

Squares & Gardens

Public squares where events take place include **Vor Frue Plads**, at the side of Vor Frue Kirke in the Latin Quarter; **Højbro Plads** and **Nytorv**, Strøget's two main squares; **Gråbrødretorv**, a historic square north of Strøget; **Kultorvet**, in the Latin Quarter; **Axeltorv**, the square fronting the Cirkus Bygningen concert hall; **Blågårds Plads**, fronting Floras Kaffe Bar in the Nørrebro area; and **Langelinie Promenaden**, along the waterfront north of the Little Mermaid.

Gardens where events take place include **Kongens Have** at Rosenborg Slot and **Frederiksberg Have** in the Frederiksberg area.

Museums, Libraries & Other Venues

There are a number of other nonconventional sites where music events also take place. These include:

Charlottenborg (☎ 33 93 20 13, Kongens Nytorv), a former palace
Christians Kirke (☎ 33 93 78 70, Strandgade 1), a Christianshavn church
Det Kongelige Bibliotek (☎ 33 93 20 13, Christians Brygge 9), the royal library
DGI-byen (☎ 33 29 80 00, Tietgensgade 65), a hotel and sports centre
Filmhusets Cinematek (☎ 33 74 34 12, Gothersgade 55), the national film institute
Hovedbibliotek (☎ 33 73 60 60, Krystalgade 15), the main public library
Højskolernes Hus (☎ 33 13 98 22, Nytorv 7), Danish folk high school offices
Musikhistorisk Museum (☎ 33 11 27 26, Åbenrå 30), the music history museum
Nationalmuseet (☎ 33 13 44 11, Ny Vestergade 10), Denmark's national museum
Tivoli (☎ 33 15 10 01, Vesterbrogade 3), the city's grand amusement park
Øksnehallen (☎ 33 86 04 00, Halmtorvet 9), an exhibition hall

ANDERS BLOMQVIST

The famed Tivoli amusement park is one of a number of nonconventional music venues.

The Music

The music at the Copenhagen Jazz Festival is nearly as varied as the venues. Traditional music sounds range from old-fashioned Dixieland jazz and Satchmo-style solo improvisation to the WWII-era swing music that reigned in Duke Ellington and Benny Goodman's day.

There's plenty of modern jazz sounds along the lines of those inspired by legendary trumpeter Miles Davis, whose innovations fused jazz with rock and blues. You can also find lots of contemporary hybrid sounds, free-jazz, acid jazz, soul jazz, jazz vocals and rhythm and blues.

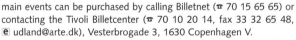

CLINT CURÉ

Tickets

Tickets can – and should – be purchased in advance for the big-name events, such as those held at the concert halls at Cirkus Bygningen and Tivoli.

If you're already in Denmark, tickets for the main events can be purchased by calling Billetnet (☎ 70 15 65 65) or contacting the Tivoli Billetcenter (☎ 70 10 20 14, fax 33 32 65 48, ⒺUdland@arte.dk), Vesterbrogade 3, 1630 Copenhagen V.

Residents of the following countries can purchase tickets from agents at home. If an agent is not listed for your country, you can order from the aforementioned Tivoli Billetcenter using a credit card.

Australia
  Showbiz (☎ 02-9327 7599, fax 9327 2966, Ⓔ admin@showbiz.com.au)
Austria
  Nol Vienna (☎ 01-533 2953, fax 535 0319)
Belgium
  Globaltickets Belgium (☎ 050-33 05 05, fax 34 698 99)
Czech Republic
  Ticketpro (☎ 2 24 81 60 20, fax 24 81 40 21) Web site: www.ticketpro.cz
France
  Edwards & Edwards Globaltickets (☎ 01 42 65 39 21, fax 01 42 65 39 10)
Germany
  Globaltickets (☎ 030-68 88 960, fax 68 88 9650)
Israel
  Castel (☎ 03-546 70 85, fax 605 07 66)
Italy
  Box Office Italia (☎ 02-54271, fax 5427909) Web site: www.ticket.it

COPENHAGEN JAZZ FESTIVAL

Japan
Curtain Call (☎ 03-3770 9496, fax 3770 4479) Web site: www .curtaincall.co.jp
Netherlands
Globaltickets (☎ 035-623 2995, fax 621 6895)
Norway
Ticket Service (☎ 22 42 62 44, fax 22 42 60 97)
Portugal
Ticket World (☎ 47 321 01 36, fax 47 321 01 37)
Spain
Ticket World (☎ 1 542 8598, 1 542 1396) Web site: www.eol.es /ticketworld
Sweden
Box Office Sweden (☎ 08-10 8800, fax 61 16299) Web site: www .boxoffice.se
UK
Edwards & Edwards Globaltickets (☎ 020-7734 4555, fax 7734 0220)
USA
Edwards & Edwards Globaltickets (☎ 212-332 2435, fax 332 2438)

Getting There & Away

The information in this chapter details the various ways of getting to Copenhagen – by air, land and sea.

As Copenhagen is one of northern Europe's main gateway cities, you'll find a multitude of flights available. In addition there are a range of boat, train and bus services connecting Copenhagen with the rest of Europe.

AIR

Copenhagen airport is Scandinavia's busiest hub, serving more than 17 million passengers a year with flights from 135 cities worldwide. There are daily direct flights to Copenhagen from numerous places in Europe, Asia and North America.

Departure Tax

Departure taxes, which equal approximately US$20, are folded in with all the other fees that you pay when you purchase your ticket. There are no separate departure taxes to pay when leaving Denmark.

Buying Tickets

An air ticket alone can gouge a great slice out of anyone's budget, but you can reduce the cost by finding discounted fares. Generally the more flexibility you have, such as a willingness to travel midweek, and the farther in advance you book, the better your odds of finding a good deal.

The Internet is a useful source for checking air fares: many travel agencies and airlines have Web sites where you can begin your search.

Some airlines sell discounted tickets direct to the customer, and it's worth contacting airlines anyway for information on routes and timetables. Sometimes there is nothing to be gained by going direct to the airline – specialist discount agencies commonly offer fares that are lower than the airline's published prices.

With deregulation, there are also an expanding number of 'no-frills' carriers, most of which sell direct. Unlike the 'full-service' airlines, the no-frills carriers often make one-way tickets available at around half the return fare, meaning that it is easy to stitch together an open-jaw itinerary. Regular airlines may also offer open jaws, particularly if you are coming from outside Europe.

Round-the-World (RTW) tickets are another possibility, and for those travelling from a great distance these can be comparable in price to an ordinary return long-haul ticket. RTWs start at about UK£800, A$1800 or US$1300, vary depending on the season, and can be valid for up to a year. Special conditions might be attached to such tickets (eg, you can't backtrack on a route). Also beware of cancellation penalties for these and other tickets.

Courier fares – cheap passage in return for accompanying an urgent package through customs – offer very low prices, however there are usually special restrictions

---

Warning

The information in this chapter is particularly vulnerable to change: prices for international travel are volatile, routes are introduced and cancelled, schedules change, special deals come and go, and rules and visa requirements are amended. Airlines and governments seem to take a perverse pleasure in making price structures and regulations as complicated as possible. You should check directly with the airline or a travel agency to make sure you understand how a fare (and any ticket you may buy) works. In addition, the travel industry is highly competitive and there are many lurks and perks.

The upshot of this is that you should get opinions, quotes and advice from as many airlines and travel agencies as possible before you part with your hard-earned cash. The details given in this chapter should be regarded as pointers and are not a substitute for your own careful, up-to-date research.

---

attached; in addition, demand for couriers is decreasing in this electronic age.

You may find that the cheapest flights are being advertised by obscure agencies. Most such firms are honest and solvent, but there are some rogue fly-by-night outfits around. Paying by credit card generally offers protection since most card issuers will provide refunds if you can prove you didn't get what you've paid for. Similar protection can be obtained by buying a ticket from a bonded agent, such as one covered by the Air Transport Operators Licence (ATOL) scheme in the UK. If you feel suspicious about a firm it's best to steer clear, or only pay a deposit before you get your ticket, then ring the airline to confirm that you are actually booked on the flight before you pay the balance. Established outfits such as STA Travel, which has offices worldwide, and Usit Campus in the UK, offer more security and are about as competitive as you can get.

The cheapest deals are only available at certain times of the year or on weekdays, and fares are particularly subject to change. Always ask about the route – the cheapest tickets may involve an inconvenient stopover. Don't take schedules for granted, either; airlines usually change their schedules twice a year, at the end of March and the end of October.

Ticketless travel, whereby your reservation details are contained within an airline computer, is becoming more common. On simple return trips the absence of a ticket can be a benefit – it's one less thing to worry about; however, if you are planning a complicated itinerary that you may wish to amend en route, there is no substitute for the good old paper version.

Travellers with Special Needs

If you have special needs of any sort – you require a vegetarian diet, are taking a baby or have a medical condition that warrants special consideration – you should let the airline know as soon as possible so that it can make arrangements accordingly. Remind it when you reconfirm your booking and again when you check in at the airport. It may also be worth ringing around the airlines before you make your booking to find out how each of them can handle your particular needs.

Most international airports will provide an escorted cart or wheelchair from check-in desk to plane where needed, and ramps, lifts, accessible toilets and reachable phones are generally available. Aircraft toilets, on the other hand, are likely to present a problem for some disabled passengers; travellers should discuss this with the airline at an early stage and, if necessary, with their doctor.

Airlines usually allow babies up to two years of age to fly for 10% of the adult fare, although a few may allow them free of charge. 'Skycots', baby food and nappies should be provided by the airline if requested in advance. Children aged between two and 12 can usually occupy a seat for half to two-thirds of the full fare.

Other Parts Of Denmark

Domestic air traffic in Denmark is quite limited. The compactness of the country and the ever-increasing efficiency of its rail system have the effect of keeping air routes to a minimum. Still, the two main carriers covering the domestic front, Maersk Air and Scandinavian Airlines (SAS), offer frequent service between Copenhagen and a few of the more distant corners of Denmark.

Maersk Air (☎ 70 10 74 74) connects Copenhagen with Billund (the site of Legoland) and Rønne on the island of Bornholm. The regular one-way fares to Copenhagen are 715kr from Rønne and 825kr from Billund. There are numerous discount schemes – for example, a return ticket purchased seven days in advance typically works out a bit cheaper than the one-way fare, as long as you stay at least two days. Other discounts include a one-way youth fare of 390kr for people aged 21 or under, and various deals for families travelling together.

SAS (☎ 70 10 30 00) flies to Copenhagen from the two largest Jutland cities, Århus and Aalborg. The one-way fare from either city is 740kr and return fares can usually be found for around the same price. Ask SAS about any other discounts that could apply such as youth fares, weekend getaway fares and special promotions.

Air Travel Glossary

Alliances Many of the world's leading airlines are now intimately involved with each other, sharing everything from reservations systems and check-in to aircraft and frequent-flyer schemes. Opponents say that alliances restrict competition. Whatever the arguments, there is no doubt that big alliances are the way of the future.

Courier Fares Businesses often need to send urgent documents or freight securely and quickly. Courier companies hire people to accompany the package through customs and, in return, offer a discount ticket which is sometimes a bargain. However, you may have to surrender all your baggage allowance and take only carry-on luggage.

Fares Airlines traditionally offer 1st class (coded F), business class (coded J) and economy class (coded Y) tickets. These days there are so many promotional and discounted fares available that few passengers pay full fare.

Lost Tickets If you lose your airline ticket, an airline will usually treat it like a travellers cheque and, after inquiries, issue you with another one. Legally, however, an airline is entitled to treat it like cash and if you lose it then it's gone forever. Take very good care of your tickets.

Onward Tickets An entry requirement for many countries is that you have a ticket out of the country. If you're unsure of your next move, the easiest solution is to buy the cheapest onward ticket to a neighbouring country or a ticket from a reliable airline which can later be refunded if you do not use it.

Open-Jaw Tickets These are return tickets where you fly out to one place but return from another. If available, this can save you backtracking to your arrival point.

Overbooking Since every flight has some passengers who fail to show up, airlines often book more passengers than they have seats. Usually excess passengers make up for the no-shows, but occasionally somebody gets 'bumped' onto the next available flight. Guess who it is most likely to be? The passengers who check in late. If you do get 'bumped', you are normally offered some form of compensation.

Reconfirmation Some airlines require you to reconfirm your flight at least 72 hours prior to departure. Check your travel documents to see if this is the case.

Restrictions Discounted tickets often have various restrictions on them – such as needing to be paid for in advance and incurring a penalty to be altered or cancelled. Others are restrictions on the minimum and maximum period you must be away.

Round-the-World Tickets RTW tickets give you a limited period (usually a year) in which to circumnavigate the globe. You can go anywhere the carrying airlines go, as long as you don't backtrack. The number of stopovers or total number of separate flights is decided before you set off and they usually cost a bit more than a basic return flight.

Ticketless Travel Airlines are gradually waking up to the realisation that paper tickets are unnecessary encumbrances. On simple one-way or return trips, reservations details can be held on computer and the passenger merely shows ID to claim their seat.

Transferred Tickets Airline tickets cannot be transferred from one person to another. Travellers sometimes try to sell the return half of their ticket, but officials can ask you to prove that you are the person named on the ticket. On an international flight, tickets are compared with passports.

The UK

London is the major centre for discounted fares in the UK. Among the agencies specialising in discount travel are: Trailfinders (☎ 020-7937 5400), 194 Kensington High St, London W8 6BD; Usit Campus (☎ 020-7730 3402), 52 Grosvenor Gardens, SW1; and STA Travel (☎ 020-7465 0484), 117 Euston Rd. The Trailfinders Web site is at www.trailfinders.com, the Usit Campus Web site is at www.usitcampus.co.uk, and STA Travel information can be found at www.statravel.com.

Plenty of other agencies advertise in the travel sections of the weekend newspapers, the listings magazine *Time Out* and the free *TNT Magazine*, which is widely available in busy public areas around London.

There are many scheduled commercial flights between Denmark and the UK. Often the cheapest flights are with Go (☎ 0845-60 54 321), which flies daily to Copenhagen from London Stansted, for around UK£65/ 100 one way/return year-round.

Other airlines flying to Copenhagen include British Airways, which flies from Heathrow; SAS, from Heathrow and Stansted; and Maersk Air, from Gatwick. All three carriers offer numerous daily flights. Unrestricted one-way fares are around UK£250, but shop around as there are often discounted promotions on this well-travelled route that can result in a return fare of about half of the full one-way price.

Continental Europe

While the cheapest way to travel between Copenhagen and the rest of continental Europe is usually by land, cheap discount flights are often available to travellers aged under 26. Generally, discounted youth fares to Copenhagen are typically around f300 from Amsterdam, DM200 from Berlin, DM300 from Frankfurt and 900FF from Paris.

There are many travel agencies throughout Europe where you can purchase discounted tickets. These include: NBBS Reizen (☎ 020-624 09 89), Rokin 66, Amsterdam; Voyages Wasteels (☎ 08 03 88 70 04), 11 rue Dupuytren, Paris; STA Travel (☎ 069-703 035), Bockenheimer Landstrasse 133, Frankfurt; STA Travel (☎ 030-311 0950), Goethestrasse 73, Berlin; SSR Travel (☎ 1 297 1111), Ankerstrasse, 112 Zurich, Switzerland; International Student and Youth Travel Service (☎ 01-322 1267), Nikis 11, Athens; and Passaggi (☎ 06-474 0923), Stazione Termini FS, Gelleria Di Tesla, Rome.

The USA

The North Atlantic is the world's busiest long-haul air corridor and flight options can be bewildering. Larger newspapers such as the *New York Times*, *Chicago Tribune* and *Los Angeles Times* produce weekly travel sections in which you'll find any number of travel agencies' ads for air fares to Europe.

You should be able to fly return to Copenhagen from major east coast cities such as New York, Washington DC or Boston for around US$500 in the low season and around US$800 in the high season. Add about US$100 for flights from the midwest and about US$200 from the west coast. You might be able to get better rates if the airlines are battling for passengers with promotional fares or you could end up with a higher fare if all the cheapest fares are booked out on the day you want to leave. Most budget fares between the USA and Copenhagen are valid for either a 30-day or a 60-day stay.

An interesting alternative to a direct flight is offered by Icelandair (☎ 800-223 5500), which allows a free stopover in Iceland's capital, Reykjavík. Its prices are usually similar to the direct Copenhagen fares offered by other airlines, though it sometimes undercuts the competition. Icelandair flies from New York, Baltimore-Washington, Boston, Minneapolis and Orlando.

There are other, less orthodox, ways of getting to Europe. For example, Airhitch (☎ 800-326 2009 in New York, ☎ 310-574 0090 in Los Angeles) specialises in standby tickets to Europe for US$169/249 one way from the east coast/west coast, but the destinations are by region (not a specific city or country). Airhitch's Web site is www.airhitch.org.

Another possibility is a courier flight, which typically costs around US$300 return to get to Copenhagen from major cities like New York. Of course, there are a lot of restrictions and you often need to be ready to go on short notice. You can find out about courier flights from the International Association of Air Travel Couriers (☎ 561-582 8320) and Now Voyager Travel (☎ 212-431 1616). Their Web sites are at www.courier.org and www.now voyagertravel.com.

Canada

For scheduled commercial flights to Copenhagen, you usually have to fly first to New York or Chicago and pick up a connecting flight. However, Air Canada (☎ 800-776 3000) has a nonstop service a few times a week from Toronto to Copenhagen.

Fares vary with the season. Because of limited competition they tend to be higher than the lowest fares available from the USA to Copenhagen. Travel CUTS offers low air fares and has offices in major cities, including Toronto (☎ 416-979 2406) at 187 College St, and Vancouver (☎ 604-659 2830) at 567 Seymour St. For other locations, or to browse Travel CUTS online, go to www.travelcuts.com.

Also, scan the budget travel agencies' ads in major newspapers such as Toronto's *Globe & Mail* and the *Vancouver Sun*.

Australia

One place to check for cheap air fares is STA Travel, which has branches in most large cities. You can call ☎ 1 300 360 960 from anywhere in Australia for the locations of all STA offices. The main Sydney branch (☎ 02-9212 1255) is at 855 George St, Ultimo; Melbourne branches include 43 Bridge St (☎ 03-9349 4344) and the University of Melbourne (☎ 03-9348 1444).

The weekend travel sections of major newspapers have many ads offering cheap fares to Europe, but don't be surprised if they happen to be sold out when you contact the agencies – they're often low-season fares on obscure airlines with conditions attached.

Discounted return fares on mainstream airlines through a reputable agency generally cost between A$1800 (low season) and A$2800 (high season).

New Zealand

Depending on which airline you choose, you may fly across Asia to Europe, with possible stopovers in India, Bangkok or Singapore, or across the USA, with possible stopovers in Honolulu, Australia or one of the Pacific islands. Worth considering is a RTW ticket, which can be around the same price as, or cheaper than, an advance-purchase return ticket. STA Travel specialises in discounted tickets and has branches around New Zealand including STA Travel (☎ 09-309 0458), 10 High St, Auckland, and STA Travel (☎ 03-379 9098), 90 Cashel St, Christchurch.

Africa

Kenya Airways flies direct from Africa to Copenhagen and there are regular connections from South Africa with Lufthansa, Turkish Airlines and British Airways.

Good places to look for cheap tickets are STA Travel (☎ 021-418 6570), 31 Riebeck St, Cape Town; there's also an office in Johannesburg (☎ 011-482 4666) at 12c Seven St, Melville.

Asia

Most Asian countries now offer fairly competitive air fare deals, but Bangkok, Singapore and Hong Kong are still the best places to shop around for discount tickets.

Discount ticket agencies in the region include: Hong Kong Student Travel Bureau (☎ 2730 3269), 8th floor, Star House, Tsimshatsui, Hong Kong; STA Travel (☎ 737 7188), Orchard Parade Hotel, 1 Tanglin Rd, Singapore; STA Travel (☎ 02-236 0262), Wall St Tower Bldg, 33/70 Surawong Road, Bangkok; and STA Travel (☎ 03-5391 2922), Nukariya Bldg, 1-16-20 Minami-Ikebukuro, Toshima-ku, Tokyo.

From India and Pakistan the cheapest flights tend to be with Eastern European carriers, but the national carriers, Air India and Pakistan International Airlines (PIA), can also offer bargains. Although you can get cheap tickets in Mumbai (Bombay) and Calcutta, Delhi is where the real wheeling and dealing goes on. In Delhi there are a number of discount travel agencies around Connaught Place.

Airline Offices

Most airline offices are either north of Central Station near the intersection of Vester Farimagsgade and Vesterbrogade, or opposite Rådhuspladsen.

The following are the office locations and reservation numbers of airlines serving Copenhagen:

Aer Lingus (☎ 33 12 60 55) Jernbanegade 4
Aeroflot (☎ 33 12 63 38) Vester Farimagsgade 1
Air Canada (☎ 33 11 45 55) Vester Farimagsgade 1
Air China (☎ 33 14 92 22) Rådhuspladsen 16
Air France (☎ 33 12 76 76) Ved Vesterport 6
Air India (☎ 33 15 70 70) Vester Farimagsgade 1
Alitalia (☎ 33 36 93 69) Vesterbrogade 6D
Austrian Airlines (☎ 33 32 16 37) Vester Farimagsgade 6
British Airways (☎ 80 20 80 20) Rådhuspladsen 16
British Midland (☎ 70 10 20 00) Hammerichsgade 1
EgyptAir (☎ 33 32 90 60) Jernbanegade 7
El Al Israel Airlines (☎ 33 14 64 17) Vesterbrogade 6D
Estonian Air (☎ 32 31 45 40) Vester Farimagsgade 7
Finnair (☎ 33 36 45 45) Nyropsgade 47
Iberia (☎ 33 12 22 22) Jernbanegade 4
Icelandair (☎ 33 12 33 88) Vester Farimagsgade 1
Kenya Airways (☎ 33 23 01 00) Trommesalen 5
KLM-Royal Dutch Airlines (☎ 32 52 74 11) Copenhagen airport
Lithuanian Airlines (☎ 32 52 81 50) Copenhagen airport
LOT Polish Airlines (☎ 33 14 58 11) Vester Farimagsgade 21
Lufthansa Airlines (☎ 33 37 73 33) Radisson SAS Royal Hotel, Hammerichsgade 1
Maersk Air (☎ 33 14 60 00) Rådhuspladsen 16
Olympic Airways (☎ 33 12 61 00) Nyropsgade 47
Pakistan International Airlines (PIA; ☎ 33 14 18 33) Vester Farimagsgade 4
Scandinavian Airlines (SAS; ☎ 70 10 20 00) Radisson SAS Royal Hotel, Hammerichsgade 1
Singapore Airlines (☎ 33 14 34 56) Vester Farimagsgade 9
South African Airways (☎ 33 14 30 31) Vester Farimagsgade 1
Swissair (☎ 33 32 16 37) Vester Farimagsgade 6
Thai Airways International (☎ 33 75 01 20) Rådhuspladsen 16
Turkish Airlines (☎ 33 14 40 55) Rådhuspladsen 16
Varig (☎ 33 11 91 22) Vester Farimagsgade 1

BUS
Other Parts of Denmark

Stiff competition from trains has left long-distance buses a very secondary mode of transport in Denmark. There are, however, daily cross-country bus routes between Copenhagen and the two largest Jutland cities, Århus and Aalborg. The fares are about 25% cheaper than taking the train.

The express bus to Copenhagen from Århus (☎ 70 21 08 88) takes three hours and costs 200kr; to Copenhagen from Aalborg (☎ 70 10 00 30) it takes five hours and costs 220kr.

Elsewhere in Europe

If you're coming from another European country and you don't already have a rail pass, it's often cheaper to get to Copenhagen by bus than it is by train or plane. Long bus rides can be tedious, so bring along a good book. On the plus side, some of the coaches are quite luxurious with a toilet, air-con and reclining seats.

Small bus companies with discount rates come along from time to time but most of them don't remain in business for more than a year or two. Ask around at student and discount travel agencies for the latest information.

Eurolines One of the biggest and most well-established express-bus services is Eurolines, connecting Copenhagen with the rest of Europe. Most of the buses operate daily (or near-daily) in summer and between two and five times a week in winter.

Sample one-way Eurolines fares from Copenhagen are 420kr to Stockholm, 445kr to Oslo, 535kr to Amsterdam, 635kr to Frankfurt, 690kr to Paris and 725kr to London. There's a discount of about 10% for

Amalienborg Slot, home of the Danish royal family since 1794

Copenhagen is famous for its parks and gardens.

Rådhuspladsen lights up at night.

City symbol on tourist information building

Night view of Central Station

Bicycle-friendly train

Bicycles are available for free in the city centre.

those aged 12 to 26 and for those over 60. Children aged four to 11 pay 50% of the adult fare and those three and under pay 20%. Return fares for all age groups are about 15% less than two one-way fares.

There's also a Eurolines pass that covers unlimited travel between 48 European cities, including the Danish cities of Copenhagen and Aalborg. Other cities that the pass covers are as far flung as Dublin, London, Paris, Madrid, Prague, Warsaw and Rome. A youth pass for travellers aged under 26 costs €232/288 for 30/60 days in the periods of 1 April to 31 May and 1 September to 31 October, €296/324 during the months of June to August, and €211/262 at other times. Travellers aged over 60 can get a senior pass at the same rates. Nonsenior adult passes are priced at approximately 25% higher than the youth passes.

Eurolines offices in Denmark are:

Aalborg (☎ 99 34 44 88) JF Kennedys Plads 1, 9000 Aalborg
Århus (☎ 86 12 36 11) Rådhuspladsen 3, 8000 Århus C
Copenhagen (Map 7, E3; ☎ 33 88 70 00) Reventlowsgade 8, 1651 Copenhagen V

Eurolines representatives elsewhere in Europe include:

Belgium (☎ 02-274 1350) CCN-Gare du Nord, 1000 Brussels
France (☎ 08 36 69 52 52) 28 Avenue du Général de Gaulle, Bagnolet
Germany (☎ 069-79 03 50) Deutsche Touring, Mannheimersbrasse, No 4 Frankfurt am Main
Netherlands (☎ 020-56 08 788) Julianaplein 5, Amsterdam
Norway (☎ 81 54 44 44) Nor-Way Bussekspress, Bussterminalen Galleriet, 0154 Oslo
Sweden (☎ 31 13 15 06) Kyrkogatan 40, 41115 Gothenburg
UK (☎ 0870-514 3219) 52 Grosvenor Gardens, London SW1W 0AU

These offices may also have information on other bus companies and deals. Advance reservations may be necessary on international buses; either call the bus companies directly or inquire at a travel agency.

Busabout This UK-based budget alternative to Eurolines is aimed at younger travellers, but has no upper age limit. During the summer season it visits 70 European cities, including Copenhagen.

It offers both consecutive day passes good for successive days of travel and flexipasses allowing for a certain number of days of travel within a set period. For example, a flexi-pass good for 10 days of travel during two months costs €209/235 for adults/youth, and a standard pass good for 21 consecutive days of travel costs €319/349. Youth passes are available to those under 26 years of age.

You can buy Busabout tickets directly from the company (☎ 020-7950 1661) or from suppliers such as Usit Campus and STA Travel. The Busabout Web site is at www.busabout.com.

TRAIN
Other Parts of Denmark
Denmark has a good, reliable train system with reasonable fares and frequent services. Most long-distance trains, such as those on the busy Copenhagen-Aalborg route, operate at least hourly throughout the day. With the exception of a few short private lines, the Danish State Railways (DSB) runs all train services in Denmark.

Rail passes such as Scanrail and Eurailpass are valid on DSB trains but cannot be used on the private lines.

DSB essentially operates two types of standard long-distance train; ticket prices are the same on both. The sleek InterCity (IC) trains have ultramodern comforts. The carriage layout resembles a more spacious version of a plane interior, complete with cushioned seats, overhead reading lights and individual music headphone jacks. IC trains also have play areas for children and roomy toilets with nappy-changing facilities. Reservations are generally required for travel on IC trains.

In addition to the standard IC trains there are also Business IC trains (designated as InterCityLyn on schedules) on certain routes, such as Copenhagen to Esbjerg, Århus and Aalborg. These are geared to business travellers, go marginally faster than standard IC trains, are a bit more posh and offer free drinks and snacks. For the pampering you'll pay a 50% surcharge over the standard train fares.

Interregional (IR) trains are older, a bit slower and more basic, but are comfortable in all respects. Reservations are optional on IR trains and in most cases you can find a seat without one, but if you're travelling a long distance or during rush hour you might prefer to make a reservation to be guaranteed a seat.

Regardless of distance travelled, the reservation fee is 15kr; on Business IC trains this fee is included in the ticket price. Train fares are reasonable: for example, to get to Copenhagen from the international port city of Esbjerg it costs 256kr and takes 3¼ hours; from the port of Frederikshavn, the farthest DSB terminal from Copenhagen, it's just 290kr and five hours by IC train.

Some people are eligible for even lower fares. People aged 65 and over are entitled to a 20% discount on Friday and Saturday and a 50% discount on other days.

Children aged 10 to 15 pay half the adult fare at all times, and kids under 10 travel free if they are with an adult. Eight or more adults travelling together are entitled to a 30% discount.

Those aged from 15 to 25 can buy an *ungdomskort* (youth card) for 150kr; it allows half-price train fares on Tuesday, Wednesday, Thursday and Saturday.

You can get free pocket-sized schedules that cover the main railway lines at any DSB train station. There's also a telephone line (☎ 70 13 14 15) that you can call for information on train travel throughout Denmark.

Elsewhere in Europe

Trains are a popular way of getting between countries in Europe; they are good meeting places and throughout northern Europe they are generally comfortable, frequent and reliable.

For comparison purposes, standard 2nd-class train fares from Copenhagen are 1005kr to Frankfurt, 400kr to Oslo and 370kr to Stockholm.

Rail Passes A multitude of rail passes are available for travel in Europe and it's important to find a travel agency familiar with the various options.

Two agencies in the USA that specialise in selling rail passes are Budget Europe Travel Service (☎ 800-441 2387), 2557 Meade Court, Ann Arbor, MI 48105, and Europe Through the Back Door (☎ 206-771 8303), 120 Fourth Ave N, PO Box 2009, Edmonds, WA 98020.

Among the agencies selling rail passes in the UK are Wasteels Travel (☎ 020-7834 7066), Victoria train station, London, and Usit Campus (☎ 020-7730 3402), 52 Grosvenor Gardens, London. In continental Europe, rail passes can be purchased at larger train stations and travel agencies.

If you buy a rail pass, read the small print. There are certain rules for validation and the pass cannot be transferred.

It's important to remember that rail passes do not cover seat reservation costs and fees for supplements such as sleepers. Also, if you are taking a high-speed train or a business-class train, there is sometimes an extra supplement.

The traveller must fill out in ink the relevant box in the calendar before starting a day's travel. Be sure that you get the date right, as tampering with the pass (which includes erasing) or failing to validate it runs the risk of fines and possible forfeiture of the pass.

We've had reports of Danish train conductors being extremely scrupulous in their checks, even examining passes with a magnifying glass.

Eurail Eurailpasses are available to residents of non-European countries, and are intended to be purchased before arriving in Europe.

Eurailpasses are valid for unlimited travel on national railways (and some private lines) in Austria, Belgium, Denmark, Finland, France, Germany, Greece, Hungary, Ireland, Italy, Luxembourg, the Netherlands, Norway, Portugal, Spain, Sweden and Switzerland. Eurailpasses are also valid for free or discounted travel on some ferries in and between these countries.

There are two Eurailpasses for travellers aged under 26. The Eurail Youth Pass is valid for unlimited 2nd-class travel for 15 days (US$388), 21 days (US$499), one month (US$623), two months (US$882) or three months (US$1089). The Eurail Youth Flexipass, also covering 2nd-class travel, is valid for freely chosen days within a two-month period: 10 days for US$458 or 15 days for US$599.

For those aged over 26, a Eurail Flexipass (available for 1st-class travel only) costs US$654 or US$862 for 10 or 15 freely chosen days within two months. The standard Eurailpass has five versions, all for unlimited travel in 1st class: US$554 for 15 days, US$718 for 21 days, US$890 for one month, US$1260 for two months and US$1558 for three months.

Two or more people travelling together can get a 15% discount by buying a Eurail Saverpass or Eurail Saver Flexipass, which work like the standard Eurailpass and Eurail Flexipass – just keep in mind that you must do all of your travelling together.

Eurailpasses for children are also available: half-fare for those aged under 12, free for those under four.

Inter-Rail These train passes are available to residents of European countries.

The Inter-Rail pass is split into zones, with the fare depending upon how many zones you plan to travel within.

Zone A comprises the UK and Ireland; B is Finland, Norway and Sweden; C is Austria, Denmark, Germany and Switzerland; D is Croatia, the Czech Republic, Hungary, Poland and Slovakia; E is Belgium, France, Luxembourg and the Netherlands; F is Morocco, Portugal and Spain; G is Italy, Greece, Slovenia and Turkey; and H is Bulgaria, Macedonia, Romania and Yugoslavia.

The price, in Danish kroner, for 22 days travel in any one zone is 1600kr for travellers aged under 26 and 2200kr for adults. Multizone passes are valid for one month: a two-zone pass costs 2000/2800kr for travellers aged under 26/adults, three zones 2300/3200kr and all zones 2600/3600kr.

Terms and conditions vary slightly from country to country, but for travel in the country of origin expect only limited discounts – if you're departing from the UK, for instance, the pass covers the channel crossing but no domestic travel.

Scanrail These rail passes cover travel in Denmark, Norway, Sweden and Finland.

Flexible and consecutive-day passes are available. For travel on any five days within a 15-day period, the pass costs US$270/200 in 1st/2nd class (US$203/150 for travellers aged under 26). Travel on any 10 days within a one-month period costs US$420/310 for 1st/2nd class (US$315/233 for those aged under 26).

For 21 consecutive days of unlimited travel, the pass costs US$486/360 for 1st/2nd class (US$365/270 for people aged under 26).

The cost for children aged under 12 is half the adult fare; children aged under four travel free.

If you're 60 years old or over, then you're eligible for a senior pass, which is valid for 1st/2nd class travel over five days in a 15-day period for US$241/178, 10 days in a one-month period for US$374/276 and 21 consecutive days for US$432/321.

To get Scanrail passes at these prices, they must be purchased before you arrive in Scandinavia.

Scanrail passes can also be purchased in Scandinavia but may cost a bit more, depending upon the exchange rate.

The Scanrail pass includes free or discounted travel on many international boats between Denmark and its neighbouring countries.

Other Discounts There are numerous other discount schemes for train travel throughout Europe, so always ask about off-peak travel, family plans and special promotions.

Many routes also have discounted return fares; if you purchase your tickets a couple of days in advance you can sometimes get a return ticket for just a bit more than the one-way fare.

CAR & MOTORCYCLE
Other Parts of Denmark

Roads in Denmark are in good condition and almost invariably well signposted. Traffic is generally quite light and the motorways efficient.

Motorway signs are colour coded: blue signs indicate exits and green signs show places that are reached by continuing along the motorway. Petrol stations, with toilets, nappy-changing facilities and minimarkets, are at 50km intervals on all Danish motorways. Motorways have emergency telephones at 2km intervals; an arrow on marker posts along the shoulder indicates the direction of the nearest phone.

Unleaded petrol costs about 8.7kr per litre, super petrol about 9kr per litre and diesel fuel about 6.9kr per litre. You'll generally find the most competitive prices at petrol stations along motorways. If you don't mind using self-service pumps, the unstaffed OK Benzin stations, which are adjacent to Brugsen grocery shops, charge about 25 øre less per litre than the name-brand stations. OK Benzin pumps are open 24 hours and accept 100kr notes and credit cards.

The Danish Road Directorate (☎ 70 10 10 40) offers a helpful 24-hour telephone service that can provide traffic forecasts and nationwide information on roadworks, detours, passes that are closed in winter and ferry cancellations; information is available in English.

The main highways into Copenhagen are the E20 from Jutland and Funen and the E47 from Helsingør. If you're coming into Copenhagen from the north on the E47, exit

Size Matters

The new Øresundsfordindelsen (Øresund Fixed Link), which provides the first 'land link' between Denmark and Sweden, ranks as the world's longest combined tunnel and bridge crossing of its kind.

It stretches nearly 16km across the Øresund from Kastrup, near Copenhagen airport, to Lernacken, near Malmö, Sweden. A 4km-long artificial island, called Peberholm, had to first be constructed halfway across the sound to provide a point where the 3.5km-long underwater tunnel could be linked with the 8km-long bridge. The whole system has two decks, with cars moving on the upper deck and trains running on the lower.

A joint construction venture undertaken by the Swedish and Danish governments, Øresundsfordindelsen opened on 1 July 2000 with a grand inauguration ceremony that featured Queen Margrethe II of Denmark and King Carl Gustaf of Sweden taking trains from their respective countries to Peberholm. There the two trains linked together and continued on to Sweden, and then, after some ceremonial ribbon cutting, the parties returned to Denmark by car.

Despite the royal regalia of the opening ceremonies, and lots of media hype proclaiming a 'new Øresund Region', Scandinavians haven't exactly flocked to the new crossing. The rail link is carrying the expected passenger-train loads, but the automobile traffic has been only half of what was anticipated, with slightly more than 6000 cars making the crossing each day. This shortcoming could spell financial disaster, since tolls are the main source of revenue for repaying the hefty financing on the US$3 billion project.

In late 2000, in a move to attract more car traffic, the 230kr auto toll was cut to 125kr for drivers willing to open a monthly account. That price cut, however, was met with an outcry of protest from car-ferry operators in Helsingør who felt they had an understanding with the government that bridge tolls would not be set at levels that competed directly with their car-ferry rates.

Views of the bridge, which has a simple but pleasing design with high pylon towers and clean linear cable patterns, can be seen from many places along the Copenhagen coast all the way north to Klampenborg. Incidentally, the view from Kastrup, near the start of Øresundsfordindelsen, isn't a particularly spectacular one, since the link begins on the Danish side as an underwater tunnel.

onto Lyngbyvej (route 19) and continue south to reach the heart of the city.

For more details on car travel within Denmark, see Car & Motorcycle in the Getting Around chapter.

Elsewhere in Europe

Until just a few years ago it was necessary to take a car ferry to get to Copenhagen, which is on the island of Zealand, from anywhere outside Denmark. All that has now changed with the construction of two ambitious bridge-tunnel links. They rank among Europe's largest civil engineering projects since the Channel Tunnel was constructed between the UK and France.

In 1998, the 18km-long Storebælts-forbindelsen (Store Bælt Bridge) was opened, connecting Zealand with the Jutland peninsula and the rest of the European mainland via Germany and the E45 motorway.

In 2000, the 16km Øresundsforbindelsen (Øresund Fixed Link) was finished, joining Copenhagen with Malmö, Sweden. Both Øresundsforbindelsen and the Storebælts-forbindelsen charge an auto toll of 230kr.

Both of these links, incidentally, are bridge-tunnel combinations with one level carrying motor vehicles and another trains.

Car ferries haven't disappeared altogether, however, and are still the most efficient way to arrive from some parts of Europe, such as Norway and the UK. For information on car ferry services to Denmark, see Boat later in this chapter.

Paperwork & Preparations Proof of vehicle ownership (such as a Vehicle Registration Document for British-registered cars) should always be carried when driving in Europe. Also carry your national driving licence, as well as an International Driving Permit (IDP) if appropriate.

Third-party motor insurance is a minimum requirement in most of Europe. Most UK motor insurance policies automatically provide third-party cover valid in EU countries and some others. Get your insurer to issue a Green Card, which is internationally recognised as proof of insurance, and check that it lists all of the countries you intend to visit. You'll need this in the event of an accident outside the country where the vehicle is insured. Also ask your insurer for a European Accident Statement form, which can simplify things. Never sign statements you can't read or understand – insist on a translation and sign that only if it's acceptable.

It's wise to have a European breakdown assistance policy, such as the RAC Eurocover Motoring Assistance plan. Ask your motoring organisation for details about free and reciprocal services offered by affiliated organisations in countries you'll be visiting.

Every vehicle travelling across an international border should display a nationality plate of its country of registration. A warning triangle, to be used in the event of a breakdown, is compulsory just about everywhere. Recommended accessories include a first-aid kit, a spare bulb kit and a fire extinguisher.

Road Rules Vehicles drive on the right in all northern European countries. Vehicles brought over from the UK or Ireland should have their headlights adjusted to avoid blinding oncoming traffic at night (a simple solution on older headlight lenses is to cover up the triangular section of the lens with tape). Priority is usually given to traffic approaching from the right in countries that drive on the right-hand side.

The British RAC publishes an annual *European Motoring Guide*, which gives an excellent summary of regulations in each country, including parking rules. Motoring organisations in other countries produce similar publications.

Take care with speed limits as they vary significantly from country to country. You may be surprised at the apparent disregard of traffic regulations in some places but as a visitor it is always best to err on the side of caution. In many European countries, driving infringements are subject to on-the-spot fines. Always ask for a receipt if you're fined.

For road rules specific to Denmark, see Road Rules under Car & Motorcycle in the Getting Around chapter.

BICYCLE
Other Parts of Denmark

Cycling is both a practical and an immensely popular way to travel in Denmark. Extensive cycling routes, both regional and national, link towns throughout the country. For instance, national cycle route 9 runs north to south through Zealand connecting Copenhagen with the port cities of Helsingør and Rødbyhavn, whereas cycle route 8 connects Copenhagen with Århus and the rest of Jutland.

CykelGuide, a brochure summarising (in Danish) the national and regional cycle routes of Denmark, is available from the Danish Road Directorate: Vejdirektoratet (☎ 70 10 10 40), Trafikantservice, Postboks 1569, Niels Juels Gade 13, 1020 Copenhagen K. This brochure can also be picked up free at tourist offices in Denmark.

It's easy to travel with a bike in Denmark, even when you're not riding it, as bicycles can readily be taken on ferries and most trains for a modest fee. On DSB trains, reservations should be made at least three hours prior to departure because bikes generally travel in a different section of the train from passengers. The DSB pamphlet *Cykler i tog*, available at larger train stations, gives details.

Always be careful locking up your bike, especially if you're travelling with an expensive model, as bike theft is common in larger cities.

For information on cycling in Copenhagen, see Bicycle in the Getting Around chapter.

From Outside Denmark

If you're flying to Copenhagen you should be able to take your bicycle along with you on the plane relatively easily. You can dismantle the bicycle and put the pieces in a bike bag or box, but it's easier to simply wheel your bike to the check-in desk, where it should be treated as a piece of baggage. You may have to remove the pedals and turn the handlebars sideways so that it takes up less space in the aircraft's hold. Check all this with the airline well in advance, preferably before you pay for your ticket.

It's also possible to send bicycles between Denmark and most other European countries via train as international luggage. The bicycle must be easy to handle; it cannot be locked and anything bulky, such as baskets and panniers, must be removed. The transport time can take as much as three days from other stations in Scandinavia and five days from elsewhere in Europe.

Still, if you have an option, the easiest and cheapest way is to take an international ferry to Denmark. You'll get to travel on the same boat as your bike, and the additional fee is usually minimal.

A primary consideration for distance cycling is to travel light, but you should take a few tools and spare parts, including a puncture repair kit and an extra inner tube. Panniers are essential to balance your possessions on either side of the bike frame. A bike helmet is also a must. Take a good lock and always use it when you leave your bike unattended.

Seasoned cyclists can average 80km a day, but there's no point in overdoing it. The slower you travel, the more local people you are likely to meet.

BOAT

If you're coming from nearby countries, ferry travel can be an economical way of getting to Denmark because it often includes overnight accommodation. It's also a pleasant way to travel as boats to Denmark are generally of a high standard. The long-distance boats usually have duty-free shops, lounges, nightclubs and both cafeterias and formal restaurants. Many of the boats between Denmark and other Scandinavian countries have floating casinos and small grocery shops on board as well.

The fares in this section are for one-way travel unless otherwise noted. There are often discounts on return tickets, particularly for people travelling by car, and occasionally there are some very good excursion deals – always ask about special promotions. If you're carrying a rail pass or a student card, be sure to flash it when you purchase a ticket, as it may entitle you to a substantial discount. A child's fare is usually half of the adult fare, and there are sometimes senior discounts available as well.

Remember that the same ferry company can have a whole host of different prices for the same route, depending upon the day of the week you travel and on the season. Note that cabin fares are quoted on a per-person (not a per-cabin) basis. Car fares given in this section are for a standard car (generally up to 6m in length and 2m in height); most fares inch up as the vehicle increases in size, and fares for camper vans are higher still.

Particularly if you're bringing along a vehicle, you should always make reservations well in advance – this is doubly true in summer and at weekends. During busy periods you'll also get the best cabin selection by booking in advance.

Ferry Companies

Following are reservation numbers for the larger ferry companies operating international routes to and from Denmark.

DFDS Seaways Here are some booking agencies:

Denmark
Copenhagen: (☎ 33 42 30 00, fax 33 42 30 11) Sankt Annæ Plads 30, 1295 Copenhagen K
Esbjerg: (☎ 79 17 79 17, fax 79 17 79 18) Englandskajen, 6700 Esbjerg
Norway
(☎ 22 41 90 90, fax 22 41 38 38) Utstikker II, Vippetangen, Oslo
Sweden
(☎ 42 26 60 00, fax 42 26 61 77) Sundsterminalen, Atlantgatan 252 25 Helsingborg
UK
London: (☎ 171-616 1400, fax 171-616 1450) 28A Queensway, London W2 3RX
Harwich: (☎ 1255-240 240, fax 1255-244 370) Scandinavia House, Parkeston Quay, Harwich, Essex CO12 4QG

Color Line Booking agencies include:
Denmark
(☎ 99 56 19 77, fax 99 56 20 20) Fergeterminalen, 9850 Hirtshals
Norway
Oslo: (☎ 81 00 08 11, fax 22 83 04 30) Postboks 1422 Vika, 0115 Oslo

Kristiansand: (☎ 38 07 88 00, fax 38 07 88 13) Fergeterminalen, Postboks 82, 4601 Kristiansand
Larvik: (☎ 33 12 28 00, fax 33 18 71 67) Ferjeterminalen, Postboks 2002, 3255 Larvik
Moss: (☎ 69 24 56 20, fax 69 24 12 55) Værlebrygga, 1531 Moss

Stena Line Booking agencies include:

Denmark
(☎ 96 20 02 00, fax 96 20 02 80) Stenaterminalen, 9900 Frederikshavn
Norway
(☎ 23 17 90 00, fax 23 17 90 60) Utstikker II Vippetangen, Oslo
Sweden
(☎ 31 85 80 00, fax 31 85 85 95) Danmarksterminalen, 405 19 Gothenburg

Germany

There are several ferry services from Germany to Denmark, however the two described below are the most direct routes to Copenhagen.

Other routes primarily take German tourists to Danish holiday destinations, such as the islands of Rømo and Bornholm. For reservations on either of the ferries that follow, call Scandlines at ☎ 33 15 15 15 in Denmark, ☎ 0381-673 12 17 in Germany.

Puttgarden to Rødbyhavn The busy train, car and passenger ferry between Puttgarden in Germany and Rødbyhavn in Denmark (the quickest way to Copenhagen) goes nearly every 30 minutes, 24 hours a day; it takes 45 minutes. If you're travelling by train, the cost of the ferry will be included in your ticket. Otherwise, the cost is 160kr for a motorcycle with two riders and 310kr for a car with up to five passengers.

Rostock to Gedser The ferry service between Rostock in Germany and Gedser in Denmark runs an average of three times a day and takes two hours. For a car with up to five people, the fare is from 445kr to 595kr, depending on the season and day of the week.

Poland

Polferries operates a year-round ferry service between the Polish city of Swinoujscie (☎ 9132-16140) and Copenhagen (☎ 33 11 46 45). The trip takes 10 hours and the boat makes the run five days a week. The fare is 340kr for a passenger, 490kr for a car with driver or 800kr for a car with up to five passengers. Motorcycles are an additional 90kr. There are good discounts on return fares and inexpensive cabins on overnight boats.

Sweden

In addition to the routes described below, the Stena Line offers daily ferry service between Gothenburg in Sweden and Frederikshavn in Denmark and between Varberg in Sweden and Grenaa in Denmark.

Helsingborg to Helsingør The cheapest ferry route between Denmark and Sweden is the shuttle between Helsingborg and Helsingør, which takes 20 minutes and costs just 16kr. Ferries depart every 20 minutes during the day and once an hour through the night. The fare for a motorcycle and driver is 95kr, while a car with up to five passengers costs 230kr. There are various car discounts, and you can often get a return ticket for around the same price as a one-way ticket. Both HH-Ferries (☎ 49 26 01 55 in Helsingør, ☎ 42 19 80 00 in Helsingborg) and Scandlines (☎ 33 15 15 15 in Helsingør, ☎ 42 18 61 00 in Helsingborg) ply this route.

There's also a frequent passenger-only hydrofoil service offered by Sundbusserne (☎ 49 21 35 45) that shaves a few minutes off the travel time but costs about twice as much.

Malmö to Copenhagen Pilen (Map 7, C7; ☎ 33 32 12 60 in Copenhagen, ☎ 40 23 44 11 in Malmö) has frequent hydrofoil service between Malmö and Copenhagen, operating hourly, except on Sunday when it leaves every other hour. The standard fare is 89kr but it's not uncommon to find specials at about half that price. The crossing takes only 45 minutes.

Flyvebådene (Map 7, C7; ☎ 33 12 80 88) also runs a hydrofoil from central Copenhagen to Malmö with frequent service and comparable fares.

Norway

DFDS Seaways runs direct from Oslo to Copenhagen, but if you're elsewhere in southern Norway, it's quicker and cheaper to take a ferry to one of Denmark's Jutland cities and catch a train onward from there to Copenhagen.

Oslo to Copenhagen DFDS Seaways (☎ 22 94 44 00) runs daily overnight ferries between Oslo and Copenhagen, with the cheapest cabin fare ranging from 550kr on winter weekdays to 930kr on summer weekends. In summer there are also reclining chairs for 640kr. With a student card, cabin fares are discounted by 25%. The cost to take a car is an additional 300kr. These boats have the cushiest service on the Denmark-Norway route; opt for the most economical cabins, as they're of the same comfortable standard as mid-priced ones. The departure in either direction is at 5 pm, with arrival at 9 am.

Bergen to Hanstholm The Fjord Line (☎ 55 54 88 00) sails year-round from Bergen to Hanstholm at 4.30 pm on Monday, Wednesday and Friday, stopping en route in Egersund, Norway, and arriving at Hanstholm the next day at 8 am. Sailings from Hanstholm to Bergen are on Sunday, Tuesday and Thursday; times vary. The Bergen-Hanstholm fare ranges from 300kr on winter weekdays to 750kr on summer weekends. Cars cost from 370kr to 680kr.

Other Ports The Color Line (☎ 22 94 44 00) runs daily ferries between Kristiansand and Hirtshals, the route with the shortest connection (four hours) and the most frequent service (three to five sailings a day in summer) between Norway and Denmark. The Color Line also operates ferries several days a week between Oslo and Hirtshals and between Moss (via Larvik) and the Danish ports of Frederikshavn and Hirtshals.

Fares on all the routes are the same, ranging from 160kr on winter weekdays to 390kr on summer weekends for a passenger, from 200kr to 555kr for a car.

The UK

DFDS Seaways operates car ferries between Harwich in the UK and the Jutland city of Esbjerg.

From May to September, one boat sets sail in each direction every second day; during the rest of the year boats leave Esbjerg on Monday, Wednesday and Friday and Harwich on Tuesday, Thursday and Saturday. Throughout the year the boats depart from Harwich at 4 pm, except on Saturday when they sail at 8 pm, and depart from Esbjerg at 6 pm. The crossing takes 19 hours.

These are pleasant boats with full amenities. Fares vary according to the season and the day of week, ranging from 448kr to 1098kr for a reclining chair, and from 948kr to 1798kr for a bed in a two-berth cabin. You can save between 10% and 30% by travelling between Sunday and Wednesday.

It costs an additional 480kr to take a car, 235kr for a motorcycle. There are discounts on return tickets and for senior travellers, students and children.

Iceland & the Faroe Islands

The Smyril Line (☎ 33 16 40 04) runs weekly ferries, from mid-May to early September, between the Danish port of Hanstholm and Tórshavn (Faroe Islands) and Seyðisfjörður (Iceland).

The boat departs from Seyðisfjörður at noon Thursday, arriving in Tórshavn at 6 am Friday and in Hanstholm at 4 pm Saturday.

Midsummer fares for a couchette are 1410kr from Tórshavn and 2200kr to Seyðisfjörður; these fares are 30% less for travel outside midsummer. There's a 25% discount for students under 26. You can bring along a motorcycle for about 500kr and a car for about 85% of the couchette fare.

Cruise Ships

Copenhagen is popular as a cruise ship stopover, usually as part of a larger Scandinavian, Baltic or Western European tour.

Between mid-May and mid-September over 200 cruise ships call at Copenhagen's Langelinie harbour (Map 4, D10), just north of the Little Mermaid (Map 4, F10).

Companies operating cruises stopping in Copenhagen include Costa Cruises, Crystal Cruises, Cunard Line, EuroCruises, the Fred Olsen Line, Orient Lines, Princess Cruises and Renaissance Cruises.

There are various itineraries. The Fred Olsen Line, for instance, offers a 13-day cruise from Dover in UK which includes Copenhagen, Oslo, St Petersberg, Tallinn, Stockholm, Kiel, and costs from US$3000.

Travel agencies, particularly those specialising in cruises, can detail all the possibilities and pile you high with brochures. They can also give you the lowdown on special promotions and discounts, such as those for early booking, which can cut as much as 25% to 40% off the standard fares.

TRAVEL AGENCIES

Kilroy Travels (Map 8, D4; ☎ 33 11 00 44) at Skindergade 28, Wasteels (Map 8, E4; ☎ 33 14 46 33) at Skoubogade 6 and STA Travel (Map 8, C4; ☎ 33 14 15 01) at Fiolstræde 18 all specialise in student and budget travel. All three are north of Strøget, just a few minutes' walk from each other.

There are many general travel agencies around the city, including Inter-Travel (Map 8, G4; ☎ 33 15 00 77) at Frederiksholms Kanal 2, opposite the Use It office (Map 8, G4), and Albatros (Map 8, A4; ☎ 33 32 24 88) at Kultorvet 11 in the Latin Quarter.

ORGANISED TOURS

If time is limited, there are various package tours that include transport to Copenhagen, hotel accommodation and, in most cases, sightseeing. Standard tours can be arranged through your travel agency or SAS airlines.

An array of package tours that include hotels can also be arranged through the large ferry companies, such as Stena Line and DFDS Seaways, the addresses of which are listed under Ferry Companies earlier in this chapter.

The Danish Cultural Institute arranges study tours to Denmark; contact addresses are listed under Useful Organisations in the Facts for the Visitor chapter.

Getting Around

COPENHAGEN AIRPORT

Located in Kastrup, 10km south-east of Copenhagen city centre, Copenhagen airport (airport code CPH) is a thoroughly modern facility that was recently voted the best airport in Europe by *Business Traveller Magazine*.

In the arrival hall, just beyond customs, there's a tourist information desk that can provide general information on Copenhagen and help you book a room.

You'll find foreign exchange booths in the arrival hall just beyond the tourist information desk as well as on the 2nd floor of the departure hall. The booths are open 6.30 am to 10 pm daily. The VAT refund bureau is on the 2nd floor of the departure hall.

The post office, in the arrival hall beyond the car rental desks, is open 10 am to 5 pm weekdays.

There's a left-luggage room (☎ 32 47 47 32) near the post office where you can store luggage for 30kr per piece per day; it's open 6 am to 10 pm daily. Self-service lockers, which cost 20kr for 24 hours, can be found nearby.

The airport has numerous eateries, espresso stands and pubs, ranging from international fast-food places such as Burger King and Pizza Hut to more Danish influenced choices such as the Salmon House and Café Karen Blixen.

It also has an extensive shopping area, with lots of speciality shops such as Georg Jensen, Royal Copenhagen and Gucci as well as the usual tax-free perfume and alcohol shops.

If you have a flight delay, there's a simple minihotel (☎ 32 31 24 55) with showers, saunas and 'slumber cabins' where you can nap.

It can be a bit of a haul before you reach customs, so when you get off the plane grab one of the free and ubiquitous baggage trolleys to cart your luggage around.

If you're waiting for a flight, note that this is a 'silent' airport and there are no boarding calls, although there are numerous monitor screens throughout the terminal.

TO/FROM THE AIRPORT

A new rail system links the airport arrival terminal directly with Copenhagen's Central Station. The airport station is just 50m beyond customs.

Trains run every 20 minutes until midnight from 4.55 am on weekdays, 5.35 am on Saturday and 6.35 am on Sunday. The trip takes just 12 minutes and costs 18kr.

If your baggage is light, you could also take local bus No 250S, which runs frequently between Rådhuspladsen and the airport terminal (Map 1, F5) – but it costs the same as the train and takes about three times longer.

By taxi, it takes about 15 minutes to get between the airport and the city centre, as long as traffic isn't too heavy. The cost is about 150kr.

PUBLIC TRANSPORT

Copenhagen has an extensive public transit system consisting of a metro rail network called S-train, whose 10 lines pass through Central Station (København H), and a vast bus system called HT, whose main terminus is at Rådhuspladsen, a couple of blocks to the north-east.

Buses and trains use a common fare system based on the number of zones you pass through.

The basic fare of 12kr for up to two zones covers most city runs and allows transfers between buses and trains on a single ticket as long as they're made within an hour. Third and subsequent zones cost 6kr more with a maximum fare of 42kr for travel throughout North Zealand.

On buses, you board at the front and pay the fare to the driver (or stamp your clip card in the machine next to the driver). On S-trains, tickets are purchased at the station and then punched in the yellow time clock on the platform before boarding the train.

Instead of buying a single destination ticket, you can buy a *klippekort* (clip card) which is valid for 10 rides in two zones (80kr) or three zones (110kr), or you can get a 24-hour ticket valid for unlimited travel in all zones (70kr).

Passengers who are stopped and found to be without a stamped ticket are liable to a fine of 500kr.

Up to two children aged under 10 travel free when accompanied by an adult. Otherwise, children aged under 16 must buy a child's ticket, which is approximately half the price of an adult fare.

All rides on Copenhagen's regional buses and trains are free for visitors holding a valid Copenhagen Card (see the boxed text 'Card Does the Trick' in the Things to See & Do chapter).

Trains and buses run from about 5 am (6 am on Sunday) to around 12.30 am, though buses continue to run through the night (charging double the usual fare) on a few main routes.

The free Copenhagen city maps distributed by the tourist office show bus routes (with numbers) and are very useful for finding your way around the city. If you plan to use buses extensively, you might want to buy HT's hefty timetable book *Busser og tog* (40kr), which comes with a colour-coded bus route map (covering the entire HT route throughout North Zealand), or get just the map for 5kr. Both are sold at HT's booth on Rådhuspladsen.

Throughout this book the bus numbers of some of the more frequent buses to individual destinations are listed, but since there can be as many as a dozen buses passing any particular place, our listing is often only a partial one. In addition to the HT buses and the S-trains, Denmark's national railroad, DSB, also includes its local lines in the common fare system as far north as Helsingør and west to Roskilde.

For schedules and other information on HT buses call ☎ 36 13 14 15 between 7 am and 9.30 pm daily; for S-trains call ☎ 33 14 17 01 between 6.30 am and 11 pm daily; for DSB trains call ☎ 70 13 14 15 between 7 am and 10 pm daily.

CAR & MOTORCYCLE

With the exception of the weekday-morning rush hour, when traffic can bottleneck coming into the city (and vice versa around 5 pm), traffic in Copenhagen is usually manageable. Getting around by car is not problematic, except for the usual challenge of finding an empty parking space in the most popular places.

To explore sights in the centre of the city, you're best off on foot or using public transport, but a car is quite convenient for reaching suburban sights or going farther afield.

Road Rules

In Denmark vehicles are driven on the right-hand side of the road. Cars and motorcycles must have dipped headlights on at all times and drivers are required to carry a warning triangle.

Seat belt use is mandatory. Children aged under three must be secured in a child seat or other approved child restraint appropriate to the child's age, size and weight. Children aged from three to six may use a child seat or booster seat instead of seat belts. Motorcycle riders must wear helmets.

Speed limits are generally 50km/h in towns and built-up areas, 80km/h on major roads and 110km/h on motorways. However, if you're towing a trailer the maximum speed you can travel on major roads and motorways is 70km/h.

Fines for speeding and other traffic offences, which can be collected on the spot, are costly. As an example, for each person in the car that isn't wearing a seat belt there's a 500kr fine. Using a hand-held mobile phone while driving is illegal and that too warrants a 500kr fine. Going through a red light carries a 1000kr fine. As for speeding it varies with the offence but, for example, driving 20km over the speed limit in a 50km/h zone can set you back a hefty 2000kr. Breaking a speed limit by more than 70% can trigger fines of up to 8000kr and the immediate confiscation of your driving licence. Although the latter occurrence may be a rare case of madness, Danish drivers do commonly exceed speed limits by a good 10km/h to 20km/h, so don't rely upon the flow of traffic as an indication of whether your speed is within legal limits.

The authorities are very strict about driving under the influence of alcohol. It's illegal to drive with a blood-alcohol concentration of 0.05% or greater; driving under the influence will render drivers liable to stiff penalties and a possible prison sentence.

Parking

To park on the street in Copenhagen centre, you usually have to buy a ticket from a kerbside machine, labelled *billetautomat*. This automated ticket machine has an LCD read-out showing the current time and as you insert coins the time advances. Put in enough money to advance the read-out to the time you desire and then push the button to eject the ticket from the machine. Place the ticket, which shows the exact time until which you can stay, face up inside the car windscreen.

The billetautomat only charges for hours when a ticket is required, so if you were to park your car at 5 pm and leave it overnight in a space where tickets are required from 8 am to 6 pm, and put in sufficient coins for two hours, the ticket would be valid until 9 am the next morning.

Copenhagen parking is zoned so that the spaces most in demand, such as those in the central commercial area, are the most costly. Your best bet is to search out a blue zone where parking costs just 7kr per hour. If you can't find an empty blue space then opt for a green zone where the fee is 12kr per hour. Avoid red zones where it's a steep 20kr per hour. Parking fees must be paid on weekdays from 8 am to 6 pm (to 8 pm in red zones), and also on Saturday from 8 am to 2 pm in red and green zones.

If you cannot find street parking, there are multistorey car parks at the main department stores, at the Radisson SAS Royal Hotel, and on Jerbanegade east of Axeltorv, among other places. Car parks charge around 12kr per hour.

In the suburbs and in smaller towns, most locations are delightfully free of coin-hungry billetautomats and street parking is free within the time limits posted. These parking spaces will be marked by a blue sign with the letter 'P'; beneath it will be the time limit for free parking (*1 time* is one hour, *2 timer* is two hours).

You will, however, need to use a windscreen parking disk. This is a flat plastic card with a clock face and a movable hour hand which must be set to show the time you parked the car. Parking disks can be picked up for a nominal fee from tourist offices and petrol stations.

Parkering forbudt means 'no parking' and is generally accompanied by a round sign with a red diagonal slash. You can, however, stop for up to three minutes to unload bags and passengers. A round sign with a red 'X', or a sign saying *Stopforbud*, means that no stopping at all is allowed.

Rental

Rental cars are expensive in Denmark. This is one area where it certainly can save you a bundle to do a little research in advance. You'll generally get the best deal on a car rental by booking through an international rental agency before you arrive in Copenhagen. Be sure to ask about promotional rates, prepay schemes and the like, then compare the options.

Otherwise, if you just show up at the counter at Copenhagen airport you're likely to find the rates for the cheapest cars (including VAT, insurance and unlimited kilometres) beginning at about 650kr per day, or 500kr per day for rentals of two days or more.

One of the better car rental deals which doesn't require booking before you arrive is the weekend rate offered by some companies. This typically allows you to keep the car from Friday afternoon to Monday morning for around 1000kr, including VAT and insurance. Request a plan that includes unlimited kilometres, as some plans begin tacking on an extra fee after 250km. As we went to press, Europcar was offering the most flexible weekend deal, allowing you to choose any 72-hour period as long as a Saturday overnight was included in the rental period and it was charging a bit less than the competition as well.

The following car hire companies have booths at the airport in the international terminal. Each also has an office in central Copenhagen:

Avis (Map 7, C3; ☎ 33 15 22 99) Kampmannsgade 1
Budget (Map 7, E2; ☎ 33 55 05 00) Helgolandsgade 2
Europcar (Map 7, D2; ☎ 33 55 99 00) Gammel Kongevej 13
Hertz (Map 7, D3; ☎ 33 17 90 21) Ved Vesterport 3

Peugeot (☎ 38 33 40 04), Frederiksborgvej 59, hires out motor scooters for between 250kr and 400kr per day.

TAXI

Taxis are readily available in the city centre at places such as train stations and shopping areas. If you see a taxi with a lit *fri* sign, you can wave it down, but you can always phone for a taxi as well.

Two large companies are Københavns Taxa (☎ 35 35 35 35) and Taxa Motor (☎ 38 10 10 10). The cost is 22kr at flagfall, plus about 10kr per kilometre (11kr to 13kr at night and at weekends). Most taxis accept credit cards. A service charge is included in the fare, so tips are not expected.

BICYCLE

Three out of four Danes own bicycles, and half use them on a regular basis. Postal workers are more likely to deliver mail by bicycle than by motor vehicle, and it's not uncommon to see well-heeled executives beating the rush hour by cycling through city traffic.

Despite all its motor traffic, Copenhagen is a great city for getting around by bicycle. There are separate cycle lanes along many of the main roads and bicycle racks can be found at museums and other public places. One caveat – if you're travelling with a bicycle, be careful, as expensive bikes are hot targets for thieves on Copenhagen streets.

Except during weekday rush hours, it's possible to carry bikes on S-trains (buy the 12kr ticket from the red machine). You can load your bicycle in any carriage that has a cycle symbol and you must stay with the bike at all times.

For more information, including a suggested cycling tour, see Cycling under Activities in the Things to See & Do chapter.

Rental

If you didn't bring a bike with you, there are several places around Copenhagen where they can be hired.

In addition to rental rates, expect to pay a refundable deposit of around 300kr for a regular bike, 1000kr for a mountain bike or tandem.

One of the most convenient bicycle rental places is Københavns Cykler (☎ 33 33 86 13) at the Reventlowsgade side of Central Station. It's open 8 am to 6 pm weekdays and 9 am to 1 pm Saturday; in summer, it's also open 10 am to 1 pm Sunday. The cost is 50kr per day or 225kr per week for a regular bike, 200kr per day or 900kr per week for a mountain bike or a tandem bike. A sister operation, Østerport Cykler (☎ 33 33 85 13) at Østerport S-train station near track 13, has the same rates and hours as Københavns Cykler, except that it's closed on Sunday year-round.

Københavns Cykelbørs (Map 7, A4; ☎ 33 14 07 17) at Gothersgade 157, not far from Rosenborg Slot, rents bikes for 40kr per day, 185kr per week. It's open 8.30 am to 5.30 pm weekdays, 10 am to 1.30 pm Saturday.

For a bargain bike, Danwheel (Map 7, E3; ☎ 33 21 22 27), Colbjørnsensgade 3, a couple of blocks north-west of Central Station, hires older bikes for 35kr per day, 165kr per week. It's open 9 am to 5.30 pm weekdays, to 2 pm at weekends.

Free Copenhagen Bikes

The city of Copenhagen has a generous scheme, called Bycykler (City Bikes), in which anyone can borrow a bicycle for free. It's motivated in part by an effort to control motor-vehicle traffic in the heart of the city. Sponsors, who paint the bikes with their logos, include private businesses, the local tourism office and the city council. In all there are some 2000 bikes available each summer.

Although these bicycles are not streamlined and are certainly not practical for long-distance cycling, that's part of the plan – use of the cycles is limited to the city centre. To deter theft and minimise maintenance, the bicycles have a distinctive design that includes solid spokeless wheels with puncture-resistant tyres. The bikes can be found at 125 widely scattered street stands in public places, including S-train stations.

The way it works is that if you're able to find a free bicycle, you deposit a 20kr coin in the stand to release the bike. When you're done using the bicycle, you can return it to any stand and get your 20kr coin back.

Cycle Regulations

Cycling is taken seriously in Denmark, and Danish cyclists steadfastly follow prescribed cycle regulations. Before setting out you should become familiar with the following:

• All traffic in Denmark, both bicycle and motor vehicle, is on the right-hand side of the road.
• Cyclists are obliged to obey traffic lights, pedestrian right-of-ways and most other road rules that apply to motor vehicles.
• When making a left turn at crossings, a large left turn is mandatory; that is, you must cycle straight across the intersecting road, staying on the right, before turning left into the right-hand lane of the new road. Do not cross diagonally.
• Use hand signals to indicate turns: a left arm outstretched for a left turn, and a right arm outstretched for a right turn.
• When entering a roundabout (traffic circle), yield to vehicles already on the roundabout.
• If you're transporting children, the bicycle must have two independent brakes. A maximum of two children under the age of six can be carried on the bicycle or in an attached trailer.

BOAT

Canal boats can be a fine traffic-free way of getting to some of Copenhagen's famous waterfront sites.

Public transit company HT has recently started ferry service along Copenhagen's canals. The boats operate every 20 minutes from early morning until about 7 pm year-round, weather permitting. Stops include Nyhavn, the south-eastern side of Churchillparken, the Royal Library and a couple of locales in Christianshavn. Tickets cost 24kr, can be purchased on the boat and are valid for one hour.

In addition, DFDS Canal Tours (Map 7, C6) operates a summertime water bus that runs along a route similar to its guided tours (see Organised Tours later in this chapter) but has no commentary. These boats leave Nyhavn every 30 minutes daily from 10.15 am to 4.45 pm between mid-May and mid-September (to 5.45 pm in July and August), and make 10 stops, including Slotsholmen, Christianshavn and the Little Mermaid (Map 4, F10). A day pass, which costs 40kr for adults and 20kr for children, allows you to get on and off as often as you like. You can also ride from just one stop to another for 30kr.

WALKING

Copenhagen is a good city for getting around on foot, as many of its leading sights are close together in the city centre. Get hold of a detailed map, such as the free one distributed by the tourist office, and just set out.

Two self-guided walking tours can be found in the Things to See & Do chapter later in this book.

In addition, the tourist office usually has a couple of free brochures with suggested walking tours.

For information on joining a guided walk, see Organised Tours later in this chapter.

HITCHING

Hitching is never entirely safe in any country in the world, and we don't recommend it. Travellers who decide to hitch should understand that they are taking a small but potentially serious risk. People who do choose to hitch will be safer if they travel in pairs and let someone know where they are planning to go.

At any rate, hitching is not a common practice in Denmark and generally not a very rewarding one. Keep in mind that hitching is illegal on motorways. Incidentally, most

Danes who do hitch usually only do so when travelling outside their own country.

ORGANISED TOURS
Bus Tours
Copenhagen is so easy to get around that there's little need to consider a sightseeing bus tour. However, Copenhagen Excursions (☎ 32 54 06 06) does offer various guided tours of the city and surrounding areas. The cheapest tour, in splashy pink-and-yellow double-decker buses with open tops, costs 100kr, lasts one hour and cruises by some of the city's main sights, such as Amalienborg Slot (Map 7, A7), Slotsholmen, the Little Mermaid and Nyhavn.

Other tours include a 2½-hour 'grand tour' that takes in a broader swath of city sights and costs 170kr, and a 360kr day-long castle tour of North Zealand that visits Kronborg Slot in Helsingør, the royal summer palace in Fredensborg and Frederiksborg Slot in Hillerød.

Boat Tours
For a different angle on the city, hop on to one of the boat tours that wind through Copenhagen's canals. Although most of the passengers are usually Danes, multilingual guides give a lively commentary in English as well.

All the tours follow a similar loop route, passing by Slotsholmen, Christianshavn and the Little Mermaid.

The biggest company, DFDS Canal Tours (☎ 33 42 30 00), operates from April to late October. Boats leave twice an hour from two locations – one at the head of Nyhavn and the other on Gammel Strand, north of Slotsholmen (see the Slotsholmen map). Tours, which last 50 minutes, run from 10 am to 5 pm, except in July and August when the Nyhavn departures extend to 7.30 pm; the cost is 50kr for adults, 20kr for children.

A better deal is with Netto-Bådene (Map 7, C7; ☎ 32 54 41 02), which charges just 20kr for adults, 10kr for children, and operates from mid-April to mid-October. Its cruises, which last an hour, leave from Holmens Kirke, east of Slotsholmen (see the Slotsholmen map), as well as from Nyhavn, between two and four times an hour from 10 am to 5 pm, with the greatest frequency in the summer high season.

Walking Tours
From June to late August a 'night watchman' dressed in period clothing and carrying a lantern and spiked mace makes his rounds of the older quarters of the city, with sightseers in tow. The one-hour tours, which are conducted in English and Danish, take place on Friday. It's touristy, but colourful and free. Meet at 9 pm at Gråbrødre Torv, the small square fronting Peder Oxe restaurant.

Copenhagen Information (Map 7, D3), the city tourist office at Bernstorffsgade 1, arranges guided walking tours in English during the months of May to September. The tours, which last two hours and leave from the tourist office at 10.30 am Monday to Saturday, visit various historic parts of the city. The cost is 50kr.

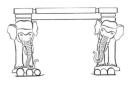

Things to See & Do

HIGHLIGHTS

There are hundreds of different things to do in Copenhagen, but whatever you do, don't miss out on some of the following:

- Let yourself go at Tivoli, the famed amusement park in the city centre
- Enjoy shopping and the street entertainment on Strøget, the world's longest pedestrian mall
- Visit the grand Ny Carlsberg Glyptotek, whose collections range from Egyptian mummies to Gauguin paintings
- While away a sunny afternoon over a cold beer at one of Nyhavn's canalside cafes
- Jump aboard a canal boat for a guided tour of the historic waterfront
- Club-hop your way through Copenhagen's spirited nightlife scene
- Marvel at the sparkling crown jewels and other regalia displayed at Rosenborg Slot
- Take a walk past the famed Little Mermaid and through Kastellet, the city's historic citadel
- Spend some time at Nationalmuseet with its amazing Bronze Age and Viking-era finds
- Wheel your way around on one of the 'City Bikes', free-use bicycles available in the city centre
- Enjoy the lunchtime herring buffet at the quintessentially Danish cafe Nyhavns Færgekro
- Party your way through the Copenhagen Jazz Festival, which transforms the city into a 10-day musical cornucopia

WALKING TOURS

Setting out on foot is a good way to explore this grand city and its numerous historic sights.

Walking Tour 1: Rådhuspladsen to the Amalienborg Area

Taking a half-day's walk from rådhus (city hall) to the neighbourhood around Amalienborg Slot, the royal palace, will not only get you oriented to Copenhagen, but also enable you to take in many of the city's central sights. As you stroll along the narrow streets, be sure to look up now and then to appreciate the gargoyles and other ornamentations that decorate many of the older buildings.

The walk starts (2 on Walking Tour map) at **Rådhuspladsen**, the central city square fronting city hall. Rådhuspladsen is also the spot where most city buses converge, so it's a cinch to get to or from any part of Copenhagen.

At the south-western side of the square you'll find a **statue of Hans Christian Andersen** (4) and a **water fountain** (3) with spouting dragons, while on the eastern side, as you face the Palace Hotel, there's a noteworthy column capped with a bronze **statue of two Vikings** (6), blowing *lurs* (horns).

From Rådhuspladsen, be sure to look over at the Unibank building on the north-western corner of Vesterbrogade and HC Andersens Blvd. The building is topped with a unique **barometer** (1) that displays a girl on her bicycle when the weather is fair or with an umbrella when rain is predicted. This charming bronze sculpture was created in 1936 by the Danish artist E Utzon-Frank.

Before leaving Rådhuspladsen, you might want to visit the century-old **rådhus** (5). For details on touring city hall, walking to the top of its tower and viewing its unusual Jens Olsen's clock, see the Rådhuspladsen & Around heading later in this chapter.

From Rådhuspladsen walk down **Strøget** which, after a couple of blocks, cuts between two spirited pedestrian squares, **Gammel Torv** and **Nytorv**. A popular summertime gathering spot in Gammel Torv is the gilded **Caritas Fountain** (7), erected in 1608 by Christian IV and marking what was once the old city's central market. As in days past, pedlars still sell jewellery, flowers and fruit on the square.

On the south-western corner of Nytorv is **Domhuset** (8), a columned neoclassical building that once served as the city hall and now houses the city's law courts. Inscribed above the entrance are the words 'Med Lov Skal Man Land Bygge' (With law shall a land be built), which are taken from the Jutland Code that codified laws in Denmark in 1241.

Continuing down Strøget, you'll pass **Helligåndskirken** (9, the Church of the Holy Ghost), one wing of which dates from medieval times, though most of the building was rebuilt after a fire in 1732. Also along the Amagertorv section of Strøget are some of the city's finest speciality shops, including **Royal Copenhagen Porcelain** (10) and **Georg Jensen** (11). The Georg Jensen shop houses a small, free museum featuring early 20th-century silverwork.

The WØ Larsen pipe shop, diagonally opposite Georg Jensen at Amagertorv 9, boasts another little free speciality exhibition, the **Tobaksmuseet** (12, Tobacco Museum), which displays a curious collection of antique tobacco and opium pipes.

The adjacent square, **Højbro Plads**, marked by a water fountain with bronze storks, is a popular venue for street musicians. At the southern end of this elongated square is a **statue** (13) of city founder Bishop Absalon on horseback; behind it, the appropriate backdrop is Slotsholmen, where the bishop erected Copenhagen's first fortress.

If you look due east from Højbro Plads you'll see the steeple of **Nikolaj Kirke** (14). The tower of this church dates from the 16th century, although most of the church was rebuilt in 1915. No longer consecrated, the church is now owned by the municipality and is used for contemporary art exhibits.

At the end of Strøget you'll reach **Kongens Nytorv**, a square boasting an equestrian statue of its designer, Christian V, and circled by gracious old buildings. Notable from Christian V's era are **Charlottenborg** (17), a 17th-century Dutch baroque palace that houses Det Kongelige Kunstakademi (The Royal Academy of Fine Arts), and the 1685 **Thott's Palæ** (18, Thott's Mansion), which now houses the French embassy.

There are also some attractive 100-year-old buildings, including the department store **Magasin du Nord** (15), with its ornate cupola, and **Det Kongelige Teater** (16, the Royal Theatre), which is fronted by statues of the playwrights Adam Oehlenschläger and Ludvig Holberg. The theatre, home to Den Kongelige Ballet (the Royal Danish Ballet) and Den Kongelige Opera (the Royal Danish Opera), has two stages, one on either side of Tordenskjoldsgade. An **archway** with a mosaic depicting Danish poets and artists spans the road connecting the two stages.

To the east of Kongens Nytorv is **Nyhavn** canal, one of the city's most scenic waterfront quarters, with its attractive 18th-century buildings and moored sailboats. The cafes along its north side make an invitingly atmospheric place to break for lunch or a frosty beer.

From the northern side of Nyhavn, head north along Toldbodgade, turn right onto Sankt Annæ Plads, left onto Larsens Plads and continue walking north along the waterfront. You'll pass a couple of **18th-century warehouses** that have been converted for modern use. One of them is now the Copenhagen Admiral Hotel (19), whose lobby is worth a peek.

When you reach the fountain that graces **Amaliehaven** (Amalie Gardens), turn inland to get to **Amalienborg Slot** (21), home of the royal family since 1794. The palace's four nearly identical rococo mansions, designed by architect Nicolai Eigtved, surround a central cobblestone square and an immense **statue** (20) of Frederik V (1746–66) on horseback sculpted by JFJ Saly. One of the mansions has exhibits that are open to the public and the square is the site of a noontime changing of the guard; both are detailed later in this chapter.

Looking west from the square you'll get a head-on view of the imposing **Marmorkirken** (22, Marble Church), which was designed in conjunction with the Amalienborg complex as part of an ambitious plan by Frederik V to extend the city northward by creating a new district geared to the affluent. From here walk north along Bredgade, where there are some historic churches and museums – **Alexander Newsky Kirke** (23), **Medicinsk-Historisk Museum** (24), **Sankt Ansgars Kirke** (25) and **Kunstindustrimuseet** (26) – which are described later in this chapter.

If you feel like extending the walk, continue north to **Churchillparken**, where Walking Tour 2 begins.

Headless Statue of Topless Lady

In 1909 the Danish beer baron Carl Jacobsen was so moved after attending a ballet performance of *The Little Mermaid* that he commissioned sculptor Edvard Eriksen to create a statue of the fairy-tale character to grace Copenhagen's harbourfront.

The face of the famous statue was modelled after the ballerina Ellen Price, while Eline Eriksen, the sculptor's wife, modelled for the body.

The Little Mermaid (Map 4, F10) survived the Great Depression and the WWII occupation unscathed but modern times haven't been so kind to Denmark's leading lady.

In January 1998, in the middle of the night, someone took a saw and decapitated the bronze statue. The next day, international news services spread the gory scene around the world, as divers searched the waters around the statue for clues to no avail. Three days later the severed head mysteriously turned up in a box outside a Copenhagen TV station – and it was speedily reattached.

That wasn't the first time the gentle lady had been the subject of undesired attention. In 1964 the original head was lopped off and in 1983 an arm was sawn off – neither were ever found again and both appendages had to be recast and welded back on.

Walking Tour 2: Churchillparken to Botanisk Have

In contrast to Walking Tour 1, which passes through the heart of the city, this second walking tour takes in quiet green spaces, gardens and less hurried neighbourhoods. Walking Tour 2 also includes a couple of the city's best-known sights, the Little Mermaid and Rosenborg Slot.

The walk starts (27) at **Churchillparken**, a quiet green space at the north side of the city centre.

On Esplanaden, at the southern end of Churchillparken, you'll find **Frihedsmuseet** (28) a museum dedicated to the Danish resistance movement of WWII. Nearby is the attractive Gothic **St Alban's Church** (29), which serves the city's English-speaking Anglican community. The church's location, in the midst of a public park, may seem a bit curious – the site was provided by Christian IX following the marriage of his daughter to the Prince of Wales, who later ascended the British throne as King Edward VII.

Beside the church sits the immense **Gefionspringvandet** (30, Gefion Fountain), a monument to yet another overseas relationship. According to Scandinavian mythology, when the Swedish king offered the

goddess Gefion as much land as she could plough in one night, Gefion turned her four sons into powerful oxen and ploughed the entire area that now comprises the island of Zealand.

The bronze statue in the fountain depicts the goddess and her oxen at work.

A 10-minute walk through the park past the fountain and along the waterfront will lead you to the statue of the **Little Mermaid** (31, Den Lille Havfrue), which was designed by Edvard Eriksen in 1913. Inspired by Hans Christian Andersen's fairy tale, the statue depicts a mermaid who had fallen in love with a prince but had to wait for 300 years to become human.

This much-photographed bronze figure, perched on a rock at the water's edge, has a certain grace, but don't expect a monument – the mermaid is indeed little, and sports a rather drab industrial harbour backdrop.

From the Little Mermaid continue on the road inland. After just a few minutes you'll reach steps leading down to a wooden bridge that crosses a moat into **Kastellet**, a citadel built by Frederik III in the 1660s. Stepping across the moat is like walking back in history – the grounds and buildings have been preserved in their original character and the

WALKING TOURS

WALKING TOUR 1 · · · ·
1 Bicycle Barometer
2 Start of Walk 1
3 Water Fountain
4 Hans Christian Andersen Statue
5 Rådhus
6 Viking Statue
7 Caritas Fountain
8 Domhuset
9 Helligåndskirken
10 Royal Copenhagen Porcelain
11 Georg Jensen
12 Tobaksmuseet
13 Bishop Absalon Statue
14 Nikolaj Kirke
15 Magasin du Nord
16 Det Kongelige Teater
17 Charlottenborg
18 Thott's Palæ
19 Copenhagen Admiral Hotel
20 Frederik V Statue
21 Amalienborg Slot
22 Marmorkirken
23 Alexander Newsky Kirke
24 Medicinsk-Historisk Museum
25 Sankt Ansgars Kirke
26 Kunstindustrimuseet

WALKING TOUR 2 ------
27 Start of Walk 2
28 Frihedsmuseet
29 St Alban's Church
30 Gefionspringvandet
31 Little Mermaid
32 Christian IV Statue
33 Nyboder Houses
34 Nyboders Mindestuer
35 Davids Samling
36 Rosenborg Slot
37 Botanisk Museum
38 Palmehus

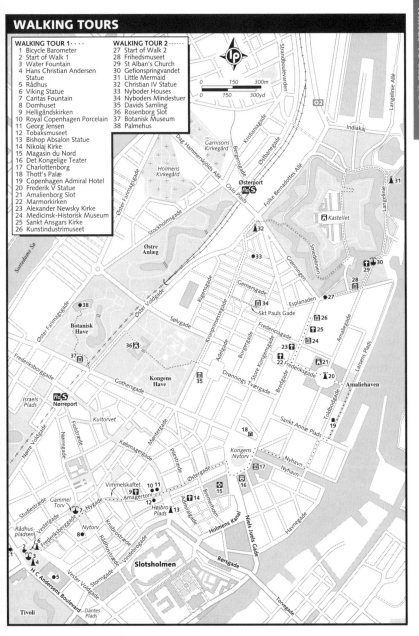

fortress is still surrounded by centuries-old ramparts. Although the fortress barracks remain in use by the Danish military, the park-like grounds are open to the public from 6 am to sunset daily. Walk south through Kastellet and you'll pass its main row of historic buildings before reaching a second bridge that spans the moat and leads back into Churchillparken.

Once you cross the moat, take the path to the right and you can walk along the outer moat ramparts north-west until you reach a side path leading to the intersection of Grønningen and Folke Bernadottes Allé. Cross Grønningen and walk south-west along Øster Voldgade and you'll soon come to a streetside **statue of Christian IV** (32). In the 1630s the king, who was expanding his military in response to threats from Sweden, developed this area to provide housing for his naval staff.

If you proceed south on Kronprinsessegade you'll pass **Nyboder** (33), which is comprised of row after row of long mustard-coloured houses with tiled roofs that once housed some 2200 naval personnel. Most of these buildings have been converted to public housing but if you turn left onto Sankt Paulsgade, the building at No 20 has been preserved as a museum called **Nyboders Mindestuer** (34). The museum (10kr), which contains period furnishings, is open afternoons on Wednesday and Sunday year-round as well as on Friday in summer.

Return to Kronprinsessegade and you can continue south to **Davids Samling** (35), a splendid little museum with an eclectic art collection. Opposite Davids Samling is **Kongens Have**, the lovely public gardens backing **Rosenborg Slot** (36), a former royal residence that's open to the public. During daylight hours you can walk

Card Does the Trick

The Copenhagen Card, a tourist pass, allows unlimited travel on buses and trains in Copenhagen and throughout North Zealand, as well as free admission to most of the region's museums and attractions.

Copenhagen attractions offering free admission to cardholders include Tivoli, Ny Carlsberg Glyptotek (Map 7, E4), Nationalmuseet (Map 7, D4), Statens Museum for Kunst (Map 7, A5), Rundetårn (Map 8, B5), the Vor Frelsers Kirke tower (Map 7, E7), Arken (Map 1, G1), Copenhagen Zoo (Map 6, E2), Den Hirschsprungske Samling (Map 4, F7), Orlogsmuseet (Map 7, D8), Jens Olsen's clock, Kunstindustrimuseet (Map 7, A7), Musikhistorisk Museum (Map 7, B5), Arbejdermuseet (Map 7, A4), Guinness World of Records Museum (Map 8, C9), Ripley's Believe It or Not! (Map 8, G2), Louis Tussaud's Wax Museum (Map 7, D4), Den Kongelige Afstøbningssamling (Map 7, A8), Gammel Dok (Map 7, D7), Københavns Bymuseum (Map 7, E1), Post & Tele Museum (Map 8, C6), Zoologisk Museum (Map 4, D4) and all of the Slotsholmen sights except De Kongelige Repræsentationslokaler.

The card also confers free admission to the Viking Ship Museum and cathedral in Roskilde, Frederiksborg Slot in Hillerød, Karen Blixen Museet in Rungsted, Louisiana in Humlebæk, Frilandsmuseet (Map 1, B3) in Lyngby, Danmarks Akvarium (Map 3, A4) in Charlottenlund and the museums in Køge.

In addition, the card offers discounts on a few other sights, such as Rosenborg Slot (Map 7, A5), Amalienborg Slot (Map 7, A7), Dansk Design Center (Map 7, D4), De Kongelige Repræsentationslokaler, the Omnimax cinema at Tycho Brahe Planetarium (Map 7, D2) and the Experimentarium (Map 3, G3) in Hellerup. There are also discounts on Scandlines canal tours and boats to Sweden.

A Copenhagen Card valid for one/two/three days costs 155/255/320kr for adults and 75/125/160kr for children aged from five to 11 years. Cards can be purchased at Central Station, at tourist offices and in some hotels.

If you want to run through a lot of sightseeing in a few days, the Copenhagen Card can be a real bargain. However, for a more leisurely exploration of select places it may work out cheaper to pay individual admission charges and use one of the transport passes (see the Getting Around chapter for details).

through the gardens, across the moat and past the castle to Øster Voldgade.

If you proceed south on Øster Voldgade you'll reach the entrance to the **Botanisk Have**, which has peaceful paths, a resplendent selection of native and exotic plants, and a walk-through tropical glasshouse called **Palmehus** (38). The gardens also hold the **Botanisk Museum** (37), which has some exhibits on plants but is only open in summer.

If you're up for more sightseeing there are a number of museums in the area you could visit, including the national gallery **Statens Museum for Kunst**, which is opposite the north-east end of the gardens. Otherwise, you can pick up a bus outside the gardens to Rådhuspladsen or other points in the city.

More details on the Botanisk Have, Kongens Have, Rosenborg Slot, Davids Samling and other nearby museums is in the Rosenborg Slot & Around section later in this chapter.

VESTERBRO

Despite the fact that the Vesterbro district boasts few conventional sightseeing attractions, for many visitors to Copenhagen it's the first place they'll see, as it's home to both Central Station and the city's main hotel district.

Vesterbro has a varied character that's readily observed by walking along its best-known street, Istedgade, which runs west from Central Station. The first few blocks are lined with rows of respectable hotels that soon give way to the city's red-light area. When Denmark became the first country to legalise pornography in the 1970s, Vesterbro's porn shops and seedy nightclubs became a magnet for tourists and voyeurs. Although it's not necessarily any tamer these days, liberalisation in other countries has made the area less of a novelty.

About halfway down Istedgade the red-light district recedes and the neighbourhood becomes increasingly multiethnic, with a mix of Pakistani and Turkish businesses. Vesterbro, together with the adjacent Nørrebro, is home to much of the city's immigrant community and abounds with good restaurants serving international cuisine.

Københavns Bymuseum
(Map 7, E1)

The Copenhagen City Museum (☎ 33 21 07 72), Vesterbrogade 59, features displays about the history and development of Copenhagen, mainly in the form of paintings and scale models. The exhibits begin with the city's origins from a seaside trading post in the 11th century, detail its blossoming as a Renaissance capital under Christian IV and wrap up with the industrial revolution and founding of the welfare state.

One curiosity is the small exhibit dedicated to the religious philosopher Søren Kierkegaard, who was born in Copenhagen in 1813, maintained an often turbulent relationship with local authorities and died in a city hospital at the age of 42. The collection includes a handful of the philosopher's personal possessions and some unflattering caricatures exaggerating Kierkegaard's spinal deformity that appeared in the local media of the day.

The museum is open 10 am to 4 pm daily, except Monday, from May to September and 1 to 4 pm from October to April. Admission is free for adults on Friday and 20kr at other times, and free for children at all times. It's about a 20-minute walk from Central Station or you can get there via bus No 6, 28 or 550S.

Tycho Brahe Planetarium
(Map 7, D2)

This planetarium (☎ 33 12 12 24) at Gammel Kongevej 10, about 750m north-west of Central Station, has a domed space theatre that offers shows of the night sky using state-of-the-art equipment capable of projecting more than 7500 stars, planets and galaxies. The planetarium's 1000-sq-metre screen also hosts Omnimax natural science films on subjects ranging from astronauts in the space shuttle to divers exploring tropical reefs.

The planetarium was named after the famed Danish astronomer Tycho Brahe (1546–1601), whose creation of precision astronomical instruments allowed him to make more exact observations of planets and stars and paved the way for the discoveries made by later astronomers.

These days, the most popular shows are the Omnimax films, which last about 50 minutes, but are usually followed by a 10-minute show featuring the night sky. There is also a planetarium-only show but it's just shown a couple of times a week, so call ahead for the schedule. The cost is 75kr for adults, 56kr for children, to see either an Omnimax film or the planetarium show, plus 15kr for a headphone setup that allows you to listen in English.

There are also some general astronomy exhibits (15kr) that include a small moon rock and photos of planets, satellites and astronauts. It's open 10.30 am to 9 pm daily.

RÅDHUSPLADSEN & AROUND

This large central square, flanked on one side by city hall and on another by Copenhagen's municipal bus terminus, marks the heart of Copenhagen. The bustling shopping street Strøget begins at the north-east side of Rådhuspladsen and the famed amusement park Tivoli glitters to the south-west.

For the Term of Your Sightseeing Life

Here are some key words and phrases you'll come across while sightseeing in Copenhagen:

kirke	church
have	garden
slot	castle
kongelige	royal
kongens	king's
museet	museum
samling	collection
udstilling	exhibition
særudstilling	special exhibition
kunst	art
entré	admission fee
rabatt	discount
handicap adgang	handicapped access
omvisninger	conducted tours
åbningstiden	opening hours
lukke-dag	closing days
daglig	daily
helligdage	holidays

Rådhuspladsen sees more foot traffic than anywhere else in Copenhagen and consequently the square is laid out in an open format without barriers, which tends to give it a rather barren appearance. The unobstructed openness of the square, however, makes it a great place to stop and observe the classic buildings that surround it. See Walking Tour 1 (which starts in Rådhuspladsen) earlier in this chapter for more details on the square.

Rådhus (Map 7, D4; City Hall)

Copenhagen's grand red-brick city hall had its groundwork laid in 1892 and was completed in 1905. Designed by the Danish architect Martin Nyrop, it reflects many of the trends of its period, displaying elements of 19th-century national Romanticism, medieval Danish design and northern Italian architecture, the last-mentioned most notable in the central courtyard.

Adorning the facade above the main entrance is a golden statue of Bishop Absalon, who founded the city in 1167. The entrance leads to the main hall, a grand room that serves as a polling station during municipal elections. With a capacity to seat up to 1200 people, the theatre-like hall is also sometimes used for official receptions and concerts. Near the hall's main portal you'll find a bust of Nyrop, along with busts of three of the city's leading citizens: writer Hans Christian Andersen, sculptor Bertel Thorvaldsen and nuclear physicist Niels Bohr.

You can poke into the main hall on your own but to tour the rest of the building, which includes the city council meeting hall, a formal banquet hall and committee rooms, you'll need to join a tour. Rådhus tours cost 30kr and take place year-round at 3 pm weekdays and at 10 and 11 am Saturday.

Another sightseeing option is to make the climb up the 105m clock tower that tops city hall, but expect a decent workout as there are some 300 steps along the way. Guided tours of the tower cost 20kr and are given at noon Monday to Saturday from October to May. During summer, tower tours are at 10 am, noon and 2 pm weekdays and at noon only on Saturday.

Jens Olsen's Clock

This elaborate clock, designed by Danish astro-mechanic Jens Olsen (1872–1945) and built at a cost of one million krone, is of special note to chronometer buffs. The clock displays not only the local time, but also solar time, sidereal time, sunrises and sunsets, firmament and celestial pole migration, planet revolutions, the Gregorian calendar and even changing holidays, such as Easter. Of its numerous wheels, the fastest turns once every 10 seconds, while the slowest will finish its first revolution after 25,753 years.

The clock was first put into motion in 1955 and its weights are wound weekly. It can be viewed in a side room off the foyer of rådhus (city hall) 10 am to 4 pm weekdays and 10 am to 1 pm Saturday. Admission is 10kr for adults and 5kr for children.

Ny Carlsberg Glyptotek
(Map 7, E4)

This exceptional museum on HC Andersens Blvd, south-east of Tivoli, houses an excellent collection of Greek, Egyptian, Etruscan and Roman sculpture and art. It was built a century ago by beer baron Carl Jacobsen, who was an ardent collector of classical art. The museum's century-old main building, designed by Danish architect Vilhelm Dahlerup, is centred around a glass-domed conservatory replete with palm trees and Mediterranean greenery, creating an atmospheric complement to the antiquities collections it exhibits.

The museum's extensive sculpture displays are arranged to depict the history of Western sculpture from 3000 BC to the end of the Roman Empire. Particularly notable is the Greek collection – in terms of its breadth and calibre it's the finest in northern Europe.

Although Ny Carlsberg Glyptotek was originally, and primarily remains, dedicated to classical art, a later gift of more than 20 paintings by Paul Gauguin led to the formation of an impressive 19th-century French and Danish art collection. The Danish collection includes numerous works by JC Dahl, CW Eckersberg, Jens Juel and Christian Købke.

The French collection is centred around the Gauguin works, which now number 50. These are displayed alongside pieces by Cézanne, Van Gogh, Pissarro, Monet and Renoir in a new wing of the museum that opened in 1996. This 'French Wing' also boasts one of only three complete series of Degas bronzes.

Ny Carlsberg Glyptotek is open 10 am to 4 pm daily, except Monday. Admission is 30kr for adults, free for children, but it's free to all on Wednesday and Sunday.

If you're visiting in the off season, consider attending one of the chamber concerts given on Sunday from October to March in the museum's columned concert hall, which is lined by life-size statues of Roman patricians.

And you don't have to pay a penny for this high-brow treat since the concerts, like Sunday admission itself, are gratis. For details on the chamber concert schedule, call the museum at ☎ 33 41 81 41.

Dansk Design Center
(Map 7, D4)

The Dansk Design Center (☎ 33 69 33 69), HC Andersens Blvd 27, opened in 2000 as a place to display Danish industrial design alongside international design trends.

The five-storey building was designed by senior Danish architect Henning Larsen and incorporates a double-glass wall of windows. Larsen originally intended for the windows to hold a layer of liquid crystal that would allow the building's streetside exterior to act as a huge video screen, but to his chagrin that concept was axed as too costly.

The centre has a dual function, providing a meeting place for people in the field of design, as well as display space for exhibitions. The ground floor holds an exhibit of classic Danish chairs, while upstairs are changing exhibits on topics such as the development of fashion trends and the history of the avant-garde audiovisual company Bang & Olufsen.

It's open 10 am to 5 pm weekdays and 11 am to 4 pm Saturday, Sunday and holidays. Admission is 25kr for adults and 15kr for children. The lobby has a cafe and gift shop.

Louis Tussaud's Wax Museum (Map 7, D4)

At this wax museum at HC Andersens Blvd 22 celebrities such as Elvis and Frankenstein can be found in the company of Danish notables, including the royal family, Søren Kierkegaard and Karen Blixen. Young kids will enjoy the scenes from Hans Christian Andersen's 'Snow Queen', but then they'll have to make their way through the creepy house of horrors that wraps up the show.

It's open 10 am to 11 pm daily from late April to mid-September and 10 am to 6 pm the rest of the year. Admission is a pricey 65kr for adults, 25kr for children.

Ripley's Believe It or Not! (Map 8, G2)

This cliched museum at Rådhuspladsen 57 displays the expected collection of unexpected oddities from around the world (such as a six-legged calf) replicated in wax figures and tableaus. It's open 9.30 am to 10.30 pm daily from June to August and 10 am to 6 pm September to May. Admission costs 69kr for adults, 33kr for children.

TIVOLI

Situated right in the heart of the city, Tivoli is a tantalising combination of flower gardens, food pavilions, amusement rides, carnival games and open-air stage shows. This genteel entertainment park, which dates from 1843, is delightfully varied. Visitors can ride the roller coaster, take aim at the shooting gallery, enjoy the pantomime of Commedia dell'Arte or simply sit and watch the crowds stroll by.

During the day children flock to Tivoli's Ferris wheel, carousel, bumper cars and other rides. In the evening Tivoli takes on a more romantic aura as the lights come on and the cultural activities unfold, with one stage hosting traditional folk dancing as another prepares a theatrical performance.

Each of Tivoli's numerous entertainment venues has a different character. Perhaps best known is Commedia dell'Arte, the open-air pantomime theatre, which features mime and ballet and was built in 1874 by Vilhelm Dahlerup, the Copenhagen architect who also designed the royal theatre. Tivoli also has an indoor cabaret theatre and a large concert hall (Koncertsal) featuring performances by international symphony orchestras and ballet troupes.

Between all the neon and action, Tivoli is a fun place to stroll around, and if you feel like a splurge there are some good restaurants that enjoy stage views and make for a memorable dining experience (see the Places to Eat chapter).

Wednesday and Saturday are the best nights to visit as they include a fireworks display shot off shortly before the clock strikes midnight.

Anyone for Vertigo?

We have three favourite places for enjoying views of Copenhagen, each one quite unlike the others.

In terms of the overall experience, top honour goes to Christianshavn's Vor Frelsers Kirke (Map 7, E7) where some 400 stairs lead to the crest of the church's 95m tower. The thrill is in the last 160 steps, which run along the outside rim of the spiral tower, narrowing to the point where they literally disappear at the top. Assuming you're not prone to vertigo, it's lots of fun and the tower tip offers an unbeatable view of Christianhavn's canals and the city's harbourfront buildings.

For those who prefer to do their climbing on the tamer inside of a building, there's the Rundetårn (Map 8, B5; Round Tower), where a ramped walkway gently winds up the tower's hollow core to a rooftop observatory. Because it sits in the heart of the old city, it makes a splendid vantage point for observing the historic buildings that comprise the city centre.

Not as well known is the rooftop cafe above the Post & Tele Museum (Map 8, C6) on Købmagergade. It isn't imbued with the centuries-old historic charm of the other two buildings, and access is via an ordinary elevator, but the view is similar to that from the top of the Rundetårn and here you can admire the cityscape while lingering over afternoon tea or a cold beer.

Tivoli (☎ 33 15 10 01) is open 11 am to midnight Sunday to Thursday and 11 am to 1 am Friday and Saturday from mid-April to late September.

Admission costs 49kr for adults and 25kr for children from mid-June to mid-August; there's a slight discount at other times. Amusement ride tickets cost 10kr (many rides require two tickets), but there are multiticket schemes and passes as well.

The numerous open-air performances are free of charge, however, there's usually an admission fee for the indoor performances. For more detailed information see the En-

tertainment chapter, or visit the Web site at www.tivoligardens.com.

Tivoli also opens for a few weeks prior to Christmas for holiday festivities, a Christmas market and ice-skating on the lake. Some of Tivoli's restaurants reopen for that period, serving traditional Danish Christmas fare.

STRØGET & AROUND

Billed as 'the world's longest pedestrian street', Strøget runs through the city centre between Rådhuspladsen and Kongens Nytorv, the square at the head of the Nyhavn canal.

TIVOLI

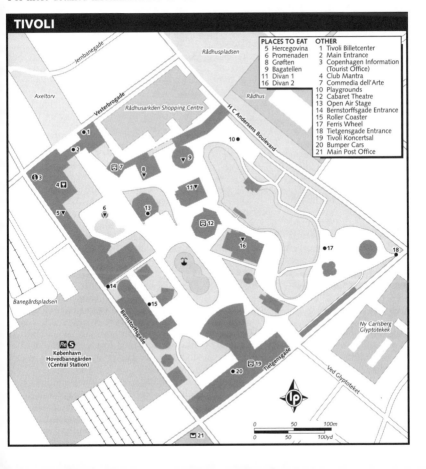

PLACES TO EAT
5 Hercegovina
6 Promenaden
8 Grøften
9 Bagatellen
11 Divan 1
16 Divan 2

OTHER
1 Tivoli Billetcenter
2 Main Entrance
3 Copenhagen Information (Tourist Office)
4 Club Mantra
7 Commedia dell'Arte
10 Playgrounds
12 Cabaret Theatre
13 Open Air Stage
14 Bernstorffsgade Entrance
15 Roller Coaster
17 Ferris Wheel
18 Tietgensgade Entrance
19 Tivoli Koncertsal
20 Bumper Cars
21 Main Post Office

Strøget, which abounds with shops, eateries and entertainment venues, is actually made up of five continuous streets: Frederiksberggade, Nygade, Vimmelskaftet, Amagertorv and Østergade.

Strøget is a fun place to stroll, its broad squares bustling with street musicians, tourists and urbanites who play off each other's energies. It's a particularly vibrant scene on sunny days, when people seem to pour out of the woodwork. For details on sights along Strøget see Walking Tour 1 earlier in this chapter.

Guinness World of Records Museum (Map 8, C9)

This touristy attraction on Strøget at Østergade 16 uses displays, photos and videos to depict the world's superlatives – the tallest, fastest, oddest and so on. It's open 9.30 am to 10 pm daily in summer and 10 am to 6 pm the rest of the year. Admission costs 69kr for adults and 28kr for children.

Post & Tele Museum (Map 8, C6)

The Post & Tele Museum (☎ 33 41 09 00) a few minutes' walk north of Strøget at Købmagergade 37, depicts the history of the Danish postal and telecommunications system with displays of historic postal vehicles, uniforms, letter boxes, radio equipment etc. It also boasts a fine stamp collection.

It's open 10 am to 5 pm (to 8 pm Wednesday) daily, except Monday. Admission is 30kr for adults, free for children; it's free to all on Wednesday. The building also has a pleasant rooftop cafe with a city view, Café Hovedtelegrafen, which can be visited without paying museum admission.

Museum Erotica (Map 8, D7)

In a country where hardcore porn is standard late night TV fare, there's got to be some recognition of the art of erotica.

The mantle is picked up by the Museum Erotica, two blocks north of Strøget at Købmagergade 24. A cross between a museum and a peep-show, it's chock-full of erotic paintings, photographs, pin-ups, statues and sex toys. These range from hand-coloured daguerreotype photographs from the 1850s to a multiscreen video room playing modern-day porn movies. Museum Erotica is open 10 am to 11 pm daily between May and September, and 11 am to 8 pm between October and April. Admission costs 65kr.

LATIN QUARTER

With its cafes and second-hand bookshops, the area north of Strøget surrounding the old campus of Københavns Universitet (Copenhagen University) is good for ambling around. The university, which was founded in 1479, has largely outgrown its original quarters and moved to a new campus (Map 7, G7) on Amager, but parts of the old campus, including the law department, remain here.

At the north side of the Latin Quarter is Kultorvet, a lively pedestrian plaza and summertime gathering place with beer gardens, flower stalls and produce stands. On sunny days you'll almost always find impromptu entertainment here, which can range from Andean flute playing to local street theatre and dancing.

University Library (Map 8, C4)

Ascend the stairs of the university library (enter from Fiolstræde) to see one quirky remnant of the 1807 British bombardment of Copenhagen: a glass case containing a British cannonball in five fragments and the target it ironically hit, a book titled *Defensor Pacis* (Defender of Peace). The library is open 10 am to 7 pm weekdays.

Vor Frue Kirke (Map 8, D3)

Opposite the university is Vor Frue Kirke (Our Lady's Church), Copenhagen's cathedral, which was founded in 1191 and rebuilt on three occasions after devastating fires. The current structure dates from 1829 and was designed in neoclassical style by architect CF Hansen, who also designed Domhuset, the city's law courts.

With its high vaulted ceilings and columns, Vor Frue Kirke seems as much museum as church – quite apropos because it also displays sculptor Bertel Thorvaldsen's statues of Christ and the 12 apostles, his most acclaimed works, which were completed in 1839. Thorvaldsen's depiction of Christ, with comforting open arms, became the most popular worldwide model for statues of Christ and remains so today.

There are occasional organ recitals throughout the year, including at noon on Saturday in July and August.

The cathedral, which is entered from Nørregade, is open 8 am to 5 pm daily, except Sunday when it's open noon to 5 pm. Admission is free.

Sankt Petri Kirke (Map 8, D3) & Synagogen (Map 8, C4)

In addition to Vor Frue Kirke, there are two other noteworthy places of worship in the Latin Quarter.

Sankt Petri Kirke (St Peter's Church), on the corner of Nørregade and Sankt Pedersstræde, dates from the 15th century and is the oldest church building in Copenhagen. Since 1585 it has served the city's German Lutheran congregation and services are still held in German today. Recently renovated, the church is open to the public 11 am to 3 pm Tuesday to Saturday.

Synagogen (the synagogue), two blocks to the east at Krystalgade 12, was built in 1831 in neoclassical style and restored in 1958. The main synagogue for the Jewish community, it can be viewed from the exterior, but the ornate interior with its Doric columns and carved woodwork is not open to the general public.

Rundetårn (Map 8, B5)

The Rundetårn (Round Tower), Købmagergade 52, is a great vantage point from which to admire the old city's red-tiled rooftops and abundant church spires. This vaulted brick tower, 35m high, was built by Christian IV in 1642 and used as an astronomical observatory in conjunction with the nearby university. Although the university erected a newer structure in 1861, amateur astronomers have continued to use the Rundetårn each winter, which gives credence to its claim to be the oldest functioning observatory in Europe.

A 209m spiral walkway winds up the tower around a hollow core; about halfway up is a small exhibition hall housing changing displays of art and culture.

The Rundetårn (☎ 33 73 03 73) is open 10 am to 8 pm daily (from noon Sunday) during the summer and 10 am to 5 pm daily (from noon Sunday) between September and May. Admission costs 15kr for adults and 5kr for children.

Winter visitors who'd like to view the night sky from the 3m-long telescope that's mounted within the rooftop dome should make inquiries at the ticket booth; the observatory is generally open Tuesday and Wednesday nights.

Musikhistorisk Museum (Map 7, B5)

The Music History Museum (☎ 33 11 27 26), housed in a couple of 18th-century buildings at Åbenrå 30 just north of Kultorvet, contains a quality collection of antique musical instruments dating from AD 1000 to 1900.

There's a particularly large collection of stringed instruments.

The exhibits are grouped according to themes, such as folk music of the Middle Ages, Renaissance instruments, 19th-century military music etc, some accompanied by musical recordings that you can listen to on headphones.

The museum is open 1 to 3.45 pm daily, except Thursday, from May to September and on Monday, Wednesday, Saturday and Sunday from October to April. Admission costs 20kr for adults, 5kr for children. There are occasional concerts and special presentations.

NYHAVN & AROUND

The picturesque Nyhavn canal was dug in the 17th century to allow traders to bring their wares into the heart of the city. Long a haunt for sailors and writers (including Hans Christian Andersen, who lived in the house at No 67 for nearly 20 years), Nyhavn today is half salty and half gentrified. The canal is lined with restored gabled townhouses and trendy pavement cafes that pack in a crowd whenever the weather is warm and sunny.

At the head of the canal is a huge frigate anchor that commemorates the Danish seamen who died in WWII serving with the Allied merchant marines.

Charlottenborg (Map 8, C10)

Fronting Kongens Nytorv, south-west of Nyhavn, is Charlottenborg, which was built in 1683 as a palace for the royal family. Since 1754 Charlottenborg has housed Det Kongelige Kunstakademi, the Royal Academy of Fine Arts. Its exhibition hall (☎ 33 13 40 22) on the eastern side of the central courtyard features changing exhibitions of modern art by Danish and international artists. It's open 10 am to 5 pm daily (to 7 pm Wednesday). Admission is 20kr for adults, free for children.

House of Amber (Map 7, B6)

The House of Amber (☎ 33 11 04 44), Kongens Nytorv 2, is an amber jewellery shop at the head of Nyhavn canal that maintains a small museum on its upper floor.

It gives the lowdown on various types of amber, with examples of clear drops, white amber and curious specimens that encapsulate different insects. There's also an 8.8kg piece of Baltic amber that's one of the largest of its types and various pieces of amber carved into jewellery, chess sets and the like.

It's open 10 am to 8 pm daily from May to mid-September and 10 am to 6 pm the rest of the year. Admission is 20kr for adults, 10kr for children.

SLOTSHOLMEN & AROUND

Slotsholmen is the seat of Denmark's national government and a repository of historical sites. Located on a small island separated from the city centre by a moat-like canal, Slotsholmen's centrepiece is Christiansborg Slot, a rambling neobaroque palace that now contains government offices.

Several short bridges link Slotsholmen to the rest of Copenhagen. If you walk into Slotsholmen from Ny Vestergade, you'll cross the western part of the canal and enter Christiansborg's large main courtyard, which was once used as a royal riding ground. The courtyard still maintains a distinctively equestrian character, overseen by a statue of Christian IX (1863–1906) on horseback and flanked to the north by stables and to the south by carriage buildings.

The stables and buildings surrounding the main courtyard date back to the original Christiansborg palace, which was built in the 1730s by Christian VI to replace the more modest Copenhagen Castle that previously stood there. The grander west wing of Christian VI's palace went up in flames in 1794, was rebuilt in the early 19th century and was once again destroyed by fire in 1884. In 1907 the cornerstone for the third (and current) Christiansborg palace was laid by Frederik VIII and, upon completion, the national parliament and the Supreme Court moved into new chambers there.

Folketinget

The parliamentary chamber, called Folketinget, is where the 179 members of parliament meet to debate national legislation. From July to late September, free tours in English are given at 2 pm daily. The rest of the year the tours are given on Sunday on the hour from 10 am to 4 pm, but are in Danish only. In addition to the parliamentary chamber, the tour also takes in Wanderer's Hall, which contains the original copy of the Constitution of the Kingdom of Denmark.

De Kongelige Repræsentationslokaler

The grandest part of Christiansborg is De Kongelige Repræsentationslokaler (Royal Reception Chambers; ☎ 33 92 64 92), an ornate Renaissance hall where the queen holds royal banquets and entertains heads of state.

Of particular note are the colourful grand wall tapestries depicting the history of Denmark, created by tapestry designer Bjørn Nørgaard to celebrate the queen's 50th birthday in 1990.

The chambers are closed to the public when in official use. Otherwise, tours with commentary in English are conducted at 11 am and 1 and 3 pm daily from May to September and 11 am and 3 pm Tuesday, Thursday, Saturday and Sunday from October to

April. Admission costs 40kr for adults, 10kr for children.

Kongelige Stalde & Kareter

At Kongelige Stalde & Kareter (the Royal Stables & Coaches), visitors can view a collection of antique coaches, uniforms and riding paraphernalia, some of which are still used for royal receptions. You can also see the royal family's carriage and saddle horses. The collection is open 2 to 4 pm Saturday and Sunday year-round; it's also open 2 to 4 pm Friday from May to September. Admission costs 10kr for adults, 5kr for children.

Ruins under Christiansborg

A walk through the crypt-like bowels of Slotsholmen offers a unique perspective on Copenhagen's lengthy history. In the basement of the current palace, beneath the tower, are the remains of two earlier castles. The most notable are the ruins of Absalon's fortress, Slotsholmen's original castle, built by Bishop Absalon in 1167. The excavated foundations, which consist largely of low limestone sections of wall, date back to the founding of the city.

Absalon's fortress was demolished by Hanseatic invaders in 1369. Its foundations,

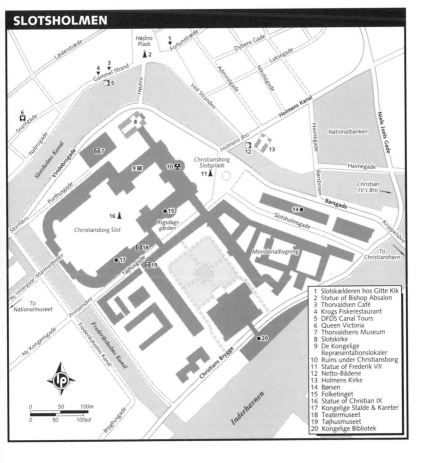

SLOTSHOLMEN

1 Slotskælderen hos Gitte Kik
2 Statue of Bishop Absalon
3 Thorvaldsen Café
4 Krogs Fiskerestaurant
5 DFDS Canal Tours
6 Queen Victoria
7 Thorvaldsens Museum
8 Slotskirke
9 De Kongelige Repræsentationslokaler
10 Ruins under Christiansborg
11 Statue of Frederik VII
12 Netto-Bådene
13 Holmens Kirke
14 Børsen
15 Folketinget
16 Statue of Christian IX
17 Kongelige Stalde & Kareter
18 Teatermuseet
19 Tøjhusmuseet
20 Kongelige Bibliotek

as well as those of the Copenhagen Castle that replaced it and stood for more than three centuries, were excavated when the current tower was built in the early 20th century.

The ruins can be explored 9.30 am to 3.30 pm daily from May to September and Tuesday, Thursday, Saturday and Sunday from October to April. Admission costs 20kr for adults, 5kr for children.

Teatermuseet

This museum occupies the Hofteater (Old Court Theatre), which dates from 1767 and drips with historic character. Performances over the years have ranged from Italian opera and pantomime to shows by local ballet troupes, one of which included fledgling ballet student Hans Christian Andersen. The theatre, which took on its current appearance in 1842, drew its final curtain in 1881 but was later reopened as a museum.

The stage, boxes and dressing rooms can be examined, along with displays of set models, drawings, costumes and period posters tracing the history of Danish theatre.

It's open 2 to 4 pm Wednesday and noon to 4 pm Saturday and Sunday year-round. Admission costs 20kr for adults, 5kr for children.

Thorvaldsens Museum

This museum (☎ 33 32 15 32) at Porthusgade 2 exhibits the works of famed Danish sculptor Bertel Thorvaldsen (1770–1844), who was heavily influenced by Greek and Roman mythology. After four decades in Rome, Thorvaldsen returned to his native Copenhagen and donated his private collection to the Danish public. In return the royal family provided this site for the construction of a museum to house Thorvaldsen's drawings, plaster moulds and statues. The museum also contains antique art from the Mediterranean region that Thorvaldsen collected during his lifetime.

Thorvaldsens Museum is open 10 am to 5 pm Tuesday to Sunday year-round. Admission is 20kr, except on Wednesday when it's free. In July and August the museum offers English-language guided tours at 3 pm Sunday. The entrance is on Vindebrogade.

Tøjhusmuseet

Accessed from Tøjhusgade is Tøjhusmuseet (the Royal Arsenal Museum), which contains an impressive collection of historic cannons, hand weapons and armour. The 163m-long building that houses the arsenal was constructed by King Christian IV in 1600 and boasts Europe's longest vaulted Renaissance hall. It's open noon to 4 pm Tuesday to Sunday year-round. Admission costs 20kr for adults, 5kr for children; it's free to all on Wednesday.

Christiansborg Slotskirke

Christiansborg Slotskirke, Slotsholmen's domed church, was built in 1826 in the neoclassic style by architect CF Hansen.

It was in the final stages of restoration in 1992 when stray fireworks set fire to the construction scaffolding encompassing the dome and set the roof ablaze. The entire dome collapsed into the church, but much of the church interior, including a frieze of angels by Bertel Thorvaldsen that rings the ceiling just below the dome, miraculously survived. The restorers went back to work and the church was reopened to the public in January 1997 with a service commemorating the 25th anniversary of Queen Margrethe II's reign.

The church is open to the public free noon to 4 pm Sunday year-round and daily in the month of July.

Kongelige Bibliotek

This library is a curious merger of the classic Royal Library building near parliament and a new ultramodern extension on the waterfront. The seven-storey extension, dubbed the 'Black Diamond', sports a shiny black granite facade, smoked black windows and a leaning cube-like design. Opened in late 1999, on the eve of the new millennium, this sleek canalside addition gives the once solidly historic waterfront a curious futuristic juxtaposition.

The Royal Library, which dates from the 17th century, is the largest library in Scandinavia. It not only serves as a research centre for scholars and university students, but also doubles as a repository for rare books,

An Author's Burden

In 1834, Hans Christian Andersen applied for work at the Royal Library in Copenhagen 'to be freed from the heavy burden of having to write in order to live'. Apparently the library administrators weren't too impressed with his résumé, as he was turned down. Ironically, Andersen's unsuccessful application is now preserved as part of the library's valued archives, along with many of his original manuscripts. They can be viewed with advance notice.

manuscripts, prints and maps. As Denmark's national library it contains a complete collection of all Danish printed works produced since 1482 and houses some 21 million items in all.

The place is well worth a visit. There's a spacious lobby with canal views, a 210-sq-metre ceiling mural by Danish artist Per Kirkeby and exhibition areas. Everything is ultramodern – researchers now do their reference searches on computers, which line the library's corridors, and place all of their requests to the librarian online. The lobby contains a bookshop, cafe and restaurant.

An enclosed overhead walkway straddles the motorway on Christians Brygge and connects the Black Diamond with the library's historic building. The old wing preserves its period character with arched doorways, chandeliers and high-ceilinged reading rooms.

The Royal Library is open 10 am to 7 pm Monday to Saturday and has to be entered at the waterfront on Christians Brygge. There are lovely flower gardens backing the historic end of the library that can be entered from Rigsdagsgården, just west of Tøjhusmuseet.

Børsen

Another striking Renaissance building is Børsen, the stock exchange, at the eastern corner of Slotsholmen on Børsgade. Constructed in the 1620s, it's of note particularly for its ornate spire, formed from the entwined tails of four dragons, and for its richly embellished gables.

This still-functioning stock exchange, which first opened during the bustling reign of Christian IV, is the oldest in Europe.

Holmens Kirke

Just across the canal to the north-east of Slotsholmen is Holmens Kirke (Church of the Royal Navy). This historic brick structure, with a nave that was originally built in 1562 to be used as an anchor forge, was converted into a church for the Royal Navy in 1619. Most of the present structure, which is predominantly in Dutch Renaissance style, dates from 1641. The church's burial chapel contains the remains of some important naval figures, including Admiral Niels Juel, who beat back the Swedes in the crucial 1677 Battle of Køge Bay.

It was at Holmens Kirke that Queen Margrethe II took her marriage vows in 1967. The interior of the church, which has an intricately carved 17th-century oak altarpiece and pulpit, can be viewed 9 am to 2 pm (to noon Saturday) daily, except Sunday, from May to September, and 9 am to noon the rest of the year. Admission is free.

Nationalmuseet (Map 7, D4)

If you want to learn more about Danish history and culture, you couldn't do better than spending an afternoon at Nationalmuseet (the National Museum) at Ny Vestergade 10, opposite the western entrance to Slotsholmen.

The National Museum has first claims on virtually every antiquity found on Danish soil, whether it be unearthed by a farmer ploughing his field or excavated in a government-sponsored archaeological dig. Consequently this quality museum boasts the most extensive collection of Danish historical artefacts in the world. These range from the Upper Palaeolithic period to the 1840s and include Stone Age tools, Viking weaponry and impressive Bronze Age, Iron Age and rune-stone collections.

Don't miss the exhibit of bronze lurs, some of which date back 3000 years and are still capable of blowing a tune, and the finely crafted 3500-year-old Sun Chariot, unearthed in a Zealand field a century ago.

There are also sections on the Norsemen and Inuit of Greenland, collections of 18th-century Danish furniture and a 'Please Touch' exhibit for sight-impaired visitors. And naturally, considering the Danes' fascination for playthings, the museum has a noteworthy collection of historic toys, along with other fun items that comprise a special children's wing.

The museum also has a noteworthy coin collection containing Greek, Roman and medieval coins and a Classical Antiquities section complete with Egyptian mummies.

There's a cafe and a gift shop inside the museum, and ramps and lifts provide access for disabled visitors. Interpretive signs are in English as well as Danish.

The newest addition to the National Museum is the Victorian Home, a circa 1850 house just east of the main museum building. A flat in the home that was owned by a successful merchant has been preserved with its original furnishings and decor, encapsulating a slice of 19th-century life. The kitchen has a peat fired stove, the stairways are adorned with marble dadoes and the woodwork and upholstery are classic patterns of their day. The Victorian Home can only be visited on a guided tour and there's no additional charge beyond the National Museum's regular admission fee, but you must book ahead as the number of visitors is limited; call the museum (☎ 33 13 44 11) for more details.

The National Museum is open 10 am to 5 pm Tuesday to Sunday year-round. On Wednesday admission is free for all; on other days it costs 40kr for adults, free for children. The museum maintains a Web site at www.natmus.dk.

AMALIENBORG & KASTELLET AREA

The Amalienborg area, also known as Frederiksstaden for Frederik V who laid out the neighbourhood in the mid-18th century, has upmarket residences, including that of the royal family, a grand marble church and other historic sites. The adjacent Kastellet area includes a 17th-century citadel and the city's best-known statue, the Little Mermaid. More detail on the Kastellet area is under Walking Tour 2 earlier in this chapter.

Amalienborg Slot (Map 7, A7)

Most of this palace, which is the residence of Queen Margrethe II, is not open to the public, but visitors can enter one wing that features exhibits of the royal apartments used by three generations of the monarchy from 1863 to 1947.

The rooms, faithfully reconstructed in the styles of the period, are decorated with heavy oak furnishings, gilt-leather tapestries, family photographs and old knick-knacks. They include the study and drawing

Changing of the Guard

When the queen is in residence at Amalienborg Slot (Map 7, A7), mainly from December to April, a colourful changing of the guard takes place in the palace square at noon. The ceremony begins with a procession from Rosenborg Slot (Map 7, A5) by the Royal Guard, bedecked in full regalia and marching to the tune of fifes and drums.

The guard contingent leaves the Rosenborg Slot gardens at 11.30 am and marches to Amalienborg Slot on a curving route that takes them to Kultorvet in the Latin Quarter, south on Købmagergade and then east along Østergade to Kongens Nytorv. From there they continue to Amalienborg Slot along Bredgade, Sankt Annæ Plads and Amaliegade.

Upon reaching the square, the old guards are ceremoniously relieved of their duties by their fresh replacements, who take up sentry posts in front of the palace. The relieved guards then join the marching band and return to their barracks at Rosenborg Slot, via a route that takes them along Frederiksgade, Store Kongensgade and Gothersgade.

In spring and early summer, when the queen takes up residence at her summer palace in Fredensborg, a version of the changing of the guard occurs there instead.

Strøget, the world's longest pedestrian mall

Stately neobaroque Marmorkirken

Marmorkirken's famous circular nave

Rowhouse facade along Nyhavn

Nyhavn's waterfront is popular with tourists.

The barracks at Kastellet, a 17th-century citadel, remain in use.

Strolling along a quiet backstreet

Rosenborg Slot, a museum and treasury

Palmehus, Botanisk Have (Botanical Gardens)

room of Christian IX (1863–1906) and Queen Louise, whose six children married into nearly as many royal families – one eventually ascending the throne in Greece and another marrying Russian tsar Alexander III. Also displayed is the study of Frederik VIII (1906–12), who decorated it in a lavish neo-Renaissance style, and the study of Christian X (1912–47), the grandfather of Queen Margrethe II.

The exhibit is open 10 am to 4 pm daily from May to October and 11 am to 4 pm Tuesday to Sunday the rest of the year. Entry is 40kr for adults, 5kr for children.

Marmorkirken (Map 7, A7)

The Marble Church, also known as Frederikskirken, is a stately neobaroque church on Frederiksgade, a block west of Amalienborg Slot. The church's massive dome, which was inspired by St Peter's in Rome and measures more than 30m in diameter, is one of Copenhagen's most dominant skyline features.

The original plans for the church were ordered by Frederik V and drawn up by Nicolai Eigtved as part of a grand design that included the Amalienborg mansions. Although church construction began in 1749, it encountered problems as costs spiralled, due in part to the prohibitively high price of Norwegian marble, and the project was soon shelved.

It wasn't until Denmark's wealthiest 19th-century financier, CF Tietgen, bankrolled the project's revival that it was eventually completed and it was consecrated as a church in 1894.

Marmorkirken's exterior, recently scrubbed clean of a century's worth of soot, is ringed by statues of Danish theologians and saints.

The church interior, with its immense circular nave, can be viewed free 10.30 am to 4.30 pm Monday to Saturday (to 6 pm Wednesday) and noon to 4.30 pm Sunday. Note that the church closes for events such as weddings, however, so it's best not to plan your visit for a Saturday in spring!

You can join a guided tour of the dome, which offers a broad view of the city from its rim, at 1 and 3 pm weekdays from mid-June through August and at 1 pm Saturday and Sunday the rest of the year. The tour costs 20kr for adults, 10kr for children.

Kunstindustrimuseet (Map 7, A7)

Kunstindustrimuseet (Museum of Decorative Art; ☎ 33 14 94 52), Bredgade 68, is housed in the former Frederiks Hospital, circa 1752. This large, rambling place feels much like an oversized antiques shop, with an eclectic collection of nearly 300,000 items from Asia and Europe.

Some of the rooms contain fine English furniture, which provided much of the inspiration for Danish designs that followed, and others hold theme exhibits.

The displays include a fairly extensive collection of Danish silver and porcelain and lots of coverage of innovations in contemporary Danish design.

One exhibit, for example, shows Denmark's contribution to chair design, displaying chairs by influential 20th-century designers Kaare Klint, Hans Wegner and Arne Jacobsen.

The museum is open 10 am to 4 pm Tuesday to Friday and noon to 4 pm Saturday and Sunday. Admission is 35kr for adults, free for children. The museum has a Web site at www.mus-kim.dk.

Other Bredgade Sights

In addition to Kunstindustrimuseet, there are a cluster of sights on Bredgade north of Marmorkirken.

First up is **Alexander Newsky Kirke (Map 7, A7)**, Bredgade 53, built in the Russian Byzantine style in 1883 by Tsar Alexander III, who was married to a Danish princess. Its ornate exterior is topped by three gold onion-shaped domes. Today the church continues to serve Copenhagen's Russian Orthodox community. It's usually open only for services.

Next to the north is **Medicinsk-Historisk Museum (Map 7, A7)**, Bredgade 62, which is housed in a former surgical academy dating from 1787 and deals with the history of medicine, pharmacy and dentistry over the past three centuries. It's open only for guided tours, which are offered at 11 am and 1 pm Wednesday, Thursday, Friday and Sunday; in July and August, the 1 pm tours are conducted in English. Admission is free.

Copenhagen's Roman Catholic cathedral, **Sankt Ansgars Kirke (Map 7, A7)**, 64 Bredgade, has a colourfully painted apse and a small museum on the history of Danish Catholicism. Admission is free and it's usually open for viewing 10 am to 4 pm Tuesday to Friday.

Den Kongelige Afstøbningssamling (Map 7, A8)

Den Kongelige Afstøbningssamling (The Royal Cast Collection; ☎ 33 74 85 75) in an old waterfront warehouse at Toldbodgade 40 exhibits plaster casts of some of the world's greatest sculptures.

The casts, about 2000 in all, were originally used as models for teaching Danish art students and include such things as Michaelangelo's *Venus de Milo*, reliefs from medieval churches and statues from the Acropolis. Indeed, art students still make up the lion's share of visitors here.

The museum is open 10 am to 4 pm Wednesday and Thursday and 1 to 4 pm Saturday and Sunday year-round. Admission is 20kr for adults, free for children, except on Wednesday when it's free for all.

Frihedsmuseet (Map 7, A8)

This museum (☎ 33 13 77 14) in Churchillparken, south of Kastellet, features exhibits on the Danish resistance movement from the time of the German occupation in 1940 to liberation in 1945. There are displays on the Danish underground press, the clandestine radio operations that maintained links with England, and the smuggling operations that saved Danish Jews from capture by the Nazis.

Admission to the museum is free. It's open 10 am to 4 pm Tuesday to Saturday and 10 am to 5 pm Sunday between May and mid-September.

It's open 11 am to 3 pm Tuesday to Saturday and 11 am to 4 pm Sunday during the rest of the year.

ROSENBORG SLOT & AROUND

This neighbourhood is home to a royal castle, three worthwhile art museums and a couple of the city's finest gardens. Not surprisingly, it draws lots of visitors from both Copenhageners and tourists alike. As many of the sights, including the gardens, are adjacent to each other, this is a great area to explore on foot. For more on walking possibilities see Walking Tour 2 earlier in this chapter.

Rosenborg Slot (Map 7, A5)

This early 17th-century castle, with its moat and garden setting, was built in Dutch Renaissance style by Christian IV to serve as his summer home. A century later Frederik IV, who felt cramped at Rosenborg, built a roomier palace north of the city in the town of Fredensborg. In the years that followed, Rosenborg was used mainly for official functions and as a place in which to safeguard the monarchy's heirlooms.

In the 1830s the royal family decided to open the castle to visitors as a museum, while still using it as a treasury for royal regalia and jewels. It continues to serve both functions today.

The 24 rooms in the castle's upper levels are chronologically arranged, housing the furnishings and portraits of each monarch from Christian IV to Frederik VII. However, the main attraction lies on the lower level – the dazzling collection of crown jewels. These include Christian IV's ornately designed crown; the jewel-studded sword of Christian III; and Queen Margrethe II's emeralds and pearls, which are kept here when the queen is not wearing them to official functions. These items are considered such a national treasure that the queen is not permitted to take the royal jewels with her when she travels outside Denmark.

Rosenborg Slot is open 10 am to 4 pm daily between 1 May and 30 September, 11 am to 3 pm daily in October and 11 am to 2 pm daily, except Monday, the rest of the year. Admission costs 50kr for adults, 10kr for children.

You can get to Rosenborg Slot by taking the S-train to Nørreport station and walking north for two blocks, or via numerous buses including Nos 14, 16, 31, 42 and 43.

The main entrance to the castle is off Øster Voldgade. There is also entry from the adjacent gardens via a moat footbridge when the castle is open.

Kongens Have The expansive green space behind Rosenborg Slot is the city's oldest public park and is known both as Kongens Have (King's Gardens) and Rosenborg Slotshave (Rosenborg Castle Gardens).

Created to complement the castle, the gardens were designed by Christian IV incorporating Renaissance features, including a rectangular grid of walking paths that still provides the main pattern today. But many other features of the gardens, which once doubled as the king's private vegetable patch, have evolved over the centuries. In the early 18th century, the royal family opened the gardens to the public.

These pleasant gardens have manicured box hedges, lovely rose beds, the requisite statues, a fun children's playground and many shaded areas. The Grønnebro (Green Bridge), which leads over the moat to the castle, is flanked by copper lions. The gardens are a popular picnic spot with Copenhageners and the site of a free marionette theatre that performs on summer afternoons.

Botanisk Have

In the 10-hectare Botanisk Have (Botanical Garden) to the west of Rosenborg Slot you can wander along fragrant paths amid arbours, terraces and rock gardens.

The garden encompasses part of the now-defunct city ramparts, creatively incorporating some of the old walls to hold rock-garden plants and giving the old moat a second life as a garden pond, replete with water lilies and marsh plants.

Originally developed in 1874 for Copenhagen University's botanical studies, the garden now holds some 20,000 species of plants from around the world.

Within the botanical garden is the **Palmehus** (Map 7, A4; Palm House), a large walk-through glasshouse containing a lush collection of tropical plants.

These are divided into different groupings, including tropical rainforest plants such as banana trees and palms, tropical savannah plants with ferns and pepper vines, and subtropical plants such as coffee trees and citrus.

There's also an orchid greenhouse with some 500 different species and a cactus house with more than 1000 species.

The botanical garden is open 8.30 am to 6 pm daily between April and October and 8.30 am to 4 pm during the rest of the year. The Palmehus is open 10 am to 3 pm daily year-round, though the cactus house and orchid greenhouse are open only 1 to 3 pm Wednesday, Saturday and Sunday. Admission to all are free.

The gardens are completed encircled by a fence and there are only two entrances, one at the intersection of Gothersgade and Øster Voldgade and the other off Øster Farimagsgade. For information on public transport, see Rosenborg Slot earlier in this chapter.

Botanisk Museum The modest Botanical Museum (Map 7, A4), Gothersgade 130, at the southern corner of the Botanisk Have, features exhibits of plants from Denmark and Greenland.

It is open only on summer afternoons, from noon to 4 pm daily between mid-June and mid-August. Admission is free.

Geologisk Museum The Geology Museum (Map 7, A5), Øster Voldgade 5, at the eastern corner of the Botanisk Have, is Denmark's foremost geological museum, covering the geology of both Denmark and Greenland.

An affiliate of Copenhagen University, it has all the usual exhibits of fossils, minerals, crystals and rocks. In addition it houses some interesting Danish displays, such as a 4.5kg chunk of amber, and some quite notable finds from Greenland; a highlight is the world's sixth-largest iron meteorite, which weighs in at 20 tonnes.

The museum is open 1 to 4 pm daily, except Monday, year-round. Admission is 20kr for adults, 10kr for children, except on Wednesday when it's free to all.

Davids Samling (Map 7, B6)

Davids Samling is a private collection that once belonged to Christian Ludvig David, a successful barrister who died in 1960, and is now maintained by a foundation he established. It occupies David's former home, a neoclassical mansion dating from 1806 just east of Kongens Have at Kronprinsessegade 30. The scale is intimate and the displays tastefully presented, creating an atmosphere that's more like visiting a well-to-do private home than rambling through a museum.

Davids Samling is best known for housing Scandinavia's largest collection of Islamic art, which occupies its entire 4th floor. It includes ceramics, silks, tapestries, jewellery and such exquisite works as an Egyptian rock crystal jug from AD 1000 and a 500-year-old Indian dagger inlaid with rubies.

The 1st floor of the museum is given over to Danish fine and applied arts, including 18th-century furniture, porcelain, silverware and paintings by such notable artists of the day as Jens Juel and CW Eckersberg.

The 2nd floor is largely dedicated to French furniture and porcelain of the same period, while the 3rd floor contains English Chippendale, lacquerware and chinoiserie.

Davids Samling is open 1 to 4 pm daily, except Monday. Admission is free. Public buses No 31, 42 and 43 stop along Gothersgade not far from the museum.

Statens Museum for Kunst (Map 7, A5)

Denmark's national gallery, Statens Museum for Kunst (Royal Museum of Fine Arts; ☎ 33 74 84 94), Sølvgade 48, was founded in 1824 to house art collections belonging to the royal family.

Originally sited at Christiansborg Slot, the museum opened in its current location in 1896. Statens Museum, which was recently renovated and doubled in size, now lays claim to being the largest art museum in Denmark.

Its collection covers seven centuries of European art, ranging from medieval works with stylised religious themes to free-form modern art. There's an interesting collection of old masters by Dutch and Flemish artists, including Rubens, Breughel and Frans Hals, as well as more contemporary European paintings by Matisse, Picasso and Munch. The museum also has an extensive collection of drawings, engravings and lithographs representing the works of such prominent artists as Piranesi, Degas and Toulouse-Lautrec.

As might be expected, Statens Museum also contains one of the world's best collections of Danish art. Classic works by Jens Juel, including a self-portrait, highlight the 18th century.

There's a whole room of works, nearly 60 in all, by the leading 19th-century 'Golden Age' artist CW Eckersberg, and his best-known student Christen Købke. The early 20th century is represented in the paintings of the Skagen artists PS Krøyer and Michael Ancher, whose seaside images are among the most recognised artworks in Denmark.

The splendid new modern art wing has numerous works by Danish artist Richard Mortensen, as well as pieces by such international contemporaries as Sam Taylor Wood and Donald Judd.

The museum is open 10 am to 5 pm Tuesday to Sunday (to 8 pm Wednesday) year-round. Except on Wednesday, when it's free to all, admission is 40kr for adults, free for children. Among the many buses that stop near the museum are Nos 10, 14, 40, 42 and 43.

Den Hirschsprungske Samling (Map 4, F7)

This museum (☎ 35 42 03 36) dedicated to Danish art of the 19th and early 20th century is at Stockholmensgade 20, in Østre Anlæg, the same park that holds the Statens Museum for Kunst.

Den Hirschsprungske Samling is a cosy place with a delightfully personal scale, which makes it a fun spot to visit after the commodious Statens Museum.

Originally the private holdings of tobacco magnate Heinrich Hirschsprung, the collection contains works by painters of Denmark's 'Golden Age', such as Christen Købke and CW Eckersberg, as well as pieces by the Danish symbolists and the Funen painters.

Hirschsprung was a sponsor for some of the Skagen painters and hence there's also a notable collection of works by PS Krøyer and Anna and Michael Ancher.

Hirschsprung turned his collection over to the city with the stipulation that Copenhagen build a suitable site to house it. The museum opened in 1911, three years after Hirschsprung's death.

Pause in the entrance room, which is itself a work of art, with a mosaic floor depicting the tobacco plant encircled by smoke, and a portrait of Hirschsprung by PS Krøyer.

The museum is open 11 am to 4 pm daily year-round, except Tuesday when it's closed and Wednesday when it's open 11 am to 9 pm. Admission is 25kr for adults and free for children, except on Wednesday when it's free to all. For information on buses, see Statens Museum for Kunst earlier in this chapter.

NØRREPORT & AROUND

Nørreport is not a big tourist area but it does have the city's main outdoor produce market, Israels Plads, and a museum dedicated to the working class.

Nørreport takes its name from the fact that it was once the site of the northern gate to the city.

The gate, which was situated near the intersection of Nørre Voldgade and Nørregade, is long gone but that area still plays a significant role in providing access to the city as it is home to a bustling metro station.

Arbejdermuseet (Map 7, A4)

Arbejdermuseet (the Workers' Museum; ☎ 33 93 25 75), Rømersgade 22, occupies the site of an old union hall and pays homage to the working class with exhibits portraying the lives of Danish labourers in the 19th and 20th centuries.

It's open 10 am to 4 pm daily, except Monday in winter. Admission costs 35kr for adults, 20kr for children.

You can get there by taking the S-train to Nørreport station and walking west on Frederiksborggade or by catching bus No 5, 14, 16, 31 or 40.

NØRREBRO

The Nørrebro quarter of the city developed in the mid-19th century as a working-class neighbourhood. More recently it has attracted a large immigrant community and become a haunt for students, musicians and artists. It boasts lots of interesting Middle Eastern and Asian restaurants and some of Copenhagen's hottest nightspots. There are a number of second-hand clothing shops in the streets radiating out from Sankt Hans Torv, antique shops along Ravnsborggade, and a Saturday morning flea market a few blocks to the west on Nørrebrogade along the wall of the Assistens Kirkegård.

Assistens Kirkegård

This cemetery in the heart of Nørrebro is the burial place of some of Denmark's most celebrated citizens, including philosopher Søren Kierkegaard, physicist Niels Bohr, authors Hans Christian Andersen and

Closed for 250 Years

From the 1600s to the 1850s, Copenhagen was enclosed by a ring-shaped fortification of earthen ramparts, making it necessary to pass through a guarded gate in order to enter or leave the city. There were four such gates – Amagerport, Vesterport, Nørreport and Østerport – the last three of these at the sites of present-day S-train stations.

Until 1821, each gate was literally locked at night with a big iron key, and the keys were taken to the king's castle where they were kept until dawn. Over the next few decades the policy was relaxed a bit, but residents still had to present a special pass to the night watchman to be able to leave the city after 10 pm.

The gates served more than just a security purpose. The Nørreport gate, which provided a beeline along Nørregade to the city market at Gammel Torv, doubled as a busy toll station where farmers had to pay duty to bring their produce to market.

Martin Andersen Nexø, and artists Jens Juel, Christen Købke and CW Eckersberg. It's an interesting place to wander around – as much a park and garden as it is a graveyard. There are tall trees, green lawns and quiet spaces where people come on summer days to sunbathe.

The cemetery is divided into sectors, which helps in locating specific sites. A good place to start is at the main entrance on Kapelvej, which has an office, generally open 9 am to 2 pm weekdays, where you can pick up a brochure mapping famous grave sites.

Even without the brochure you should be able to meander your way along the paths to some of the big-name graves. From the office turn south-west (left) just before the chapel and continue for a couple of minutes in that direction to reach Hans Christian Andersen's grave at P1; you'll pass Martin Andersen Nexø's en route at H2. To get to Søren Kierkegaard's grave turn right instead of left at the chapel and walk a few minutes to the north-east until you reach A17; Jens Juel (A21) and Christen Købke (A9) are nearby.

If you want to dig deeper into cemetery lore, the Assistens Kirkegårds Formidlingscenter (☎ 35 37 19 17), a cultural group based inside the main entrance at Kapelvej 2 (and whose motto is 'Meet the Danes – both the living and the dead!'), arranges guided tours. Its main tour (25kr) is conducted at 1 pm Sunday and typically given in Danish, but it can also arrange private tours in English.

The cemetery is open 8 am to 8 pm daily between May and August, to 6 pm in March, April, September and October and to 4 pm from November to February; admission is free. Bus Nos 5 and 16 stop nearby.

OSTERBRØ

The Osterbrø section of the city, which extends north from Nørrebro, is largely residential and a bit upmarket. Nonetheless it has the distinction of being home to Copenhagen's largest and oldest summer hostel, the national sports stadium Parken (Map 4, D6), the inviting public park Fælledparken and a number of theatres.

Zoologisk Museum (Map 4, D4)

This modern zoological museum on the corner of Jagtvej and Universitetsparken displays all sorts of stuffed animals, from North Zealand deer to Greenlandic polar bears. There are also interesting dioramas, recorded animal sounds, a 14m-long bowhead whale skeleton and various insect displays.

It's open 11 am to 5 pm Tuesday to Sunday. Admission costs 25kr for adults and 10kr for children. Bus Nos 18, 42, 43 and 184 run to the museum.

CHRISTIANSHAVN

Christianshavn, on the eastern flank of Copenhagen, was established by Christian IV in the early 17th century as a commercial centre and a military buffer for the expanding city. It's cut with a network of canals, modelled after those in Holland,

---

Dying to Get In

Assistens Kirkegård, which translates as 'assistant or auxiliary cemetery', was established in 1760 to provide an overflow for the more prestigious burial places in central Copenhagen. In those days Nørrebro was considered well beyond the city limits and the new cemetery was so shunned by Copenhagen's elite that during its first few decades it was little more than a pauper's burial ground.

By 1800 churches in crowded Copenhagen were restricting new burials and city folk began to warm to the Nørrebro cemetery's garden-like setting. The widely held image of the place changed so dramatically that Assistens Kirkegård suddenly became a fashionable resting place for the well-heeled.

Although people from all walks of life are buried here, there's simply no other place in Denmark that can claim the bones of so many famous 19th- and 20th-century Danes.

which leads Christianshavn to occasionally be dubbed 'Little Amsterdam'.

Still surrounded by its old ramparts, Christianshavn today is a hotchpotch of newer apartment complexes and renovated period warehouses that have found second lives as upmarket housing and restored government offices. The neighbourhood attracts an interesting mix of artists, yuppies and dropouts. Christianshavn is also home to a sizable Greenlandic community and was the setting of the public housing complex in the popular novel and movie *Smilla's Sense of Snow*.

To get to Christianshavn, you can walk over the Knippelsbro bridge from the northeastern part of Slotsholmen, take the canal Water Bus or catch bus No 8 or 2 from Rådhuspladsen. If you're going to Christiania first, bus No 8 is the best, as it stops near the main gate on Prinsessegade.

Christiania

In 1971 an abandoned 41-hectare military camp on the eastern side of Christianshavn was taken over by squatters who proclaimed it the 'free state' of Christiania, subject to their own laws. Police tried to clear the area but it was the height of the 'hippie revolution' and an increasing number of alternative folk from throughout Denmark arrived, attracted by communal living and the prospect of reclaiming military land for peaceful purposes.

The momentum became too much for the government to hold back and, bowing to public pressure, the community was allowed to continue as a 'social experiment'. About 1000 people settled into Christiania, turning the old barracks into schools and housing, and starting their own collective businesses, workshops and recycling programs.

As well as hosting progressive happenings, Christiania also became a magnet for runaways and junkies. Although Christiania residents felt that the conventional press played up an image of decadence and criminality – as opposed to portraying Christiania as a self-governing, ecology-oriented and tolerant community – they did, in time, find it necessary to modify

their free-law approach. A new policy was established that outlawed hard drugs in Christiania, and the heroin and cocaine pushers were expelled.

Still, Christiania remains controversial. Some Danes resent the community's rent-free, tax-free situation and many neighbours want sections of Christiania turned into public parks and school grounds. But the Christiania community has managed to hold its own over the years.

Although the police don't regularly patrol Christiania, they have staged numerous organised raids on the community and it's not unknown for police training to include a tactical sweep along Pusherstreet.

Visitors are welcome to stroll or cycle through car-free Christiania, though large dogs may intimidate some free spirits. Photography is frowned upon, and outright forbidden on Pusherstreet, where marijuana joints and hashish are openly (though not legally) sold and smoked.

Christiania has a small outdoor market where pipes and T-shirts are sold, a few craft shops, a bakery and several eateries. It also has a casual bar called Woodstock **(Map 7, D8)**, where joints replace cigarettes and the crowd is about as wasted as you'll find anywhere, and a large, popular nightclub called Loppen.

The main entrance **(Map 7, D8)** into Christiania is on Prinsessegade, 200m northeast of its intersection with Bådsmandsstræde. Pusherstreet and most shops are within a few minutes' walk of the entrance.

If you want to learn more about Christiania (☎ 32 95 65 07), informative guided tours (25kr; meet inside the main entrance) are held at noon and 3 pm daily in summer.

Vor Frelsers Kirke (Map 7, E7)

A few minutes south-west of Christiania is the 17th-century Vor Frelsers Kirke (Our Saviour's Church), Sankt Annæ Gade 29. This church, which once benefited from close ties with the Danish monarchy, has a grand interior.

Take a good look at the immense pipe organ, built in 1698, which contains some 4000 pipes and is decorated with elaborate wood carvings. Also noteworthy is the ornate baroque altar adorned with marble cherubs and angels, designed by the Swede Nicodemus Tessin in 1695.

For a panoramic city view, make the dizzying 400-step ascent up the church's 95m spiral tower – the last 150 steps run along the outside rim of the tower, narrowing to the point where they literally disappear at the top. This colourful spire was added to the church in 1752 by Lauritz de Thurah, who took his inspiration from Boromini's tower of St Ivo in Rome.

Admission to the church is free. It costs 20kr for adults and 10kr for children to climb the tower. It's open 11 am to 4.30 pm daily from April to August and 11 am to 3.30 pm from September to March. If you'd like to hear the organ, it's used in church services, including an English-language one that's held at noon on Sunday.

Orlogsmuseet (Map 7, D8)

Orlogsmuseet (The Royal Danish Naval Museum) occupies a former naval hospital at Overgaden oven Vandet 58 on Christianshavn Kanal. This museum houses more than 300 model ships, many dating from the 16th to the 19th century.

Some were built by naval engineers to serve as design prototypes for the construction of new ships; consequently the models take many forms, from cross-sectional ones detailing frame proportions to full-dressed models with working sails.

The museum also displays a collection of figureheads, navigational instruments, ship lanterns, a Fresnel lens from a lighthouse and the propeller from the German U-boat that sank the *Lusitania*.

It's open noon to 4 pm Tuesday to Sunday year-round. Admission costs 30kr for adults, 20kr for children.

Christians Kirke (Map 7, E6)

Christians Kirke, Strandgade 1, was designed by Danish architect Nicolai Eigtved and completed in 1759. This church once served the local German congregation and has an expansive, theatre-like rococo interior with tiered galleries.

It's open 8 am to 6 pm (to 5 pm Friday and Saturday) daily from March to October and 8 am to 5 pm in winter, except during church services. Admission is free.

B & W Museum (Map 7, E7)

The B & W Museum (☎ 32 54 02 27), Strandgade 4, displays the history of Burmeister & Wein, the shipbuilding company that was founded in 1843 and in 1912 pioneered the use of diesel engines in ocean-going ships. In January 1943 Burmeister & Wein became the target of the first Allied air raid on Copenhagen, when British bombers levelled the company's Christianshavn factory to put an end to its production of German U-boat engines.

The museum is open 10 am to 1 pm weekdays (and the first Sunday of each month) year-round. Admission is free.

Gammel Dok (Map 7, D7)

Gammel Dok (☎ 32 57 19 30), Strandgade 27B, houses the Dansk Arkitektur Center, a foundation devoted to the advancement of architecture. The site features changing exhibitions of Danish and international architecture, design and industrial art.

The building itself is suitably atmospheric – a renovated early 18th-century warehouse on the site of Copenhagen's first dock (Gammel Dok means Old Dock).

It's open 10 am to 5 pm daily year-round. Admission to the exhibitions is 30kr for adults, free for children.

HELLERUP

This is largely a suburb of the city, but it does have one site that's noteworthy for those travelling with children.

Experimentarium (Map 3, G3)

This extensive hands-on technology and natural science centre is housed in a former bottling hall of Tuborg Breweries at Tuborg Havnevej 7. The centre contains some 300 hands-on exhibits.

It's a fun place for kids, featuring time-honoured standards such as the hall of mirrors, and computer-enhanced activities that make it possible to compose water music, stand on the moon or take a ride on an inverted bicycle. All the exhibits have instructions in both English and Danish.

It's open 10 am to 5 pm daily from mid-June to early August, 9 am to 5 pm Monday, Wednesday and Friday, 9 am to 9 pm Tuesday and 11 am to 5 pm at weekends during the rest of the year. Admission costs 79kr for adults and 57kr for children. To get there catch bus No 6 from central Copenhagen. The Experimentarium maintains a Web site at www.experimentarium.dk.

CHARLOTTENLUND

This well-to-do coastal area lies at Copenhagen's northern outskirts. Despite being so close to the city, it has a decent sandy beach, although the smokestacks of Hellerup to the south are part of the backdrop.

Just inland from the beach is the moat-encircled Charlottenlund Fort, which now harbours a camping ground. There's not much left of the old fort other than some cannons, but it's a pleasant place with swans, ducks and lots of birdsong.

Danmarks Akvarium (Map 3, A4)

Danmarks Akvarium (☎ 39 62 32 83), an aquarium at Kavalergården 1, is 500m north of Charlottenlund Fort. By Scandinavian standards it's a fairly large aquarium and the well-presented collection includes cold-water fish, tropical fish, live corals, nurse sharks, sea turtles, electric eels, crocodiles and piranhas. There's also a 'touch pool' section for children that's open at weekends and school holidays.

The aquarium is open 10 am to 6 pm daily from mid-February to mid-October and 10 am to 4 pm weekdays and 10 am to 5 pm at weekends the rest of the year. Admission costs 60kr for adults, 30kr for children. There's a cafeteria. Bus No 6 from central Copenhagen stops near the aquarium.

Charlottenlund Slotspark

From the aquarium car park a path leads directly into Charlottenlund Slotspark (Charlottenlund Castle Park), where there are gardens and an attractive three-storey manor house called Charlottenlund Slot (Map 3, A2) that once belonged to the royal family. The last royal resident was Princess Louise, the wife of Frederik VIII, who lived here until her death in 1926. An obelisk monument at the rear of the manor house commemorates the couple.

Since the 1930s the building has been the headquarters of the Danish Institute for Fisheries Research. Walkways lead around the park-like grounds, making for an enjoyable stroll.

KLAMPENBORG

Klampenborg, being only 20 minutes from Central Station on the S-train's line C, is a favourite spot for Copenhageners on family outings.

Its main attractions are a large amusement park, a wooded deer park crisscrossed with trails and Bellevue beach (Map 1, B4), a sandy stretch that gets packed with sunbathers in summer; all are within walking distance of one another.

Dyrehaven

Dyrehaven (Deer Park), more formally called Jægersborg Dyrehave, is an expansive 1000-hectare area of beech trees and meadows crisscrossed by an alluring network of walking and cycling trails. Dyrehaven was established as a royal hunting ground in 1669 and has evolved into the capital's most popular picnicking area.

At the centre of Dyrehaven is the manor house Eremitagen (Map 1, A4), which was built as a hunting lodge by Christian VI in 1736; a relief of the king adorns the western facade. Located on a grassy knoll, it's a great vantage point from which to spot herds of grazing deer.

In all, there are about 2000 deer in the park, mostly fallow deer, but also red deer and Japanese sika deer. Among the red deer are a few rare white specimens, descendants of deer imported in 1737 from Germany, where they are now extinct. Eremitagen can be reached by walking 2km north of Bakken along the main route, Kristiansholmsvej, although it can also be reached from numerous other points in the park as most of the largest trails radiate out like spokes from Eremitagen.

Hackney carriages provide horse-drawn rides into the park from the intersection of Peter Lieps Vej and Kristiansholmsvej opposite the back entrance of Bakken. The carriage rides cost 200kr for 30 minutes; the coaches carry up to five passengers, but it's most romantic with two!

Bakken (Map 1, B4)

The 400-year-old Bakken (☎ 39 63 35 44) at the southern edge of Dyrehaven lays claim to being the world's oldest amusement park. A blue-collar version of Tivoli, it's a honky-tonk carnival of bumper cars, roller coasters, slot machines and beer halls. All in all, there are more than 100 different amusements, with rides taking the shape of Viking ships, swans and the like. It also has all the requisite fast-food stalls and carnival games.

Bakken is open noon to midnight daily between late March and late August. Admission is free. Children's rides cost around 15kr, adult rides about double that, and there are discounted multiuse passes. Bakken is a 10-minute walk west from Klampenborg station. If you come by car, parking is available for 30kr.

Ordrupgaard (Map 1, B4)

Ordrupgaard (☎ 39 64 11 83), Vilvordevej 110, is a small art museum specialising in French art, primarily from the impressionist period, and includes works by Gauguin, Degas, Monet, Renoir and Cezanne. It also has a collection of Danish contemporary art. The museum occupies the former home of its wealthy founder, Wilhelm Hansen, who bequeathed both his house and his private art collection to the people of Denmark.

It's open 1 to 5 pm daily, except Monday. Admission is 25kr for adults, free for children, except on Wednesday when it's free to all. Bus No 388 from Klampenborg station stops nearby.

LYNGBY

The main sight of interest in Lyngby is Frilandsmuseet, a sprawling open-air museum

of old countryside dwellings, workshops and barns that have been gathered from sites around Denmark.

The Lyngby area also has a number of lakes, including Furesø, the deepest lake in Denmark. For information on hiring canoes and rowing boats on the lakes, see Activities later in this chapter.

Frilandsmuseet (Map 1, B3)

Frilandsmuseet (☎ 45 85 02 92) consists of 110 historic buildings arranged in 40 different groupings to provide a sense of Danish rural life as it was in various regions and across different social strata. The houses range from rather grand affairs to meagre, sod-roofed cottages. Many of the buildings are furnished from the period: the smithy is equipped with irons and a hearth and the post mill still has functioning sails. Grazing farm animals, selected from old Danish breeds, and costumed field workers add an element of authenticity to the setting.

There's a light schedule of demonstrations such as folk dancing, weaving and pottery making, mostly at weekends.

Visitors will need to set aside several hours to explore; in keeping with its rural nature, the sites are widely spread across the grounds. To avoid distracting from the period feel, buildings are not labelled or posted with descriptive signs. The main brochure maps out the sights and gives brief descriptions, but it is only in Danish; be sure to ask for the English translation that corresponds to the map key.

Frilandsmuseet is open 10 am to 5 pm between Easter and September and 10 am to 4 pm for the first three weeks of October; it's closed on Monday and in winter. Except on Wednesday when it's free for all, admission is 40kr for adults, free for children. There's a kiosk selling ice cream and hot dogs and a cafeteria with more substantial food.

The museum, at Kongevejen 100, is a 10-minute signposted walk from Sorgenfri station, which is 25 minutes from Central Station on the S-train's line B. You can also take bus No 184 or 194, both of which stop at the entrance.

RUNGSTED

Rungsted on the exclusive Øresund coast is lined with the seaside homes of some of Copenhagen's wealthiest residents. It's also the site of Rungstedlund, the estate which houses the Karen Blixen museum.

Rungstedlund was originally built as an inn around 1500. King Karl XII of Sweden stayed there in 1700 and the Danish lyric poet Johannes Ewald, who wrote Denmark's national anthem, was a boarder from 1773 to 1776. The property was later turned into a private residence and in 1879 was purchased by Karen Blixen's father, Wilhelm Dinesen. Blixen was born at Rungstedlund in 1885 and lived there off and on until her death in 1962.

There's a tourist information kiosk at the intersection of Rungstedvej and Rungsted Strandvej, opposite Rungsted's large yacht harbour. If you're up for a meal, there are numerous places to eat at the yacht harbour.

Karen Blixen Museet

Karen Blixen's former home, now a museum, is furnished in much the way she left

---

Out of Rungsted

Karen Blixen was born Karen Christenze Dinesen on 17 April 1885 in Rungsted, a well-to-do community north of Copenhagen. She studied art in Copenhagen, Rome and Paris. In 1914, when she was 28 and eager to escape the confines of her bourgeois family, she married her second cousin Baron Bror von Blixen-Finecke, after having a failed love affair with his twin brother Hans. It was a marriage of convenience – she wanted his title and he needed her money.

The couple then moved to Kenya and started a coffee plantation, which Karen was left to manage. The baron, who had several extramarital affairs, eventually infected Karen with syphilis. She came home to Denmark for medical treatment, but subsequently returned to Africa and divorced the baron in 1925. In 1932, after her coffee plantation had failed and the great love of her life, Englishman Denys Finch-Hatton, had died in a tragic plane crash, Karen Blixen left Africa and returned to the family estate in Rungsted, where she began to write. Danes were slow to take to Blixen's writings, in part because she consistently wrote about the aristocracy in approving terms and used an old-fashioned idiomatic style that some thought arrogant. Her insistence on being called 'Baroness' also took its toll on her popularity in a Denmark bent on minimising class disparity.

Following rejection by publishers in Denmark and England, her first book, *Seven Gothic Tales*, a compilation of short stories set in the 19th century, was published in New York in 1934 (under the pseudonym Isak Dinesen) and was so well received that it was chosen as a Book-of-the-Month selection. It was only after her success in the USA that Danish publishers took a serious interest in her works.

In 1937, Blixen's landmark *Out of Africa*, the memoirs of her life in Kenya, was published in both Danish and English. This was followed by *Winter's Tales* in 1942, *The Angelic Avengers* in 1944, *Last Tales* in 1957, *Anecdotes of Destiny* in 1958 and *Shadows on the Grass* in 1960. Three of Blixen's books were published after her death: *Daguerreotypes and Other Essays*, *Carnival: Entertainments and Posthumous Tales* and *Letters from Africa 1914-1931*. Two of Blixen's works were turned into the Oscar-winning films *Out of Africa* and *Babette's Feast*.

A few years before her death, Blixen arranged for her estate to be turned over to the private Rungstedlund Foundation. For years the foundation had only enough money to maintain the grounds as a bird sanctuary, but the posthumous book sales that were spurred by the success of the films made it possible to turn her former home into a museum in 1991.

MARTIN HARRIS

it and has photographs, paintings, Masai spears and shields and other mementoes of her time in Africa. In the exhibition room is the old Corona typewriter that Blixen used to write her novels.

One wing of the museum, a converted carriage house and stables, houses a library of Blixen's books in many languages, a cafe and a bookshop; there's also an audiovisual presentation on Blixen's life.

The grounds contain gardens and a wood, part of which has been set aside as a bird sanctuary.

Blixen lies buried in a little clearing shaded by a sprawling beech tree, her grave marked by a simple stone slab inscribed with just her name.

The museum is open 10 am to 5 pm daily between May and September. It's also open 1 to 4 pm Wednesday, Thursday and Friday, and 11 am to 4 pm Saturday and Sunday between October and April. Admission is 35kr for adults, free for children.

All Copenhagen-Helsingør trains stop at Rungsted; from Central Station it takes 30 minutes and costs 42kr.

The museum is at Rungsted Strandvej 111, opposite the yacht harbour and 1.25km from the train station.

To get there, walk north from the train station up Stationvej, turn right at the lights onto Rungstedvej and then at its intersection with Rungsted Strandvej walk south about 300m and you'll come to the museum; the whole walk takes about 15 minutes.

If you'd like to walk through the museum's bird sanctuary on the way back to the train station, ask at the museum desk for the *Garden and Bird Sanctuary* brochure, which maps out the route.

FREDERIKSBERG

Frederiksberg is a pleasant, upmarket area with an abundance of green space, the most notable of which is Frederiksberg Have (Frederiksberg Garden).

This large park encircles the zoo, is crisscrossed with walking trails and holds large shade trees, a meandering canal and sunny lawns popular with sunbathers and picnickers.

Zoologisk Have (Map 6, E2; Copenhagen Zoo)

This national zoo (☎ 36 30 20 01), Roskildevej 32, which dates from 1859, has the standard collection of caged creatures, including elephants, lions, zebras, hippos, gorillas and polar bears. Special sections include the Tropical Zoo, the Children's Zoo, the Ape Jungle, the African Savannah and the South American Pampas.

It's open 9 am to 6 pm daily from June to August, 9 am to 5 pm in spring and autumn and 9 am to 4 pm from November to March. Admission costs 70kr for adults, 35kr for children. Bus No 28 from Rådhuspladsen stops outside the gate.

Carlsberg Brewery (Map 6, G3)

The Carlsberg Visitors Center, Gamle Carlsberg Vej 11, adjacent to Carlsberg brewery, has an exhibition area on the history of Danish beer from 1370 BC (yes, they carbondated a bog girl who was found in a peat bog caressing a jug of well-aged brew!). Dioramas, in English as well as Danish, give the lowdown on the brewing process and en route to your final destination you'll pass antique copper vats and see the stables that still keep a team of Jutland drayhorses.

The self-guided tour ends, apropos, at a little pub where you get your choice of two free beers – make one of them the Carls Special, a deliciously smooth dark malt that's a local favourite.

The visitor centre is open 10 am to 4 pm weekdays; admission is free. Worthy of note as you enter the brewery grounds is the Elephant Gate (Map 6, F3), two stone elephant pillars that span Ny Carlsberg Vej, the main road through the complex. You can get to the brewery by taking bus No 6 westbound from Rådhuspladsen.

Royal Copenhagen (Map 6, C2)

Founded in 1775, Royal Copenhagen, Denmark's leading porcelain company, moved its operations to this Frederiksberg site in 1884. The factory complex (☎ 38 14 92 97), Smallegade 45, is so large that the company refers to it as a community. If you're curious to see how the porcelain is produced,

Potent Patron of the Arts

The brewer Carl Jacobsen (1842-1914) was a great supporter of culture and the arts. After a fire swept the Frederiksborg castle, north of Copenhagen, Jacobsen took on the task of restoring the badly damaged building and converting it into a national museum. In 1876 he established the Carlsberg Foundation to provide the financial support to maintain that museum.

Despite his vast wealth, Jacobsen believed that great works of art were treasures that should be available to the general public rather than items to be held as private trophies by the rich. In the late 19th century he founded the Ny Carlsberg Glyptotek and donated his own exceptional collection of art to the museum.

In 1902, with the permanent home of the Ny Carlsberg Glyptotek (Map 7, E4) under construction, Jacobsen donated his brewery to the Carlsberg Foundation, making it the most richly endowed private foundation in Denmark. To this day, that foundation is still the majority shareholder in Carlsberg Brewery. So if you want to support the arts, you know which beer to order!

the finer pieces of which are still hand-painted, you can join a one-hour multilingual guided tour. The tours are given at 9, 10 and 11 am and 1 and 2 pm Monday to Friday and cost 25kr.

The adjacent factory shop sells seconds at prices that are up to 50% off what you'd pay in stores. It's open 9 am to 5.30 pm weekdays and 9 am to 2 pm Saturday. Take bus No 1 or 14 from Rådhuspladsen.

ISHØJ

In contrast to the upmarket coastal suburbs at the north side of Copenhagen, the southerly suburbs are more diverse, with a sizable concentration of Middle Eastern immigrants. The entire Ishøj community, not only its housing and commercial centre but even its beach, which is built upon reclaimed land dredged from the bay, has been developed over the past few decades.

Most of what Ishøj has to offer visitors is along the coast where there's a vast sandy beach with good windsurfing, a modern art museum, a harbourfront camping ground and a brand new hostel.

Arken (Map 1, G1)

Arken (the Ark; ☎ 43 54 02 22) is a large contemporary art museum that opened in 1996 on the coast at Skovvej 100. The stark modernistic building rises above Ishøj beach and is as much a work of art as the exhibits inside.

The Arken collection features the works of leading Danish and Nordic artists since 1945, with an emphasis on photo-based art, sculpture and installations. There are also changing exhibits such as works by artists from the regional COBRA (COpenhagen-BRussels-Amsterdam) movement and by the Norwegian artist Edvard Munch.

Arken is open 10 am to 5 pm Tuesday to Sunday (to 9 pm Wednesday). Admission costs 40kr for adults and 15kr for children. You can get to Arken by taking the S-train to Ishøj station and boarding bus No 128 there.

DRAGØR

If Copenhagen begins to feel crowded, consider an afternoon excursion to Dragør, an old maritime village on the island of Amager, a few kilometres south of the airport. In the early 1550s Christian II allowed Dutch farmers to settle in Amager to provide his court with flowers and produce, and the town of Dragør still retains a bit of Dutch flavour.

You can get to Dragør via bus No 30, 33 or 350S from central Copenhagen.

Dragør Museum

The Dragør Museum (☎ 32 53 93 07) is in a half-timbered house adjacent to the harbourfront tourist office. This quaint little museum displays model ships, antique ship paraphernalia and period furnishings from sea captain's homes.

It's open noon to 4 pm Tuesday to Sunday from May to September. Admission costs 20kr for adults, 10kr for children.

Historic Buildings

A fun thing to do in Dragør is to wander the narrow, winding cobblestone streets leading up from the harbour, which are lined with the thatch-roofed, mustard-coloured houses comprising the old town.

One interesting little ramble is to take Strandgade, a pedestrian alley that begins opposite the museum, and continue up to Badstuevælen, an old cobbled square lined with some attractive houses dating from the 1790s.

Of particular interest on Strandgade, at its intersection with Magstræde, is Dragør Kro, built by JH Blichmann, who designed many of Dragør's finest homes. Of note on Badstuevælen square are houses at Nos 8 and 12, also built by Blichmann. Take a look, too, at the square's stone obelisk erected in Christian VII's day to mark the distance to central Copenhagen – 1.5 Danish miles or, in more contemporary measurement, 10.5km.

Returning to the waterfront via Kongevejen, note building No 11, now a pharmacy and bookshop. It originally belonged to the customs inspector and still sports the relief of Denmark's national arms.

COPENHAGEN FOR FREE

In egalitarian Denmark some of the finest things in life are free – at least one day a week – so you might want to plan your museum browsing accordingly.

Every Wednesday, the Statens Museum of Kunst, Nationalmuseet, Den Hirschsprungske Samling, Tøjhusmuseet, Post & Tele Museum, Geologisk Museum, Thorvaldsens Museum, Frilandsmuseet and Ny Carlsberg Glyptotek turn off their cash registers and open their doors gratis to all. Ny Carlsberg Glyptotek is also free on Sunday.

The Københavns Bymuseum is free on Friday. In addition, there are a handful of Copenhagen museums that never charge for admission: Frihedsmuseet, Davids Samling, Georg Jensen Museum, B & W Museum, Tobaksmuseet and the Medicinsk-Historisk Museum.

And of course, the city's lovely parks and gardens, including the botanical garden with its tropical Palmehus, are free for strolling every day. Copenhagen churches are free of entrance charges and some, such as the city's cathedral, Vor Frue Kirke, are virtual museums unto themselves.

If you're up for playtime, Bakken, the amusement park in Klampenborg, never charges admission. And in this delightful city you can even enjoy a couple of free glasses of beer as the finale of a free tour at Carlsberg Brewery.

ACTIVITIES
Swimming

Beaches The greater Copenhagen area has a number of bathing beaches, if brisk water doesn't deter you. Even in July, ocean temperatures average just 17°C, so most beachgoers are Scandinavians and Germans rather than visitors from warmer climes. Those who prefer more tepid waters should choose from one of Copenhagen's indoor swimming pools.

Ocean waters are tested regularly, and if sewage spills or other serious pollution occurs the beaches affected are closed and signposted.

A popular beach south of Copenhagen is Amager Strandpark, which can be reached by bus No 12 or 13. Playground facilities and shallow waters make it ideal for children. Deeper waters can be accessed by walking out along the jetties. There's another beach, Sydstranden, in Amager along the southern side of Dragør; take bus No 33 or 34.

The most easily accessible beaches north of central Copenhagen are the Charlottenlund beach and the Bellevue beach **(Map 1, B4)** at Klampenborg; both can be reached via bus No 6.

Topless bathing is *de rigueur* at all Danish beaches, but nude bathing is typically limited to certain areas; the main rule of thumb is to follow local custom. One place that is popular with nude sunbathers is the north side of Bellevue beach.

Pools DGI-byen (**Map 7, E3**; ☎ 33 29 80 00), Tietgensgade 65, just minutes from Central Station, has a wonderful new swim centre called Vandkulturhuset with several different indoor pools. The main pool is a grand affair with a unique ellipse shape and 100m lanes. Others include a deep 'mountain pool' with a climbing wall, a wet trampoline and diving platforms; a hot water pool; and a children's pool. Use of the pools and sauna costs 40kr for adults, 25kr for children. If you didn't pack a swimsuit you can borrow one for 20kr, but grab a towel from your hotel or you'll have to pay another 20kr to use one here. It's open 7 am to 7 pm Monday, Wednesday and Friday and at least 10 am to 5 pm on other days. The complex is run by DGI, the Danish Sports and Gymnastic Association.

If you don't need such fancy digs, scattered throughout Copenhagen are a handful of public swimming pools and saunas that you can use. Each charges around 25kr for adults, half that for children. These include:

Frederiksberg Svømmehal (**Map 6, B3**; ☎ 38 14 04 04), Helgesvej 29, Frederiksberg; open 8 am to 8 pm weekdays and 8 am to 2 pm Saturday

Fælledbadet (**Map 4, D5**; ☎ 35 39 08 04), Borgmester Jensens Allé 50 at Fælledparken in Østerbro; variable hours, roughly 7 am to 6 pm weekdays and 9 am to 3 pm at weekends

Vesterbro Svømmehal (**Map 6, G4**; ☎ 33 22 05 00), Angelgade 4 in the Vesterbro area; open daily, with variable hours on weekdays and 9 am to 2 pm at weekends

Bellahøj Friluftsbad (**Map 5, C2**; ☎ 38 60 16 66) at the intersection of Bellahøjvej and Frederikssundsvej (within walking distance of the hostel and camping ground); open summer-only

Fitness Clubs
If you want to get a good work-out while you're in Copenhagen, there are a handful of fitness clubs where visitors can pay a 75kr fee to use the weights and fitness machines.

Form & Fitness (☎ 33 32 10 02) in the Scala complex at Vesterbrogade 2, in the city centre, is open daily, 24 hours a day. In the Østerbro area, there's Form & Fitness

(**Map 4, D6**; ☎ 35 55 00 78) at Parken, Øster Allé 42, that's open 8 am to 9.30 pm Monday to Thursday, 6.30 am to 8 pm Friday and 8 am to 5 pm at weekends.

The fitness club at the Radisson SAS Falconer Hotel (**Map 6, C3**; ☎ 38 10 90 70), Falkoner Allé 9, in the Frederiksberg area, is open 7 am to 9 pm Monday to Thursday, 7 am to 7 pm Friday, 9 am to 5 pm Saturday and 10 am to 6 pm Sunday.

The fitness club at Radisson SAS Scandinavia Hotel (**Map 7, F6**; ☎ 32 54 28 88), Amager Blvd 70, in the Amager area, is open 7 am to 10 pm Monday to Thursday, 7 am to 9 pm Friday, 7 am to 7 pm Saturday and 8 am to 7 pm Sunday.

Badminton & Squash
There are a couple of places in Copenhagen where you can play badminton and squash. Both charge 50kr an hour for badminton, 65kr an hour for squash. Racquets can be hired for 25kr an hour.

Grøndal Centret (**Map 5, E2**; ☎ 38 34 11 09), Hvidkildevej 64, in the Bellahøj area near the hostel and camping ground, is open 8 am to 11 pm weekdays and 9 am to 6 pm at weekends.

Nørrebrohallen (**Map 4, D1**; ☎ 35 83 10 01), Bragesgade 5, in the Nørrebro area, is open at least 8 am to 9 pm daily.

Boating
There are a number of possibilities for hiring boats and rowing your way around scenic waterways.

If you want to explore Christianshavn's historic canals, Christianshavns Bådudlejning og Café (**Map 7, E7**; ☎ 32 96 53 53) at Overgaden neden Vandet 29 hires rowing boats on the canal for 60kr an hour. It's open 10 am to sunset daily from early May to about mid-September.

For those who prefer a more rural setting, the Lyngby area has a series of substantial lakes, including Furesø, the deepest lake in Denmark. It's possible to hire rowing boats or canoes for 60kr per hour at Holte Havn (**Map 1, A2**; ☎ 45 42 04 49), a waterside kiosk at 22 Vejlesøvej, and row around either Furesø or the smaller Vejlesø, which

THINGS TO SEE & DO

are connected by a channel. Holte Havn is open 10 am to at least 9 pm (sometimes as late as midnight) daily from mid-April to late September and is a two-minute walk from Holte S-train station.

Frederiksdal Kanoudlejning (**Map 1, B2**; ☎ 45 85 67 70) at Nybrovej 520 (by the locks) hires out canoes and rowing boats for use on the river Mølleåen and the lakes Lyngby Sø, Bagsværd Sø and Furesø, which are interconnected. Boat hire costs 60kr per hour. It's open 10 am to 6 pm daily, except Monday. To get there, get off at Sorgenfri S-train station and take bus No 191.

Windsurfing
The beaches at Amager and Ishøj offer decent windsurfing conditions and both have windsurfing operations. Surf & Snowboard (☎ 32 84 04 53), Amager Strandvej, is at Amager Beach and Nautic Surf & Ski Ishøj (☎ 43 54 00 19), Søhesten 6A, is at Ishøj. Expect to pay about 350kr for a one-day course, use of gear included.

Cycling
Cycle lanes are found along many city streets and virtually all of Copenhagen can be toured by bicycle, except for pedestrian-only streets such as Strøget.

When touring the city, cyclists should be cautious of bus passengers who commonly step off the bus into the cycle lanes, and of pedestrians (particularly tourists) who sometimes absent-mindedly step off the kerb and into the path of oncoming cyclists. This is particularly a problem on roads such as Nørregade, where cyclists are allowed to ride against the one-way traffic.

Cycling maps, including a 1:50,000 scale map of the greater Copenhagen area called *Københavns Amt*, are produced by the Danish cycling federation, Dansk Cyklist Forbund (**Map 7, B3**), and can be readily purchased at bookshops.

Information on bicycle hire can be found under Bicycle in the Getting Around chapter.

Cycle Tour The most popular self-guided cycling tour in the Copenhagen area is the 12km ride north to Dyrehaven. There's a cycle path the entire way, much of it skirting the Øresund coast.

To begin, take Østerbrogade north from the city. After passing the S-train station Svanemøllen, the road continues as Strandvejen, passing through the busy suburb of Hellerup, where intersections have blue-marked crossings to indicate cyclist rights-of-way, and then up through the quiet coastal village of Charlottenlund. Here the cycle lane widens. There's a beach, an old fort and an aquarium for interesting diversions. Once you reach Klampenborg station, a bike path leads into Dyrehaven, a woodland crossed by a network of trails, and a

---

Dining with Danes

The best way to get to know a place is through contact with its people – but at meaningful levels that's sometimes easier said than done. Thanks to a new program run through the tourist office, visitors to Copenhagen now have an opportunity to share an evening at home with a Danish family.

The way it works is that you pick up a booking application at your hostel, hotel or the tourist office, or simply contact the program coordinator, Anette Haargaard (☎ 33 12 40 44 ext 204 or ☎ 26 85 39 61, ⓔ ahaargaard.organiser@get2net.dk). Do this at least two days ahead of the day you'd like to meet with a family (though earlier is better) and give Anette a little background on your interests. Anette then tries to match guests up with families with similar interests.

There are currently about 45 Danish families participating in the program, most living in or near the city, a few in the Zealand countryside. There are gay families in the program as well. Once the arrangements are made, you'll be given train and/or bus directions and the meeting time. Guests pay a 225kr fee for each adult, 125kr for each child aged 6 to 14 (under 6 free); the money is used to cover program expenses and meal costs.

Two views of the famed Tivoli amusement park, which takes on a romantic night-time aura.

No cars or motorcycles in Christiania

Mailbox in the 'free state' of Christiania

Exhibit at liberated Museum Erotica

One of 110 historic rural buildings featured at Frilandsmuseet

perfect place for a picnic. If you want to continue farther north, an off-road cycling path runs parallel to the coastal road to Rungsted. Either way, you have the choice of returning on the same route, taking an alternative route such as the inland road Bernstorffsvej, or putting your bike on the S-train and making it a one-way tour.

Ice Skating

Copenhageners know how to have fun, even when the mercury plunges. The busy public square Kongens Nytorv, at the head of the Nyhavn canal, is flooded during the winter to form an outdoor ice skating rink. If you don't have your own skates, they can be rented for 35kr right at Kongens Nytorv during the season, which is typically from early November to the first weekend in March.

In addition, during the pre-Christmas season opening of Tivoli, the amusement park's lake becomes a winter playground for ice skaters as well.

Golf

Københavns Golfklub (**Map 1, A4**; ☎ 39 63 04 83), Dyrehaven 2, is an 18-hole golf course at the northern end of Dyrehaven park in Klampenborg. Green fees are 280kr weekdays, 350kr at weekends.

COURSES
Folk High Schools

Scandinavia's unique *folkehøjskole*, literally 'folk high school' (the 'high' denoting an institute of higher learning), provides a liberal education within a communal living environment. Folk high schools got their start in Denmark, inspired by philosopher Nikolai Grundtvig's concept of 'enlightenment for life'. The curriculum includes such things as drama, peace studies and organic farming.

People aged 17½ and older can enrol; there are no entrance exams and no degrees.

Tuition, including room and board, averages 820kr a week. For more information, including a catalogue of the nearly 100 schools, contact Højskolernes Sekretariat (☎ 33 13 98 22, e hs@grundtvig.dk), Nytorv 7, 1450 Copenhagen K. The Web site is at www.folkehojskoler.dk/old/int.

While most folk high schools teach in Danish, the International People's College (☎ 49 21 33 61), Montebello Allé 1, 3000 Helsingør, has students and teachers from around the world, and most instruction is given in English.

Foreigners are welcome to enrol in short-term courses that typically last for two to eight weeks and in summer these include an intensive Danish language and culture program. The college has its Web site at www.ipc.dk.

Danish Language Courses

Contact the Danish Cultural Institute (see Useful Organisations in the Facts for the Visitor chapter) for information on Danish language courses that might be offered in your home country.

In Denmark, there are a number of schools set up to teach Danish to foreigners, but most focus on teaching immigrants or other long-term residents. For others, a good place to try first is HOF, a private school that has a relatively open enrolment; courses typically meet three times a week, last two months and cost around 800kr.

Following are four of the schools that offer Danish language courses to foreigners:

AOF (☎ 39 16 82 00), Lersø Park Allé 44, 2100 Copenhagen Ø
HOF (☎ 33 11 88 33), Købmagergade 26, 1150 Copenhagen K
KISS (☎ 35 36 25 25), Nørregade 32, 2200 Copenhagen N
Studieskolen (☎ 33 14 43 22), Antonigade 6, 1106 Copenhagen K

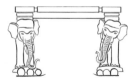

Places to Stay

Copenhagen offers good accommodation options in every price range and you don't have to pay a premium to be in the city centre.

The main hotel quarter (and, incidentally, the city's red-light district) is along the west side of Central Station, where rows of six-storey century-old buildings house one hotel after the other. Despite the neighbourhood's porn shops and streetwalkers, the area is neither unpleasant nor notably dangerous, at least not by the standards of large cities elsewhere in Europe. Still, if you prefer a better neighbourhood, there are numerous options that are also central, as well as others that offer a quieter suburban setting.

Copenhagen is a popular convention city and if you happen to arrive without reservations when one is taking place, finding a room can be a challenge. These conventions, referred to in Denmark as congresses, can occur at any time of the year and the largest ones can book out virtually every hotel in the city. There are some new hotel projects under way aimed at increasing the city's room capacity, but whether that will ultimately provide relief from the convention crunches or just attract more and larger conventions remains to be seen. If you don't like to take chances, your best bet is to book well in advance.

Some hotels consistently apply their listed rates, but with many hotels the rates are upped when they expect to be very busy and lowered when things slack off. As a general rule, you can expect the best deals in the off season and the highest rates during summer. The hotel rates given in this section include service charge, the 25% value-added tax (VAT) and, except where noted, a complimentary buffet-style breakfast.

It's worth considering buying a Scan+ Hotel Pass which costs 100kr and offers handsome discounts on weekend and summer rates at participating hotels (Hotel Imperial and Ascot Hotel in Copenhagen) in major Scandinavian cities. It can be purchased at the hotels and is valid for a year.

Booking Services

The city tourist office, **Wonderful Copenhagen** (☎ 70 22 24 42, Bernstorffsgade 1) north of Central Station, has an accommodation counter that books unfilled hotel rooms at discounts off the published rates. These commonly range from around 100kr off for budget hotels to as much as 50% off for top-end hotels – a situation that can sometimes make a splurge only slightly more costly than going budget. These discounts, however, are based purely on supply and demand and are not always available during busy periods. Still, if there are no big conventions happening in the city or other forces causing a run on rooms you'll often find tempting deals. There's a 50kr fee per booking. The counter is open 9 am to 8 pm Monday to Saturday and 10 am to 8 pm Sunday from 1 May to 31 August; it's also open 9 am to 4.30 pm weekdays and 9 am to 1.30 pm Saturday the rest of the year.

The **Tourist Information** desk situated in the arrival area at Copenhagen airport, just outside customs, also books unfilled Copenhagen hotel rooms at similarly discounted rates and for a 50kr booking fee. If you're arriving by air this is the more convenient option and it typically has shorter queues. The airport information desk is open 6 am to 11 pm daily.

PLACES TO STAY – BUDGET
Camping

Camping is very popular in Denmark. Although most camping grounds are in the countryside, Copenhagen has a handful of sites within commuting distance of the city centre.

Danish camping grounds require that campers be in possession of a camping pass. If you don't have a valid Camping Card International, then you can purchase a Danish carnet at the first camping ground you visit or from tourist offices. The cost for an annual pass is 45kr for an individual or 75kr for a family.

As well as providing tenting and caravan space, some camping grounds rent cabins. These typically sleep four to six people. They often have cooking facilities, but bed linen and blankets are rarely provided so it's best to bring your own sleeping bag.

Camping is regulated in Denmark and is only allowed in established camping grounds, or on private land with the owner's permission. While it may seem tempting, camping in a car or caravan at the beach, in a car park or along the street is prohibited and can result in an immediate fine.

Ratings Camping grounds in Denmark are rated by the Danish Camping Board using a star system, with the number of stars relating to the facilities. You'll find this rating displayed at the camping ground, as well as in literature that lists camping areas.

One-star camping grounds fulfil minimum standards, such as providing running water, toilets, at least one shower and at least one electric outlet for shavers.

Two-star places have a minimum of one shower for every 25 sites, a kitchen with hot tap water and hotplates, as well as a playground for children. To qualify for a two-star rating, the site must also be within 2km of a grocery store.

All sites classified two-star or higher are equipped to service caravans with facilities for emptying toilets, cleaning tanks and replenishing drinking water.

Camping grounds with three stars, the most common rating, have more elaborate facilities, including hot water in the washbasins, a communal lounge, a larger play area for children, nursing rooms for babies, and sinks or washing machines for laundry. Also, they must be within 1km of a grocery store.

In recent years the system was expanded to make way for four-star and five-star ratings. The higher standards required to earn the additional stars are mostly along the lines of greater creature comforts, but these higher ratings also require that there be a separate pitch area for tents and an equipped bicycle repair area. Currently only a few camping grounds – and none in the immediate Copenhagen area – have received the new top ratings.

Camping Grounds The *Bellahøj Camping* (**Map 5, E2**; ☎ 38 10 11 50, *fax 38 10 13 32, Hvidkildevej 66, 2400 Copenhagen NV*) is a simple one-star place in a grassy field at the side of a busy road about 5km west of the city centre in the Bellahøj area. A summer-only operation, this camping ground is open from 1 June to 31 August. It has showers and cooking facilities and there's a supermarket within walking distance. The cost is 57kr per person. From Rådhuspladsen take bus No 11, which stops right at the camping ground.

The more developed *Absalon Camping* (**Map 1, E2**; ☎ 36 41 06 00, *fax 36 41 02 93*, e *absalon@dcu.dk, Korsdalsvej 132, 2610 Rødovre*) is a two-star facility 9km west of the city centre in the Rødovre suburb, near Brøndbyøster station on S-train line B. Facilities include a coin laundry, food kiosk, group kitchen and playground. In addition to camping sites, which cost 56kr per person, caravans and five-person cabins can be rented from 200kr per day, plus the per-person camping fee. Absalon Camping is open year-round.

A delightful alternative is *Charlotten-lund Strandpark* (**Map 3, B4**; ☎ 39 62 36 88, *fax 39 61 08 16*, e *camping-fort@ mail.dk, Strandvejen 144B, 2920 Charlottenlund*), 8km north of central Copenhagen. This friendly camping ground, on Charlottenlund beach, is appealingly set in the tree-lined grounds of an old moat-encircled coastal fortification. The cost is 65kr per person but space is limited so advance bookings are recommended. There's a snack kiosk, showers and a coin laundry on site; a bakery and a supermarket are just a few hundred metres away. The frequent bus No 6 connects the camping ground with Copenhagen city centre. It's open from 15 June to 15 September.

Tangloppen Camping (**Map 1, G1**; ☎ 43 54 07 67, *fax 43 54 07 64*, e *c-tanglopp en@fdm.dk, Tangloppen 2, Ishøj Havn, 2635 Ishøj*) is another waterside option, this one 14km south-west of central Copenhagen. It's right on Ishøj harbour and just a short walk from a sandy beach and the Arken modern art museum. Rated three stars, it has full amenities, including cooking and laundry facilities, TV lounge, food kiosk and opportunities for fishing and windsurfing. The cost is 58kr per person. There are also waterfront cabins from 390kr a day in summer, 225kr in the off season. Tangloppen is open from late April to mid-September. To get there, take the S-train to Ishøj station and then change to bus No 128.

Hostelling International

Two hostels *(vandrerhjem)* in the Copenhagen suburbs and two more just outside the city are members of the Hostelling International (HI) organisation, known in Denmark as Danhostel.

HI is the current name for the worldwide hostel organisation that in previous years was known as International Youth Hostel Federation (IYHF) or Youth Hostels Association (YHA). The switch to HI was made in part to attract a wider clientele and move away from the heavy emphasis on 'youth'. Some countries are still making the transition to HI, so if your home hostel card says IYHF, HI or YHA, it's all the same thing.

Travellers who don't have an international hostel card can buy one once they arrive in Denmark for 160kr (annual fee) or pay 30kr extra for each night's stay. If you're not sure whether you'll be staying at hostels often enough to make it worth buying an annual card, ask for a sticker each time you pay the 30kr per-night fee; if you accumulate six stickers you'll have yourself an annual hostel card.

Most of Denmark's HI hostels have private rooms in addition to dormitory rooms, which makes them a good-value alternative to hotels. Danish hostels appeal to a wide range of guests in all age categories and are oriented as much towards families and groups as they are to backpackers, students and other budget travellers.

Facilities in hostels vary, but most newer hostels have two-bed and four-bed rooms and thus are well suited for use by couples or small groups of friends travelling together.

HI hostels are categorised by a star system, from one to five stars. One-star hostels meet the basic requirements, whereas two-star hostels add on luggage storage facilities

and a small shop. Three-star hostels also have a TV lounge. Four-star and five-star hostels fancy up the facilities and have a minimum of 75% of their rooms with private shower and toilet.

With few exceptions, Denmark's HI hostels have single bunk-style beds with comfortable foam mattresses. Blankets and pillows are provided at all hostels, but if you don't bring your own sheets you'll have to hire them for around 40kr per stay. Sleeping bags are not allowed. A handy, lightweight pouch-style sleeping sheet with an attached pillow cover can be purchased at many hostels worldwide and will save you a bundle on sheet-rental charges.

In the summer and other holiday periods, hostels often book out entirely, so it's always a good idea to make advance reservations.

You can pick up the handy, 200-page *Danhostel Danmarks Vandrerhjem* guide free from hostels or tourist offices; it gives information on individual hostels, including each hostel's facilities and a simple sketch map showing its location.

All Danish hostels provide an all-you-can-eat breakfast for 40kr and many also provide dinner (65kr maximum). Most hostels also have guest kitchens with pots and pans where you can cook your own food.

Denmark's hostelling association's headquarters is: Danhostel (**Map 7, E2**; ☎ 33 31 36 12, fax 33 31 36 26, ℮ ldv@danhostel .dk), Vesterbrogade 39, 1620 Copenhagen V. The association's Web site is at www .danhostel.dk. To join HI before you leave home, ask at your nearest hostel or contact your national hostelling association. Some national offices are:

Australia
   Australian Youth Hostel Association (☎ 02-9565 1699, ℮ yha@yha.au), Level 3, 10 Mallett St, Camperdown NSW 2050
Canada
   Hostelling International – Canada (☎ 613-237 7884, ℮ info@hostellingintl.ca), 205 Catherine St, Suite 400, Ottawa, Ontario K2P 1C3
England & Wales
   Youth Hostels Association (☎ 01727-855215, ℮ customerservices@yha.org.uk), Trevelyan House, 8 St Stephen's Hill, St Alban's, Hertfordshire AL1 2DY

Ireland
An Oige, Irish Youth Hostel Association
(☎ 01-8304555, e anoige@iol.ie), 61 Mountjoy St, Dublin 7
New Zealand
Youth Hostels Association of New Zealand
(☎ 03-379 9970, e info@yha.org.nz), PO Box 436, 193 Cashel St, Third Floor, Union House, Christchurch
Northern Ireland
Youth Hostel Association of Northern Ireland
(☎ 2890-315435, e info@hini.org.uk), 22 Donegall Road, Belfast BT12 5JN
Scotland
Scottish Youth Hostels Association (☎ 0786-891400, e info@syha.org.uk), 7 Glebe Crescent, Stirling FK8 2JA
USA
Hostelling International – American Youth Hostels (☎ 202-783 6161, e hiayhserv@hiayh.org), 733 15th St NW, Suite 840, Washington, DC 20005

The four HI Copenhagen-area hostels are:

Copenhagen Bellahøj Hostel (Map 5, E1; ☎ 38 28 97 15, fax 38 89 02 10, e bella hoej@danhostel.dk, Herbergvejen 8, 2700 Brønshøj) in the quiet suburban neighbourhood of Bellahøj, 4km north-west of the city centre, is a cosy place. Rated three stars, it's open from 1 March to 15 January and has 250 beds costing 95kr in a dorm. There are a limited number of family rooms for 240kr a double. Facilities include a laundry room, guest kitchen, email access, lounge, TV room, table tennis and wheelchair accessibility. Breakfast and dinner are available, and there's a bakery and other eateries nearby. From Central Station take bus No 11 or from Rådhuspladsen take bus No 2-Brønshøj and get off at Fuglsangs Allé.

Copenhagen Amager Hostel (Map 1, F4; ☎ 32 52 29 08, fax 32 52 27 08, e copenhagen-amager@danhostel.dk, Vejlands Allé 200, 2300 Copenhagen S) is in an isolated part of Amager just off the E20, 5km from the city centre. This three-star facility is one of Europe's largest hostels with 528 beds in a series of low-rise wings containing cells of two- and five-bed rooms. It costs 90kr per person in a dorm. One thing that distinguishes Amager from other hostels is that it's relatively easy to

get a private room here; a double costs 240kr, a triple 310kr. There's a laundry room, guest kitchen, a setup for checking email and accessibility for people in wheelchairs. You may want to bring food supplies, as the hostel is a long haul from shops and restaurants if you're on foot; the hostel cafeteria serves breakfast and dinner. Copenhagen Amager is open 15 January to 30 November. Take the S-train to Sjælør station, then change to bus No 100S, which stops in front of the hostel. On weekdays until 5 pm, bus No 46 runs from Central Station directly to the hostel.

Ishøj Strand Vandrerhjem (Map 1, G1; ☎ 43 53 50 15, fax 43 53 50 45, e hotel@pilem.dk, Ishøj Strandvej 13, 2635 Ishøj) is a brand new five-star hostel in the seaside community of Ishøj, 15km south-west of central Copenhagen. It has 191 beds in 40 rooms; each room has its own toilet and bath. The cost is 100kr for a dorm bed, 325kr for a private single room, 350kr for a double and 450kr for a room that holds a family of five. Open year-round, the hostel has a restaurant which offers three meals a day, bicycle rental, online computers and wheelchair-accessible facilities. There's a beach with swimming and windsurfing possibilities just 1km away. Restaurants and a grocery store are within walking distance. The hostel is 800m east of Ishøj station, a stop on the S-train; the travel time from Copenhagen's Central Station is just 15 minutes if you take the E line, 20 minutes on the A line.

A similar distance from the centre of Copenhagen, but more remote, is *Lyngby Vandrerhjem* (Map 1, A4; ☎ 45 80 30 74, fax 45 80 30 32, Rådvad 1, 2800 Lyngby), which is nestled in a small hamlet at the northern side of Dyrehaven. This older, one-star hostel occupies a manorlike house that can accommodate 94 people, mostly in rooms with four to six beds. Open from 1 April to late October, it costs 95kr for a dorm bed, 240kr for a double; meals are available. The area is quite pretty, with swan-filled ponds, and it's within walking distance of the house where silversmith Georg Jensen was born in 1866; however, it's not a terribly practical place to make a base if your main focus is exploring central Copenhagen. If you don't have a car, travel time from Copenhagen takes at least an hour as it requires taking the S-train to Lyngby then catching a bus. Bus No 187 runs from the Lyngby S-train station to the hostel, but it's an infrequent weekday-only bus, so check the schedule in advance. Otherwise it's a 2km walk between the hostel and the nearest regularly serviced bus stop in Hjortekær.

Independent Hostels

Even when the HI hostels are full you can almost always find a bed at one of the city-sponsored or private hostels. Although the larger ones tend to be more of a crash-pad scene than the HI hostels, and standards can be pretty low, they're also more central, don't require hostel membership and do allow the use of sleeping bags.

Unlike HI hostels, which are year-round operations, most of the following hostels are summertime facilities set up to handle the influx of young budget travellers descending upon the city from June to August.

City Public Hostel (**Map 7, E1**; ☎ *33 31 20 70, fax 33 23 51 75, Absalonsgade 8, Vesterbro, 1658 Copenhagen V*) is an elementary place with 200 beds. There's one 68-bed dorm, but other rooms contain from six to 12 beds each. It's open from early May to mid-August, has 24-hour reception and costs 120kr per person. Breakfast is available for 20kr, there's a guest kitchen and you'll find some good, reasonably priced restaurants within a few blocks of the place. To get to City Public Hostel from Central Station, walk west along Vesterbrogade for about 10 minutes; it's less than 1km.

City-run *Sleep-In* (**Map 4, D6**; ☎ *35 26 50 59, fax 35 43 50 58,* [e] *copenhagen@ sleep-in.dk, Blegdamsvej 132A, 2100 Copenhagen Ø)* a few kilometres north of the city centre in the Østerbro district is open from late June to 31 August. This is Copenhagen's largest summer hostel with some 286 beds occupying a sports hall that's curtained off into 'rooms' with four to six beds; there are no doors, but the curtains offer a little privacy. A bed costs 80kr. This

well-run facility has free lockers, a guest kitchen and a cafe. You can use your own sleeping bag or rent bed linen for 30kr. Reception is open 24 hours. It's about a 15-minute ride from the city centre; take bus No 1, 6 or 14, get off at Trianglen and then walk 300m south-west on Blegdamsvej. You can also take night bus No 85N or 95N or take the S-train to Østerport station, from where the hostel is about a 1km walk to the north-west. A bakery, a grocery store and restaurants are within easy walking distance.

Sleep-In Green (**Map 4, G4**; ☎ *35 37 77 77, Ravnsborggade 18, 2200 Copenhagen N)* is in the Nørrebro area, close to cafes and the nightlife. Open from late May to late September, it has 68 dorm beds for 85kr. The place takes its name from its ecological orientation, and guests are welcome to help themselves to a healthy breakfast of organic fare for 30kr. Internet access is available. Take bus No 5 or 16, or walk north-west on Frederiksborggade over the canal.

Privately run *Sleep-In Heaven* (**Map 7, A1**; ☎ *35 35 46 48,* [e] *morefun@sleepin heaven.com, Struenseegade 7, 2200 Copenhagen N)* in the Nørrebro area and open year-round charges 100kr for one of its 76 beds in a basement dorm. There's no group kitchen, however, there are a number of cheap eating places which are within walking distance. Breakfast is available for 35kr, sheets for 20kr. Take bus No 8 to the Kapelvej stop.

The smallest operation, *YMCA Interpoint* (**Map 7, E1**; ☎ *33 31 15 74, Valdemarsgade 15, 1665 Copenhagen V)*, in the Vesterbro district, is open from the end of June to early August. There are only 28 dorm beds (80kr) in all, so it fills early; call ahead for reservations. Bedsheets (15kr) and breakfast (25kr) are available; there's no kitchen but there are plenty of affordable eating options nearby. Reception is open 8.30 to 11.30 am, 3.30 to 5.30 pm and 8 pm to 12.30 am. Guests have access to the YMCA gym. It's about a 15-minute walk from Central Station (take Vesterbrogade west to Valdemarsgade), or take bus No 6 or 16.

A fun alternative south-west of the city limits is the *Belægningen Avedørelejren*

(Map 1, F2; ☎ *36 77 90 84, fax 36 77 95 87,* e *info@belaegningen.dk, Avedøre Tværvej 10, 2650 Hvidovre)*, a new municipal-owned hostel in the renovated barracks of a former military camp. Staff are friendly, the standards are high and cosy rooms with just a few beds have clean linen and towels included in the rate. Dorm beds cost 100kr, singles 250kr and doubles 350kr. Breakfast is available for 40kr at the complex's restaurant and the hostel offers free Internet access, cheap bicycle rentals and a group kitchen. There are good cycling options nearby, including Vestvolden, a tree-lined bike path leading to central Copenhagen. As an added perk you just might spot some of Denmark's hottest screen stars, as the camp's rear buildings have been turned into a Danish 'Hollywood' housing the country's main movie companies. The hostel's reception is open 7 am to 1 pm and 3.30 to 11 pm. There's a grocery store, bakery and cheap eateries 1km away. From Central Station it's a 20-minute ride (get off at Avedøre School) on bus No 650S, which runs at least three times an hour until midnight.

Also see *Hotel Jørgensen*, which offers dorm beds year-round, in Nørreport & Around under Hotels later in this chapter.

Private Rooms

The accommodation counter at the city tourist office, *Wonderful Copenhagen* (☎ *70 22 24 42, Bernstorffsgade 1, 1630 Copenhagen V)*, north of Central Station, books rooms in private homes. Singles cost from 200kr to 250kr, doubles from 300kr to 350kr. There's a 50kr fee per booking. The counter is open 9 am to 8 pm Monday to Saturday and 10 am to 8 pm Sunday from 1 May to 31 August; it's also open 9 am to 4.30 pm weekdays and 9 am to 1.30 pm Saturday the rest of the year.

Use It (☎ *33 73 06 20, Rådhusstræde 13, 1466 Copenhagen K)* books rooms in private homes, costing from 150kr to 200kr for singles and from 225kr to 300kr for doubles. There's no booking fee. It's open 9 am to 7 pm daily from mid-June to mid-September, and 11 am to 4 pm (to 2 pm Friday) weekdays the rest of the year.

Dossing Down in Denmark

Here are some words you'll come across on hotel and hostel brochures:

værelse room
enkeltværelse single room
dobbeltværelse double room
eget bad og toilet with shower and toilet
bad og toilet på gangen shower and toilet in the hallway
morgenmad inkl i prisen breakfast included in the price
senge; køjsenge beds; bunk beds
med opredning with extra bed
lejlighed flat, apartment
adgang til køkken access to kitchen
vaskemaskine og tørretumbler washing machine and tumbler drier

---

Dansk Bed & Breakfast (☎ *39 61 04 05, Bernstorffsvej 71A, 2900 Hellerup)* handles 300 homes throughout Denmark, offering private rooms from around 200/300kr for singles/doubles. Its members include some homes in the greater Copenhagen area that each have a room or two for rent. It will make the bookings for you or you can order a brochure (90kr) listing the homes and book them directly yourself. Dansk Bed & Breakfast has a Web site at www.bbdk.dk.

Hotels

It's a bit of a stretch to use the term 'budget' and 'hotel' in the same sentence for Copenhagen. It's an expensive city for hotel owners to do business in, and that's reflected in the cost at all hotels. Curiously, the price difference between places categorised here as Budget and many of those in the Mid-Range section isn't all that great, so travellers on a flexible budget may want to look at the listings in both sections. The following listings are for places that have double rooms for 600kr or less year-round.

Vesterbro The four hotels that follow are all within walking distance of Central Station. Turisthotellet, Saga and Selandia are closest to the station but also in the dingier part of Vesterbro. Løven, on the other hand, is a farther walk from the station but in a good, ethnically diverse neighbourhood.

The cheapest place, **Turisthotellet** (**Map 7, E3**; ☎ *33 22 98 39, Reverdilsgade 5, 1701 Copenhagen V*), is very basic with a handful of small, shabby rooms. Despite the term 'hotel' there's no front desk or hotel amenities – it's more like a run-down boarding house. The rates posted in the window are from 200/300kr for singles/doubles with shared bath, but the quoted rates are often higher.

Løven (**Map 7, E2**; ☎ *21 80 67 20, fax 33 15 86 46, Vesterbrogade 30, 1620 Copenhagen V*) is a new place that rates as one of the city's best deals. The building, which for decades was leased exclusively to a Jutland business group to use as accommodation when it had work in Copenhagen, is now a mix of renovated guestrooms and spacious flats. While it's not fancy, there are lots of pleasant touches such as natural wood floors and the manager is adding soundproof glass to compensate for the busy streetside location. A room with shared bath and access to a guest kitchen costs 350/450kr for singles/doubles, though lower rates are sometimes available. There are also flats with full facilities for 550kr a double (for more details see Serviced Apartments later in this chapter). Breakfast is available for 40kr and a bakery and cheap Turkish restaurants are just outside the front door.

Saga Hotel (**Map 7, E3**; ☎ *33 24 49 44, fax 33 24 60 33,* e *booking@sagahotel.dk, Colbjørnsensgade 18, 1652 Copenhagen V*) has 76 rooms, most of which have been renovated. There's no lift and it's multistorey, so you may have to climb some stairs, but the minimalist approach to lobby amenities helps keep the rates relatively low. The rooms are straightforward, but they are tidy and have a phone and TV. In the summer, singles/doubles cost 420/580kr with shared bath, 625/850kr with private bath; the rest of the year rates begin at 380/480kr with shared bath, 480/580kr with private bath.

Selandia Hotel (**Map 7, E2**; ☎ *33 31 46 10, fax 33 31 46 09,* e *hotel-selandia @city.dk, Helgolandsgade 12, 1653 Copen-*

hagen V) has 84 rooms, each with a desk, sink and TV. Cheapest are the 27 rooms with shared bath costing 500/600kr in summer, 450/540kr in winter. Rooms with private bath start at 725/900kr in summer, 640/740kr in winter. Inquire about the 10% discount for Internet bookings and the unpublished weekend specials. The hotel has a Web site at www.hotel-selandia.dk.

Nyhavn The Nyhavn canal area is a fun part of the city to be in, particularly in summer when it's lined with pavement cafes and colourful sailing boats. The following hotel is right on the canal and makes a great budget option.

Sømandshjemmet Bethel (**Map 7, C7**; ☎ *33 13 03 70, fax 33 15 85 70, Nyhavn 22, 1051 Copenhagen K)* calls itself a seamen's hotel but is open to all. This cosy little place has a nice location, a lift to all floors, and two dozen good-sized rooms with an eclectic variety of furnishings. All have TV and those with private bath also have a phone. Many also have unbeatable views of Nyhavn – for the best, ask for a corner room, well worth the extra 150kr. Singles/doubles cost 395/495kr with shared bath and start at 495/595kr with private bath.

Nørreport & Around The Nørreport area, which extends westward from Nørreport station, is a bit of an alternative community with the city's main flea market and its two gay-oriented hotels.

Hotel Jørgensen (**Map 7, B3**; ☎ *33 13 81 86, fax 33 15 51 05,* e *hotel@post12 .tele.dk, Rømersgade 11, 1362 Copenhagen K)* is popular with gay travellers but open to all. Simple singles/doubles with shared bath and cable TV cost 425/525kr. The hotel also has 13 dorm rooms with 150 beds at 115kr. Rates for both the dorms and private rooms include breakfast. There are lockers for dorm guests and a coin laundry is just metres away. Hotel Jørgensen is within easy walking distance of Nørreport station and a variety of eating options. It has a Web site at www.hoteljorgensen.dk.

One block to the east is **Hotel Windsor** (**Map 7, B4**; ☎ *33 11 08 30, fax 33 11 63 87,*

[e] *hotelwindsor@inet.uni-c.dk, Frederiksborggade 30, 1360 Copenhagen K)*, an exclusively gay hotel in an older building opposite Israels Plads. The hotel's two dozen rooms are straightforward and a bit worn but all have TV and some have VCRs and refrigerators. Singles/doubles cost 450/600kr.

Frederiksberg This sizable area begins at the west side of the city lake Sankt Jørgens Sø and extends several kilometres west. The hotels that follow are at the east side of Frederiksberg, within walking distance of central Copenhagen.

*Hotel Euroglobe (*Map 7, C1; *☎/fax 33 79 79 54,* [e] *discount@hoteleuroglobe.dk, Niels Ebbesens Vej 20, 1911 Frederiksberg C)*, which has 28 budget rooms, is in an old building that's been splashed with a fresh coat of paint. Rooms are basic, with two beds, an end table and a washbasin; bathrooms are shared. Singles/doubles cost 350/450kr. Hotel Euroglobe is about a 20-minute walk from Central Station, or take bus No 3 or 29, which stop a few blocks away.

Modern *Cab-Inn Scandinavia (*Map 7, B2; *☎ 35 36 11 11, fax 35 36 11 14,* [e] *cab-inn@cab-inn.dk, Vodroffsvej 57, 1900 Frederiksberg C)* has 201 sleekly compact rooms that resemble cabins in a cruise ship, complete with upper and lower bunks. Although small, the rooms are otherwise comfortable and have cable TV, phone, complimentary tea and a bathroom. Singles/doubles cost 475/585kr; basement parking is available for 45kr a day. Breakfast is not included in the room rate, but it is available in the hotel cafe for an extra 45kr.

A few blocks to the south-west is the 86-room *Cab-Inn Copenhagen (*Map 7, C1; *☎ 33 21 04 00, fax 33 21 74 09, Danasvej 32, 1900 Frederiksberg C)*, which has the same type of rooms and the same rates as Cab-Inn Scandinavia. Both hotels have rooms that are accessible to people in wheelchairs and are about a 20-minute walk from Rådhuspladsen.

*Hotel Sankt Jørgen (*Map 7, B1; *☎ 35 37 15 11, fax 35 37 11 97,* [e] *st.jorgen@ teliamail.dk, Julius Thomsens Gade 22, 1632 Copenhagen V)* is family-run and

Green Dreams

Ecology-minded Denmark has instituted a system known as Den Grønne Nøgle, or the Green Key, to acknowledge environmentally friendly hotels and hostels.

Numerous criteria must be fulfilled for a place to be awarded the Green Key. These include limiting water consumption by using water-saving shower heads, using low-energy light bulbs and ecology-friendly detergents, recycling wastes, having smoke-free rooms and serving at least two organic products at breakfast.

Places that qualify for the Green Key display a special logo that looks like a smiling green-coloured key standing on end.

pleasantly old-fashioned. There are 19 spacious doubles for 600kr and two rather cramped singles for 500kr. If space is available, single travellers are usually given a double room at the single price. Most rooms have three to six beds, so they can easily accommodate families – add 150kr for each person beyond two. Some rooms have TV and refrigerator, others don't, so if either are important to you request them when you book. All bathrooms are shared. It's about a 20-minute walk from the centre.

Airport The *Transithal-hotel (*☎ *32 31 24 55, fax 32 31 31 09)*, in the basement of the airport's international terminal, has simple rooms with private facilities geared for those in transit. Singles/doubles cost 255/360kr for a four-hour stay, 360/530kr for an eight-hour stay, 540/755kr for up to 12 hours.

PLACES TO STAY – MID-RANGE

The hotels that comprise the mid-range section have standard rates for double rooms priced between 600kr and 1200kr.

Vesterbro

This area at the western side of Central Station has a convenient central location and most of the city's mid-range accommodation.

*Missionshotellet Nebo (*Map 7, E3; *☎ 33 21 12 17, fax 33 23 47 74,* [e] *nebo@email.dk,*

Istedgade 6, 1650 Copenhagen V) is very convenient, a mere stone's throw from Central Station. The 96 rooms are small but perfectly adequate with a sink, TV and phone, and the common areas include large, clean showers. In summer, singles/doubles cost 450/650kr with shared bath, 850/890kr with private bath; winter rates are 400/510kr with shared bath, 640/700kr with private bath. The hotel has a Web site at www.nebo.dk.

At 253-room *Absalon Hotel (*Map 7, E3*; ☎ 33 24 22 11, fax 33 24 34 11, ⓔ info@ absalon-hotel.dk, Helgolandsgade 15, 1653 Copenhagen V)* the cheaper rooms are in a separate annex that has less sparkle than the rest of the hotel. Some of these annex rooms are quite large and have TV and a sink; all have shared baths and cost 450/600kr for singles/doubles in summer, 400/500kr in winter. The pricier rooms in the main hotel are pleasant with private baths and full amenities, and cost 825/1050kr in summer, 690/790kr in winter. The hotel has a Web site at www.absalon-hotel.dk.

*Copenhagen Triton Hotel (*Map 7, E3*; ☎ 33 31 32 66, fax 33 31 69 70, Helgolandsgade 7-11, 1653 Copenhagen V)* has 123 rooms with faded Scandinavian decor. The rooms have TV, phone, minibar, desk and private bath. One plus – the rear rooms face a courtyard and are quieter than most in this bustling neighbourhood. Its singles/doubles cost 695/795kr on weekdays, 595/695kr at weekends, but there are sometimes specials that cut the weekend rate by about 100kr. The hotel is scheduled for an overdue renovation and is in the process of becoming an affiliate of the French hotel chain Accor, in its Ibis category of economy-priced properties.

*Hotel Hebron (*Map 7, E2*; ☎ 33 31 69 06, fax 33 31 90 67, ⓔ tophotel@hebron.dk, Helgolandsgade 4, 1653 Copenhagen V)* is a quiet hotel with 100 cosy, renovated rooms, each with a desk, TV and phone. Singles/doubles with private bath cost 680/880kr. The hotel also has roomier suites which cost 1040/1220kr for two/three people. The hotel has a Web site at www.hebron.dk.

*Tiffany (*Map 7, E3*; ☎ 33 21 80 50, fax 33 21 87 50, ⓔ tiffany@hotel-tiffany.dk,*

Colbjørnsensgade 28, 1652 Copenhagen V) is a pleasant little all-suite hotel. The 24 rooms each have a TV, a phone, a trouser press, a private bath and a kitchenette with refrigerator and microwave oven. Singles/doubles cost 645/795kr in winter, 795/945kr in summer. A buffet breakfast is not included, but coffee, tea and fresh pastries are available each morning. The hotel has a Web site at www.hotel-tiffany.dk.

*Savoy Hotel (*Map 7, E2*; ☎ 33 26 75 00, fax 33 26 75 01, Vesterbrogade 34, 1620 Copenhagen V)* is a century-old hotel that's recently been renovated but still retains some of its period character and Art Nouveau decor. Although the hotel fronts a busy road, all of its 66 rooms face a quiet courtyard. Each room has cable TV, a minibar, coffee maker and private bath. Standard singles/doubles cost 945/1095kr, while suites are priced from 1495kr.

*DGI-byen Hotel (*Map 7, E3*; ☎ 33 29 80 50, fax 33 29 80 59, ⓔ hotel@dgi.dk, Tietgensgade 65, 1704 Copenhagen V)* is part of a new sports complex 200m south of Central Station. The hotel consists of 104 rooms on three storeys of the complex. The rooms have modern Scandinavian decor with blond hardwood floors and sleek but sparse furnishings. Rates for standard rooms with TV and private bath are 1195/1395kr on weekdays and 795/895kr at weekends. For 100kr more you can opt for a superior room, which is slightly larger and has a bathtub rather than a shower. There's Internet access via the TV in all rooms plus ISDN links for those travelling with their own laptops. Hotel guests have complimentary access to the complex's oversized swimming pool.

Nyhavn

The Nyhavn area has much to offer visitors, including a lively cafe scene and proximity to central sights.

*Sophie Amalie Hotel (*Map 7, B7*; ☎ 33 13 34 00, fax 33 11 77 07, ⓔ anglehot@ remmen.dk, Sankt Annæ Plads 21, 1021 Copenhagen K)* is popular with business travellers. The 134 rooms are modern and each has the standard amenities, including a desk, minibar, cable TV and private bath.

Regular singles/doubles cost 700/1000kr. Much more interesting are the 6th floor split-level suites with harbour views; each has a living room with a sofa bed on the lower level and a loft bedroom above, and costs 1395kr for two people, 100kr more for a third or fourth person. An optional breakfast costs an extra 95kr per person. There's a 10% discount for payment by cash or travellers cheque. The hotel has a Web site at www.remmen.dk.

Hotel City (**Map 7, C7**; ☎ *33 13 06 66, fax 33 13 06 67, Peder Skramsgade 24, 1054 Copenhagen K*) is a relatively small hotel with 81 pleasant rooms, each with cable TV, phone, trouser press and private bath. Most contain two single beds, placed side by side. The regular rates for singles/doubles are 895/1095kr. The hotel, which is a Best Western affiliate, also has a more tempting weekend rate of 725kr but it's only available in winter. About a five-minute walk from the hydrofoil docks, Hotel City is convenient for visitors travelling by boat to Malmö or Bornholm.

Copenhagen Strand (**Map 7, C7**; ☎ *33 48 99 00, fax 33 48 99 01,* **e** *copenhagen strand@arp-hansen.dk, Havnegade 37, 1958 Copenhagen K*) is a new mid-range hotel overlooking Copenhagen Harbour. The 174 rooms, which have a maritime decor, are equipped with cable TV, minibar and private bath, and cost from 995/1195kr for singles/ doubles. Nonsmoking rooms are available. There's an onsite business centre and a lobby bar. The hotel has a Web site at www.copenhagenstrand.dk.

Hotel Maritime (**Map 7, C7**; ☎ *33 13 48 82, fax 33 15 03 45,* **e** *hotel@maritime.dk, Peder Skramsgade 19, 1054 Copenhagen K*) has 64 rooms that are on the small side, but otherwise adequate, with TV, phone and private bath. The standard rate for singles/ doubles is a pricey 950/1250kr, but you can sometimes get rooms for around half that rate at the airport or tourist office roombooking services.

Nørreport & Around

Both of the hotels that follow are about a 10-minute walk west of Nørreport station

in a quiet neighbourhood, close to the city lakes.

Ibsens Hotel (**Map 7, B3**; ☎ *33 13 19 13, fax 33 13 19 16,* **e** *hotel@ibsenshotel.dk, Vendersgade 23, 1363 Copenhagen K*) has 103 rooms spread across four floors of a renovated period building. The place has the character of a 'boutique hotel' with creative decor and no two rooms looking exactly the same. Some rooms have contemporary Scandinavian design, others are furnished with antiques but all boast a comfortable bed, TV and private bath. Singles/doubles cost from 845/1050kr and there are also suites with kitchenettes for 1900kr. The hotel has a Web site at www.ibsenshotel.dk.

Hotel Kong Arthur (**Map 7, A3**; ☎ *33 11 12 12, fax 33 32 61 30,* **e** *hotel@kong arthur.dk, Nørre Søgade 11, 1370 Copenhagen K*) is a 107-room establishment in an attractive 19th-century building that fronts the lake Peblinge Sø. Room amenities include TV, minibar, trouser presses and newly renovated bathrooms. Standard rates for singles/doubles are 1055/1280kr, but if you book online there's a discount of around 10%. The hotel's Web site is located at www.kongarthur.dk.

Amalienborg & Kastellet Area

The residents of this upmarket section of the city centre include the royal family.

The 117-room *Hotel Esplanaden* (**Map 7, A7**; ☎ *33 48 10 00, fax 33 48 10 66, Bredgade 78, 1260 Copenhagen K*), a Choice Hotels affiliate, is a sister hotel to the top-end Neptun Hotel. Located opposite Churchillparken, Hotel Esplanaden is a nice choice for those who want to be near green space but still close to central sights. The hotel is a pleasant, older place offering modernised rooms with private bath, TV and a phone with voice mail. Its singles/ doubles cost 830/1100kr, but there's a special 750kr rate that's available when things are slow.

PLACES TO STAY – TOP END

In this section you'll find Copenhagen's pricier hotels, where the standard weekday rates for a double cost upwards of 1200kr.

PLACES TO STAY

Naturally in this category you can always count on all the rooms including private bathrooms.

Vesterbro

The places that follow are all within a short walk of Central Station on the northern extreme of Vesterbro and well outside the red-light district that embraces most mid-range Vesterbro hotels.

*Grand Hotel (*Map 7, D3*; ☎ 33 27 69 00, fax 33 27 69 01,* e *grandhotel@arp-han sen.dk, Vesterbrogade 9, 1620 Copenhagen V)* is conveniently located just north of Central Station. This pleasant 100-year-old hotel has 160 rooms, each with desk, minibar, TV and phone. Nonsmoking rooms are available. Standard singles/doubles start at 1125/1460kr, but there are various discount schemes and you can sometimes get a steeply reduced last-minute price through the tourist office's room-booking counter. There's a bar and restaurant on site. The hotel has a Web site at www.grandhotelco penhagen.dk.

Despite its rather nondescript facade, *Hotel Imperial (*Map 7, D2*; ☎ 33 12 80 00, fax 33 93 80 31,* e *imperial@imperialho tel.dk, Vester Farimagsgade 9, 1606 Copenhagen V)* opposite the Vesterport S-train station has one of the best reputations for service among Copenhagen's top-end establishments. Each of the 163 rooms has modern decor with a desk, phone, cable TV, minibar and a deep Japanese-style bathtub. Standard singles/doubles start at 1355/1775kr, but discounted Scan+ Hotel Pass rates of 765/970kr are offered at weekends year-round and daily in summer. The hotel has a Web site at www.imperialhotel.dk.

First Hotel Vesterbro Copenhagen (Map 7, E2*; ☎ 33 78 80 00, fax 33 78 80 80,* e *info@firsthotels.se, Vesterbrogade 23, 1620 Copenhagen V)* is a new 403-room hotel catering to high-end travellers. It has a smart Scandinavian decor that's elegant yet low keyed. The rooms are allergen free with wood floors instead of carpeting and fully half of them are set aside for nonsmokers. All are equipped with the latest amenities including voice mail, an

ISDN outlet, and Internet access via the TV; they also have minibars, room safes, air-conditioning and trouser presses. There's a bar, a restaurant and a business centre. Singles/doubles cost 1648/1898kr on weekdays, but at weekends they drop to a reasonable 948/1148kr.

The 472-room *Scandic Hotel Copenhagen (*Map 7, D2*; ☎ 33 14 35 35, fax 33 32 12 23, Vester Søgade 6, 1601 Copenhagen V)* near the Tycho Brahe Planetarium is a well-regarded chain hotel with all the expected facilities, including a health club, a concierge and secretarial services. Regular rates begin around 1200/1700kr for singles/doubles, but there are often cheaper promotional deals available.

*Radisson SAS Royal Hotel (*Map 7, D3*; ☎ 33 42 60 00, fax 33 42 61 00, Hammerichsgade 1, 1611 Copenhagen V)* is a centrally located, 265-room, multistorey hotel that's popular with well-to-do business travellers and visiting dignitaries. Rooms are modern with full amenities. The hotel has computer work stations with Internet access, restaurants and a fitness centre. Nonsmoking rooms are available. Singles/doubles cost 2050/2350kr, but discount schemes are numerous, including a weekend rate of 1190/1390kr, and half-price discounts for seniors aged 65 or older. In addition to the rooms, there are fancy suites costing upwards of 7000kr.

Rådhuspladsen

The area around Rådhuspladsen, the central city square, is a convenient place to be based, as it's near the head of Strøget and within a short walk of some of the city's leading sights.

*Ascot Hotel (*Map 7, D3*; ☎ 33 12 60 00, fax 33 14 60 40,* e *hotel@ascot-hotel.dk, Studiestræde 61, 1554 Copenhagen V)* occupies a former bathhouse erected 100 years ago by the same architect who designed Copenhagen's city hall. The lobby boasts some interesting bas-reliefs depicting scenes from the bathhouse days. Most of the 155 rooms are large, each has a deep soaking tub in the bathroom, and some have a kitchen. Singles/doubles start at 1090/1390kr, though that rate drops to 635/820kr at weekends and in summer if you have a Scan+ Hotel Pass. Free parking is provided for guests.

Hotel Kong Frederik (Map 8, F1; ☎ 33 12 59 02, fax 33 93 59 01, e anglehot@ remmen.dk, Vester Voldgade 25, 1552 Copenhagen V) is a classic hotel with a solidly historic character including dark woods, antique furnishings and paintings of Danish royalty. Recently renovated, the 110 rooms are poshly comfortable and each has a TV, phone, minibar and hairdryer. Singles/ doubles start at 1220/1320kr; breakfast costs an extra 105kr per person. The hotel has a Web site at www.remmen.dk.

Palace Hotel (Map 8, G2; ☎ 33 14 40 50, fax 33 14 52 79, e booking@princi- pal.dk, Rådhuspladsen 57, 1550 Copen- hagen V) is in a picturesque period building overlooking Rådhuspladsen. The 162 rooms are spacious, each with a TV, phone, room safe, minibar and desk. The decor is old-fashioned, with upholstered chairs, heavy curtains and brass lamps. It'd be a pleasant place to stay if the price was right, and when things are slow the rate can be discounted by as much as 50% for last- minute customers. The regular rates for singles/doubles begin at 1525/1725kr.

Nyhavn & Around

The Nyhavn area is a trendy location with some of the city's top hotels and a good proximity to some fine restaurants as well.

Hotel Opera (Map 7, C6; ☎ 33 47 83 00, fax 33 47 83 01, e hotelopera@arp-hansen .dk, Tordenskjoldsgade 15, 1055 Copen- hagen K), just south of Det Kongelige Teater, has an inviting old-world character befitting its theatre district location. Although it's not as fancy as other top-end period hotels, the rates are a bit lower and the 91 rooms are pleasant, each with phone and TV. Singles/ doubles begin at 990/1390kr; weekend rates are 850/1115kr. The hotel has a Web site at www.operahotelcopenhagen.dk.

For nautical atmosphere, it's hard to beat **Copenhagen Admiral Hotel** (Map 7, B7; ☎ 33 74 14 16, fax 33 74 14 15, e admiral@ admiral-hotel.dk, Toldbodgade 24-28, 1253 Copenhagen K) on the waterfront between Nyhavn and Amalienborg Slot. The hotel oc- cupies a renovated 18th-century granary and is replete with brick archways and sturdy old beams of Pomeranian pine. Each of the 366 rooms has a nice blend of period charm and modern conveniences, including a TV, a desk and a bathroom with bidet. The junior suites are split level, with a queen-size bed in the loft and a sitting area with a sofa bed below. The hotel has a sauna, a solarium and a restaurant. Regular singles/doubles cost 985/1195kr, or for 100kr more you can opt for a harbourview room. Junior suites cost 1415kr for two people, 1495kr for three. Breakfast costs an extra 95kr.

71 Nyhavn Hotel (Map 7, C7; ☎ 33 43 62 00, fax 33 43 62 01, e 71nyhavnho tel@arp-hansen.dk, Nyhavn 71, 1051 Copenhagen K) has 82 rooms in a reno- vated 200-year-old harbourside warehouse. It too has incorporated some of the build- ing's period features and standard singles/ doubles cost 1250/1495kr, superior rooms with views cost 1350/1695kr and waterfront corner suites with great views of both the harbour and Nyhavn canal cost 2995kr. Weekend rates begin at 1065/1270kr. The hotel has a Web site at www.71nyhavnho telcopenhagen.dk.

Neptun Hotel (Map 7, B7; ☎ 33 96 20 00, fax 33 96 20 97, e info@neptun-group.dk, Sankt Annæ Plads 18, 1250 Copenhagen K) is a well-regarded 1st class hotel a block north of Nyhavn. Each of the 122 rooms and 12 suites has TV, phone, an electronic room safe, a minibar and a trouser press. Regular singles/doubles start at 1385/1490kr, but there's a weekend and summer special of 1125kr for a room sleeping up to two adults and two children. The Neptun is an affiliate of Choice Hotels.

Phoenix (Map 7, B7; ☎ 33 95 95 00, fax 33 33 98 33, e phoenixcopenhagen@arp- hansen.dk, Bredgade 37, 1260 Copenhagen K), a block north of Nyhavn, is one of the city's more fastidious deluxe hotels. The 212 plush rooms have heavy carpets, upholstered chairs, chandeliers and the like. There's a restaurant and pub on site. Singles/doubles start at 1290/1650kr on weekdays, 950/ 1250kr at weekends. The roomy junior suites have jacuzzi bathtubs and cost 3000kr on weekdays, 2150kr at weekends. The hotel's Web site is at www.phoenixcopenhagen.dk.

Visiting celebrities often opt for the exclusive *Hotel d'Angleterre* (**Map 8, C9**; ☎ 33 12 00 95, fax 33 12 11 18, e angle hot@remmen.dk, Kongens Nytorv 34, 1050 Copenhagen K), which has chandeliers, marble floors and a history dating back to the 17th century. It also has Copenhagen's highest rates, starting at 1955/2295kr for singles/doubles and reaching 12,995kr for a two-bedroom royal suite. And breakfast is an extra 125kr per person. Despite its lengthy history, the hotel no longer enjoys the solidly pre-eminent reputation it once had among Copenhagen's top hotels.

Frederiksberg

Frederiksberg is generally more residential than central Copenhagen but it does have the following top-end hotel.

The 166-room *Radisson SAS Falconer Hotel* (**Map 6, C3**; ☎ 38 15 80 01, fax 38 15 80 02, Falkoner Allé 9, 2000 Frederiksberg) is situated west of Copenhagen's centre near the Frederiksberg S-train station. The hotel, which is a popular convention spot, has a large banquet hall, a health club, a restaurant and a bar. Some rooms have been specially adapted for disabled people and all have modern amenities like TVs, minibars, hairdryers and trouser presses. Nonsmoking rooms are available. Singles/doubles cost 1400/1750kr, but there's a 50% discount for seniors year-round and a similarly discounted summer family rate.

Amager & the Airport

Most people staying in the Amager do so for convenience to the airport.

Radisson SAS Scandinavia Hotel (**Map 7, F6**; ☎ 33 96 50 00, fax 33 96 55 00, Amager Blvd 70, 2300 Copenhagen S) is in a high-rise building in the northern part of Amager. It offers free parking, services for business travellers, a pool and fitness centre, squash courts, several restaurants, a bar and Copenhagen's only casino. Its 542 rooms, which have full 1st class amenities, typically

cost 1750kr a double, but there's a weekend rate of 1300kr and various other discounts.

The 197-room *Radisson SAS Globetrotter Hotel* (**Map 1, F5**; ☎ 32 87 02 02, fax 32 87 02 20, 171 Engvej, 2300 Copenhagen S) in a rather nondistinct area just 2km north of the airport is popular with airline personnel and others in transit. There are services for business travellers, a restaurant and bar, a swimming pool and a fitness centre. Its singles/doubles cost 1350/1650kr, but ask about discount schemes when you book.

Nearing completion is the new four-star *Hilton Copenhagen Airport* (**Map 1, F5**; ☎ 32 50 15 01, fax 32 52 85 28, Ellehammersvej 20, 2770 Kastrup) located beside the airport rail terminal. The hotel will have 375 rooms, a fitness centre, a swimming pool, conference facilities and the expected amenities when it opens in 2001.

LONG-TERM RENTALS
Finding a Flat

The housing market in Copenhagen is a tight one and landing a long-term flat rental at a reasonable price can be a challenge. Prices vary according to the condition of the flat, the neighbourhood and its proximity to the city centre, but generally begin around 3500kr a month for a small flat with a kitchen, bath and separate bedroom.

Good places to look for listings are in the classified sections of Copenhagen's main newspapers, *Politiken* and *Berlingske Tidende*; in both papers the greatest number of listings appear in the Sunday editions. Another good source is *Den Blå Avis*, which comes out twice weekly, on Monday and Thursday, and has lengthy listings. All three of these papers are in Danish only, so if you don't read Danish you'll need to get a friend to help with the translations. You can also look in the classified section of *The Copenhagen Post*, which is in English and published on Friday, but the apartment listings there are usually quite meagre.

Another source, particularly if you're looking for a place for less than six months, is to stop by Use It, Rådhusstræde 13, which maintains files on places available for subleasing.

Serviced Apartments

Apartments can be a good deal, especially for those who want to cut expenses by preparing their own meals rather than frequenting restaurants. They can be anything from a one-room setup with a microwave, refrigerator and hotplate to a commodious flat with a fully equipped kitchen, a living room with stereo and cable TV and a bedroom or two.

In recent years a couple of Copenhagen businesses have surfaced that specialise in arranging apartment rentals for visitors. Some of these rentals are places that have been set aside permanently for this purpose, but many others, including the ones that tend to be more economically priced, are people's private flats that they put up for hire while they're away on travels of their own. So curiously, by staying in one of these flats you might not only be landing a good deal for yourself, but may also be helping travelling Danes subsidise their journeys! The first two businesses that follow specialise in such places and generally have more units available in summer, as that's the peak time for Danes to be away on holiday.

Hay-4-You (☎ *33 33 08 05,* [e] *hay4you@ cool.dk, Vimmelskaftet 49, 1161 Copenhagen K)* has a pool of about 120 units and some of the best prices. Summer rates for small apartments start around 350kr a day, with a three-day minimum, or from 2000kr a week. The rest of the year rates can be as low as 275/1500kr a day/week. Prices include sheets, towels and utilities. Hay-4-You has a Web site at www.scanhomes.com.

Let A Flat (☎ *33 25 61 12,* [e] *letaflat@ worldonline.dk, Valdemarsgade 57, 1665 Copenhagen V)* is a similar but much smaller operation that handles about a dozen apartments. A typical unit is a one-bedroom flat with a small kitchen that can accommodate two to three people for 400kr a day. There's a minimum stay of five to seven days.

Løven (**Map 7, E2**; ☎ *21 80 67 20, fax 33 15 86 46, Vesterbrogade 30, 1620 Copenhagen V)* has a dozen well-equipped flats with kitchens, private bath and cable TV at its main Vesterbro location and another eight units in the Latin Quarter. These are rented on a daily basis for 550kr a double, or 225kr per person for larger groups; there may be some price flexibility for longer-term stays – particularly in the off-season.

Citilet Apartments (☎ *33 25 21 29, fax 33 91 30 77,* [e] *citilet@citilet.dk, Fortunstræde 4, 1065 Copenhagen K)* specialises in top-end places that are clustered in a couple of buildings right in the city centre. It's a fixed group of apartments and functions like a hotel in some ways, with daily cleaning service and breakfast included in the rates. Studio units cost 950/6500kr a day/week and one-bedroom apartments average 1300/ 8500kr a day/week.

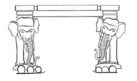

Places to Eat

FOOD

Copenhagen offers plenty of good dining options for every budget. The selections are varied. You can find old-fashioned Danish pubs with meat and potatoes grub; trendy cafes serving a blend of Danish food spiced with Asian influences; and fancy restaurants offering authentic international cuisines.

Generally the most prominent top-end restaurants feature what's dubbed 'Danish-French' cuisine, a creative fusion combining the flavourful sauces that signature French fare with the addition of fresh Danish vegetables and seafood that aren't typical in traditional French recipes.

Shoring up the mid-range category are the traditional Danish restaurants offering items such as *smørrebrød* (literally buttered bread), herring specialities and other seafood and meat dishes.

Among the cheapest places to eat well are those specialising in Mediterranean buffets and the numerous Italian restaurants that serve the standard pizza-and-pasta fare. Simple Greek eateries selling inexpensive *shawarma*, a filling pitta-bread sandwich of shaved meat, are a favourite alternative to generic fast food. You can also find a cheap, if not particularly healthy, munch at one of the ubiquitous *pølsemandens*, the wheeled carts that sell a variety of hot dogs and sausages.

Two common terms you'll find on menu cards are *dagens ret*, which means 'daily special' and is typically the best deal on the menu, and *børnemenu*, which means children's menu.

Danish Cuisine

Nothing epitomises Danish food more than smørrebrød, an open-faced sandwich that ranges from very basic fare to elaborate sculpture-like creations. Typically it's a slice of rye bread topped with either roast beef, tiny shrimps, roast pork or fish fillet and finished off with a variety of garnishes.

Although smørrebrød is served in most restaurants at lunch time, it's cheapest at bakeries or at specialised smørrebrød take-away shops found near train stations and office buildings.

Also distinctively Danish is the *koldt bord* (literally cold table), a buffet-style spread of cold foods, including salads, cold cuts, smoked fish, cheeses, vegetables, condiments, breads and crackers, and usually a few hot dishes such as meatballs and fried fish. The cornerstone of the cold table is herring, which comes in pickled, marinated and salted versions.

An abbreviated version of the koldt bord, with the addition of cereals and fruit, is served as a complimentary breakfast at most hotels.

Danish cuisine relies heavily on fish, meat and potatoes. The following are some of the more popular Danish dishes:

flæskesteg – roast pork, usually with crackling and served with potatoes and cabbage

frikadeller – fried ground-pork meatballs, commonly served with boiled potatoes and red cabbage

fyldt hvidkålshoved – ground beef wrapped in cabbage leaves

gravad laks – cured or salted salmon marinated in dill and served with a sweet mustard sauce

hakkebøf – a ground-beef burger that's usually covered with fried onions and served with boiled potatoes, brown sauce and beets

hvid labskovs – Danish stew made of square cuts of beef boiled with potatoes, bay leaves and pepper

kogt torsk – poached cod, usually in a mustard sauce and served with boiled potatoes

mørbradbøf – small pork fillets, commonly in a mushroom sauce

stegt flæsk – crisp-fried pork slices, generally served with potatoes and a parsley sauce

stegt rødspætte – fried, breaded plaice, usually served with parsley potatoes

DRINKS

In terms of beer, the locally brewed Carlsberg and Tuborg labels are the undisputed hometown favourites in Copenhagen. Beer *(øl)* can be ordered as draught beer *(fadøl)*, lager *(pilsner)*, light beer *(lyst øl)*, dark lager *(lagerøl)* or stout *(porter)*.

The most popular spirit in Denmark is the Aalborg-produced aquavit *(akvavit)*. There are several dozen types, the most common of which is spiced with caraway seeds. In Denmark, aquavit is not sipped but is swallowed straight down as a shot and most commonly followed by a chaser of beer. A popular Danish liqueur, made of cherries, is Peter Heering, which is excellent sipped straight or served over vanilla ice cream.

Common wine terms are *hvidvin* (white wine), *rødvin* (red wine), *mousserende vin* (sparkling wine) and *husets vin* (house wine). *Gløgg* is a mulled wine that's a favourite speciality during the Christmas season.

Beer, wine and spirits are served in most restaurants and cafes. They can be purchased at grocery stores during normal shopping hours and prices are quite reasonable. The minimum legal age for purchasing alcoholic beverages is 18 years.

VESTERBRO

This district, which encompasses Central Station and extends west, has numerous places to eat, including some good, inexpensive ethnic choices.

Restaurants

For an inexpensive all-you-can-eat deal there's *Astor Pizza (Map 7, D3; Vesterbrogade 7)* just north of Central Station, which has a reasonable pizza-and-salad bar for 39kr from 11 am to 5 pm, 49kr after 5 pm.

Restaurant Shezan (Map 7, E2; ☎ 33 24 78 88) on the corner of Viktoriagade and Istedgade serves a full menu of authentic Pakistani food. At this popular neighbourhood restaurant, vegetarian dishes such as *dhal turka* (spiced lentils) or *chana* (chickpea) curry cost a reasonable 50kr, while a range of chicken and lamb dishes average 60kr. It's open noon to 11 pm daily.

Ankara (Map 7, E2; ☎ 33 31 92 33, Vesterbrogade 35) is a casual 2nd-floor restaurant with a good-value buffet of numerous cold and hot traditional Middle Eastern dishes, including calamari, chicken, lamb and salads. The cost is just 39kr from noon to 4 pm and 59kr from 4 pm to midnight. If you prefer to eat light, Ankara also has a fast-food bar on the street level, which offers a pitta-bread felafel sandwich served with a soda for 20kr.

For a more upmarket setting there's *Sifa (Map 7, E2; ☎ 33 25 10 10, Vesterbrogade 39)*, which has good buffets for 49kr before 4 pm and 69kr after 4 pm. Or order a three-course meal that includes a choice of starter, main dish and dessert for 69kr at lunch,

PLACES TO EAT

Grinning from Beer to Beer

Danes are great producers and drinkers of beer. Denmark's United Breweries, an amalgamation of Carlsberg and Tuborg breweries, is the largest exporter of beer in Europe. Not all of the brew makes its way out of Denmark however. Danes down some seven million hectolitres (roughly two billion bottles) of brew a year, ranking them sixth among the greatest beer drinkers worldwide.

The best-selling beers in Denmark are pilsners, lagers with an alcohol content of 4.6%, but there are scores of other beers to choose from as well. These range from light beers with an alcohol content of 1.7% to hearty stouts that kick in at 8%.

You'll find the percentage of alcohol listed on the bottle label. Danish beers are classified with ascending numbers according to the amount of alcohol they contain, with *klasse 1* referring to the common pilsners and *klasse 4* to the strongest stouts.

88kr at dinner. Either way there are a wide variety of Middle Eastern dishes to select from. It's open 11 am to midnight, and has belly dancing at weekends.

Restaurant Koh-I-Noor (Map 7, E2; ☎ 33 24 64 17, Vesterbrogade 33) offers candlelight dining and a tasty Indian buffet that includes curried lamb, beef and chicken dishes, naan bread, soup and salad for 79kr, served nightly from 5 to 10 pm. There's also an a la carte menu, which includes vegetarian dishes, priced from 75kr to 100kr.

Restaurant Teaterkælderen (Map 7, E2; ☎ 33 25 75 00, Gammel Kongevej 29), one of the city's most unusual dining options, occupies the converted prop cellar of the century-old Det Ny Teater. The place is thick with character, its red brick walls are adorned with photos of former stage stars and the waiters double as performers, stopping between serving courses to sing, play guitar or perform magic tricks. The restaurant caters to theatregoers wanting to wine and dine before or after plays, so non-theatregoers get the place to themselves between 7.30 and 10 pm when shows take place upstairs. The Danish-French menu changes every few months and costs 215kr for a two-course meal, 245kr for three courses. Add 160kr for a bottle of house wine. Ask about the special *tæppefaldsanretning* (curtain menu) available after the show for 125kr.

Fast Food, Bakeries & Markets

Central Station has a number of fast-food eateries, including a *McDonald's* and a *Subway* sandwich shop.

More interesting is the station's *Gourmet Marked*, a little food court with a half-dozen deli-style eateries, where 30kr buys a slice of pizza and a beer, or a quarter-chicken with fries; it's open 10 am to 10 pm daily.

Kringlen bakery, in the north-eastern corner of the station, sells good breads and pastries; it's open 6.30 am (7 am on Sunday) to 6 pm daily.

Central Station also boasts a couple of railway-affiliated restaurants. Best value among these is *Spise Hjørnet*, a DSB cafe-

teria open 6.30 am to 10 pm, which offers a daily hot special costing 39kr on weekdays, 49kr at weekends. These are filling but unexciting meals. You can also make your own single-serving salad from a limited salad bar for 23kr including bread.

Also in Central Station is a *supermarket* open 8 am to midnight daily and a small *fruit stand* with slightly shorter hours.

ISO (Map 7, E2; Vesterbrogade 25) is the closest large grocery store to the main hotel district and has cheap bakery items and sandwiches. It's open 9 am to 8 pm weekdays, 8 am to 5 pm Saturday.

Bon Appetit (Map 7, E2; Vesterbrogade 17) is a favourite of office workers looking for a cheap lunch. It specialises in good takeaway sandwiches, either smørrebrød-style or on a bulky roll, from 20kr. Opening hours are 7 am to 4 pm Monday to Thursday, 7 am to 1 pm Friday.

Oasen Kebab (Map 7, E2; Istedgade 58), a popular place with the immigrant community, has felafels (15kr), kebabs (23kr), cheap chicken dishes and long opening hours.

Café Konditoriet (Map 7, E2; Vesterbrogade 32), a small bakery with a few tables in the back, provides an inexpensive option for morning coffee and pastries. It's open 6.30 am to 6 pm weekdays, 7 am to 4 pm at weekends.

RÅDHUSPLADSEN & AROUND

Rådhuspladsen, the large square that fronts city hall and serves as the city's main bus terminal, has a couple of hot-dog wagons and a fruit stand that set up right on the plaza. The rest of the places that follow are within a short walk. Places to eat inside Tivoli, the amusement park opposite Rådhuspladsen, are listed in a separate section.

Restaurants

Hard Rock Cafe (Map 7, D3; ☎ 33 12 43 33, Vesterbrogade 3) near the tourist office features American-style fare along with rock memorabilia decor that includes one of Michael Jackson's gloves and Bob Dylan's guitars. Either a vegie burger or beef burger, served with fries, costs 79kr, while barbecued ribs are priced at 139kr.

Nourishing Nonmeat Nosh

While strictly vegetarian restaurants are relatively few in number, vegetarians should nonetheless be able to get by fairly comfortably in Copenhagen.

Three good solely-vegetarian restaurants are **Govindas** (Map 7, A4; Nørre Farimagsgade 82), a Hare Krishna operation near the botanical garden; **Den Grønne Kælder** (Map 8, B7; Pilestræde 48), a reasonably priced central spot; and **Morgenstedet** (Map 7, D8), a cosy place in the alternative community of Christiania. The menu at all three places includes vegan dishes.

RizRaz (Map 8, F5; Kompagnistræde 20), south of Strøget, has tempting, reasonably priced vegetarian buffets of Mediterranean food, in addition to serving meat and fish dishes to order.

Other restaurants specialising in Mediterranean buffet-style meals also offer a wide choice of vegetarian dishes such as salads, sauteed vegetables, rice and couscous. While these spreads typically have dozens of different items, about a third of the dishes usually include meat or seafood items – so you'll need to choose carefully. Recommended among these places are the Greek restaurant **Samos** (Map 8, D4; Skindergade 29), just north of Strøget, and the two branches of the Turkish restaurant **Ankara** (Map 7, E2) at Vesterbrogade 35 in Vesterbro and Krystalgade 8 (Map 8, C4) in the Latin Quarter.

In addition, most Danish cafes offer a decent variety of salads, many of them meat-free, and some also offer a hot vegetarian dish. Among those popular with vegetarian diners are **Atlas Bar** (Map 8, E2; Larsbjørnstre18) in the Latin Quarter and **Picnic** (Map 4, F4; Fælledvej 22) in the Nørrebrogade area.

Most Italian restaurants have vegetarian pasta options, and for those who eat cheese, there are scores of pizza places throughout Copenhagen. And of course, all Indian and Pakistani restaurants have some vegetarian-only items.

There's a happy hour from 5.30 pm with half-price cocktails. It's open noon to at least midnight daily. And, of course, it sells its logo T-shirts.

Brasserie on the Square (☎ 33 14 40 50, Rådhuspladsen 57) in the lobby of the Palace Hotel offers a Danish buffet, including herring dishes, salmon pâté and salads, from noon to 4 pm daily. Although it's not an elaborate affair, it has a pleasant upmarket setting and is a reasonable deal, costing 129kr. At dinner the best value is the special menu, which changes monthly, but features a three-course meal for 228kr.

Taj Indian Restaurant (Map 7, D3; ☎ 33 13 10 10, Jernbanegade 5) is widely regarded as the best Indian restaurant in Copenhagen. Prices are on the high side, with multicourse dinners from 150kr to 500kr, but the food gets top-notch reviews. It's open noon to midnight daily.

Cafes

Café Bjørg (Map 8, F1; ☎ 33 14 53 20, Vester Voldgade 19), an upmarket cafe a block north of Rådhuspladsen, has creative sandwiches such as Cajun chicken for around 50kr, Caesar salad for 65kr and chicken satay for 92kr. It's open 11 am to at least midnight daily.

For those who are museum browsing, **Ny Carlsberg Glyptotek** (Map 7, E4) on HC Andersens Blvd has a pleasant atrium cafe, overlooking the museum's palm garden, serving pastries, sandwiches, coffee and wine. Expect a crowd at weekends.

Fast Food, Bakeries & Markets

Facing Rådhuspladsen on its eastern side is a **7-Eleven** (Map 8, G2) convenience store that's open 24 hours and sells snacks and cheap coffee. Also facing the square on Vester Voldgade is a **KFC** (Map 8, G2) with its standard fast-food chicken.

Scala (Map 7, D3), on Vesterbrogade opposite Tivoli, is a multistorey building chock-a-block with fast-food eateries, though few are notable. The best bets include **Matahari**, offering wok-cooked East Asian dishes for around 50kr, and **Italian Corner**, with various pasta plates for 39kr. All of the food can be ordered for eating in or takeaway and Scala is open daily for lunch and dinner.

Rådhusarkaden, a large indoor shopping centre on Vesterbrogade near Rådhuspladsen, has an *Irma* grocery shop and the *Conditori Hans Christian Andersen*, which offers good sandwiches, pastries and coffee.

TIVOLI

Tivoli boasts more than 30 places to eat. These range from simple stalls offering typical amusement-park fare such as ice cream and hot dogs to some of the city's more respected eating establishments. You'll need to pay Tivoli admission (or have a Copenhagen Card) to eat at these places – and they only operate during the Tivoli season. Most of the restaurants open around noon and stay open late, closing about a half-hour before Tivoli does. For the locations of the following, see the Tivoli map.

Hercegovina (☎ 33 15 63 63) specialises in Bosnian and Hercegovinian food and often has roaming musicians performing ethnic music. In the evenings there's a buffet of salads and grilled meats costing 159kr – this is moderate by Tivoli standards, but the food is no more inspired than some of the Mediterranean restaurants outside Tivoli that charge a fraction of the price. However, if you eat between 5 and 6 pm (but be careful, as you must pay the bill by 6 pm!) the price drops to a more reasonable 99kr.

If you're a big meat eater, a good, moderately priced choice is *Promenaden* (☎ 33 75 07 70), which enjoys a view of the open-air stage and serves spareribs and steaks averaging 125kr at lunch, 170kr at dinner.

Also popular is *Grøften* (☎ 33 12 11 25). The speciality here is a type of smørrebrød with tiny fjord shrimps spiced with lime and fresh pepper that cost 85kr; other smørrebrød are priced from 36kr apiece. The menu also includes two-course meals featuring salmon or steak for 195kr.

Bagatellen (☎ 33 75 07 51) is one of Tivoli's trendier choices, combining Mediterranean and Californian influences and offering both indoor dining and outdoor pondview tables. There are three-course deals at lunch for 145kr, at dinner for 365kr.

Or you can order a la carte with main courses such as grilled lobster for 195kr and rack of lamb for 250kr.

If money is not an issue, *Divan 2* (☎ 33 12 51 51) is widely considered to be Tivoli's finest restaurant for both food and service. In operation since Tivoli opened in 1843, this restaurant serves gourmet French food and has a vintage wine collection. Its sister restaurant, *Divan 1* (☎ 33 11 42 42), has a similar history and garden setting and also enjoys a reputation for good food, but with a menu emphasising Danish and international fare. A meal at either Divan could easily set you back at least 500kr.

STRØGET & AROUND

There are scores of dining options on and around this famed pedestrian street that marks the heart of Copenhagen, with choices running the gamut from cheap fast food to top-rated fine dining.

Restaurants

Pizza Hut (Map 8, E6) on Amagertorv beside the Tobacco Museum offers a pizza-and-salad buffet for 49kr from 11 am to 4 pm, or the chain's usual pizzas to order until 11 pm daily.

Cheaper is the nearby *Café de Paris* (Map 8, E5) pizzeria in the arcade at Vimmelskaftet 39, which has a simple pizza and salad buffet for just 39kr. In the same arcade at *Restaurant Eastern* (Map 8, E5) a buffet of Indian and Pakistani dishes costs 49kr from 11 am to 5 pm and 79kr after 5 pm.

Samos (Map 8, D4; *Skindergade 29*) has a top-notch buffet featuring 12 Greek hot dishes and a fresh salad bar for just 39kr from noon to 5 pm, 79kr from 5 to 11 pm daily. You can also order reasonably priced a la carte dishes such as lamb cutlets or moussaka.

Den Grønne Kælder (Map 8, B7; ☎ 33 93 01 40, *Pilestræde 48*) is a strictly vegetarian restaurant. At lunch, served until 5 pm, you can select two salads and a simple hot dish or quiche for 50kr. At dinner there's a wider selection of hot dishes, and a full meal costs around 100kr. It's open 11 am to 10 pm Monday to Saturday.

The mainstay at **Pasta Basta** (**Map 8, D5**; ☎ *33 11 21 31, Valkendorfsgade 22*) is a self-service buffet of various cold pasta and salad dishes costing 69kr. You can also order from the main menu, which includes hot pasta dishes served with the likes of red snapper; most cost from 70kr to 115kr. The restaurant is open 11.30 am to 3 am weekdays, until 5 am at weekends, making it a popular spot with night owls looking for a late meal or drink.

Jensen's Bøfhus (**Map 8, D5**; ☎ *33 32 78 00*), a Danish-chain steak restaurant, is in a period house fronting Gråbrødre Torv (Greyfriars' Square), a pleasant cobblestone plaza. Although the food is average, prices are cheap and on warm summer days you can sit out on the square. For lunch, served from 11.30 am to 4 pm, there's a steak and baked potato deal for 39kr. Dinner steaks average 130kr, but there's usually a special for under 100kr.

Nearby **Peder Oxe** (**Map 8, D5**; ☎ *33 11 00 77, Gråbrødre Torv 11*), which fronts the square, offers affordable fine dining with a Danish country ambience. It has tasty fish and organic meat dishes, served with a good salad buffet, for around 150kr. It also has a house wine deal – you pay for only as much of the bottle as you end up drinking. Copenhagen's oldest monastery was built on this site in 1238 and the restaurant's wine cellar retains part of the old stone foundations. It's open 11.30 am to at least 10.30 pm daily.

Restaurant Gråbrødre Torv 21 (**Map 8, D5**; ☎ *33 11 47 07, Gråbrødre Torv 21*) has excellent Danish food and is a good choice for a night of fine dining. Main courses such as lamb or fresh fish are priced around 150kr, or you can get the three-course meal of the day for 268kr. It's open for dinner 6 to 10 pm daily.

Konrad (**Map 8, C7**; ☎ *33 93 29 29, Pilestræde 12*) is a posh restaurant and bar with good contemporary Danish cuisine and attentive service. The menu varies as it incorporates items that are seasonally fresh. Expect beef and fish main courses to be priced around 200kr. It's open for lunch noon to 3 pm and for dinner 6 to 10 pm (to 11 pm on Friday and Saturday).

Kommandanten (**Map 8, B9**; ☎ *33 12 09 90, Ny Adelgade 7*), just west of Kongens Nytorv, has received numerous accolades, including the Michelin Guides' highest rating among Copenhagen's restaurants. The a la carte main courses such as rack of lamb or duck in cabernet sauce cost around 250kr, and there is a changing three-course menu for 360kr. It's open 5.30 to 10 pm daily except Sunday.

Cafes

For an old-fashioned high-brow treat visit **La Glace** (**Map 8, E4**; *Skoubogade 3*), a classic konditori-style cafe that has been serving tea and fancy cakes to socialites for more than a century. It's open 8 am to 5.30 pm weekdays, with shorter weekend hours.

Huset med det Grønne Træ (**Map 8, E3**; ☎ *33 12 87 86*) is at the north-western corner of Gammel Torv and beside the linden tree from which it takes its name. This little lunch cafe, housed in a period building dating from 1796, offers quintessential Danish fare, with smørrebrød sandwiches, draught beer and a dozen brands of schnapps. Sandwiches cost around 40kr, a lunch plate with herring, liver pâté, roast beef, cheese, and potato salad costs 101kr. It's open 11 am to 3 pm weekdays year-round as well as noon to 3 pm on Saturday in winter.

Also abundant in local character is **Café Sorgenfri** (**Map 8, E4**; ☎ *33 11 58 80, Brolæggerstræde 8*), a corner pub serving good Danish food. Traditional cold dishes such as smørrebrød and pickled herring cost around 45kr. Hot dishes, including tasty roast pork, are a few kroner more; or you can jump in and sample it all with a variety plate (110kr) that includes herring, roast pork and meatballs with beets, cheese and other items. The kitchen is open noon to 8.30 pm daily.

RizRaz (**Map 8, F5**; ☎ *33 15 05 75, Kompagnistræde 20*) is just south of Strøget and conveniently located around the corner from Use It. At this pleasant cafe you can feast on a Mediterranean-style vegetarian buffet (49kr), including felafel, pasta, hummus and salads, served daily from 11.30 am to 5 pm (to 4 pm at weekends). At dinner, from 5 to 11 pm, the buffet costs 59kr. You

PLACES TO EAT

can also order from the menu: lamb kebabs, grilled fish or fried calamari cost 99kr, including the buffet.

Café Hovedtelegrafen (☎ 33 41 09 00, *Købmagergade 37*) on the upper level of the Post & Tele Museum has a splendid rooftop view of the city and a decent menu as well. You can enjoy a bowl of gazpacho soup, an organic feta cheese salad or a grilled chicken sandwich, each priced around 60kr, or just linger over a beer or cappuccino. It's closed on Monday, but otherwise open 11 am to 5 pm daily (to 8 pm on Wednesday).

Fast Food, Bakeries & Markets

Strøget has many cheap eateries, including ice-cream, hamburger and hot-dog stands as well as numerous hole-in-the-wall kebab joints selling felafels for under 30kr.

For a cheap treat try *Shawarma Grill House* (Map 8, F2) at the western end of Strøget, a two-minute walk from Rådhuspladsen. This bustling, unpretentious eatery serves Strøget's best shawarma (28kr), a pitta-bread sandwich of shaved beef and lamb topped with a yoghurt dressing. It also makes inexpensive felafel and kebabs. It's open 11 am to midnight daily (to 5 am at weekends) and has a sit-down counter on the ground floor and a dining room upstairs. More mundane options in the same price range can be found at *McDonald's* (Map 8, G2) and *Burger King* (Map 8, G2) on the opposite side of the street.

China Box (Map 8, F2) on Østergade opposite Mikkel Bryggers Gade sells inexpensive takeaway Chinese food, with an emphasis on things deep-fried. For 27kr, you get your choice of three items, such as fried rice, noodles and deep-fried shrimp.

An excellent bakery is *Reinh van Hauen*, which uses mainly organic ingredients and has branches at the eastern end of Strøget (Map 8, D9) at Østergade 22 and on a side street at the western end of Strøget (Map 8, G2) at Mikkel Bryggers Gade 2.

For a French influence, there's *Croissant'en* (Map 8, D7; *Østergade 59*), which sells croissants and inexpensive takeaway quiches and sandwiches.

Netto supermarket (Map 8, C8), near the eastern end of Strøget, has relatively cheap grocery prices. For a more upmarket selection, try the bakery and grocery shop on the ground floor of *Magasin du Nord* department store (Map 8, D9), a block south of Østergade at the eastern end of Strøget.

McGrails (Map 8, E3), a small health-food shop on the north-eastern corner of Gammel Torv, sells snacks, vitamins and organic wines and cereals.

LATIN QUARTER

In this section of the city centre, which caters largely to college students and the gay community, the cafes tend to gear their menus to the health conscious.

Cafes

Studenterhuset (Map 8, B5; ☎ 35 32 38 61, *Købmagergade 52*) is a low-key student hang-out near the Round Tower. It features drinks and light eats, including vegetarian or meat sandwiches for 30kr, and is open noon to midnight on weekdays.

Atlas Bar (Map 8, E2; ☎ 33 15 03 52, *Larsbjørnsstræde18*), a casual basement cafe in the heart of the gay district, has a changing chalkboard menu that includes salads and other vegetarian items for around 60kr and chicken dishes for about twice that. Many of the dishes use organic ingredients. It's open 11 am to 10 pm Monday to Saturday.

Café Sommersko (Map 8, C7; ☎ 33 14 81 89, *Kronprinsensgade 6*) is a trendsetter, popular for both drinks and food. The menu offers sandwiches, omelettes and light meals such as vegetarian soba or salmon with pasta for 50kr to 90kr. The cafe also serves cakes, desserts and breakfast pastries at moderate prices. It's open at least 9 am to midnight daily.

The 2nd-floor cafe *Klaptræet* (Map 8, B4; ☎ 33 13 31 48, *Kultorvet 11*) overlooking Kultorvet square serves burgers, chilli con carne and salads for less than 50kr. There's also a daily home-made soup with bread (34kr). It's open 10 am until at least midnight daily. In summer, Klaptræet sets up outdoor tables and a draught beer tap right on the square.

Restaurants

Ankara (Map 8, C4; ☎ 33 15 19 15, Krystalgade 8), a Turkish restaurant, offers surprisingly good food for the money as well as a pleasant setting with candlelit tables. There's a generous buffet of salads, rice and numerous hot and cold dishes that costs just 39kr until 4 pm, 59kr from 4 to 11 pm.

Ristorante Italiano (Map 8, D4; ☎ 33 11 12 95, Fiolstræde 2) at the back of Vor Frue Kirke has authentic Italian food and decor. Lunch specials, including lasagne or pizza, cost 39kr to 49kr, and prices on the dinner menu range from 59kr for pizzas to 159kr for seafood. In the summer the outdoor cafe tables are an agreeable sunny-day option.

Det Lille Apotek (Map 8, C4; ☎ 33 12 56 06, Store Kannikestræde 15) is a standby for traditional Danish food at moderate prices. Multi-item meals that include pickled herring, fish fillet and smørrebrød cost from 75kr to 110kr at lunch and a three-course dinner costs 168kr. By some claims, Det Lille Apotek, which traces its history to 1720 (it was a pharmacy, or *apotek*, before that), is the oldest restaurant in Copenhagen. It's open 11.30 am until at least 10 pm daily.

St Gertruds Kloster (Map 8, A4; ☎ 33 14 66 30, Hauser Plads 32) just off Kultorvet is an elegant restaurant in a former medieval monastery, sections of which date from the 14th century. The most popular of the four dining rooms is the one occupying the cellar, which has arched brick walls and is lit by some 1500 candles. The restaurant specialises in Danish-French cuisine. Starters, including smoked salmon and escargot, are priced from 150kr to 250kr, while main dishes begin around 250kr. On Sunday, there's also a fixed-price, three-course dinner served with wine for 348kr. The restaurant is open 4 pm to midnight daily and reservations are requested.

NYHAVN & AROUND

In the summer season the places that front the northern side of scenic Nyhavn canal set tables outside, turning the street into a line of pavement cafes. On sunny days this is a favourite spot for Copenhageners to sit with friends and linger over a cold beer.

Restaurants

Restaurant Shezan (Map 7, C7; ☎ 33 91 46 46, Havnegade 33) serves authentic Pakistani food with a complete range of both vegetarian-only dishes and chicken and lamb dishes. It's a fun place to dine if you have a few people sharing orders – expect the bill to run around 100kr per person. It's open noon to 11 pm daily.

If you're into formal dining, **Els** (Map 7, B7; ☎ 33 14 13 41, Store Strandstræde 3) has good food in a classic upmarket Danish setting. Although the decor is solidly 19th century, the menu blends contemporary Danish and French influences. A two-course lunch (served from noon to 3 pm daily) costs around 200kr; a three-course dinner (5.30 to 10 pm), costs 388kr.

The neighbourhood's other top-end restaurant, **Leonore Christine** (Map 7, C7; ☎ 33 13 50 40, Nyhavn 9), is in a cosy historic building fronting the canal. The menu here also features a mingling of French and Danish cuisines, with starters priced around 100kr and a la carte main dishes around 250kr. It's open noon to midnight daily.

Cafes

The exhibition hall at **Charlottenborg** (Map 8, C10), near Kongens Nytorv, has an arty cafe with a changing chalkboard menu of reasonably priced light eats. Smørrebrød sandwiches are around 50kr, a herring plate is 68kr and the cafe also serves cakes, coffee and beer. It's open 11 am to 4 pm, the same hours as the museum.

For a thoroughly Danish experience, don't miss the herring buffet at **Nyhavns Færgekro** (Map 7, B7; ☎ 33 15 15 88, Nyhavn 5), an atmospheric cafe right on the canal. This all-you-can-eat buffet has 10 different kinds of herring, including baked, marinated and rollmops, with condiments to sprinkle on top and boiled potatoes to round out the meal; it costs 89kr and is available from 11.30 am to 5 pm daily. If you're not a herring lover, there's also a variety of smørrebrød for around 50kr. Dinner, served from 5 to 11.30 pm, betrays French influences and is pricier.

Another canal favourite is **Cap Horn** (Map 7, C7; ☎ 33 12 85 04, Nyhavn 21), which

PLACES TO EAT

specialises in Danish fare and uses mainly organic ingredients. A lunch plate of three open-faced sandwiches costs 69kr or a two-course meal of herring, steak and potatoes is 105kr. It's open daily for lunch from 11.30 am to 5 pm and for dinner until the crowds die down, which is usually late.

Fast Food

Apart from the *hot-dog wagon* that customarily sets up on Kongens Nytorv, the cheapest eats in the Nyhavn area can be found at *Pizzabageren* (Map 7, C7), a fast-food joint on the corner of Nyhavn and Toldbodgade, which serves pitta-bread sandwiches, burgers and chips – nothing notable, but you can quiet your stomach for 30kr or so. *Jasmin* (Map 7, C7), next to Pizzabageren, serves takeaway Thai food, with various combinations available for 40kr.

SLOTSHOLMEN & AROUND

While there's no place to eat within the historic quarters of Slotsholmen there are some interesting options just beyond.

Restaurants

A good option for fine dining is *Krogs Fiskerestaurant* (Slotsholmen Map; ☎ 33 15 89 15, Gammel Strand 38), north of Slotsholmen Kanal. It specialises in fresh seafood served with organic produce; starters

A Treat by Any Name

Bakeries abound in Copenhagen, all selling those sinfully rich breakfast pastries that are so synonymous with Denmark they're known around the world simply as 'Danish'.

Curiously, Danes look elsewhere to give credit. In Denmark, those same mouthwatering treats – flaky butter-laden pastry with a dollop of icing or jam – are called *wienerbrød*, which translates as 'Vienna bread'.

As legend has it, the naming of the pastry can be traced to a Danish baker who moved to Austria in the 18th century, where he perfected a version of pastry in a style that has since been known to the Danes as wienerbrød and to the rest of the world as 'Danish'.

average 150kr, main courses 300kr. The restaurant is open for dinner from 5.30 to 10.30 pm Monday to Saturday.

Søren K (☎ 33 47 49 49) off the lobby of the sleek new Royal Library has become a fashionable place for an upmarket meal. It offers a fine canal view. At lunch you can get things such as beef carpaccio or tuna salad for around 100kr. The pricier dinner menu features such dishes as dill salmon, beef tornadoes and Norwegian lobster; expect dinner to total around 500kr per person. It's open 11 am to 11.30 pm daily.

Cafes

Øieblikket, an espresso bar in the lobby of the Royal Library, has reasonably priced muffins, quiche, sandwiches, coffee and beer, with tables overlooking the canal.

Nationalmuseet (Map 7, D4; Ny Vestergade 10) has a stylish 2nd-floor cafe offering creative sandwiches, salads, light meals and desserts – or you can just relax over a glass of wine. The prices are reasonable, the opening hours mirror those of the museum and if you just want to dine you won't need to pay museum admission.

Slotskælderen hos Gitte Kik (Slotsholmen Map; ☎ 33 11 15 37, Fortunstræde 4) a few minutes' walk from Folketinget is a snug little lunch spot where you can literally rub shoulders with members of parliament. Quintessentially Danish, its menu features smørrebrød, with the sandwiches priced from 34kr to 75kr. It's open 11 am to 3 pm weekdays only.

Thorvaldsen Café (Slotsholmen Map; ☎ 33 32 04 00, Gammel Strand 34) opposite the canal is a bit pricey, but it has good salads, sandwiches and Spanish-influenced fare. On sunny days the pavement tables are the place to be. It's open 11.30 am to midnight daily.

AMALIENBORG & KASTELLET AREA

This area, which includes the royal palace and the Little Mermaid, has some recommendable places to eat among its famed sightseeing attractions.

Restaurants

One of the trendiest places in the neighbourhood is *Restaurant Olsen (Map 7, B7; ☎ 33 93 91 95, Store Kongensgade 66)*. This pleasant restaurant has a mixed menu of classic Danish meat and potato dishes as well as European provincial fare with French, German and Swiss accents. Expect a three-course meal to cost around 250kr. It's open noon to midnight Monday to Saturday.

For something different, there's *KGB (Map 7, B6; ☎ 33 36 07 70, Dronningens Tværgade 22)*, a modish Russian-themed restaurant and vodka bar, complete with wall portraits of Cold War-era Soviet leaders. It offers three-course dinners for 225kr, with such items as borscht, mussel soup and various cod preparations. It's open 7.30 pm to at least midnight daily.

Langelinie Pavillonen (Map 4, F10; ☎ 35 26 01 11, Langelinie) 150m south of the Little Mermaid statue is an upmarket 2nd-floor restaurant with a good harbour view. Lunch choices include a club sandwich for 90kr or a two-course meal of the day for 168kr. At dinner there's a changing menu of Danish-French fare, with a three-course meal priced at 298kr. Because of its waterview setting it sometimes books out to private parties, but otherwise is open noon to midnight daily.

Cafes

Ida Davidsen (Map 7, A7; ☎ 33 91 36 55, Store Kongensgade 70) is widely considered the top smørrebrød restaurant in Denmark. It has a nearly limitless variety of open-faced sandwiches. The prices average 50kr, however, more exotic versions can cost up to 150kr each. It's open 10 am to 5 pm weekdays only, with the last order taken at 4 pm.

Nearby *Amadeus (Map 7, B6; ☎ 33 32 35 11, Store Kongensgade 62)* combines an organic bakery that has wonderful breads with a smart cafe specialising in fresh, wholesome food. This is one of those low-profile gems that visitors seldom discover. At lunch, 11 am to 4 pm daily, creative salads and a variety of tempting sandwiches, ranging from club to smørrebrød, are priced

around 85kr for eat-in or 60kr for takeaway. At dinner (4.30 to 11.30 pm) the chef prepares seasonal Danish dishes, offering a three-course menu for a reasonable 169kr. There's dining both indoors and in a rear courtyard.

ROSENBORG SLOT & AROUND

The neighbourhood around Rosenborg Slot has a couple of appealing cafes that cater to sightseers.

Cafes

Traktørstedet Rosenborg Slot (Map 7, A5; ☎ 33 15 76 20) at the Øster Voldgade entrance to Rosenborg Slot is a pleasant cafe offering both standard sandwiches and Danish smørrebrød for around 50kr. There's also a Danish lunch plate for 125kr and a few speciality salads. You can dine at cosy cafe tables inside or in a garden setting outdoors. It's open 11 am to 4 pm daily, except on Monday in winter.

Statens Museum for Kunst (Map 7, A5; ☎ 33 74 84 94, Søvgade 48) has a lobbyside cafe with modern Scandinavian decor and a garden view. Every day there's an 85kr special that typically includes a salmon dish, salad, bread and a seafood appetiser. The menu also has soup, sandwiches and salads. It's open 10 am to 5 pm daily, except on Wednesday when it closes at 8 pm.

On sunny days the *Botanical Garden* operates a little outdoor cafe behind the Palmehus that serves ice cream, pastries and sandwiches.

NØRREPORT & AROUND

The area around Nørreport station has quite a few fast-food options and there are more substantial restaurants near the hotels situated to the west.

Restaurants

Restaurant Broadway (Map 7, B4; ☎ 33 93 99 77, Linnesgade 14) will be mostly of interest to people staying at nearby Hotel Jørgensen, as similar restaurants elsewhere in the city offer a more exciting spread. Still, this Turkish restaurant features a buffet of Middle Eastern fare with salads and hot dishes for a reasonable 39kr from 11 am to 4 pm and 49kr from 4 pm to midnight.

Govindas (Map 7, A4; ☎ 33 33 74 44, *Nørre Farimagsgade 82)* serves savoury Indian-style vegetarian food in a pleasant setting with mellow music. At this alternative restaurant, Hare Krishna devotees cook up an all-you-can-eat meal of basmati rice, soup, salad and a few hot dishes such as eggplant casserole for 55kr. Govindas is run as a business rather than a venue for converting new members, so there's no religious hard-sell, just good, wholesome food. It's open noon to 8.30 pm Monday to Saturday.

Sticks 'N' Sushi (Map 7, B3; ☎ 33 11 14 07, *Nansensgade 59)* is a fun cross-cultural place run by a family of mixed Japanese and Danish descent. It's added some local twists to its Japanese menu to make things more appealing to Danes. Many of the items, such as sushi rolls, are served on sticks popsicle-style, similar to the way grilled items such as yakitori (grilled chicken) are served in Japan. The extensive menu includes Western favourites such as California maki (avocado roll sushi) and traditional items such as tuna sashimi and yakitori. You can order a la carte, but the best deal is the set-course plates that include at least 10 items and cost from 200kr to 350kr. Cold Kirin beer on tap and warm Japanese sake are available. It's open 6 pm to midnight daily.

Sticks 'N' Sushi Takeaway (Map 7, B3; ☎ 33 16 14 07, *Nansensgade 47)* is the fast-food branch of the aforementioned restaurant and it too serves good Japanese fare. Prices are substantially lower here, with a multi-item menu from 75kr to 150kr. Although it's largely takeaway the place has a small bar and a couple of tables, so you could eat-in. It's open 2 to 10 pm daily.

Fast Food, Bakeries & Markets

Tempting among the cheap eateries clustered along Nørre Voldgade is *Taffelbay's Konditori* (Map 7, B4; *Nørre Voldgade 92)*, which has generous sandwiches and luscious fruit tarts and strudel, and is open 6 am daily. There's also a *Netto* grocery store

(Map 7, B4) located just north of the bakery, a *McDonald's* (Map 7, B4) a block to the south, and a little coffee shop, *Café au Lait* (Map 7, B4), directly across the street.

The city's main *produce market* is situated at Israels Plads, a few minutes' walk west of Nørreport station. Stalls are set up at the market until 5 pm weekdays and until 2 pm Saturday, when it doubles as a flea market.

NØRREBRO

The Nørrebro area, with its mix of students and immigrants, has a nice variety of eating options. The area around Sankt Hans Torv has developed into one of the city's newest and most youthful cafe scenes and in summer the square itself is thick with outdoor tables.

Restaurants

Indian Corner (Map 4, G3; ☎ 35 39 28 02, *Nørrebrogade 59)* is a pleasant little neighbourhood restaurant serving good Indian food. Vegetarian dishes cost around 60kr and specialities such as tandoori prawns or tikka chicken cost 80kr to 90kr; add another 20kr for rice. It's open for dinner 4 to 11 pm daily, except Tuesday.

Quattro Fontane (Map 4, F4; ☎ 35 39 39 31, *Guldbergsgade 3)* just west of Sankt Hans Torv has good pizza and pasta dishes averaging 60kr and a few meat and fish dishes for around double that price; there's also a 28kr children's menu. It's open 4 pm to midnight daily.

Ayuttaya Thai Restaurant (Map 7, A1; ☎ 35 37 38 68, *Griffenfeldsgade 39A)* serves good, reasonably priced Thai food. There's a wide variety of dishes, including curries and noodles. Prices for most chicken, beef and pork dishes are 63kr, while fish and shrimp dishes are 69kr. It's open noon to 11 pm Tuesday to Saturday and 5 to 11 pm Sunday.

Mexicali (Map 7, B2; ☎ 35 39 47 04, *Åboulevard 12)* offers Mexican vegetarian dishes such as a cheese burrito or enchilada with rice for around 80kr; meat dishes cost a bit more. It's open 5 pm to midnight Monday to Saturday.

Cafes

The popular *Floras Kaffe Bar* (Map 7, A2; ☎ 35 39 00 18, Blågårdsgade 27) is a kicked-back place offering a full range of coffees, good desserts and reasonably priced soups, sandwiches and salads. There are usually a couple of hot meal specials for around 65kr and much of the fare is organic. In summer you can sit outside and soak up the sunshine. It's open 10 am to around midnight daily.

Sebastopol (Map 4, F4; ☎ 35 36 30 02, Sankt Hans Torv) is a stylish cafe on the square offering sandwiches, salads, vegetarian lasagne, nachos and other light eats, mostly in the 60kr to 90kr price range. It packs in a crowd on Sunday when brunch is accompanied by live jazz music. It's open 9 am until at least 1 am daily.

Nearby *Picnic* (Map 4, F4; ☎ 35 39 09 53, Fælledvej 22) is a small, casual operation with deli-style dishes, including a variety of vegetable and Mediterranean salads, for 50kr to 75kr. Most everything they serve is organic. Picnic, which is open 11 am (noon at weekends) to 10 pm daily, also has Turkish coffees and teas.

Propaganda (Map 7, A2; ☎ 35 39 49 00, Nørrebrogade 13), a night venue, serves Asian-influenced food such as Thai curry chicken or Szechuan beef noodles for around 90kr. The menu also includes vegetarian noodle dishes. It's open 5 pm to at least midnight daily.

Pussy Galore's Flying Circus (Map 4, F4; ☎ 35 24 53 00, Sankt Hans Torv) is one of Nørrebro's trendiest digs, with both indoor seating and alfresco tables on the square. Its varied menu includes salads, sandwiches and generous burgers for around 60kr and international fare such as Goa spiced lamb or Yucatan barbecue pork for 100kr. On weekday mornings until 10 am there's a breakfast buffet of eggs, muesli and fresh bread for 30kr and on Sunday until 4 pm there's a pricier but popular brunch menu. It's open 8 am to 2 am weekdays, 9 am to 2 am at weekends.

Fast Food, Bakeries & Markets

Byens Konditori (Map 4, G4; Nørrebrogade 42) has good pastries, is centrally located and is open daily. *The Bagel Company* (Map 4, G4; Elmegade 14) on a side street near Sankt Hans Torv is a small operation selling a variety of bagels for 6kr to 8kr and bagel sandwiches for 30kr. Opening hours are 10 am to 8 pm weekdays, 10 am to 6 pm at weekends.

Sheik Shawarma (Map 4, F3; ☎ 35 37 40 48, Nørrebrogade 98) is a little hole in the wall with just three cafe tables, but this family-run operation makes some of the best shawarma sandwiches in Copenhagen. A large meal-sized version costs just 20kr, a regular size 15kr. It also has 10kr felafels and inexpensive chicken. Sheik Shawarma is open 11 am to 11 pm daily. Pick up a honey-laden baklava (3kr) for dessert at the adjacent *Aladdin Bageri* (Map 4, F3).

Health-food shops include *Naturbutik* (Map 4, G3; Nørrebrogade 57), which stocks an array of bulk and prepackaged foods, teas and vitamins, and *Solsikken* (Map 7, A2; Blågårdsgade 33), which sells the usual health-food products and has produce, wine and crystal sections. There are also conventional grocery stores in the same neighbourhoods; you'll find a *Netto* (Map 7, A2) on Blågårdsgade diagonally opposite Solsikken, and a *Super Brugsen* (Map 4, G3) on Nørrebrogade a few metres southeast of Naturbutik.

BELLAHØJ

Bellahøj is a residential suburb with dining options catering to local neighbours and will be of interest mostly to those staying at the Copenhagen Bellahøj hostel.

Bodgenhoff Bageri (Map 5, F1) on the corner of Bellahøjvej and Næsbyholmvej has good pastries and bread. It's just a five-minute walk from the hostel and is open daily.

There are a handful of affordable places along Godthåbsvej, about 1km south-east of the hostel. Popular is *Restaurant Lazio* (Map 5, G2; ☎ 38 87 35 93, Godthåbsvej 191), a small Italian eatery with inexpensive sandwiches, a wide variety of pizzas and calzones for around 40kr, lasagne and pastas for 50kr and a handful of lunch specials served until 4 pm for just 30kr. It's open noon to 11 pm daily. If you're at the hostel and prefer to eat-in, delivery can be arranged for an extra 15kr.

If you want to prepare your own meals, you'll find fresh produce at *Centrum Frugt* (Map 5, G2; *Godthåbsvej 205*) and reasonably priced groceries at *Netto* (Map 5, G2; *Godthåbsvej 195*).

CHRISTIANSHAVN

Places to eat in Christianshavn include atmospheric canalside spots as well as businesses within the walls of the alternative community of Christiania. In addition to the places that follow, Christiania also has a handful of informal spots selling coffee, juice, alcohol and sandwiches.

Restaurants

Restaurant Gammel Dok (Map 7, D7; ☎ *32 57 19 30, Strandgade 27B*) on the waterfront in the Dansk Arkitektur Center offers sandwiches for around 50kr, a Danish lunch platter for 99kr and pricier three-course meals. It's open 10 am to 5 pm weekdays, 11 am to 4 pm at weekends and holidays.

Base Camp Holmen (Map 7, C9; ☎ *70 23 23 18, Halvtolv 12*) is a hot new restaurant, bar and entertainment venue. Occupying a former military base warehouse, it can seat nearly a thousand people and, particularly at weekends, packs in a crowd. One section has barbecue setups where diners grill their own steaks and seafood – expect a full meal to cost around 250kr. There's also a cheaper cafeteria-style restaurant with light eats for under 100kr. Popular is the jazz brunch, from 11 am to 3 pm most Sundays; it costs 90kr, which includes fruit, bacon, eggs, cheese and coffee, and is accompanied by live music.

You might be surprised to find an upmarket dinner restaurant in the alternative world of Christiania, but *Spiseloppen* (Map 7, D8; ☎ *32 57 95 58, Bådsmandsstræde 43*) is just that and it draws plenty of city folk from the fancier parts of town. The chefs hail from New Zealand, Ireland, Lebanon and Denmark, and the food is fusion-style, mixing different cuisines. The menu is a la carte and changes nightly; the main dishes always

include one vegetarian, one fish and four meat options and typically cost around 160kr. Soup, salads and desserts average around 45kr. Spiseloppen is a large hall-like place, but nonetheless often fills, so reservations are recommended, particularly at weekends. It's open 5 to 10 pm Tuesday to Sunday.

Cafes

Morgenstedet (Map 7, D8) on Langgaden, in the centre of Christiania, is a delightful little place serving only vegetarian dishes, including some vegan. The food is tasty and fresh, using mostly organic ingredients and prepared home-style. The menu changes daily, but there are always half a dozen salads at 12kr a serving and hot soup with bread for 30kr. The daily special includes two salads with a hot dish, such as chilli and corn bread, for 50kr at lunch, 60kr at dinner. In winter, a wood-burning stove makes the place cosy. Smoking (tobacco or pot) is not allowed. It's open noon to 9 pm daily, except Tuesday.

Other cheap places in Christiania include *Oasen Café* (Map 7, D8), a kicked-back coffee shop tucked in among the hashish shops on Pusherstreet; and *Grønsagen* (Map 7, D8), a greengrocer at the far end of Pusherstreet, which makes inexpensive takeaway sandwiches.

A pleasant spot on sunny summer days is *Christianshavns Bådudlejning og Café* (Map 7, E7; ☎ *32 96 53 53, Overgaden neden Vandet 29*), an informal open-air cafe on Christianshavn canal adjacent to the boat rental dock. You can sit right at the edge of the water and snack on inexpensive cakes, croissants, sandwiches or salads. This seasonal operation is open 10 am to midnight daily roughly from May to October.

Café Wilder (Map 7, D7; ☎ *32 54 71 83, Wildersgade 56*) is an inviting neighbourhood cafe with both vegetable and pasta salads for around 50kr and lunch-time sandwiches for 35kr. At dinner, served from 6 to 9.45 pm, fish dishes average 115kr, but there's a daily special for 85kr. It's also a popular late-night spot to linger over a drink. The cafe is open 9 am to 2 am weekdays, 10 am to 2 am at weekends.

Oven Vande Café (Map 7, D7; ☎ *32 95 96 02, Overgade Oven Vandet 44)* is an upmarket cafe with a solidly French kitchen. Lunches cost around 100kr and dinner could easily run double that though there's usually a daily meal for 130kr. It's open 11 am to midnight daily.

ØSTERBRO
Although Østerbro is largely a residential area, some travellers end up in the neighbourhood, especially those staying at Sleep-In, Copenhagen's premier summer hostel.

Restaurants
Restaurant New Garden (Map 4, D7; ☎ *35 26 21 92, Østerbrogade 74)* at the east side of Trianglen offers 12 different Chinese lunches for 49kr until 3 pm weekdays. At other times, there's a full menu of Chinese standards for around 90kr. It's open 11.30 am to 11.30 pm daily.

Cafes
Park Café (Map 4, C7; ☎ *35 42 62 48, Østerbrogade 79)* is a cavernous place that also doubles as a night spot. Its varied menu includes moderately priced sandwiches, salads and snacks. It attracts a young crowd, serves both vegetarian and meat items and offers a popular Sunday brunch for around 85kr. It's open for meals 11 am to 10 pm daily.

Fast Food, Bakeries & Markets
Sleep-In guests will find a number of fast-food options nearby, including a 24-hour *7-Eleven (Map 4, D7; Østerbrogade 74)* that offers a coffee and doughnut deal for just 10kr. For better quality pastries there's *Pariser Konditori (Map 4, D7; Østerbrogade 88A)*, a bakery a block to the north. If you prefer to go organic, *Det Rene Brød (Map 4, D7; Rosenvængets Allé 17)*, a block east of Trianglen, specialises in hearty 'ecological' breads. You can also find some organic foods at *Irma (Map 4, E7; Østerbrogade 52)*, a chain grocery store. There's a *McDonald's* **(Map 4, C7)** 500m north of Trianglen on the corner of Østerbrogade and Nøjsomhedsvej.

CHARLOTTENLUND & HELLERUP
The adjacent northern communities of Charlottenlund and Hellerup don't see many tourists so aren't as tightly packed with restaurants as Copenhagen centre, but you'll never have to travel too far to find something to eat.

Taffelbay's Konditori (Map 3, C3; Strandvejen 155) on the main road south of Charlottenlund Fort has good takeaway sandwiches and tempting pastries.

Jorden Rundt Café (Map 3, A5; ☎ *39 63 73 81, Strandvejen 152)* is a popular old-fashioned eatery serving sandwiches, chilli con carne and other simple fare; it's on the main road just north of the aquarium. It's open 11 am to 8.30 pm daily.

Sticks 'N' Sushi (Map 3, E3; ☎ *39 40 15 40, Strandvejen 195)* is midway between Charlottenlund and the Experimentarium in Hellerup. As the name implies it specialises in Japanese fare; prices are moderate to slightly expensive. It's open 11.30 am to 11 pm daily.

In addition, the two main visitor sights in the area, the Experimentarium **(Map 3, G3)** in Hellerup and Danmarks Akvarium **(Map 3, A4)**, the aquarium in Charlottenlund, both have simple cafes.

KLAMPENBORG
Most of the eateries in this area are inside Bakken amusement park, though Klampenborg's most popular restaurant is located just outside its gates.

Restaurants
Peter Lieps Hus (☎ *39 64 07 86, Dyrehaven 8)* sits in Dyrehaven park outside the northern entrance to Bakken. Occupying an historic thatch-roofed house, this classic restaurant is so renowned among Copenhageners that it's commonly featured as a setting in contemporary Danish novels. The restaurant is nearly as romantic as the buggy carts, though expect a crowd at dinner time. Naturally the menu is Danish, with meals ranging from the traditional plate of herring, fish fillet, roast beef and potato salad for 126kr to a multicourse

venison meal for 348kr. There are also lunch specials for around 100kr, or simply snack on moderately priced smørrebrød sandwiches and beer. Lunch is from 11.30 am to 5.30 pm and dinner 5.30 to 8 pm; it's closed on Monday.

Fast Food

Bakken has a plethora of cheap eats ranging from cotton-candy stalls and hot-dog stands to some unpretentious sit-down restaurants. Among the latter are *Bøgely*, which features smørrebrød and Danish fare, and *Skovroen*, which specialises in spareribs and offers 10kr beer during its happy 'hour' that amusingly runs from noon to midnight daily. The fare served at many other places in Bakken is as apparent as their names: *Burgerbar*, *Pølserkroens Grill*, *Crepes Baren* and *Schnitzel House*.

RUNGSTED

Numerous eating options can be found at Rungsted's large yachting harbour. These include *kiosks* selling burgers, beer and ice cream; *Røgeriet*, a casual seaside spot specialising in smoked fish; and *Sejiklubbernes*, a substantial waterfront restaurant with a varied menu including daily specials for under 100kr. There are waterfront picnic tables where you can sit and eat, and a convenient coastal walkway leads between the harbour and the Karen Blixen museum.

FREDERIKSBERG

MG Petersens Familiehave (Map 6, E3; ☎ 36 16 11 33, Pile Allé 16), south-east of Frederiksberg Have, is one of the more interesting places to eat in Frederiksberg. In keeping with this neighbourhood's garden character, this large, casual 140-year-old eatery serves Danish family fare at outdoor tables. Specialities include fried pork and boiled potatoes for 65kr, beef rib roast and chips for 75kr and a 98kr multi-item platter with marinated herring, fish fillet, boiled shrimp, Danish meatballs, roast pork, pâté, cheese and bread. It's a seasonal operation, open 11 am to 11 pm daily from April to September. In the evening there are often musicians playing old-fashioned Danish tunes.

At the other end of the dining spectrum is *Formel B* (Map 6, E4; ☎ 33 25 10 66, Vesterbrogade 182), which offers intimate formal dining and a seven-course menu of the day for 575kr. The food is a merge of French and Danish cuisine that utilises seasonally fresh items. It's open 6 to 10 pm Monday to Saturday, for dinner only.

DRAGØR

This quaint seaside village, south of Copenhagen airport, has a good selection of eating options in keeping with its nautical character.

Restaurants

The 200-year-old *Dragorr Kro* (☎ 32 53 00 53, Strandgade 30) is hard to beat for atmosphere. Lunch, 11.30 am to 4 pm, offers dishes such as a fish fillet or an omelette for around 60kr. At dinner there's a vegetarian meal for 89kr, or you can try the Danish favourite, a 200g steak with potatoes and salad, for 159kr.

Beghuset (☎ 32 53 01 36, Strandgade 14), Dragør's top restaurant, features traditional Danish dishes and French-influenced fare. At lunch, served from noon to 3 pm, there are multi-item Danish plates for around 150kr and sandwiches for about half that. At dinner, 6 to 9.45 pm, full-course meals cost around 250kr. It's closed on Monday.

Cafes

Pakhuset (☎ 32 53 93 07, Gamle Havn) at the harbour, behind the Dragør Museum, is the village's newest cafe. A small museum-run place, it has sandwiches and light eats such as a herring plate or smoked shrimp with salad for around 70kr. It's open noon to 4 pm Tuesday to Sunday.

Fast Food, Bakeries & Markets

There's a small bakery, *Laura Ella* (Kongevejen 13), in the town centre. There's a *fruit stand* next door and a *Super Brugsen* grocery store across the street.

Dragør Is, opposite the harbour, won the 'golden scoop award' for dishing out the most ice cream in Denmark. And for 17kr, you can join the crowd and walk out with a couple of scoops of your own.

Entertainment

Copenhagen is a 24-hour party city. For free entertainment simply stroll along Strøget, especially between Nytorv and Højbro Plads, which in the late afternoon and evening is a bit like an impromptu three-ring circus with musicians, magicians, jugglers and other street performers.

Copenhagen has scores of backstreet cafes and clubs with live music, so there's no shortage of places to have a drink or hit the dance floor. Danes tend to be late-nighters and many places don't really start to get going until 11 pm or midnight.

The free entertainment publication *Nat & Dag* lists concerts, club schedules and cafe events in detail; it can be found at Use It, the tourist office and various clubs.

Each summer the Copenhagen area hosts two world-renowned music festivals: the Copenhagen Jazz Festival, which takes place in scores of venues throughout the capital, and the Roskilde Festival, a huge Woodstock-like rock event that takes place in the ancient city of Roskilde, a short train ride from central Copenhagen.

Information on the Copenhagen Jazz Festival is in a special section. Details on the Roskilde Festival are under Rock in this chapter.

BOOKING OFFICES

Tivoli Billetcenter (Tivoli Map; ☎ 38 88 22 22, fax 38 88 22 23, *Vesterbrogade 3*) at the Tivoli main entrance is a good first stop when looking for tickets of any kind. Billetcenter is the box office for ARTE, which handles tickets for plays in Copenhagen; an agent for BilletNet, which sells tickets for concerts, dance productions and music festivals nationwide; and the box office for productions at the Tivoli concert hall. Tivoli Billetcenter is open 10 am to 8 pm daily, but closed on Sunday in the low season.

Post offices are also agents for BilletNet. You can get schedule information for concerts and theatre productions on the Web sites at www.billetnet.dk and www.arte.dk.

If you want to make bookings while overseas, you can call the Tivoli Billetcenter directly at its international booking number (☎ 38 88 70 14) and pay by credit card. The tickets can be mailed to you overseas for a fee, or you can pick them up at the office once you arrive in Copenhagen.

If you're up for a last-minute theatre experience, it's possible to get half-price tickets for unsold seats in the city's theatres. These discounted tickets are sold at the Tivoli Billetcenter starting at noon for performances taking place that same day.

PUBS & CAFES

When Danes want to go out for a drink, they head for a cafe. Copenhageners are fond of cosy places and consequently cafes play a leading role in the city's social scene. Cafes are generally places where you can go and stay for hours – they not only serve alcohol, but if you've an inkling for a meal, dessert or coffee, you can order those as well. And some cafes add music to the mix, particularly at weekends.

As for pubs – there's not necessarily much to differentiate them from cafes. The general trend here is that most places that refer to themselves as a pub have an Irish or British theme.

Vesterbro

Bang & Jensen Café (Map 7, F1; ☎ 33 25 53 18, *Istedgade 130*) is a popular place with people in their 20s. At the site of a former chemist shop, it sports eclectic furniture and old pinball machines. The place is busiest on Saturday when there's Latin music.

A few of the area's largest hotels have lobby bars, including *Radisson SAS Royal Hotel* (Map 7, D3; ☎ 33 42 60 00, *Hammerichsgade 1*) at the north-eastern side of Vesterbro.

Rådhuspladsen & Around

Café Bjørg (Map 8, F1; ☎ 33 14 53 20, *Vester Voldgade 19*) situated a block north of Rådhuspladsen is a stylish Danish cafe offering a quiet venue for an evening drink.

Bustling *Hard Rock Cafe (Map 7, D3; ☎ 33 12 43 33, Vesterbrogade 3)* near the tourist office has the expected rock and roll theme, Carlsberg draught on tap and a happy hour from 5.30 pm with half-price mixed drinks.

If you prefer a British accent and brew, there's *Old English Pub (Map 7, D3; ☎ 33 32 19 21)* at Vesterbrogade 2B and neighbouring *Rosie Mcgee's (Map 7, D3; ☎ 33 32 19 23)*, a Scottish-style pub at Vesterbrogade 2A. Also in the area is *Shamrock Inn (☎ 33 14 06 02)*, an Irish pub in the Scala complex, on Vesterbrogade opposite Tivoli.

Strøget & Around

Absalon's Bar (Map 8, G2) at the western end of Strøget is a small local watering hole best known for its curious basement toilet, which has a couple of stones embedded in the wall that are thought to have once belonged to a 12th-century church constructed by Bishop Absalon.

Australian Bar (Map 8, E2; ☎ 33 15 04 80) at the rear of Vestergade 10, one block north of Strøget, is a casual place with a Down Under decor and a half-dozen pool tables.

Café Europa (Map 8, E7; ☎ 33 12 04 28, Amagertorv 1), a continental-style cafe, sets up tables right on Højbro Plads when it's sunny, making it a great place for people-watching.

For local flavour there's *Café Sorgenfri (Map 8, E4; ☎ 33 11 58 80, Brolæggerstræde 8)*, which is a typical neighbourhood establishment that serves Danish schnapps and beer.

The Dubliner (Map 8, E7; ☎ 33 32 22 26, Amagertorv 5) on the western side of Højbro Plads is a trendy pub with Danish and Irish brews, live Irish folk music and big-screen sports TV.

Konrad (Map 8, C7; ☎ 33 93 29 29, Pilestræde 12) is an upmarket bar inside one of the area's fancier restaurants – the bar is pricey but with lots of style and late hours.

Trendy *Krasnapolsky (Map 8, E2; ☎ 33 32 88 00, Vestergade 10)* west of Gammel Torv boasts the longest bar in Copenhagen and attracts a large late-night crowd.

Peder Oxe (Map 8, D5; ☎ 33 11 00 77, Gråbrødre Torv 11) has an atmospheric wine cellar that incorporates some of the stone walls from Copenhagen's oldest monastery, which was built on this site in 1238.

Latin Quarter

Atlas Bar (Map 8, E2; ☎ 33 15 03 52, Larsbjørnstre18), a cafe in the gay district, is a cosy place for an afternoon or evening drink.

Britannia (Map 8, C6; ☎ 33 14 89 69, Løvstræde 4) two blocks south of the Round Tower is not only a dance club, but also has a bar with darts and eight pool tables.

Café Sommersko (Map 8, C7; ☎ 33 14 81 89, Kronprinsensgade 6) draws a high-energy university crowd and serves a wide variety of drinks, including 50 different brands of beer.

Klaptræet (Map 8, B4; ☎ 33 13 31 48, Kultorvet 11), a cafe overlooking Kultorvet square, has a casual unpretentious atmosphere. Kultorvet itself becomes a popular beer garden in summer, when some of the nearby businesses, including Klaptræet, set up tables in the square and sell beer on tap.

Kul-Kaféen (Map 8, D1; ☎ 33 32 17 77, Teglgårdsstræde 5) is geared to a youthful crowd, with night-time activities including everything from slam poetry to music.

Sabines Cafeteria (Map 8, D1; ☎ 33 14 09 44, Teglgårdsstræde 4) is an inviting cafe that attracts a mixed crowd.

Studenterhuset (Map 8, B5; ☎ 35 32 38 61, Købmagergade 52) near the Round Tower is a student haunt with cheap drinks and live jazz or rock music on Thursday and Friday.

Nyhavn & Around

Nyhavn 17 (Map 7, C7; ☎ 33 12 54 19, Nyhavn 17) is a popular pub right on Nyhavn canal. There are plenty of other places to have a cold beer on Nyhavn as well, and in the late spring and summer months cafes such as *Nyhavns Færgekro (Map 7, B7; ☎ 33 15 15 88, Nyhavn 5)* and *Cap Horn (Map 7, C7; ☎ 33 12 85 04, Nyhavn 21)* set up outdoor beer gardens on the pavement.

Beer aficionados will think they've staggered into paradise.

Fine dining on Gråbrødre Torv

The boys are back in town.

Sisters are doing it for themselves.

Quality Holmegaard glass

Herring buffet at Nyhavns Færgekro

Inside Royal Copenhagen's shop on Strøget

Diners enjoy the pleasant ambience of Café Sommersko in the Latin Quarter.

Amalienborg & Kastellet Area

At *KGB* (Map 7, B6; ☎ 33 36 07 70, *Dronningens Trærgade 22*), a restaurant and vodka bar, you can sample a variety of Russian drinks under the watchful eyes of Cold War-era Soviet leaders whose portraits line the walls.

Nørreport & Around

Globe Irish Pub (Map 8, B2; ☎ 33 32 08 60, *Nørregade 43*), an authentic Irish pub about 200m south of Nørreport station, has live music and football games on big-screen TV.

Stereo Bar (Map 7, B4; ☎ 33 13 61 13, *Linnesgade 16A*) is a late-night club that has a small dance floor with DJ music and attracts a predominantly young crowd.

Nørrebro

Café Blågåds Apotek (Map 7, A2; ☎ 35 37 24 42, *Blågårdsgade 20*) is a smoky bar that's a venue for folk, blues and swing music.

A favourite mellow place for a drink is nearby *Floras Kaffe Bar* (Map 7, A2; ☎ 35 39 00 18, *Blågårdsgade 27*), a casual cafe with outdoor seating on sunny days.

Propaganda (Map 7, A2; ☎ 35 39 49 00, *Nørrebrogade 13*), formerly the Banana Republic, is a late-night bar and dance venue.

Nørrebro's trendiest cafe, *Pussy Galore's Flying Circus* (Map 4, F4; ☎ 35 24 53 00, *Sankt Hans Torv*), is a popular place for drinks and snacks. On sunny summer days tables are placed on the square out front.

Also stylish is nearby *Sebastopol* (Map 4, F4; ☎ 35 36 30 02, *Sankt Hans Torv*), which occasionally has live jazz music; it, too, spills outside onto the square when the weather permits.

Christianshavn

Base Camp Holmen (Map 7, C9; ☎ 70 23 23 18, *Halvtolv 12*) is a former military base warehouse that's been converted into a happening entertainment and dining venue. This huge, cavernous place attracts large crowds at weekends when there's live music.

For those who prefer a mellower scene there's *Café Wilder* (Map 7, D7; ☎ 32 54 71 83, *Wildersgade 56*), a cosy neighbourhood cafe that's a popular late-night spot to linger over a drink.

A pleasant place on sunny summer days is *Christianshavns Bådudlejning og Café* (Map 7, E7; ☎ 32 96 53 53, *Overgaden neden Vandet 29*), a friendly outdoor cafe right on the edge of Christianshavn canal at the boat rental dock.

Woodstock (Map 7, D8), a seedy bar on Pusherstreet in Christiania, is in some ways a tattered remnant of the '60s with unapologetic marijuana smoking, but also heavy drinking by some down-and-out souls.

Østerbro

Park Café (Map 4, C7; ☎ 35 42 62 48, *Østerbrogade 79*) is the neighbourhood's most happening night venue. Its cafe section often has live entertainment and there are also a couple of large dance floors.

DISCOS & CLUBS

Copenhagen's club scene is a late one. Don't expect much to be happening before 10 pm, and things generally don't get into full swing until at least midnight.

For the latest club schedules, pick up a copy of the free *Musik Kalenderen*, a foldout monthly brochure found at the tourist office and entertainment venues around the city.

Rust (Map 4, F4; ☎ 35 24 52 00, *Guldbergsgade 8*) in the Nørrebro area is a bustling place that attracts one of the largest club crowds in Copenhagen. It has a couple of dance floors, a wide variety of current music, and occasional international performers. Wednesday features Club Lust with hot techno music.

Also in the Nørrebro area is *Stengade 30* (Map 7, A2; ☎ 35 36 09 38, *Stengade 18*), which has a lively alternative scene with everything from new wave and hip hop to techno and big-name rock.

Vega (Map 6, F5; ☎ 33 25 70 11, *Enghavevej 40*), in the Vesterbro area, occupies an old trade union building with an engaging 1950s ambience. It's now one of Copenhagen's hottest spots with big-name rock and jazz bands performing on its main stage, called Store Vega, and underground acts on its smaller Lille Vega stage.

Loppen (Map 7, D8; ☎ 32 57 84 22) in an old warehouse in Christiania is a popular spot with some of the city's top bands, ranging from funk and soul to punk rock. It's open Tuesday to Saturday. At weekends, the live concerts are followed at 2 to 5 am by a disco.

Subsonic (Map 8, D5; ☎ 33 13 26 25, *Skindergade 45)* in the Latin Quarter is a huge place with a large dance floor and DJs spinning pop and rock music from the '80s and '90s. It sports three bars and an offbeat modern decor.

Britannia (Map 8, C6; ☎ 33 14 89 69, *Løvstræde 4)* in the Latin Quarter, two blocks south of the Round Tower, is a multilevel dance venue with '70s and '80s music in the basement and techno and British pop on the upper floor.

Park Café (Map 4, C7; ☎ 35 42 62 48, *Østerbrogade 79)*, the Østerbro area's main night spot, has a couple of large dance floors – the upper level one with live music and the basement floor with a DJ. The music is varied but progressive and the crowd tends to be young and stylish.

Barcelona (Map 4, G4; ☎ 35 35 76 11, *Fælledvej 21)* in the Nørrebro area is heavily into rhythm and blues, hip hop and soul; there's a dance floor and DJ from Thursday to Saturday.

Tex Hot' N' Rock (Map 8, E2; ☎ 33 91 39 13, *Vestergade 7)* north of Strøget, near Gammel Torv, specialises in '70s and '80s jams with theme nights that perform the music of a single group, such as the Rolling Stones, Bon Jovi or Black Sabbath.

In (Map 8, E3; ☎ 33 11 74 78, *Nørregade 1)* between Strøget's Gammel Torv and the Latin Quarter's Vor Frue Kirke has a disco that attracts a young crowd; it plays current chart toppers and some world music.

Club Mantra (Tivoli Map; ☎ 33 11 11 13, *Bernstorffsgade 3)*, a disco at Tivoli, features reggae on Thursday and rhythm and blues on Friday and Saturday.

Pumpehuset (Map 7, D3; ☎ 33 93 14 32, *Studiestræde 52)* in the city centre features live rock and pop bands, with occasional theme nights highlighting the music of performers such as David Bowie or Tom Jones.

GAY & LESBIAN VENUES

Copenhagen has one of the liveliest gay and lesbian scenes in Europe. There are numerous gay bars, clubs and cafes, many of them concentrated along Studiestræde in the two blocks between Vester Voldgade and Nørregade.

In addition Landsforeningen for Bøsser og Lesbiske (Map 8, D1; LBL; ☎ 33 13 19 48, ⓔ lbl@lbl.dk), the national organisation for gay men and lesbians, has its headquarters in the heart of the gay district at Teglgårdstræde 13. It provides a wide range of services to the gay and lesbian community. (More on LBL can be found under Gay & Lesbian Travellers in the Facts for the Visitor chapter.)

Once you arrive in the city be sure to pick up a copy of *PAN-bladet*, published by LBL and available at its headquarters or at any of the businesses and clubs listed in this section. This monthly gay magazine has the latest information on gay organisations, entertainment venues and other places of interest. For the summer visitors, a handy English-language version, *PAN's Guide to Gay and Lesbian Denmark*, is published each June. Also worth picking up is the free foldout map *Copenhagen Gay Life Welcomes You*, which maps out gay sites and has ads by gay businesses.

Dancing

The main mixed gay and lesbian dance spot is *Pan* (Map 8, E4; ☎ 33 11 37 84, *Knabrostræde 3)* at the south side of Strøget, which has three bars and two dance floors. Typically one disco spins the latest sounds and the other focuses on camp pop and romantic music. Pan is open 8 pm (the discos open at 10 pm) until at least 5 am Wednesday to Saturday.

Trendy *Never Mind* (Map 7, C3; ☎ 33 11 88 86, *Nørre Voldgade 2)* is a dance bar that attracts a mixed late-night crowd; it's open 10 pm to 6 am daily.

Cafes & Clubs

Cosy Bar (Map 8, E1; ☎ 33 12 74 27, *Studiestræde 24)* is a late-night meeting place that attracts mostly men, with the largest crowds

And a Gay Time Is Had by All

Copenhagen's annual gay pride parade, called Mermaid Pride, is the city's biggest and splashiest gay event of the year.

Typically, upwards of 2000 gay men and lesbians strut their way through the city as thousands of cheering spectators line the parade route. It's a wildly colourful event with brilliant floats and a varied group of paraders – some of the guys dress solely in body paint and others are decked out in fine threads like a queen headed for a royal ball. Participants include 'dykes on bikes', men into leather and costumed folks who look like they're ready for a Rio Carnival.

Mermaid Pride usually takes place on the first or second Saturday in August. The parade begins at 1 pm at the parking area of Landbohøjskolen, a veterinarian school on Thorvaldsenvej, about 1km west of the lake Sankt Jørgen Sø. From there it loops west briefly along Hostrupsvej, heads south on Falkoner Allé and Allégade and then turns east into the city along Vesterbrogade, HC Andersens Blvd and Stormgade to its final destination at Slotsholmen. The whole route takes about 3½ hours to complete.

CLINT CURÉ

At Slotholmen's Christianborg Slotsplads, the square fronting parliament, parade organisers and gay rights activists hand out awards and give speeches, interspersed with live music and dancing.

The event then moves to Tivoli, where gay ballroom dancing takes place at 10 pm at Tivoli's main stage. In addition, all of the city's gay bars stay open until 5 am on this day and many of them offer special activities of their own.

The organisers of the Mermaid Pride parade have a Web site at www.mermaidpride.dk.

after 3 am. It's open midnight to 6 am weekdays and 11 pm to 7 am at weekends.

Masken (Map 8, E1; ☎ 33 91 09 37, Studiestræde 33), open 4 pm to 2 am daily, has a mellow atmosphere with cheap beer and good sandwiches; it's mainly a hang-out for gay men, but Thursday is Ladies Night. At weekends it attracts a young mixed crowd.

Copenhagen Men's Bar (Map 8, D1; Teglgårdsstræde 3) in the gay district around the corner from Studiestræde is the place to go for guys into leather. It's open 3 pm to 2 am daily.

Pan Bogcafé (☎ 33 13 19 48, Teglgårdstræde 13) at the LBL complex is an informal gay bookshop and cafe selling coffee, beer and soft drinks; it's open 5 to 7 pm weekdays only.

Popular *Sebastian (Map 8, E5; ☎ 33 32 22 79, Hyskenstræde 10)* on a side street leading south from Strøget is a pleasant bar and cafe that attracts a mixed crowd of gay men and lesbians. It's open noon to 2 am daily with 'gay hour' discounted drinks 5 to 9 pm.

Centralhjørnet (Map 8, F3; ☎ 33 11 85 49, Kattesundet 18) just south of Strøjet is Copenhagen's oldest gay bar, dating back some 75 years. Its 1950s decor and corner jukebox attracts an older, lively crowd. It's open 11 am (3 pm on Sunday) to 1 am daily.

A block to the east is *Can-Can (Map 8, G3; ☎ 33 11 50 10, Mikkel Bryggers Gade 11)*, which also has a jukebox and attracts mostly gay men.

Café Intime (Map 6, D3; ☎ 38 34 19 58, Allégade 25) in the Frederiksberg area is an old-fashioned piano bar owned by a Swedish woman named Monica who leads sing-alongs. The place attracts a mixed crowd of lesbians and drag queens. It's open 5 pm (8 pm on Saturday) to 2 am Wednesday to Sunday.

Queen Victoria (Slotsholmen Map; ☎ 33 91 01 91, Snaregade 4) between Strøget and Slotsholmen is a bar and restaurant operated by one of the city's best-known drag queens. It's open 5 pm to midnight daily.

ENTERTAINMENT

In addition to the preceding gay businesses, some places that aren't predominantly gay venues also stage occasional gay entertainment. For instance, ***Britannia*** *(Map* **8, C6**; ☎ *33 14 89 69, Løvstræde 4)* in the Latin Quarter has drag shows every Friday.

Cruising

Ørstedsparken, a couple of blocks northwest of Studiestræde, is a popular gay cruising site but those visiting the park should be cautious as anti-gay gangs occasionally come through the park as well. The trees at Ørstedsparken have unique 'bird houses', which are lidded boxes stocked with condoms by safe-sex volunteers. The gay clubs and bars also distribute free condoms.

In addition to the bars and clubs listed in this section, Copenhagen has a handful of gay saunas, video rooms and sex clubs; the aforementioned publications list them.

ROCK

Most of the Copenhagen clubs that feature live music and dancing have rock bands at least part of the time. Three leading Danish groups to keep an eye out for are Aqua, D-A-D and Kashmir. The greater Copenhagen area also features some noteworthy open-air concerts during the summer season.

Roskilde Festival

The grand Roskilde Festival rocks sleepy Roskilde, a 25-minute train ride west of central Copenhagen, for four consecutive days each summer on the last weekend in June.

Inspired by the Woodstock and Isle of Wight festivals, the first Roskilde Festival was held in 1971, with some 20 bands performing to a gathering of 10,000. Since that time it's mushroomed into northern Europe's largest rock music festival, with more than 150 rock, techno and ethnic bands playing on seven stages.

Recent festival line-ups have included such headliners as Black Sabbath, the Beastie Boys, Bob Dylan, Iggy Pop, Marilyn Manson, Tori Amos, Lou Reed, The Cure and Nine Inch Nails. Over the years, the promoters have also been particularly astute at presenting new trends in rock and

at booking lesser-known groups (such as UB40 and Talking Heads) who have later gone on to stardom.

The Roskilde Festival is more than just music – it's a huge spirited bash with lots of drinking and partying. The average age of the festivalgoers is 24 and about half come from other countries, particularly Germany, Sweden, Finland, the Netherlands, Norway and Belgium. There are stalls selling everything from tattoos to fast food, but you may want to bring some food supplies of your own as prices are high.

Although it's always been a big party scene, the festival organisers have prided themselves in running a safety-conscious event. Nonetheless, tragedy befell the festival in 2000, when nine concertgoers suffocated as they were pressed forward by a crush of fans trying to get closer to a midnight performance by Pearl Jam. The grounds were muddy from rain and the victims, all young men, apparently slipped and fell as the crowd pushed forward.

What the 2000 tragedy will mean for the Roskilde Festival in the future remains to be seen, but it's possible that audience sizes will be reduced. Some 74,000 tickets were sold for the 2000 festival and an estimated 50,000 people were in the Pearl Jam audience.

All of the profits from the Roskilde Festival are distributed to charitable causes both at home and abroad. Festival tickets cost around 900kr, including camping at the site, and can be purchased in Denmark through BilletNet (☎ 38 88 70 22).

Tickets can also be obtained by calling ☎ 050-3135055 in the Netherlands, ☎ 03-231-1865 in Belgium, ☎ 0115 912 9116 in the UK or ☎ 0600 11616 in Finland. Advance sales typically start in December. The latest information can be obtained on the festival Web site at www.roskilde-festival.dk.

Other Open-Air Concerts

Throughout the summer numerous concerts are held in Copenhagen's parks and squares; most are free, though some charge small fees. The tourist office can give you the latest on where the smaller events are taking place. The two leading outdoor venues that have scheduled entertainment throughout the summer are Pavillonen and Femøren.

Beachside open-air concerts take place on Saturday afternoon from mid-May to early August at *Femøren park* (☎ 32 59 79 33) on the coast of Amager. Admission fees range from 50kr to 160kr, depending upon the group. The music is rock or pop, usually by top Danish groups, and each summer there are a few well-known international names such as Tower of Power, Robert Plant and the James Taylor Quartet. Femøren has a Web site at www.5-oeren.dk.

Pavillonen (Map 4, D5; ☎ 35 26 01 11), an open-air cafe at Fælledparken, a large park in the Østerbro district, stages free music all summer long. The entertainment varies with the day of the week, but can be anything from tango to blues or rock. At weekends, which is the busiest time, there's live music 8 to 10 pm, followed by a DJ until 5 am. It's closed on Tuesday. Pavillonen has a Web site at www.pavillonen.dk.

JAZZ & BLUES

Copenhagen Jazz House (Map 8, D6; ☎ 33 15 26 00, Niels Hemmingsensgade 10) is the city's leading jazz spot, featuring top Danish musicians and occasional international performers. The music runs the gamut from bebop to fusion jazz, and there's a large dance floor. The main nights are Thursday, Friday and Saturday, but there can be performances on other nights as well.

JazzHuset Vognporten (Map 8, G4; ☎ 33 15 20 02, Rådhusstræde 13), another significant jazz venue in the city centre, has lots of Danish performers but also musicians from the USA and UK.

La Fontaine (Map 8, F5; ☎ 33 11 60 98, Kompagnistræde 11) is a casual late-night venue for swing and mainstream jazz musicians, including visiting artists who sometimes end up jamming together.

Mojo (Map 7, D4; ☎ 33 11 64 53, Løngangstræde 21) is the city centre's hot spot for blues, with live entertainment nightly.

SALSA

If you're up for something with a Latin twist, the following two places offer salsa dancing on Thursday, Friday and Saturday nights.

Sabor Latino (Map 7, D4; ☎ 33 11 97 66, Vester Voldgade 85) features Cuban-style salsa and merengue, and you can dance sometimes to disco, sometimes to live Latin bands. Neophytes should arrive at 10 pm for an hour of free dance instruction.

Newer *Columbus* (Map 7, A2; ☎ 35 37 00 51, Nørrebrogade 22) in the ethnically diverse Nørrebro area has a salsa disco.

CINEMAS

Danish movie theatres mainly feature the latest in big-name international films, with a heavy dose of Hollywood, but they also mix in some classics, art films and Danish titles. Movies are shown in their original language with Danish subtitles.

At most cinemas, ticket prices vary with the time of the day and the day of the week, ranging from around 40kr for weekday matinee shows to about 75kr for movies after 6 pm at weekends.

The majority of Copenhagen's cinemas are clustered within a few blocks of each other right in the city centre, convenient to both Central Station and the Rådhuspladsen bus terminal. Collectively, they have a couple of dozen screens so there's always a wide variety of flicks to choose from.

The two largest multiscreen cinemas – *Scala* (Map 7, D3; ☎ 33 13 81 00, Axeltorv 2) and *Palads* (Map 7, D3; ☎ 70 13 12 11, Axeltorv 9) – are near each other along Vesterbrogade opposite Tivoli.

Other multiscreen cinemas in the same neighbourhood are *Palladium* (☎ 70 13 12 11, Vesterbrogade 1) in the Rådhusarkaden shopping centre; *Dagmar Teatret* (Map 7, D3; ☎ 33 14 32 22, Jernbanegade 2); and *Grand Teatret* (Map 8, G3; ☎ 33 15 16 11, Mikkel Bryggers Gade 8) just off Strøget.

For those staying in the Østerbro area, *Park Bio* (Map 4, C6; ☎ 35 38 33 62, Østerbrogade 72) screens both contemporary and classic films.

In addition to these places, Det Danske Filminstitut, the same organisation that helps bankroll most Danish films, runs informal *Filmhusets Cinematek* (Map 7, B5;

ENTERTAINMENT

☎ *33 74 34 12, Gothersgade 55)* at the northern end of the Latin Quarter. It shows a mix of Danish and classic international films daily, except Monday, and has low prices.

The city also has an Omnimax theatre, in the *Tycho Brahe Planetarium (*Map 7, D2*; ☎ 33 12 12 24, Gammel Kongevej 10)*, which shows fast-moving nature and adventure films on a giant screen. For more information see Tycho Brahe Planetarium in the Things to See & Do chapter.

BALLET & OPERA

Den Kongelige Ballet (the Royal Danish Ballet) and Den Kongelige Opera (the Royal Danish Opera) perform at *Det Kongelige Teater* (Map 8, D10; the Royal Theatre) at Kongens Nytorv. The season runs from mid-August to late May, skipping the main summer months.

The Royal Danish Ballet performs classic works, such as *Giselle*, *Swan Lake* and August Bournonville's *La Sylphide*. It also presents contemporary ballets, some choreographed specifically for the Royal Danish Ballet. Likewise, the Royal Danish Opera not only performs classics by Wagner, Puccini and Verdi, but also stages a couple of innovative new operas each season.

An English-language brochure with the season schedule is available from the tourist office, or write to The Royal Theatre, Box Office, PO Box 2185, 1017 Copenhagen K.

If booking from abroad, you can charge the tickets to a credit card and have them mailed to you. For bookings and information call ☎ 33 69 69 69 between 1 and 7 pm Monday to Saturday; send a fax to 33 69 69 30; or go online to www.kgl-teater.dk and email your request. Keep in mind that refunds will only be given in case of cancellation of the performance or a change of repertoire.

Standard ticket prices are from 50kr to 300kr, but there are some discounts to be found. One is a last-minute deal – whenever there's a performance that hasn't been sold out by 5 pm, the box office will begin selling the remaining tickets for that evening's show at 50% off. In addition, those aged under 26 or over 67 are entitled to 50% off all standard ticket prices at any time.

THEATRE

Copenhagen theatres have been suffering in recent years from cuts in government subsidies, dwindling private support and shrinking audiences. In addition, critics have tended to be tough on theatres, taking them to task for producing plays that have been slanted to the mainstream and lacking artistic innovation.

That said and done, Copenhagen does have a number of theatres that maintain regular production schedules, so there are always at least a few plays to select from at any one time.

Note that plays are usually produced in Danish – which might be amusing if you've always wondered what *Don Quixote* sounds like in a foreign tongue, but it's apt to leave most visitors scratching their heads, particularly if it's a play that they're not already familiar with.

Current productions are listed in the brochure *Teater Kalenderen* and the magazine *Copenhagen This Week*, both produced monthly and available free at the tourist office.

For information on getting half-price same-day theatre tickets, see Booking Offices earlier in this chapter.

Performances take place at the following theatres:

*Betty Nansen (*Map 6, E4*; ☎ 33 21 14 90, Frederiksberg Allé 57)* in the Frederiksberg area

*Café Teatret (*Map 8, C5*; ☎ 33 12 58 14, Skindergade 3)* in the Latin Quarter

*Cirkus Bygningen (*Map 7, D3*; ☎ 38 88 70 22, Jernbanegade 8)* in the city centre

*Dansescenen (*Map 4, C6*; ☎ 35 43 58 58, Østerfælled Torv 34)* near Fælledparken in Østerbro

*Det Kongelige Teater (*Map 8, D10*; ☎ 33 69 69 69, Kongens Nytorv)* in the Nyhavn area

*Det Ny Teater (*Map 7, E2*; ☎ 33 25 50 75, Gammel Kongevej)* in the Vesterbro area

*Folke Teatret (*Map 8, B2*; ☎ 33 12 18 45, Nørregade 39)* in the Latin Quarter

*Husets Teater (*Map 7, E2*; ☎ 33 25 13 76, Halmtorvet 9)* south-west of Central Station in the Vesterbro area

*Kanonhallen (*Map 4, C6*; ☎ 35 43 20 21, Serridslevvej 2)* near Fælledparken in Østerbro

*Mammutteatret (*Map 4, E8*; ☎ 33 12 58 14, Livjægergade 17)* in the Østerbro area

*Nørrebros Teater (*Map 7, A2*; ☎ 35 39 27 11, Ravnsborggade 3)* in the Nørrebro area

*Østre Gasværk Teater (*Map 4, B7*; ☎ 39 27 71 77, Nyborggade 17)* in the Østerbro area

*Private Teatret (*Map 7, D2*; ☎ 33 32 33 33, Nyropsgade 41)* in the Vesterbro area

*Teater Sthyr & Kjær (*Map 8, G4*; ☎ 35 15 20 07, Magstræde 14)* next to Use It

Of special interest for children are the free marionette shows performed during the months of June, July and August at the eastern side of Kongens Have, the public gardens near Rosenborg Slot. These puppet shows last a half-hour and begin at 2 and 3 pm daily, except Monday.

TIVOLI

The *Tivoli Koncertsal* (concert hall) is the venue for symphony orchestra, string quartet and other classical music performances by Danish and international musicians. There's a ballet festival each season featuring top international troupes, as well as cabaret performances. It also has modern dance performances by such big names as the Alvin Ailey dance troupe. Tickets are sold at the Tivoli Billetcenter (☎ 33 15 10 12), Vesterbrogade 3, near the main Tivoli entrance.

Tivoli also hosts numerous free performances to parkgoers, including the Italian-influenced *Commedia dell'Arte*, which is a pantomime that plays nightly at the open-air pantomime theatre near the Vesterbrogade entrance. For the locations of these venues, see the Tivoli map.

CASINO

If you want to try your hand with the high rollers, *Casino Copenhagen (*☎ 33 96 59 65)* at Radisson SAS Scandinavia Hotel (Map 7, F6), Amager Blvd 70, in the northern part of Amager, has slot machines, stud poker, blackjack tables and both American and French roulette. It's open 2 pm to 4 am daily. Admission is restricted to those aged 18 and over, and there's a cover charge to get in.

SPECTATOR SPORTS

The national sport is football and Denmark's national football team has fared fairly well in recent years. If you're keen to watch an international match, games are played at *Parken (*Map 4, D6*; ☎ 35 43 31 31)*, Denmark's national stadium in Copenhagen, which is at the eastern side of Fælledparken in the Østerbro area. That's also the leading Copenhagen venue for national league play, which occurs between late July and early December and from early March to late May.

If you're interested in horse races, there's the *Charlottenlund Travbane*, a trotting (harness racing) track in Charlottenlund, and *Klampenborg Galopbane* (Map 1, B4), a horse-racing track immediately south of Bakken in Klampenborg.

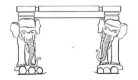

Shopping

When it's time for a shopping spree many Danes prefer to go outside their own country to places such as Germany where things are cheaper, so you shouldn't expect a lot of bargains while shopping in Copenhagen.

On the plus side, most visitors have an advantage over Danes in that they can get a refund on most of the 25% value-added tax (VAT), as long as they make their purchases at shops that participate in the 'Tax Free Shopping Global Refund' scheme. Those shops that participate sport a 'Tax Free Shopping' emblem in their windows, and these include most of the tourist-oriented shops along Strøget. For details on the VAT rebates see Taxes & Refunds under Money in the Facts for the Visitor chapter.

Cutting down the tax will help drop prices to more reasonable levels, but it still won't make many things cheap, since most of the items you'll find in speciality shops – from porcelain to down comforters – are of a pricey calibre to begin with.

Simply put, Danes are relatively wealthy and quite stylish so they tend to be discriminating shoppers who demand high quality. In the shops of Copenhagen you certainly can find many things that you'd be happy to own.

WHAT TO BUY
Porcelain & Crystal

One of the world's most famous sets of porcelain is the Flora Danica dinner service. The original set dates from 1790 and consists of 1800 unique pieces, each hand-painted with a different native Danish flower or plant, and rimmed with gold. Pieces of that original set are on display at Copenhagen's Rosenborg Slot (Map 7, A5). You can also see examples – or if money is no obstacle, purchase your own reproduced set – at the Royal Copenhagen porcelain shop (Map 8, D6) on Strøget.

The other leader in Danish porcelain is Bing & Grøndahl, founded in 1853. It too has a variety of tableware, much of it decorated with finely painted floral designs. Bing & Grøndahl is perhaps most widely known for its annual Christmas plates, which it has been issuing for more than a hundred years. These plates, which are cobalt blue and white with a traditional winter design, are collected by millions of people worldwide.

Denmark's principal producer of quality glassware and crystal is Holmegaard, founded in 1825.

Both Holmegaard glass and Bing & Grøndahl porcelain are now affiliated with Royal Copenhagen and you can find products of all three companies at Royal Copenhagen's shop on Strøget at Amagertorv 6 near Højbro Plads.

For the latest trends in European porcelain and crystal, such as Gianni Versace tableware, Sweden's Orrefors crystal, Danish art glass and ceramic figurines, take a look at Rosenthal StudioHaus (Map 8, F2; ☎ 33 14 21 01) at Frederiksberggade 21 on Strøget.

If, on the other hand, you're looking for a bargain, head out to Royal Copenhagen's factory at the western side of the city. The factory has a shop where it sells its slightly flawed seconds for up to 50% off department store prices. Items such as cups or teapots can be purchased inexpensively by the piece. The factory shop (☎ 38 34 10 04) is at Smallegade 47 in the Frederiksberg area. For information on touring the factory, see the Frederiksberg section in the Things to See & Do chapter.

Silver

With its clean lines and its skilful merging of aesthetics and function, Danish silverwork is prized both in Denmark and abroad. The chief design criteria are that the item be attractive yet simple, as well as easy to use.

The father of modern Danish silverwork was sculptor and silversmith Georg Jensen, who artistically incorporated curvilineal designs; his namesake company is still a leader in Danish silverwork today. Two of Jensen's students, Kay Bojesen and Henning Koppel, are also leading names in Danish silverwork.

The Georg Jensen shop (**Map 8, D7**; ☎ 33 13 71 81), Amagertorv 4, features fine silverwork, including cutlery, candleholders, jewellery and designer art pieces. It also has museum-quality displays that are worth a look whether you're a shopper or not.

Traditional Jewellery

The Vikings made ornate jewellery that incorporated lots of curving, intertwined shapes resembling the tails of serpents and dragons. These days a company called Museums Kopi Smykker reproduces Viking designs with many of the pieces moulded after Viking-era jewellery.

You can get bracelets, necklaces, pins and earrings in bronze, gold or sterling silver at Museums Kopi Smykker's shop (**Map 8, B9**; ☎ 33 32 76 72) at Grønnegade 6, north of Strøget, or at its airport shop (☎ 32 50 03 10).

Another jewellery shop that specialises in traditional Danish design with historic influences is Strædets (**Map 8, E7**), Læderstræde 10, near Højbro Plads.

For more on replicated historic jewellery see Nationalmuseet under Gifts & Souvenirs later in this chapter.

Amber

Amber is fossilised tree resin that is translucent and brittle. It's usually golden yellow, but it can appear in other hues, such as reddish brown. Some pieces of amber contain fossilised ferns or insects that were trapped inside the resin aeons ago when it was still sticky. No two pieces are ever alike. Most amber found in Denmark dates back at least 20 million years and is derived from the resin of the great pine forests that once blanketed the region.

Amber is polished and made into jewellery, particularly pendants, beaded necklaces, earrings and rings.

There are many shops selling amber in Copenhagen, including Amber Specialist (**Map 8, F2**; ☎ 33 11 88 03) at Frederiksberggade 28 on Strøget, and House of Amber (**Map 7, B6**; ☎ 33 11 04 44) at Kongens Nytorv 2, which also houses a small amber museum.

Gifts & Souvenirs

The gift shops at museums are great places to pick up quality Danish-made items that will remind you of your trip.

The Dansk Design Centre (**Map 7, D4**; ☎ 33 69 33 69), HC Andersens Blvd 27, has a lobby gift shop selling a variety of items. In addition to books, magazines and posters, it features contemporary objects by leading Danish designers such as a stainless steel salad set designed by Arne Jacobsen, a cream pitcher by Ursula Munch-Petersen and glass bowls by Anja Kjær.

The gift shop at Nationalmuseet (**Map 7, D4**; ☎ 33 13 41 11), Ny Vestergade 10, carries a nice selection of jewellery moulded on Viking and Iron Age finds from the museum's collection. This includes such things as a pendant in the shape of dragon heads, a brooch depicting a Viking ship and various bracelets and rings, all made at the national museum in 14-carat gold or sterling silver. The national museum's gift shop also sells other items such as Viking ship models and a variety of posters and books.

Louisiana, the modern art museum in Humlebæk, has a large gift shop with a fine array of arty gift items, including coffee cups with Andy Warhol motifs, art prints and designer toys. It also has an excellent selection of English-language art books covering both its own collection and art in general.

If you want to bring home images of some of the works you've seen at Statens Museum for Kunst (**Map 7, A5**; ☎ 33 74 84 84), Sølvgade 48, this museum has a wide assortment of books on both Danish and international art.

For those who enjoy kitsch, the tourist office sells an inexpensive Little Mermaid figure glued to a rock and decorated with a Danish flag – you can't get more cliched than that!

Contemporary Art

There's a budding contemporary art movement in Copenhagen and you can find numerous galleries throughout the city. A good place to start is at the eclectic Nikolaj Contemporary Art Center (☎ 33 93 16 26), a community-run project in the old Nikolaj church near Højbro Plads, a block south of Strøget. You can also find changing exhibits of local contemporary art in the exhibition room of the Rundetårn (**Map 8, B5**; ☎ 33 73 03 73) in the Latin Quarter.

Galerie Susanne Højriis (**Map 7, A7**; ☎ 33 14 04 41), Bredgade 63, specialises in minimalist sculpture and pictorial art by up-and-coming local artists. Gallerihuset (**Map 8, E2**; ☎ 33 15 35 52), Studiestræde 19, has a varied selection of Danish paintings and sculptures. Galleri Nørby (**Map 8, E3**; ☎ 33 15 19 20), Vestergade 8, features ceramics and other crafts, while Peter Svarrer (**Map 7, B6**; ☎ 33 32 22 41), Kronprinsessegade 34, houses its own workshop where it creates and sells handblown glass.

Galleri Bo Bjerggaard (**Map 8, B7**; ☎ 33 93 42 21), Pilestræde 48, carries the work of leading Danish artists, such as Per Kirkeby, and international contemporary art. Among the city's other leading private galleries selling both Danish and international art are Galerie Asbæk (**Map 7, B7**; ☎ 33 15 40 04), Bredgade 20; Galleri Christian Dam (**Map 7, B7**; ☎ 33 15 78 78), Bredgade 23; and Galleri Susanne Ottesen (**Map 8, A8**; ☎ 33 15 52 44), Gothersgade 49.

T-Shirts

T-shirts can make inexpensive souvenirs and many sport attractive Danish logos. T-shirt shops are numerous around the city centre so you won't have to look hard to find something that catches your fancy.

A good place to start is at Town Shop in Rådhusarkaden (**Map 7, D3**), opposite rådhus (**Map 7, D4**; city hall), which has a particularly large selection of T-shirts with both Copenhagen and Denmark images.

You can also find shirts in a few nonconventional locations – the municipal government, for instance, has a handsome black T-shirt with an abstract city skyline design that's sold in the lobby of rådhus and at the HT bus information office (**Map 8, G1**) on Rådhuspladsen. The tourist office, Bernstorffsgade 1, also sells some distinctively Copenhagen T-shirts.

And then there's Hard Rock Cafe (**Map 7, D3**), Vesterbrogade 3, which sells its usual selection of logo T-shirts with the word 'Copenhagen' front and centre.

Sweaters

Scandinavian sweaters are typically made of heavy wool, in rich blue or black colours accented with white and sporting snowflakelike designs. They are very distinctive, and ideally suited for warding off the chill in cold climates. A wide variety, including popular Norwegian styles, can be found at the Sweater Market (**Map 8, F3**; ☎ 33 15 27 73) at Frederiksberggade 15 on Strøget.

Fashion

Strøget is the place to shop for the latest in fashionable clothing. You can find leading designer names at shops such as Birger Christensen (**Map 8, D8**; ☎ 33 11 55 55), Østergade 38, which has Donna Karan, DKNY, Prada, Chanel and Hermès.

One of the latest shops on the scene is Kenzo (**Map 8, D7**; ☎ 33 14 01 10), Østergade 57, which specialises in cross-cultural designs, covering everything from sporty casualwear to silk dresses and men's suits. Sand (**Map 8, D8**; ☎ 33 14 21 21), Østergade 40, sells Danish-designed men's and women's clothing with lots of greys and blacks. For more conservative English-style clothing, there's a branch of Mulberry (**Map 8, C9**; ☎ 33 36 68 78), Østergade 13, selling handbags, wools and tweeds. All of the aforementioned places can run up a lofty credit-card balance pretty quickly.

For something that's more affordable, try Hennes & Mauritz, also known as H&M (**Map 8, E5**; ☎ 33 73 70 00), Amagertorv 21, which specialises in mass-producing contemporary clothing modelled on fashions from popular designers. Consequently, prices are quite reasonable for the neighbourhood.

Down Comforters

One treat of travelling in Denmark is cuddling under those soft goose-down comforters (known as continental quilts in Britain) that are the norm in hotels and guesthouses.

If you've taken to this cosy comfort it's possible to bring one home – unlike heavy woollen blankets, these soft, down-filled quilts compress reasonably well (they usually come with a stuff bag) and can probably be squeezed into your luggage without adding much weight or bulk.

One Strøget shop that specialises in down comforters is Ofelia Comforter Shop (**Map 8, E7**; ☎ 33 12 41 98), Amagertorv 3; the department stores also carry them.

Home Furnishings

The classic, sparse lines of Scandinavian design is popular in contemporary homes worldwide.

Modern Danish furniture focuses on the practical refinement of style and the principle that the design should be tailored to the comfort of the user.

Danish architects put such great emphasis on 'form following function' that they typically design a room only after considering the styles of furniture that are most likely to be used there. Not surprisingly many of Denmark's architects have crossed over into furniture design. One of them, Arne Jacobsen, introduced the rounded egg-shaped chair that typifies contemporary Danish chair styles.

Denmark's best-known lamp designer is Poul Henningsen, who in his work has emphasised the need for lighting to be soft, for the shade to cast a pleasant shadow, and for the lightbulb to be blocked from direct view. His PH-5 lamp is one of the most popular hanging lamps sold in Denmark today.

You can find one of the largest selections of contemporary furnishings and lamps at Illums Bolighus (**Map 8, D6**; ☎ 33 13 71 81) at Amagertorv 10 on Strøget.

The department store Illum (**Map 8, D7**; ☎ 33 14 40 02), a block to the west at Østergade 52, also has a good home furnishings section.

Electronics

Bang & Olufsen is the leading Danish name in high priced contemporary electronics. You can see some of its avant-garde stereo systems and sleekly designed televisions in its showroom (**Map 8, C9**) at Østergade 3 on the eastern end of Strøget.

Food & Drink

Illum, the Strøget department store at Østergade 52, has a basement supermarket with gourmet food items including Danish cheeses.

If you want to do your shopping where the royal family does, there are a couple of notable places that are official purveyors to the Crown. These include the centuries-old tea shop AC Perch (**Map 8, C6**) at Kronprinsensgade 5, north of Strøget, and the organic bakery Reihn van Hauen at Mikkel Bryggers Gade 2, near the western end of Strøget.

You can find organic wines in some supermarkets and at McGrails (**Map 8, E3**), a small health-food shop on the north-eastern corner of Gammel Torv. And, of course, the city makes some great beers under the Carlsberg label.

The most popular spirit in Denmark is aquavit and the most popular brand is Aalborg. There are several varieties, the most common of which is spiced with caraway seeds. Another popular Danish liqueur is cherry-flavoured Peter Heering, which is good sipped straight or served over vanilla ice cream. You can find these spirits in supermarkets or pick them up at the airport duty-free shops on your way home.

Books

Substantial bookshops stocking good selections of English-language books, travel guides and maps include GAD (**Map 8, E4**; ☎ 33 15 05 58), on Strøget at Vimmelskaftet 32, Politiken Boghallen (**Map 8, F1**; ☎ 33 47 25 60) at Rådhuspladsen 37 and Arnold Busck (**Map 8, C5**; ☎ 33 73 35 00) at Købmagergade 49 in the Latin Quarter.

GAD also has convenient branches in the lobby of the Royal Library south of Slotsholmen and in Central Station.

If you're looking specifically for international travel guidebooks, Kilroy Travels (**Map 8, D4**; ☎ 33 11 00 44), Skindergade 28, has a comprehensive selection. Nordisk Korthandel (**Map 8, E1**; ☎ 33 38 26 38), Studiestræde 26, sells guidebooks as well as an extensive range of cycling and hiking trail maps of Denmark and elsewhere in Europe. Librairie Française (**Map 8, E4**), south of Strøget at Badstuestræde 6, sells French-language books.

Book collectors will find good browsing in the antique bookshops along Fiolstræde in the block running between Krystalgade and Nørre Voldgade.

Postage Stamps

Denmark's postal service issues about 25 speciality stamps each year, and most of these are made using the old-fashioned steel engraving techniques that are favoured by collectors.

Stamp collectors can buy commemorative stamps from Post Danmark's shop Frimærkebutikken (☎ 33 41 09 00) at the Post & Tele Museum (**Map 8, C6**), Købmagergade 37. Stamps can also be purchased online at www.stamps.postdanmark.dk.

WHERE TO SHOP
Strøget

Copenhagen's main shopping street is Strøget, the famed pedestrian street that runs for more than a kilometre through the heart of the city. Along Strøget, you'll find numerous speciality shops selling everything from tacky souvenirs and fashionable jew-

Flying the Flag

The Danish flag, the Dannebrog, is the oldest national flag in the world. Legend has it that in 1219, during an invasion of Estonia by Valdemar the Victorious, a Danish defeat was turned around when a red banner with a white cross fell from the sky. A voice from the mist proclaimed that if the banner was raised, the Danes would win. The Danes followed the instructions, won their battle, and took this banner as their national flag.

These days the Danes display their flag in a surprising variety of ways. Bright red with a white cross, the Dannebrog can be seen hanging pennant-style in shopping streets, as graphics in magazine ads, and flying high on the flagpoles that stand beside virtually every home in the countryside. To Danes, displaying the flag is an equal measure of colourful adornment and national pride.

ellery and clothing to Danish porcelain, silver and electronics. It also has some of Denmark's best-known shops, including those of Georg Jensen and Royal Copenhagen, and a couple of quality department stores.

Strøget is a fun place – many of the shops are in classic period buildings, the streets are abuzz with other shoppers and the squares along the way are enlivened with street musicians and pavement cafes. If the shopping gets tiresome, there are plenty of options for tempting pastries and tea or a cold beer.

Latin Quarter

While the Strøget shops are the domain of tourists and fashion-conscious Danes, the Latin Quarter caters more to students, intellectuals and the counterculture. Instead of sleek stores with fancy window-dressing, it offers dusty secondhand shops including some antiquarian bookshops and a few small antique shops. The thickest collection of secondhand shops is on Fiolstræde in the block that runs north-east from Københavns Universitet.

Bredgade

Bredgade, the same street that houses the Kunstindustrimuseet (Museum of Decorative Art), is thick with art galleries, top-end antique shops and places specialising in estate sales. If you enjoy browsing for art and quality antiques this is the street to stroll. Between Nyhavn and Kunstindustrimuseet, virtually every second building along Bredgade houses a stylish gallery or antique shop. Keep in mind that this is the haunt of the well heeled so expect some high prices, but it'll give you a glimpse of some of the best that Copenhagen has to offer.

Department Stores

Copenhagen's largest department store, Magasin du Nord (**Map 8, D9**; ☎ 33 11 44 33), covers an entire block on the southwestern side of Kongens Nytorv and contains everything from clothing and luggage to tableware and a grocery shop. Illum (☎ 33 14 40 02), another large department store, on Strøget at Østergade 52, has a lot of avant-garde design items in the areas of fashion, sportswear, kitchenware and home furnishings.

Illums Bolighus (☎ 33 13 71 81), Amagertorv 10, stocks Danish-designed furniture, down comforters, ceramics, silverware and glass, but is also a good place to look for simple gifts such as a quality toy or a stainless steel cheese-slicer.

Flea Markets

There are a handful of flea markets around the city where you can buy jewellery and simple handicrafts. These tend to be rather small scale, but can vary by the week depending on the vendors and at any rate are fun for poking around.

Israels Plads in the Nørreport area has a casual flea market 8 am to 2 pm each Saturday from May to November.

Kongens Nytorv, the square at the head of Nyhavn, has a flea market open 10 am to 5 pm Saturday from May to October.

A somewhat more top-end flea market sets up at Gammel Strand, along the canal opposite Slotsholmen, 8 am to 5.30 pm Friday and Saturday from May to September.

In addition, the alternative community of Christiania in Christianshavn has an outdoor flea market of sorts at the entrance to Pusherstreet that sells pipes, T-shirts and jewellery. This one's open pretty much every day year-round, weather permitting.

Airport Shops

Most international airports have the requisite duty-free shops and a handful of concessionaires, but Copenhagen airport boasts a fully fledged shopping centre.

For all practical purposes, once departing passengers pass through the security station they enter a large shopping arena. There are a full 50 shops in the transfer area of the international terminal. These include tax-free shops such as Whiskey World, dealing in name-brand spirits; Wine Bar, with a selection of German and French wines; the Chocolate Shop, with top Scandinavian and Belgian sweets; and other shops selling the usual duty-free perfumes, cosmetics and cigarettes.

In addition there are numerous speciality shops. For Danish items there's a Georg Jensen silverware shop; a branch of Royal Copenhagen selling porcelain, glassware and figurines; a Lego shop with its popular toys; Museums Kopi Smykker, selling replicas of Viking jewellery; and a mini-branch of the department store Illums Bolighus, with a range of last-minute gift ideas. Of course, there are also the usual international speciality shops such as Nike and Gucci and plenty of other places selling a wide range of products, including men's and women's clothing, jewellery, electronic and audio equipment, watches, travel bags, lingerie, magazines and books.

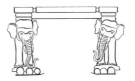

Excursions

Denmark is so compact and so convenient to get around by either train or car that virtually any place in the country makes a reasonable excursion from Copenhagen.

Certainly any place on the island of Zealand can be visited as an easy day trip. In addition, there are destinations beyond Zealand that could be taken in as full day trips or visited more leisurely as longer excursions.

North Zealand

The northern half of Zealand, the island that's home to Copenhagen, offers a wonderful variety of excursion options, with most destinations less than an hour from the city. Considering its proximity to Copenhagen, North Zealand is surprisingly rural, with small farms, wheat fields and beech woodlands. It also boasts fine beaches and some notable historic sights.

One of the most popular day trips from Copenhagen is a loop tour taking in Frederiksborg Slot in Hillerød and Kronborg Slot in Helsingør, with an optional stop at Fredensborg Slot in-between. With an early start you might even have time to continue on to one of the north shore beaches or visit Louisiana, the splendid modern art museum in Humlebæk, on the way back to Copenhagen.

And of course, if you're not tight for time, North Zealand has a number of destinations that invite a longer stay.

If you're driving up the coast to Helsingør, ignore the motorway and take the coastal road, Strandvej (route 152), which is far more scenic. The Øresund coast, which extends north from Copenhagen to the Helsingør area, is largely a run of small seaside suburbs and yachting harbours. On clear days you can look across the Øresund (Sound), which separates Denmark from Sweden, and see southern Sweden on the opposite shore.

When planning your tour, keep in mind that the Copenhagen Card allows free access to trains, buses and most sightseeing attractions throughout North Zealand (see the boxed text 'Card Does the Trick' in the Things to See & Do chapter).

HILLERØD
postcode 3400

Hillerød, 40km north-west of Copenhagen, is a small town centred around a grand lakeside castle, Frederiksborg Slot.

An administrative centre and transport hub for North Zealand, Hillerød isn't notably quaint in itself but the castle and the surrounding gardens are lovely. You can enjoy picturesque views of the castle by following the path that skirts the castle lake. If you feel like taking a longer stroll, paths run through Slotshaven, an expansive baroque-style privet garden immediately north of the castle and lake. The paths leading through Slotshaven connect with trails in the adjacent woodlands of Lille Dyrehave and Indelukket which, taken together, could easily make a pleasant one- or two-hour outing.

Information

Hillerød Turistbureau (☎ 48 24 26 26), Slangerupgade 2, is 50m south of the castle entrance. It's open 10 am to 5 pm weekdays, 10 am to 1 pm Saturday, except between mid-June and August when it's open 10 am to 6 pm weekdays, 10 am to 3 pm Saturday.

Frederiksborg Slot

This impressive Dutch Renaissance castle spreads across three islets at the eastern side of the castle lake, Slotsø. The oldest part of Frederiksborg Slot dates from the reign of Frederik II, after whom the castle is named, but most of the present structure was built in the early 17th century by Frederik II's more extravagant son, Christian IV.

As you enter the main gate you'll pass old stable buildings dating from the 1560s and then cross over a moat to the second islet, where you'll enter an expansive central courtyard with a grandly ornate Neptune

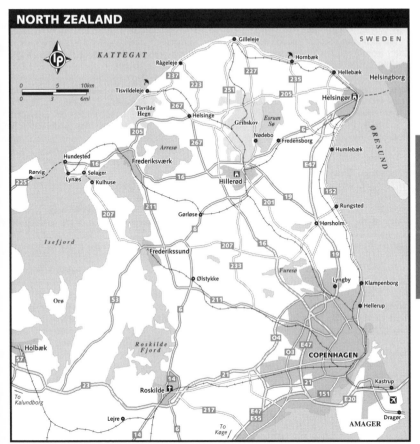

NORTH ZEALAND

KATTEGAT

SWEDEN

Gilleleje

Hornbæk

Rågeleje

Hellebæk

Helsingborg

Tisvildeleje

Tisvilde
Hegn

Helsinge

Helsingør

Gribskov

Esrum
Sø

ØRESUND

Arresø

Nødebo

Fredensborg

Humlebæk

Hundested

Frederiksværk

Rørvig

Sølager

Hillerød

Lynæs

Kulhuse

Rungsted

Gørløse

Hørsholm

Isefjord

Frederikssund

Ølstykke

Furesø

Lyngby

Klampenborg

Orø

Hellerup

Holbæk

Roskilde
Fjord

COPENHAGEN

Kastrup

To
Kalundborg

Roskilde

Lejre

Dragør

AMAGER

To
Køge

EXCURSIONS

fountain. The relatively modest wings that flank the fountain once served as residences for court officers and government officials. A second bridge crosses to the northernmost islet, the site of the main body of the castle, which served as the home of Danish royalty for more than a century.

Frederiksborg Slot was ravaged by fire in 1859. The royal family, unable to undertake the costly repairs, decided to give up the property. Carlsberg beer baron JC Jacobsen then stepped onto the scene and spearheaded a drive to restore the castle as a national museum, a function it still serves today.

The sprawling castle has a magnificent interior boasting gilded ceilings, wall-sized tapestries, period paintings and antique furnishings, with exhibits occupying 70 of its rooms. The richly embellished Riddershalen (Knights Hall) and Slotskirken (Coronation Chapel), where Danish monarchs were crowned from 1671 to 1840, are alone worth the admission fee. The chapel, incidentally, was spared serious fire damage and retains the original interior commissioned by Christian IV, including a lavish hand-carved altar and pulpit created by Mores of Hamburg in 1606 and a priceless Compenius organ built in 1610. The organ is played each Thursday between 1.30 and 2 pm.

Frederiksborg Slot is open 10 am to 5 pm daily from April to October, and 11 am to 3 pm during the rest of the year. Admission costs 45kr for adults, 10kr for children. Outside opening hours visitors are still free to stroll around the grounds and enter the castle courtyard.

If you arrive at the castle by car, there's free parking off Frederikværksgade, just west of the castle.

Places to Stay

Hillerød Camping (*☎/fax 48 26 48 54, Dyrskuepladsen*) is a three-star camping ground about a 20-minute walk directly south of the castle along Slangerupgade. It's open between May and mid-September. There are cooking facilities and a coin laundry, and cabins are available to rent.

Hotel Hillerød (*☎ 48 24 08 00, fax 48 24 08 74,* ⓔ *hotel@hotelhillerod.dk, Milnersvej 41*), about 2km south of the castle, has an atrium filled with flowering plants and 74 modern rooms with bath, TV and kitchenette. Normal rates for singles/doubles are 700/900kr but at weekends and holidays there's a reduced rate of 575/605kr.

Places to Eat

There are a number of inexpensive places to eat a few minutes' walk from the castle on Slotsgade. At No 38 there's a *McDonald's*, 200m farther east is an *Irma* grocery shop and just beyond that at No 27D is *Gonzales Cantina*, which serves the best pizza in town. Gonzales also offers good-value 29kr lunch specials (11 am to 4 pm) including lasagne, pizza or beef, while at other times steak or chicken dishes with salad and chips cost around 50kr and pitta-bread sandwiches cost 25kr. For drinks or a snack try *Hennessy's (Slotsgade 52)*, an Irish pub that serves up afternoon cake and tea (30kr) on a veranda overlooking the castle.

Getting There & Around

The S-train (A & E lines) runs every 10 minutes between Copenhagen and Hillerød (42kr), a 40-minute ride. From Hillerød sta-

tion follow the signs to the central square, Torvet, and then continue north-west along Slotsgade to the castle, a 15-minute walk in all, or grab bus No 701 (12kr), which can drop you at the gate.

The little ferry *Frederiksborg* sails across the castle lake about every 30 minutes from 11 am to 5 pm daily from June to August, landing at three small piers: one just north of Torvet, another near the castle entrance and the third north of the castle on the road to Slotshaven. The fare is 20kr for adults and 5kr for children.

FREDENSBORG
postcode 3480

Fredensborg is a quiet town with a royal palace, a lakeside location and some good walking tracks. If you're in no hurry, it's a pleasant place to stay for a day or two and unwind the clock.

Slotsgade, the road that terminates at the palace gate, has a number of historic buildings, including the classic inn **Hotel Store Kro** at No 6. **Villa Bournonville**, the former home of the 19th-century ballet master Auguste Bournonville at Slotsgade 9, is now an art gallery; **Havremagasinet**, Slotsgade 11, once served as horse stables; and **Kunstnergården**, an art and crafts gallery a bit farther south at Slotsgade 17, was originally an inn built in 1722.

Information

Fredensborg Turistinformation (*☎ 48 48 21 00, fax 48 48 04 65*), just outside the palace at Slotsgade 2, is open 10 am to 6 pm daily from late June to August, and 10 am to 4 pm weekdays and 11 am to 3 pm Sunday the rest of the year.

There are a couple of banks in the centre of town, including Den Danske Bank at Jernbanegade 5. The post office is at Helsingørvej 2 at the intersection with Jernbanegade.

Fredensborg Slot

This palace, the royal family's summer residence, was built in 1720 by Frederik IV. It was named Fredensborg, which means Peace Palace, to commemorate the peace that Denmark had recently achieved with its

Scandinavian neighbours. The palace certainly reflects the more tranquil mood of that era and is largely in the style of a country manor house, in contrast to the moat-encircled fortresses of Kronborg and Frederiksborg that preceded it.

The main mansion was designed by the leading Danish architect of the day, JC Krieger, and is in Italian baroque style with marble floors and a large central cupola. It's fronted by a large octagonal courtyard framed by two-storey buildings.

Partly because of its spread-out design, the palace is not as impressive as other Danish royal palaces in North Zealand. Fredensborg's interior can only be visited during July, when the royal family holidays elsewhere; guided tours cost 30kr for adults and 10kr for children and run every 30 minutes between 1 and 5 pm daily.

The palace is backed by 120 hectares of **wooded parkland**, crisscrossed by trails and open to the public year-round. Take a stroll through **Normandsdalen**, west of the palace, to a circular amphitheatre with 70 life-sized sandstone statues of Norwegian folk characters – fisherfolk, farmers and so on – in traditional dress. If you continue walking a few minutes' west from there you'll reach Esrum Sø, a lake skirted by another trail.

To get to Fredensborg Slot from the train station, turn left onto Stationsvej and then turn right onto Jernbanegade, which merges with Slotsgade near the palace gate; the whole walk takes about 10 minutes.

Other Attractions

The south-eastern shore of **Esrum Sø**, Denmark's second-largest lake, borders Fredensborg and offers swimming, boating and fishing. Along the shore you can sometimes spot ospreys and cormorants, and the surrounding woods are the habitat of roe deer.

It's a 10-minute walk west from the palace gate along Skipperallé to Skipperhuset (☎ 48 48 01 07), a lakeside restaurant where there's a summer ferry service and rowing boats for hire. The main beach is nearby. The ferry can take you to **Gribskov**, a forested area with trails and picnic grounds that borders the western side of Esrum Sø.

Places to Stay

The hostel, *Fredensborg Vandrerhjem* (☎ 48 48 03 15, fax 48 48 16 56, e *dan hostel@mail.dk, Østrupvej 3)*, has a prime location just 300m south of the palace; it's open year-round. Most of the 88 beds are in double rooms; some have toilets but all showers are off the hall. There's a TV room and a guest kitchen. Dorm beds cost 100kr, singles/doubles cost 195/295kr. To get there turn west off Slotsgade at Hotel Store Kro and continue for about 50m.

Staff at the tourist office can book *rooms* in private homes; doubles cost around 350kr including breakfast. There's a 25kr booking fee.

Just outside the palace gate is *Hotel Store Kro* (☎ 48 40 01 11, fax 48 48 45 61, e *re ception@storekro.dk, Slotsgade 6)*, the earliest sections of which were built by Frederik IV in 1723 to accommodate palace guests. No two rooms are alike but all have traditional decor as well as a bathroom, a TV, a phone and a minibar. Rooms cost 950/1250kr.

For an upmarket rural getaway, try *Pension Bondehuset* (☎ 48 48 01 12, fax 48 48 03 01, e *info@bondehuset.dk, Sørupvej 14, Box 6)*, which also dates from the early 18th century. By the lake on the western outskirts of Fredensborg, it has classic manor house furnishings and provides rowing boats for guests to use. Rooms with bath cost 520/840kr including breakfast, or 720/1245kr with half-board; for the lowest rates, reserve at least a week in advance.

Places to Eat

There's a good *fruit stand* and a *bakery* at Jernbanegade 20, about halfway between the train station and Fredensborg Slot, and a *Netto* grocery store is nearby. *Ciao*, a pleasant Italian cafe adjacent to Netto, serves good pizza and pasta costing 39kr between 11 am and 4 pm, and generous fish and meat dishes at dinner for about double that.

For ice cream, sandwiches and coffee, the cafe *Under Kronen (Jernbanegade 1)* is conveniently located just outside the palace gate.

Hua Fu, on Slotsgade opposite the Hotel Store Kro, has good Chinese food at moderate prices, including combination plates for 55kr at lunch, about double that at dinner. It's open 11 am to 11 pm daily.

A good top-end choice is **Restaurant Prinsessen** *(Slotsgade 3A)*, which offers traditional Danish plates and *smørrebrød* at lunch and a French-influenced a la carte Danish menu at dinner.

Getting There & Away
Fredensborg is midway on the railway line between Hillerød (12kr, 12 minutes) and Helsingør (30kr, 20 minutes). Trains run about twice hourly from early morning to around midnight.

Buses No 336 and 339 run hourly between Fredensborg train station and Hillerød (12kr, 20 minutes), stopping en route near Fredensborg Slot.

HUMLEBÆK
The coastal town of Humlebæk has a couple of harbours and bathing beaches and some wooded areas, but the main focus for visitors is the modern art museum Louisiana.

Louisiana
Louisiana, Denmark's most renowned modern art museum, is on a seaside knoll in a strikingly modernistic complex featuring sculpture-laden grounds.

The sculptures on the lawns, which include works by Henry Moore, Alexander Calder and Max Ernst, create an engaging interplay between art, architecture and landscape. Louisiana is a fascinating place to visit even for those not passionate about modern art.

Items from the museum's permanent collection of paintings and graphic art from the postwar era are creatively displayed and grouped. There are sections on constructivism, COBRA-movement (COpenhagen-BRussels-Amsterdam) artists, some abstract expressionism, minimal art, pop art and staged photography. Works on display include those by international luminaries Pablo Picasso, Francis Bacon and Alberto Giacometti. Prominent Danish artists represented are Asger Jorn, Carl-Henning Pedersen, Robert Jacobsen and Richard Mortensen.

The museum also has top-notch temporary exhibitions, which over the years have had such diverse themes as Toulouse-Lautrec & Paris, the works of Juan Muñoz and the world of Andy Warhol.

If you're travelling with kids this is one museum that can be lots of fun. It has an entire children's wing where kids can explore their artistic talents using an interactive computer and various hands-on media; ask about the free Friday afternoon workshops that attract lots of international youngsters.

The museum also presents concerts and films and has a substantial shop selling art books and quality gift items ranging from Andy Warhol motif mugs to designer toys.

Louisiana is 1km from Humlebæk train station, a 10-minute signposted walk along Gammel Strandvej. It's open 10 am to 5 pm (to 10 pm Wednesday) daily year-round. Entry is 60kr for adults and 20kr for children.

Places to Eat
The Louisiana museum's **Solarium Café** has a picturesque setting, good, reasonably priced sandwiches, burgers and cakes and a 79kr hot meal of the day.

There are a number of simple eating options along Gammel Strandvej just outside Humlebæk train station. To the south of the station is **Slagter Bagger**, a deli offering mouth-watering smørrebrød sandwiches as well as salads sold by weight. Adjacent is a good **fruit stand** and right around the corner is a small **grocery shop** and a **bakery**.

Getting There & Away
DSB trains leave Copenhagen a few times each hour for Humlebæk (42kr, 40 minutes). DSB also offers a Louisiana excursion ticket for 106kr that includes the museum admission price and the return train fare from Copenhagen. Though it's a bit slower, you could also take bus No 388, which runs between Copenhagen (42kr) and Helsingør (18kr).

HELSINGØR
postcode 3000
Helsingør (known in English as Elsinore), at the narrowest point of the Øresund, has

long been a busy port town. While the new Øresund Bridge in Amager has relieved some of the traffic, this is still Scandinavia's busiest shipping channel, with ferries shuttling to/from Sweden throughout the day.

Although Swedish shoppers hopping over on day trips comprise many of Helsingør's visitors (which accounts for the plethora of liquor shops near the harbour), the town offers enough sightseeing possibilities to make for an enjoyable half-day of touring.

Helsingør has maintained some of its historic quarters, including a block of old homes and warehouses known as Sundtoldkarreen (Sound Dues Square) at the northeastern end of Strandgade. Helsingør's top sight, perched across the harbour on the northern side of town, is the imposing Kronborg Slot, made famous as Elsinore Castle in Shakespeare's *Hamlet*.

Information
Tourist Offices The Helsingør Turistbureau (☎ 49 21 13 33, fax 49 21 15 77), Havnepladsen 3, is opposite the train station. Being a port of entry, it offers a wide range of services, including selling Camping Card International passes, Hostelling International cards and phonecards. It's open 9 am to 6 pm weekdays and 9 am to 4 pm Saturday from late June to August, and during the rest of the year it's open 9 am to 4 pm weekdays and 10 am to 1 pm Saturday.

Money & Post Den Danske Bank, Stengade 55, is open 9.30 am to 4 pm weekdays (to 6 pm Thursday). The post office, adjacent to the train station, is open 9.30 am to 5 pm weekdays and 10 am to 1 pm Saturday.

Walking Tour
This little walk through the oldest parts of Helsingør takes a scenic, and virtually direct, route to Kronborg Slot. Begin the walk at the northern side of the tourist office; stroll up Brostræde, a pedestrian alley, and then continue north along Sankt Anna Gade.

You'll soon come to the 15th-century Gothic cathedral **Sankt Olai Kirke**, which occupies the block between Stengade and Sankt Olai Gade. The cathedral has an ornate altar and baptistry.

A block farther north is **Helsingør Bymuseum**, Sankt Anna Gade 36, built by the monks of the adjacent monastery in 1516 to serve as a sailors' hospital. It did stints as a poorhouse and a town library before being converted to a history museum in 1973. The hotchpotch of exhibits includes antique dolls and a model of Helsingør as it was in 1801. The Bymuseum is open noon to 4 pm daily and admission costs 10kr.

Karmeliterklostret (Carmelite monastery), comprising the red-brick buildings north of the Bymuseum, is one of Scandinavia's best-preserved medieval monasteries. Christian II's mistress, Dyveke, is thought to have been buried at the monastery when she died in 1517.

To continue on to Kronborg Slot, follow Sankt Anna Gade to Kronborgvej, turn right and follow that road to the castle, about a 15-minute walk away. En route, at the intersection with Allégade, is a little public garden where flowers attract colourful butterflies.

Kronborg Slot
Despite the attention Kronborg has received as the setting of Shakespeare's *Hamlet*, the castle's primary function was not as a royal residence but rather as a grandiose tollhouse, wresting taxes from ships passing through the narrow Øresund. The castle's history dates from the 1420s, when the Danish king Erik of Pomerania introduced the 'sound dues' and built a small fortress, called Krogen, on a promontory at the narrowest part of the sound.

Financed by the generous revenue from shipping tolls, the original medieval fortress was rebuilt and enlarged by Frederik II between 1574 and 1585 to form the present Kronborg Slot. Much of Kronborg was ravaged by fire in 1629, but Christian IV rebuilt it, preserving the castle's earlier Renaissance style. In 1658, during the war with Sweden, the Swedes occupied Kronborg and removed practically everything of value, leaving the interior in shambles. After that, Danish royalty rarely visited the castle, although the sound dues still were collected for another

HELSINGØR

Nordhavn

ØRESUND

To Helsingør Vandrerhjem (300m),
Danmarks Tekniske Museum,
Hammermøllen & Hornbæk

PLACES TO STAY
1 Helsingør Camping
  Grønnehave
14 Hotel Hamlet

PLACES TO EAT
6 Gæstgivergården
7 Kvickly Supermarket
8 Thai Cuisine Restaurant
9 Kødbørsen
13 Kammercaféen
15 Rådmand Davids Hus
16 Bakery

OTHER
2 Marienlyst Slot
3 Kronborg Slot;
  Handels-og Søfartsmuseet
4 Karmeliterklostret
5 Helsingør Bymuseum
10 Sankt Olai Kirke
11 Den Danske Bank
12 Helsingør Turistbureau
17 Bus Stop
18 Post Office
19 Scandlines Terminal
  (Ferry to Sweden)
20 HH-Ferries Terminal
  (Ferry to Sweden)
21 Sundbusserne Terminal
  (Hydrofoil to Sweden)

To Hillerød &
Copenhagen

EXCURSIONS

200 years. In 1785 Kronborg was converted into barracks and that remained its chief function until 1922. Since then the castle has been thoroughly restored and is now open to the public as a museum.

Some of the castle's more interesting quarters include the king's and queen's chambers, which have marble fireplaces and detailed ceiling paintings; the small chamber, which boasts royal tapestries; and the great hall, one of the longest Renaissance halls in Scandinavia. The chapel is one of the best-preserved parts of the castle and has some choice wood carvings, while the gloomy dungeons make for more unusual touring.

In the dungeon you'll pass the resting statue of the legendary Viking chief Holger Danske (Ogier the Dane) who is said to watch over Denmark, ever-ready to come to her aid should the hour of need arise. The low-ceilinged dungeon includes areas that once served as soldiers' quarters and storerooms for salted fish, which these days are homes for nesting bats!

Also housed in the castle is **Handels-og Søfartsmuseet** (Danish Maritime Museum), a collection of model ships, paintings, nautical instruments and sea charts illustrating the history of Danish shipping and trade. Model ship enthusiasts will find it interesting. The remains of the original Krogen fortress can be seen in the masonry of the museum's showrooms No 21 and 22.

Both Kronborg Slot and Handels-og Søfartsmuseet are open 10.30 am to 5 pm between May and September, 11 am to 4 pm in April and October and 11 am to 3 pm between November and March; they're closed on Monday between October and April.

You can cross the moat and walk around the castle courtyard free of charge; tour the chapel, dungeon and royal quarters for 30kr (children 10kr); or buy a combined ticket costing 45kr (children 15kr) that includes entry to the maritime museum. A Copenhagen Card provides free entry to the maritime museum, which costs 25kr alone, but doesn't cover the other Kronborg sights.

Kronborg is 1km from the Helsingør train station (see the earlier Walking Tour for a suggested route) but you can also take the

To Be or Not To Be

When Shakespeare penned his tragedy *Hamlet* in 1602, he used Kronborg Slot (calling it Elsinore Castle) as its setting. There is no evidence that Shakespeare ever visited Helsingør, but when the stately Kronborg Slot was completed in 1585, word of it was heralded far and wide and it apparently struck Shakespeare as a fitting setting. Although the play was fiction, Shakespeare did include two actual Danish nobles in his plot – Frederik Rosenkrantz and Knud Gyldenstierne (Guildenstern), both of whom had visited the English court in the 1590s.

The fact that Hamlet, the Prince of Denmark, was a fictional character, has not deterred legions of sightseers from visiting 'Hamlet's Castle'. Indeed, due to the fame bestowed on it by Shakespeare, Kronborg is the most widely known castle in all of Scandinavia.

During the past few decades, Kronborg Slot has been used many times as the setting for staged performances of *Hamlet*, featuring such prominent actors as Sir Laurence Olivier, Richard Burton and Michael Redgrave.

Hornbæk-bound train to Grønnehave station and walk east for a few minutes to the castle.

Outskirts of Town

About 1.5km north-west of the town centre is **Marienlyst Slot**, a three-storey manor house. It was built in 1763 in the Louis Seize neoclassical style by French architect NH Jardin and encompasses parts of an early summer house constructed by Frederik II. The interior exhibits include local paintings and silverwork. Admission is 20kr for adults, free for children; it's open to the public noon to 5 pm daily. Hornbæk-bound trains stop at Marienlyst station, just north of the manor house.

If you'd like to examine technological inventions from the late 19th and early 20th centuries, the **Danmarks Tekniske Museum** at Nordre Strandvej 23, opposite the hostel, displays early gramophones, radios, motor vehicles and a 1906 Danish-built aeroplane that lays claim to being the first plane ever flown in Europe (it stayed airborne for 11 seconds!). The museum is open 10 am to 5 pm Tuesday to Sunday; admission costs 25kr for adults, 13kr for children. It's a short walk east from Højstrup train station, or you can take bus No 340.

Hammermøllen, 5km west of Helsingør town centre in the village of Hellebæk, is an old smithy that was founded by Christian IV and used to make muskets for the Kronborg arsenal. The current building, which dates from 1765, has also functioned as a water wheel-operated copper mill and textile mill. It's open 10 am to 5 pm Tuesday to Sunday (to 4 pm in winter). Admission costs 10kr for adults, 5kr for children. Hammermøllen is a five-minute walk south of Hellebæk train station.

Places to Stay

The two-star **Helsingør Camping Grønnehave** (☎/fax 49 21 58 56, Campingvej 1) is on the beach about 1.5km north-west of the town centre. Open year-round, it has 120 sites, a kiosk, cooking facilities and a coin laundry. To get there take a Hornbæk-bound train or bus No 340 from Helsingør station, then get off at Marienlyst train station and walk east to Campingvej.

Helsingør Vandrerhjem (☎ 49 21 16 40, fax 49 21 13 99, ℮ helsingor@danhostel.dk, Nordre Strandvej 24) is 2km north-west of the town centre in a renovated coastal manor house. This 200-bed hostel is open year-round except during December and January. Most of the rooms have baths and just two to six beds, and many are equipped for disabled visitors. Dorm beds cost 90kr, doubles cost 225kr. There's a beach nearby. From Helsingør train station catch bus No 340 or take the Hornbæk-bound train and walk north-west from Marienlyst station.

Staff at the tourist office can book **rooms** in private homes at a cost of 200/350kr for singles/doubles, plus a 25kr booking fee.

Hotel Hamlet (☎ 49 21 05 91, fax 49 26 01 30, ℮ hotelhamlet@internet.dk, Bramstræde 5) has 36 rooms with private bath, phone and TV at 645/850kr. Ask about Scan+ and other discount schemes that can sometimes lower the rate.

Places to Eat

The DSB railway terminal and the adjacent ferry terminals have simple food **kiosks**.

Kammercaféen, in the old customs house behind the tourist office, is an ecological cafe offering reasonably priced sandwiches and a few hot dishes including a 70kr steak and salad meal. A block to the south-west is **Rådmand Davids Hus** (Strandgade 70), a popular cafe housed in a 300-year-old half-timbered building. The special is the 'shopping lunch' (65kr), a generous plate of traditional Danish foods, typically salmon pâté, salad and slices of lamb, cheese and bread, served 10 am to 4 pm Monday to Saturday.

You'll find the main cluster of eateries around Axeltorv, four blocks north-west of Helsingør train station, which has a dozen places to eat as well as beer gardens selling Helsingør's own Wiibroe pilsner.

Kødbørsen, a butcher shop on the southern side of Axeltorv, makes good, inexpensive takeaway smørrebrød. Two popular, moderately priced options, both on the northern side of the square, are **Thai Cuisine Restaurant**, with a full menu of Thai specialities, and **Gæstgivergården**, which is a candlelit, pub-like place serving traditional Danish fare.

There's a **bakery** opposite Helsingør train station and another in the **Kvickly** supermarket (Stjernegade 25), a block west of Axeltorv.

Getting There & Away

Bus No 340 runs to/from Hornbæk (18kr, 25 minutes) and Gilleleje (36kr, 50 minutes) twice hourly. Bus No 388 runs to Humlebæk (18kr, 20 minutes) and Copenhagen (42kr, 75 minutes).

Train Helsingør train station has two adjacent terminals: the main DSB terminal for national trains and the Helsingør-Hornbæk-Gilleleje Banen (HHGB) terminal for the private railway that runs along the north coast. DSB trains to and from Copenhagen run about three times hourly from early morning to around midnight (42kr, 55 minutes). DSB trains to and from Hillerød (36kr, 30 minutes) run at least once hourly until around midnight. The HHGB train from Helsingør to Gilleleje via Hornbæk runs an average of twice hourly (36kr, 40 minutes), with the last train pulling out of Helsingør at 10.54 pm.

Car & Motorcycle Helsingør is 47km north of Copenhagen and 24km north-east of Hillerød. There's free parking throughout the city, including at car parks north-east of the tourist office, to the west of the Kvickly supermarket and outside Kronborg Slot.

Boat For information on the frequent ferries to Helsingborg in Sweden (16kr, 20 minutes), see the Getting There & Away chapter.

HORNBÆK
postcode 3100
The north coast of Zealand, also known as the Kattegat coast, is a pleasant mix of dunes, heathlands and coastal woodlands. Development is limited to a handful of small fishing

towns that date back to the 1500s, their backstreets bordered by half-timbered thatchroofed houses with tidy flower gardens. Although the towns have only a few thousand residents in winter, the population swells with throngs of beachgoers in summer.

Hornbæk has the best beach on the north coast, a vast expanse of soft white sands that runs the entire length of the town. It's backed by sand dunes with beach grass and thickets of *Rosa rugosa*, a wild pink seaside rose that blooms all summer. Even though it borders the town the beach is pleasantly undeveloped, with all of the commercial facilities on the inland side of the dunes.

Danish poet Holger Drachmann, who died in Hornbæk in 1908, is memorialised by a harbourside monument. These days the salty fisherfolk, about whom Drachmann often wrote, share their harbour with scores of sailing boats and yachts.

From the train station it's a five-minute walk directly north along Havnevej to the

EXCURSIONS

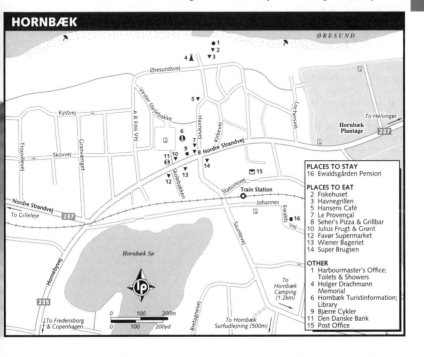

HORNBÆK

PLACES TO STAY
16 Ewaldsgården Pension

PLACES TO EAT
2 Fiskehuset
3 Havnegrillen
5 Hansens Café
7 Le Provençal
8 Seher's Pizza & Grillbar
10 Julius Frugt & Grønt
12 Favør Supermarket
13 Wiener Bageriet
14 Super Brugsen

OTHER
1 Harbourmaster's Office;
   Toilets & Showers
4 Holger Drachmann
   Memorial
6 Hornbæk Turistinformation;
   Library
9 Bjærre Cykler
11 Den Danske Bank
15 Post Office

Bravery Immortalised

In 1774, Hornbæk fishermen came to the rescue of British captain Thomas Brauwn, whose ship was being battered by a raging storm. These unhesitant Danes, braving treacherous seas, so inspired their country folk that a popular play, *Fiskerne*, was written about them by the lyricist poet Johannes Ewald. A song taken from the play became Denmark's national anthem. The rescue was also immortalised by the artist CW Eckersberg, who used it as a theme in a number of his paintings.

harbour. Climb the dunes to the left and you're on the beach.

Information

Hornbæk Turistinformation is inside the library (☎ 49 70 47 47, fax 49 70 41 42), Vester Stejlebakke 2A; to get there take the walkway at the side of Den Danske Bank. The tourist office is open the same hours as the library: 2 to 7 pm Monday, Tuesday and Thursday, 10 am to 5 pm Wednesday and Friday, and 10 am to 2 pm Saturday.

Den Danske Bank is in the town centre at Nordre Strandvej 350. The post office is opposite the train station. The library has online computers. There are public toilets and showers at the harbour.

Things to See & Do

The **beach** is Hornbæk's main attraction and offers good swimming conditions and plenty of space for sunbathing.

If you're interested in **windsurfing**, contact Hornbæk Surfudlejning (☎ 49 70 33 75), Drejervej 19, which provides gear rental (250kr a day) and lessons (480kr including gear). To charter a boat to go **fishing**, contact the tourist office or the harbourmaster's office at the southern side of the harbour; expect to pay from 400kr to 800kr depending upon boat size. You can rent **bicycles** for 50kr a day at Bjærre Cykler (☎ 49 70 32 82), Nordre Strandvej 338.

If you're up to an enjoyable nature stroll, **Hornbæk Plantage**, a public woodland that extends 3.5km along the coast east from

Hornbæk, has numerous interconnecting trails branching out either side of route 237. There are wild roses along the coast and pine trees and flowering Scotch broom inland. One trail follows the coast from Lochersvej in Hornbæk to the eastern end of the plantage. Other trails go inland, including one path that leads to Hornbæk Camping. There are several areas along Nordre Strandvej (route 237) where you can park a car and start your wanderings. A free forestry map, *Vandreture i Statsskovene, Hornbæk Plantage*, shows all the trails and is available from the tourist office.

Places to Stay

There's a three-star camping ground, **Hornbæk Camping** (☎ 49 70 02 23, fax 49 70 23 91, Planetvej 4), on the outskirts of town off Sauntevej, about 1.5km south-east of the centre. Open April to September, it has a coin laundry, a group kitchen and heated cabins for hire.

Ewaldsgården Pension (☎/fax 49 70 00 82, Johannes Ewalds Vej 5), south-east of the train station and about a 10-minute walk from the harbour, occupies an early 18th-century country house. The interior is light and airy with a cosy mix of antiques and cottage-style furnishings. All 12 rooms have a washbasin; shared showers and toilets are off the hall. Singles/doubles cost 360/550kr including breakfast.

If you're interested in renting a **summer house** by the week, the main local agency is Hornbæk Sommerhusudlejning (☎ 49 70 20 20, fax 49 70 20 98), Hornebyvej 62E.

Places to Eat

Eating opportunities down at the harbour include a *fiskehuset*, which sells peel-and-eat shrimp by weight, and **Havnegrillen**, a fast-food stand selling hot dogs, burgers, fish sandwiches and ice cream.

Seher's Pizza & Grillbar (*Nordre Strandvej 336*) serves pizza and pasta for around 40kr, as well as cheaper burgers and pitta-bread sandwiches.

Hansens Café (*Havnevej 19*) is in the town's oldest house, a sod-roofed and half-timbered building with a pleasant pub-like

EXCURSIONS

atmosphere. The handwritten menu changes daily but you can expect to find good Danish food at moderate prices. The best fine-dining option is *Le Provençal (Havnevej 1)*, a dinner restaurant featuring upmarket French food at prices to match.

You can pick up groceries at the *Super Brugsen* or the nearby *Favør* supermarket at Nordre Strandvej 349. There's a bakery, *Wiener Bageriet*, midway between the two and a good fruit stand, *Julius Frugt & Grønt*, next to Den Danske Bank.

Getting There & Away

Trains between Helsingør and Hornbæk (25 minutes) run about twice hourly on week-days, once hourly at weekends, while bus No 340 (28 minutes) does the same run hourly. Either way the fare is 18kr. Bus No 340 also runs to Gilleleje (24kr, 20 minutes) and buses No 306, 336 and 339 go to Hillerød.

GILLELEJE
postcode 3250

Zealand's northernmost town, Gilleleje has lots of attractive straw-roofed houses as well as the island's largest fishing harbour. Despite its size, the harbour has an appealing character, filled as it is with colourful wooden-hulled fishing boats.

Many of the attractions the town has to offer are in one way or another connected with fishing, including smokehouses along the harbour and a little dockside fish auction that can be viewed by early-risers.

Gilleleje played a key role during WWII in helping some 2000 Danish Jews escape Nazi-occupied Denmark. Scores of local townsfolk risked their own safety clandestinely sheltering the refugees until Gilleleje fishing boats, operating in the dark of night, could carry them to the safety of neutral Sweden.

It's a five-minute walk north from the train station to the harbour.

Information

The Gilleleje tourist office (☎ 48 30 01 74, fax 48 30 34 74) is in the town centre at Hovedgade 6F, 200m east of the train station. It's open 10 am to 6 pm daily from mid-June to August, and 9 am to 4 pm weekdays and 9 am to noon Saturday the rest of the year.

Den Danske Bank is in the centre of town at Vesterbrogade 6. The post office is at Stationsvej 6, just north of the train station.

Things to See & Do

The local museum of fishing, **Det Gamle Fiskerhus/Skibshallen** at Hovedgade 49, about 400m east of the tourist office, features a fisherman's house dating from 1850 and displays about the lives of fisherfolk from the Middle Ages onward.

Midway between the tourist office and the fishing museum, on the northern side of Hovedgade, is **Gilleleje Kirke**, originally built from timbers salvaged from ship-wrecks in the early 16th century to minister to seamen. The church boasts a 17th-century hand-carved pulpit and a painted altar from 1834. In 1943 many of the Danish Jews waiting to be rowed across to neutral Sweden took refuge in the church attic; a displayed Medal of Merit from the Jewish community honours the local efforts.

The **Gilleleje Museum**, on the western side of town at Vesterbrogade 56, is dedicated to the history of the town, from the Middle Ages to the advent of summer tourism. It also has an exhibition on the town's role in helping Danish Jews escape the Nazis.

Although not on a par with those at Hornbæk or Tisvildeleje, there are public **beaches** on either side of town.

Coastal trails head in both directions from the town centre. The trail to the west, which starts near the intersection of Nordre Strandvej and Vesterbrogade, leads 1.75km to a stone **memorial** dedicated to the Danish philosopher Søren Kierkegaard, who used to make visits to this coast.

The trail to the east, which begins off Hovedgade at the eastern side of the fishing museum, leads 2.5km to the site where two lighthouses with coal-burning beacons were erected in 1772. In 1899 the western light-house was modernised with rotating lenses and the eastern one, no longer needed, was abandoned. In 1980 the eastern lighthouse, **Nakkehoved Østre Fyr**, was restored as a museum. If you have a vehicle, you can get

EXCURSIONS

there by turning north off route 237 onto Fyrvejen.

The two museums in town and the lighthouse are open 1 to 4 pm daily except Tuesday between mid-June and mid-September; a single ticket costing 20kr (free for children) covers all three sights.

Places to Stay

There's a two-star inland camping ground, *Gilleleje Camping (☎ 49 71 97 55, Bregnerødvej 21)*, 4km south-east of the town centre.

Staff at the Gilleleje tourist office can book *rooms* in private homes at around 250/350kr for singles/doubles, plus a 25kr booking fee.

Hotel Strand (☎ 48 30 05 12, fax 48 30 18 59, Vesterbrogade 4) is in the centre of town, a short walk west from the harbour. It has 25 rooms, three that are a tad small but have showers (toilets are off the hall) and cost 410/610kr. Other rooms are larger and more modern with bath, balcony, TV and phone and cost 470/720kr. Rates include breakfast.

Places to Eat

Fish is unmistakably the speciality in Gilleleje, and every eatery of interest can be found clustered on the waterfront. *Røgeriet Bornholm*, a smokehouse on the harbour, sells smoked fish by the piece; a herring makes a tasty snack and costs about 10kr. At the nearby *Adamsen's Fisk* you can buy affordable deli items such as fish cakes, rollmops and shrimp salad to take away. *Sea-Food Gilleleje*, next door, sells good 35kr fish and chips and has a few picnic tables where you can sit and eat.

For something fancier, *Hos Karen & Marie (Nordre Havnevej 3)* is an excellent little seafood restaurant in a period building overlooking the harbour. At lunch (served until 4 pm) there's a nice 139kr sampler plate which includes pickled herring, butterfried plaice, salmon, pork tenderloin and brie. Dinner is more expensive.

Getting There & Away

Trains run between Hillerød and Gilleleje (30kr, 31 minutes) about twice hourly on weekdays, hourly at weekends, and between Helsingør and Gilleleje (36kr, 40 minutes) with similar frequency.

There's no rail link between Gilleleje and Tisvildeleje but all of the north coast towns are linked by bus. Bus No 340 connects Gilleleje with Hornbæk (24kr, 20 minutes) and Helsingør (36kr, 50 minutes). Bus No 363 connects Gilleleje with Tisvildeleje, but it's a roundabout hour-long ride (18kr). Gilleleje's bus and train stations are adjacent to each other.

TISVILDELEJE
postcode 3220

Tisvildeleje is a pleasant little seaside village with an invitingly slow pace, a comfortable hostel and fine nature walks. It's bordered by a broad stretch of sandy beach backed by low dunes; the nearest beach is just a short walk from the train station but the most glorious sweep is at the end of Hovedgaden, 1km west of the village centre. That beach has a large car park, a changing room and toilets.

Inland of the beach is Tisvilde Hegn, a windswept forest of twisted trees and heather-covered hills that extends south-west from Tisvildeleje for more than 8km. Much of this enchanting forest was planted in the 18th century to stabilise the sand drifts that were threatening to turn the area into desert.

Information

Both the post office and the seasonal tourist office (☎ 48 70 74 51) are in Tisvildeleje train station at Banevej 8. The tourist office is open 10 am to 5 pm Monday to Saturday from June to August only.

Walks in Tisvilde Hegn

From the beach parking area at the end of Hovedgaden you can walk, either along the beach or on a dirt path through the woods, about 3km south to **Troldeskoven** (Witch Wood), an area of ancient trees that have been sculpted by the wind into haunting shapes. On the way make a short detour east at Brantebjerg for a nice hill-top view.

Tisvilde Hegn has many other trails, including one to **Asserbo Slotsruin**, the moatencircled ruins of a former manor house and a 12th-century monastery, which are near the southern boundary of the forest. The south-western part of Tisvilde Hegn merges with **Asserbo Plantage**, a wooded area that borders lake Arresø. Trail maps are available free from the tourist office.

Places to Stay

The cheery 272-bed hostel, *Tisvildeleje Vandrerhjem* (☎ 48 70 98 50, fax 48 70 98 97, e *shc@helene.dk, Bygmarken 30*), is 1km east of the town centre and within walking distance of a sandy beach which is safe for children. The hostel is the centrepiece of the Sankt Helene complex, which runs nature courses for schoolchildren and other groups. Its 12-hectare grounds have walking trails, tennis courts and sports fields. Most of the complex is accessible to people in wheelchairs.

Hostel accommodation is in modern rooms, each with four beds, a little sitting area and a bathroom. Rates are 100kr for a dorm bed, 350kr for a double. There are also cabins containing up to five beds for 395kr and family-sized apartments that are rented by the week with the cost varying by season. Campers can pitch a tent in the field adjacent to the reception office for 25kr per person, including use of the showers and kitchen.

The hostel is open year-round but reservations are often essential from May to mid-September. If you're arriving by train, get off at Godhavns station, one stop before Tisvildeleje station; the hostel is just north of the tracks. If arriving by car, turn north on Godhavnsvej.

The 25-room *Tisvildeleje Strand Hotel* (☎ 48 70 71 19, fax 48 70 71 77, Hovedgaden 75) is in the centre of town and within walking distance of the beach. Its singles/doubles with shared bath cost 425/475kr, while rooms with private bath are 475kr to 750kr for singles and 550kr to 850kr for doubles; all rates include breakfast.

Places to Eat

A small cluster of eateries is in the town centre on Hovedgaden, including a good bakery, *Tisvildeleje Bageri*, at No 60, a little *grocery shop* opposite and *Tisvildeleje*

Caféen at No 55, a pub-like place with good, moderately priced fare.

Smitty's Pizzabar (Hovedgaden 78), opposite the hotel, caters to summer crowds by selling ice cream and pizza. If you're staying at the hostel there's a food kiosk on site and a reasonably priced restaurant serving three meals a day.

Getting There & Around

Bus No 363 runs between Gilleleje and Tisvildeleje (18kr, one hour) but it takes a circuitous route. Trains run between Hillerød and Tisvildeleje (30kr, 31 minutes) once an hour; there are a few extra trains in the early morning and the late afternoon.

Bicycles can be hired in the town centre from the Hydro petrol station, Hovedgaden 53, a few minutes' walk west of the train station; the cost is 50/250kr per day/week.

FREDERIKSVÆRK

postcode 3300

Frederiksværk, at the northern side of the Roskilde Fjord, is Denmark's oldest industrial town, founded in 1756 by order of Frederik V, from whom the town takes its name. At that time a canal was dug between the Roskilde Fjord and Arresø lake to provide water power for mills, a gunpowder factory and a cannon foundry.

The tourist office (☎ 47 72 30 01) is in Gjethuset, a former cannon foundry on Torvet which has been converted into a **cultural centre** with changing art exhibits.

Fittingly, Frederiksværk's two museums, both near the canal in the centre of town, are dedicated to the town's industrial history. **Frederiksværk Bymuseum**, near Torvet, features artefacts and displays on Frederiksværk's early industries, while the open-air **Krudtværksmuseum** (Gunpowder Factory Museum) on Krudtværksalleén consists of period buildings equipped with their original machinery and a working water mill. Both are open noon to 4 pm Tuesday to Sunday from June to mid-September and admission to each costs 20kr.

The town sits on the western shore of Arresø which, at 41 sq km, is the largest lake in Denmark. Leisurely **boat excursions**

(☎ 47 72 30 01) cruise the lake on summer afternoons.

Frederiksværk is 28 minutes (24kr) from Hillerød by train.

Places to Stay

If you need to break for the night, Frederiksværk has a convenient combination hostel and camping ground. *Frederiksværk Vandrerhjem & Campingplads (☎ 47 77 07 25, fax 47 72 07 66, e strandbo@image.dk, Strandgade 30)* is right by the canal in the centre of town and dorm beds cost 90kr, while singles/doubles cost 180/220kr.

FREDERIKSSUND

Frederikssund, at the narrowest part of the Roskilde Fjord, is best known for **Viking-espillene** (the Viking Plays) performed from mid-June to early July by a troupe of 200 local actors. Performances take place in a large open-air theatre on the fjord, a 10-minute walk south of the train station. Admission costs 100kr, or 140kr if you want to join the feast that follows the play. For information or bookings call ☎ 47 31 06 85.

Also in town is the **JF Willumsens Museum**, Jenriksvej 4, which contains paintings, sculpture and drawings by Jens Ferdinand Willumsen (1863–1958), one of Denmark's leading symbolists. The museum also displays some works by other artists, which belonged to Willumsen's private collection. It's open 10 am to 5 pm daily and admission costs 30kr.

Frederikssund is at the end of the S-train H line, making it a 45-minute (42kr) ride from Copenhagen.

ROSKILDE

postcode 4000

Roskilde, Denmark's first capital, was a thriving trade centre throughout the Middle Ages. It was also the site of Zealand's first Christian church, built by Viking king Harald Bluetooth in AD 980.

In 1026 Canute I, in a rage over a chess match, had his brother-in-law Ulf Jarl assassinated in that church. Ulf's widow, Canute's sister Estrid, insisted that the wooden stave church in which her husband was ambushed

be torn down, and then donated property for the construction of a new stone church. The foundations of that early stone church are beneath the floor of the present-day Roskilde Domkirke (cathedral). Estrid and her son Svend Estridsen are among many Danish royals now buried in the cathedral.

As the centre of Danish Catholicism, medieval Roskilde had a cathedral and nearly 20 churches and monasteries. After the Reformation swept Denmark in 1536, the monasteries and most of the churches were demolished. Consequently the town, which had been in decline since the capital

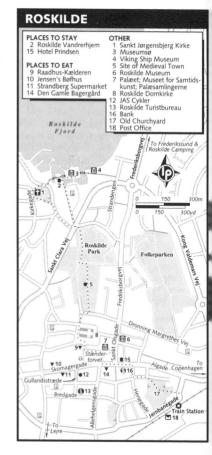

ROSKILDE

PLACES TO STAY
2 Roskilde Vandrerhjem
15 Hotel Prindsen

PLACES TO EAT
9 Raadhus-Kælderen
10 Jensen's Bøfhus
11 Strandberg Supermarket
14 Den Gamle Bagergård

OTHER
1 Sankt Jørgensbjerg Kirke
3 Museumsø
4 Viking Ship Museum
5 Site of Medieval Town
6 Roskilde Museum
7 Palæet; Museet for Samtidskunst; Palæsamlingerne
8 Roskilde Domkirke
12 JAS Cykler
13 Roskilde Turistbureau
16 Bank
17 Old Churchyard
18 Post Office

moved to Copenhagen in the early 15th century, saw its population shrink radically.

Today, Roskilde is a likeable, low-profile town with 52,000 inhabitants. Only 35km west of Copenhagen, it is on Denmark's main east-west train route. Northern Europe's largest rock music festival is held in Roskilde on the last weekend in June. Some 150 bands, including big-name international performers, attract 80,000 concertgoers.

Information

The Roskilde Turistbureau (☎ 46 35 27 00, fax 46 35 14 74) is at Gullandsstræde 15, Postboks 637. It's open 9 am to 6 pm weekdays and 9 am to 3 pm Saturday in July and August. During the rest of the year it's open 9 am to 5 pm weekdays (to 4 pm Friday in autumn and winter) and 10 am to 1 pm Saturday.

There are a couple of banks along Algade just east of Torvet. The post office is at Jernbanegade 3, to the south-west of the train station.

Walking Tour

Roskilde's main sights are within walking distance of each other. **Roskilde Domkirke** is on Torvet, a 10-minute walk north-west from the train station: cut diagonally across the old churchyard then left along Algade.

From the cathedral, you can take a 15-minute walk through the extensive green belt of city parks on the way down to the **Viking Ship Museum**. The route begins at the northern side of the cathedral and crosses a field where wildflowers blanket the unexcavated remains of Roskilde's original **medieval town**. The rectangular depression at this site marks the spot where the 12th-century church Sankt Hans Kirke was torn down during the Reformation.

After visiting the Viking Ship Museum, a five-minute walk west along the harbour will bring you to the **Sankt Jørgensbjerg quarter**, where the cobbled walkway Kirkegade leads through a neighbourhood of old thatched-roofed houses and into the courtyard of the hill-top **Sankt Jørgensbjerg Kirke**. This church, the nave of which dates from the 11th century, is one of the oldest in Denmark.

Roskilde Domkirke

Although most of Roskilde's medieval buildings have vanished in fires over the centuries, this imposing cathedral still dominates the city centre. Started in 1170 by Bishop Absalon, Roskilde Domkirke has been rebuilt and added to so many times that it represents a millennium of Danish architectural styles.

Roskilde Domkirke is a Unesco World Heritage Site. It boasts tall spires, a splendid interior and the crypts of 37 Danish kings and queens. Some of the crypts are spectacularly embellished and guarded by marble statues of knights and women in mourning, while others are simple unadorned stone coffins. There's something quite awesome about being able to stand next to the bones of so many of Scandinavia's most powerful historical figures.

Of particular interest is the chapel of King Christian IV, off the northern side of the cathedral. It contains the coffin of Christian flanked by his young son, Prince Christian, and his wife, Anne Cathrine, as well as the brass coffins of his successor, Frederik III, and his wife, Queen Sofie Amalie. The bronze statue of Christian IV beside the entranceway is the work of Bertel Thorvaldsen, while the huge wall-sized paintings, encased in trompe l'oeil frames, were created by Wilhelm Marstrand and include a classic scene depicting Christian IV rallying the troops aboard the warship *Trinity* during the 1644 battle of Kolbergerheide.

Some of the cathedral's finest pieces were installed by Christian IV, including the intricately detailed pulpit made of marble, alabaster and sandstone in 1610 by Copenhagen sculptor Hans Brokman.

The enormous gilt 'cupboard-style' altarpiece, made in 1560 in Antwerp, is adorned with 21 plates depicting the life of Christ. The story of how it came to Roskilde is as interesting as the piece. Apparently when the altarpiece was being sent to its intended destination of Gdansk, its shipper attempted to cheat on the sound dues in Helsingør by grossly undervaluing it; the shrewd customs officer, asserting his right to acquire items at their valuation price, snapped up the altarpiece.

EXCURSIONS

ROSKILDE DOMKIRKE

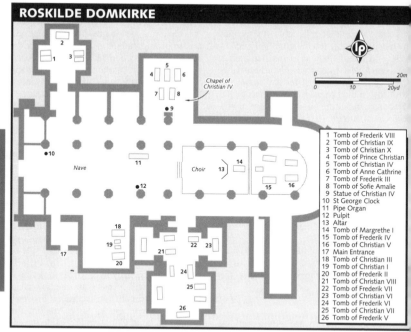

1 Tomb of Frederik VIII
2 Tomb of Christian IX
3 Tomb of Christian X
4 Tomb of Prince Christian
5 Tomb of Christian IV
6 Tomb of Anne Cathrine
7 Tomb of Frederik III
8 Tomb of Sofie Amalie
9 Statue of Christian IV
10 St George Clock
11 Pipe Organ
12 Pulpit
13 Altar
14 Tomb of Margrethe I
15 Tomb of Frederik IV
16 Tomb of Christian V
17 Main Entrance
18 Tomb of Christian III
19 Tomb of Christian I
20 Tomb of Frederik II
21 Tomb of Christian VIII
22 Tomb of Frederik VII
23 Tomb of Christian VI
24 Tomb of Frederik VI
25 Tomb of Christian VII
26 Tomb of Frederik V

An unusually lighthearted item is the cathedral's early 16th-century clock, poised above the entrance, on which a tiny St George on horseback marks the hour by slaying a yelping dragon.

The cathedral is open 9 am to 4.45 pm weekdays, 9 am to noon Saturday and 12.30 to 4.45 pm Sunday from March to September. Between October and March it's open 10 am to 3.45 pm Tuesday to Friday, 11.30 am to 3.45 pm Saturday and 12.30 to 3.45 pm Sunday.

It's not unusual for the cathedral to be closed on Saturday for weddings and occasionally on other days for funerals. You can check in advance whether it's open by calling the tourist office.

Admission costs 12kr for adults and 6kr for children. In summer, tours are conducted by multilingual guides at 11.30 am and 1.30 pm weekdays, 11 am Saturday and 1.30 pm Sunday; tours cost 30kr for adults and 10kr for children.

Free concerts given on the splendid 16th-century baroque pipe organ are held at 8 pm every Thursday in June, July and August.

Viking Ship Museum

This intriguing museum displays five reconstructed Viking ships (circa AD 1000) which were excavated from the bottom of Roskilde Fjord in 1962. The wooden ship fragments are reassembled on new skeleton frames that provide the shape. As some of the wood was lost over the centuries, none of the ships are complete but all have been reconstructed enough to provide a sense of their original features.

The ships include an 18m warship of the type used to raid England and a 16.5m trader that may once have carried cargo between Greenland and Denmark. Appropriately, the museum is at the eastern side of the harbour overlooking Roskilde Fjord which provides a scenic backdrop for the displays.

The latest addition is **Museumsø** (Museum Island), a new harbourfront facility adjacent to the main museum. At this pier-like island, craftspeople painstakingly employ Viking-era techniques and tools to build replicas of Viking ships. Three substantial replicas, *Helge Ask*, *Kraka Fyr* and *Roar Ege*, are moored in the harbour and numerous other reconstructions are in the works. Museumsø also holds an archaeological workshop where recent excavations are being preserved and analysed by researchers from the National Museum; it's open to visitors 10 am to 3 pm weekdays.

Summer is a fun time to visit as there are seasonal workshops where children can try their hand at sailmaking and other maritime crafts, and possibilities for taking short sailing trips on the fjord.

The Viking Ship Museum is open 9 am to 5 pm daily from May to September and 10 am to 4 pm October to April. Admission costs 52kr for adults and 29kr for children.

Other City Museums

The well-presented **Roskilde Museum**, Sankt Olsgade 18, covers Roskilde's history in displays ranging from the Stone Age up to the contemporary 'rock age' of the Roskilde Festival. And naturally there's coverage of Roskilde's glory days as the former capital of Denmark. It's open 11 am

Digging Up the Past

Towards the end of the Viking era, the narrower necks of Roskilde Fjord were purposely blocked to prevent raids by Norwegian fleets. The five Viking ships that are now displayed at Roskilde's Viking Ship Museum were thought to have been deliberately sunk in one such channel and then piled with rocks to make a reinforced barrier similar to an underwater stone wall. Although people had long suspected that there was a ship beneath the ridge of stones, folklore had led them to believe it was a single ship sunk by Queen Margrethe in the 15th century.

It wasn't until researchers from the national museum made a series of exploratory dives in the late 1950s that it was discovered that there were several ships at the site and that they dated from the Viking period. Excavations began in 1962, when a cofferdam was built around the ships in the middle of the fjord and pumps were used to drain seawater from the site. Within just four months archaeologists were able to unpile the mound of stones and excavate the ships, whose wooden hulks were now in thousands of pieces. The ship fragments were then reassembled within a purpose-built museum that opened on the harbourfront in 1969.

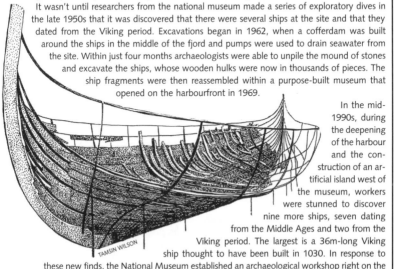

In the mid-1990s, during the deepening of the harbour and the construction of an artificial island west of the museum, workers were stunned to discover nine more ships, seven dating from the Middle Ages and two from the Viking period. The largest is a 36m-long Viking ship thought to have been built in 1030. In response to these new finds, the National Museum established an archaeological workshop right on the site where the recovered ship fragments are cleaned, preserved and documented.

TAMSIN WILSON

to 4 pm daily. Admission is 25kr for adults, free for children.

Palæet (the Palace), an attractive 18th-century baroque building fronting Torvet, is a former bishops' residence that now houses **Museet for Samtidskunst** (Museum of Contemporary Art), a small museum with changing exhibits, and **Palæsamlingerne** (Palace Collections), containing 18th- and 19th-century paintings that once belonged to wealthy Roskilde merchants. The contemporary art museum is open 11 am to 5 pm Tuesday to Friday and noon to 4 pm at weekends; admission is 20kr for adults, free for children. The Palace Collections are open 11 am to 4 pm daily between mid-May and mid-September, and 2 to 4 pm Saturday and Sunday during the rest of the year; admission is 25kr for adults, free for children.

Places to Stay

Most travellers visit Roskilde on a day trip, but should you want to stay overnight, there are a few interesting options.

The new harbourside *Roskilde Vandrerhjem* (☎ *46 35 21 84, fax 46 32 66 90,* e *danhostel.roskilde@post.tele.dk, Vindeboder 7)*, adjacent to the Viking Ship Museum, has 152 beds in 40 rooms. Some of the rooms have water views and each has its own shower and toilet. Dorm beds cost 100kr and a private room for one to three people costs 300kr. The hostel is open year-round, and has full facilities including a TV lounge, guest kitchen and laundry.

Staff at the tourist office can book *rooms* in private homes at 150/300kr for singles/doubles, plus a 25kr booking fee; rooms can be booked either in town, in the suburbs or on farms.

In the city centre is *Hotel Prindsen* (☎ *46 35 80 10, fax 46 35 81 10,* e *info@hotel prindsen, Algade 13)*, Denmark's oldest continuously operating hotel. First opened in 1695, its guest list reads like a who's who of great Danes, from King Frederik VII to Hans Christian Andersen. As befits an old hotel, the rooms are different sizes and have varied decor, but all have a bath, a phone, a TV and a minibar. The regular rates are

925/1065kr. At weekends year-round and daily from mid-June to mid-August there's a special 725kr holiday rate that covers a room for up to two adults and two children. All rates include breakfast. The hotel is a member of the Best Western chain.

Three-star *Roskilde Camping* (☎ *46 75 79 96, fax 46 75 44 26, Baunehøjvej 7, Veddelev)* is at a sandy beach on Roskilde Fjord 3km north of the Viking Ship Museum. It's open from mid-April to mid-September, and can be reached by bus No 603.

Places to Eat

Den Gamle Bagergård (Algade 6) is a good bakery with pastries and tempting takeaway sandwiches. On Wednesday and Saturday mornings there's a *market* on Torvet selling fresh fruit and vegetables as well as handicrafts and flowers.

On Skomagergade, the pedestrian street that runs west from Torvet, there are numerous places to eat. The *Strandberg* supermarket *(Skomagergade 11)* has a rooftop cafeteria with a city view and a varied menu that includes morning pastries and a 30kr chicken and fries lunch. For around 45kr, you can get a simple steak lunch at the nearby *Jensen's Bøfhus (Skomagergade 38)*.

For an atmospheric treat, *Raadhus Kælderen*, in the cellar of the old town hall (circa 1430), just south of the cathedral, offers 68kr lunch deals, including fish fillet with shrimp and asparagus, from 11 am to 5 pm. Evening meals are around 200kr but feature some creative dishes.

Getting There & Around

Trains from Copenhagen to Roskilde are frequent (42kr, 25 minutes). Trains also run between Roskilde and Køge (36kr, 25 minutes). There are lockers at the train station.

If you're coming from Copenhagen by car, route 21 leads to Roskilde. Upon approaching the city, exit onto route 156, which leads into the centre. There are convenient car parks south of Strandberg supermarket and down by the Viking Ship Museum.

Bicycles can be rented daily except Sunday from JAS Cykler (☎ 46 35 04 20), Gullandsstræde 3, for 50kr per day.

Kronborg Castle, Helsingør, boasts one of the longest Renaissance halls in Scandinavia.

Roskilde Domkirke, a World Heritage Site.

Louisiana Museum of Modern Art, Humlebæk

Ornate cypt in Roskilde Domkirke.

North Zealand's tranquil landscape

Ribe, the oldest town in Denmark

Sitting Bull at rest in Legoland

LEJRE

The countryside on the outskirts of Lejre, a village 8km south-west of Roskilde, has two sightseeing attractions that could be combined in a leisurely afternoon outing.

Lejre Forsøgscenter

This 'archaeological experimental centre' contains a reconstructed Iron Age village where Danish families can volunteer to spend their summer holidays as 'prehistoric families', using technology and dressed in clothing from that period. The reconstructed houses they live in and the tools they use are modelled on finds from archaeological excavations around Denmark.

The centre, which is a popular destination for school outings, also has craft demonstrations and a small cottage-farm area where the lives of 19th-century Danish farmers are re-enacted. During summer children can paddle dugout canoes and partake in other hands-on activities such as grinding flour and baking biscuits. Although the centre operates between 1 May and 15 September, the majority of the activities take place in the summer high season when the 'prehistoric families' are present. It's open 10 am to 5 pm Tuesday to Sunday daily mid-June to early August.

Admission to Lejre Forsøgscenter (☎ 46 48 08 78) costs 60kr for adults and 30kr for children.

Ledreborg Slot

This grand manor house, set on a knoll overlooking 80 hectares of lawns and woods, was built by Count Johan Ludvig Holstein in 1739 and has been home to the Holstein-Ledreborg family ever since. The interior has hardly changed since the house was originally decorated and consequently it's considered one of the finest period manor houses in Denmark.

Visitors are required to put on booties at the entrance to prevent damage to the marble and parquet floors.

The house is chock-full of antique furniture, gilded mirrors, chandeliers, oil paintings and wall tapestries. One of the most superb rooms is the banquet room, which was designed by architect Nicolai Eigtved, the creator of Copenhagen's Amalienborg Slot. Also in the house is a chapel, constructed by JC Krieger in 1745, which served as the parish church until 1899.

Ledreborg (☎ 46 48 00 38) is open to visitors 11 am to 5 pm daily between mid-June and August, 11 am to 5 pm Sunday only in May, early June and September. Entry is 50kr for adults and 25kr for children.

Getting There & Away

From Roskilde it's a short train ride to Lejre station, where bus No 233 continues to both Ledreborg Slot and Lejre Forsøgscenter.

If you have your own transport, from Roskilde take Ringstedvej (route 14), turn right on route 155 and then almost immediately turn left onto Ledreborg Allé. Follow the signs to Ledreborg, 6km away, where a long drive lined by old elm trees leads to the entrance. Lejre Forsøgscenter is 2km farther along the same road.

Southern Zealand

Steeped in history, southern Zealand has played an important role since the Viking era. It was a stomping ground in medieval times for Copenhagen's founder Bishop Absalon and in the 17th century the area was the stage for many of the battles in the lengthy wars between Denmark and Sweden. The most pivotal loss in Danish history was played out here in 1658 when Swedish King Gustave marched across southern Zealand en route to Copenhagen and forced a treaty that nearly cost Denmark its sovereignty.

Today the region contains a mix of peaceful towns, rural villages and patchwork farmland.

Highlights of southern Zealand include the engaging town of Køge; the medieval church at Ringsted; and the 1000-year-old ring fortress at Trelleborg, one of Denmark's most impressive Viking sites.

If you're travelling across the region with your own transport, the rural route 150 makes a fine alternative to zipping along on the E20 motorway. Not only is it a slower, greener route but it will take you right into the most interesting towns and villages.

KØGE

postcode 4600

Køge has a rich history that dates from 1288, when it was granted its municipal charter by King Erik VI. With its large natural harbour, Køge quickly developed into a thriving fishing and trade centre.

In 1677 one of the most important naval engagements of the Danish-Swedish wars was fought in the waters off Køge. Known as the Battle of Køge Bay, it made a legend of Danish admiral Niels Juel, who resoundingly defeated the attacking Swedish navy and thwarted their attempted invasion.

Today the harbour still plays an important role in Køge's economy, having been developed into a modern commercial facility.

While parts of the city have been industrialised, Køge has done a superb job of retaining the period character of its central

historic quarter. The narrow streets that radiate from Torvet, the town square, are lined with old buildings, some that survived a sweeping fire in 1633 and many others that were built in the construction boom spawned by that blaze.

Information

The Køge Turistbureau (☎ 56 65 58 00, fax 56 65 59 84), near Torvet, at Vestergade 1 distributes a free 96-page booklet, with English and German translations, describing the town's sights. The office is open am to 5 pm weekdays year-round, and Saturday 9 am to 3 pm from June to August and 10 am to 1 pm the rest of the year.

The Unibank on the northern side of Torvet has a 24-hour ATM which accepts international bank and credit cards.

The post office is at Jernstøbervænget on the western side of town. It's open 10 am to 5 pm weekdays and 10 am to 12.30 pm Saturday.

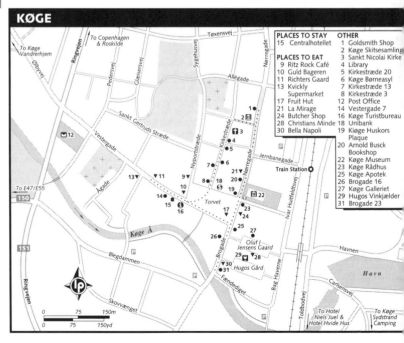

KØGE

PLACES TO STAY
15 Centralhotellet

PLACES TO EAT
9 Ritz Rock Café
10 Guld Bageren
11 Richters Gaard
13 Kvickly Supermarket
17 Fruit Hut
21 La Mirage
24 Butcher Shop
28 Christians Minde
30 Bella Napoli

OTHER
1 Goldsmith Shop
2 Køge Skitsesamling
3 Sankt Nicolai Kirke
4 Library
5 Kirkestræde 20
6 Køge Børneasyl
7 Kirkestræde 13
8 Kirkestræde 3
12 Post Office
14 Vestergade 7
16 Køge Turistbureau
18 Unibank
19 Kiøge Huskors Plaque
20 Arnold Busck Bookshop
22 Køge Museum
23 Køge Rådhus
25 Køge Apotek
26 Brogade 16
27 Køge Galleriet
29 Hugos Vinkjælder
31 Brogade 23

Walking Tour

Most of Køge's finest historic sites are within easy walking distance of each other. A pleasant little stroll of these sites can be made in about an hour, although if you take your time, stopping at the church and the two museums along the way, you could easily turn it into a half-day outing.

Begin the walk at Torvet by making a short detour west along the first block of **Vestergade**. There are two notable half-timbered houses in this area: house **No 7**, which dates from the 16th century, and **No 16** (the Richters Gaard restaurant), a well-preserved merchant's house dating from 1644, with old hand-blown glass in the doors and intricately carved detail on the timbers. From here you can return back to Torvet and head north on Kirkestræde.

At **Kirkestræde 3**, just metres from Torvet, is the house built by Oluf Sandersen and his wife Margareta Jørgensdatter in 1638, as duly noted in the lettering above the gate. Other timber-frame houses include **Kirkestræde 13**, which dates from the 16th century, and Kirkestræde 10, a 17th-century house that has served as a kindergarten, **Køge Børneasyl**, since 1856. The oldest half-timbered house in Denmark, a modest little place constructed in 1527 with a brick front and a steeply tiled roof, is at **Kirkestræde 20**. It's followed by **Sankt Nicolai Kirke** (the church and the two museums in this walking tour are detailed in the sections that follow).

If you turn right onto Katekismusgade, you'll immediately come to the **Køge Skitsesamling** art museum. In the grounds near the museum is a bronze sculpture of a young boy with scurrying lizards by Svend Rathsack.

Immediately north of the museum, at Nørregade 31, is an attractive red timbered house built in 1612 that now holds a **goldsmith shop**. Continuing south on Nørregade, you'll pass more houses built in the early 17th century: No 5, which now houses the Arnold Busck **bookshop**, and No 4, home to the **Køge Museum**.

Look for the marble plaque marked **'Kiøge Huskors'** (Kiøge and Kjøge are old spellings of Køge) on the green corner building at Torvet 2, which honours the victims of a witch hunt in the 1600s. Two residents of an earlier house on this site were among those burned at the stake.

Along the eastern side of Torvet is the yellow neoclassical **Køge Rådhus**, which boasts of being the oldest functioning town hall in Denmark. At the rear of this complex is a building erected in 1600 to serve as an inn for Christian IV on journeys between his royal palaces in Copenhagen and Nykøbing.

At Brogade 1, opposite the south-eastern corner of Torvet, is the **Køge Apotek**, a chemist shop that has occupied this site since 1660. Proceeding south, at Brogade 7 is **Oluf I Jensens Gaard**, a courtyard containing a collection of typical 19th-century merchant buildings; one of these now houses the **Køge Galleriet**, a local art gallery.

At Brogade 19 there's an older courtyard, **Hugos Gård**, with some 17th-century structures and a medieval brick building dating from the 14th century. The former wine cellar of the latter building houses a wine bar, Hugos Vinkjælder, that is an enjoyable place for a break. In the adjacent courtyard, at Brogade 17, workers unearthed a buried treasure in 1987 – an old wooden trunk filled with more than 30kg of 17th-century silver coins, the largest such find ever made in Denmark. Some of these coins are now on display at the Køge Museum.

The circa 1638 building at **Brogade 23** is decorated with cherubs carved by the famed 17th-century artist Abel Schrøder. If you cross the street and return back to Torvet along the western side of Brogade, you'll pass Køge's longest timber-framed house at **Brogade 16**, a yellow brick structure which was erected in 1636 by the town mayor.

Sankt Nicolai Kirke

This church on Kirkestræde, two blocks north of Torvet, is named after St Nicholas, the patron saint of mariners. At the upper eastern end of the church tower there's a little brick projection called the Lygten, which for centuries was used to hang a burning lantern as a guide for sailors returning to the harbour. It was from atop the church tower that Christian IV kept watch on his naval fleet as it successfully defended the town from Swedish invaders during the Battle of Køge Bay.

The church dates from 1324, but was largely rebuilt in the 15th century. Most of the ornately carved works that adorn the interior were added later, including the 17th-century altar and pulpit. From mid-June to the end of August, Sankt Nicolai Kirke is open 10 am to 4 pm weekdays and 10 am to noon Saturday. The rest of the year it's open 10 am to noon weekdays only. In midsummer you can climb the tower between 10 am and 1.30 pm.

Køge Museum

Køge Museum, Nørregade 4, occupies a lovely building dating from 1619 that was once a wealthy merchant's home and store. It now holds a few dozen exhibit rooms illustrating the cultural history of the town and surrounding region. As well as the expected period furnishings and artefacts, there's an interesting hotchpotch of displays ranging from a Mesolithic-era grave to recently discovered silver coins, part of a huge stash thought to have been hidden during the Swedish wars of the late 17th century. The museum also has a desk used by Danish philosopher NFS Grundtvig, who lived on the outskirts of Køge, and a windowpane onto which Hans Christian Andersen, during an apparently stressed-out stay at a nearby inn, scratched the words 'Oh God, Oh God in Kjøge'.

The museum is open 11 am to 5 pm daily from June to August. The rest of the year it's open 1 to 5 pm Tuesday to Friday, 11 am to 3 pm Saturday and 1 to 5 pm Sunday. Entry is 20kr for adults and 10kr for children.

Køge Skitsesamling

The Køge Skitsesamling (Art and Sketch Collection), Nørregade 29, is a unique art museum that specialises in outlining the creative process from an artist's earliest concept to the finished work. The displays include original drawings, clay models and mock-ups by several 20th-century Danish artists. It's open 11 am to 5 pm Tuesday to Sunday. The admission of 20kr for adults and 10kr for children also covers the aforementioned Køge Museum.

Places to Stay

The two-star *Køge Sydstrand Camping* (☎/fax 56 65 07 69, Søndre Badevej) is on a beach with an industrial backdrop at the southern side of the harbour. Open mid-April to late September, it's about a 20-minute walk south from the train station.

The 80-bed *Køge Vandrerhjem* (☎ 56 65 14 74, fax 56 66 08 69, Vamdrupvej 1) is in a quiet neighbourhood 2km north-west of the town centre. The hostel is open year-round, except during the Christmas holiday period. Dorm beds cost 90kr per person, and a private room for either one or two people costs 220kr. To get there from the Køge train station, take bus No 210, get off at Agerskovvej and follow the signs to the hostel, 400m away.

Staff at the tourist office can book *rooms* in private homes for 375kr to 450kr a double, plus a 25kr booking fee.

The fittingly named *Centralhotellet* (☎ 56 65 06 96, fax 56 66 02 07, Vestergade 3), adjacent to the tourist office, has a dozen rooms above a small bar and in a separate wing out back. The rooms, which are straightforward but adequate, cost 270/490kr for singles/doubles with shared bath or 590kr for doubles with private bath, breakfast included.

Hotel Niels Juel (☎ 56 63 18 00, fax 56 63 04 92, Toldbodvej 20), near the inner harbour, a couple of blocks south of the train station, is a modern 50-room hotel affiliated with the Best Western chain. The rooms, which have private bath, TV, phone and minibar, cost 880/1080kr.

There's a second Best Western, *Hotel Hvide Hus* (☎ 56 65 36 90, fax 56 66 33 14, Strandvejen 111), near the beach at the less developed southern end of town. It has 126 modern rooms costing 880/1090kr. In addition to the standard rates given, both Best Western hotels offer a special discounted weekend and summer rate of 725kr which covers up to two adults and two children. All rates include breakfast.

Places to Eat

On the eastern side of Torvet you'll find a *fruit hut* and a *butcher shop* with takeaway smørrebrød sandwiches. There's a produce, cheese and flower *market* at Torvet on Wednesday and Saturday mornings, and a *Kvickly* supermarket on Vestergade.

Our favourite spot is *Guld Bageren*, a combination bakery and self-service cafe at the western side of Torvet. It has good breads, mouthwatering fruit tarts, creative sandwiches and huge 10kr cups of coffee. Enjoy it all from the 2nd-floor dining area overlooking the square. It's open from 6 am daily.

The nearby *Ritz Rock Café (Torvet 22)* is a Tex-Mex place that doubles as a weekend disco. Featured items such as a 200g pepper steak or the chicken fajita plate cost around 100kr, but there also are burgers and lunch specials for about half that. The kitchen is open 11 am to 9.30 pm daily.

Bella Napoli (Brogade 21), a popular and somewhat upmarket Italian restaurant, has pizza and pasta dishes from around 40kr at lunch, 60kr at dinner. It's open noon to 11 pm. Cheaper is *La Mirage (Nørregade 9)*, a casual place with pizzas for 30kr until 3 pm, 40kr after that; it's open 11 am to at least 10 pm daily.

Richters Gaard (Vestergade 16), an atmospheric fine-dining restaurant in a half-timbered building dating from 1644, offers an elaborate 395kr multicourse dinner nightly from 5 pm.

Christians Minde (Brogade 7) is a more affordable fine-dining option with full course dinners for around 200kr. At lunch it features traditional open-faced sandwiches; it's open 11.30 am to 10 pm.

Getting There & Away

Køge is at the end of the E (and A+) lines, the southernmost point of greater Copenhagen's S-train network. Trains from Copenhagen run three to six times an hour, take 40 minutes and cost 42kr. Køge is also linked to Roskilde (36kr, 25 minutes) by an hourly (twice hourly during peak times) train.

Køge is 42km south-west of Copenhagen and 25km south-east of Roskilde. If you're coming by car take the E47/55 from Copenhagen or route 6 from Roskilde and then pick up route 151 south into the centre of Køge. There's free parking on Torvet with a one-hour limit during business hours and less-restricted parking off Havnen, north of the harbour.

VALLØ
postcode 4600

Vallø is a charming hamlet with cobblestone streets, a dozen mustard-yellow houses and an attractive moat-encircled Renaissance castle, Vallø Slot. Situated in the countryside about 7km south of Køge, Vallø makes an enjoyable excursion for those looking to get off the beaten path. If old-world character and mildly eccentric surroundings appeal, it could also be a fun place to spend the evening.

Vallø Slot

The red-brick Vallø Slot dates from 1586 and retains most of its original style, even though much of it was rebuilt following a fire in 1893.

The castle has a rather unusual history. On her birthday in 1737, Queen Sophie Magdalene, who owned the estate, established a foundation that turned Vallø Slot into a home for 'spinsters of noble birth'. Until a few decades ago, unmarried daughters of Danish royalty who hadn't the means to live in their own castles or manor houses were allowed to take up residence at Vallø, supported by the foundation and government social programs.

In the 1970s, bowing to changing sentiments that had previously spared this anachronistic niche of the Zealand countryside, the foundation amended its charter to gradually make the estate more accessible to the general public. For now, the castle remains home solely to a handful of ageing blue-blooded women who had taken up residence prior to 1976.

Vallø Slot is surrounded by 2800 hectares of woods and ponds and 1300 hectares of fields and arable land reaching down to the coast. Although the main castle buildings are not yet open to the public, visitors can walk in the gardens and adjacent woods.

EXCURSIONS

Hestestalden, the stables at Vallø Slot, has an exhibition on the history of the castle that's open 11 am to 4 pm daily from mid-May to August only. Entry is 10kr; free if you have a same-day Køge Museum ticket.

Places to Stay & Eat

Vallø Slotskro (☎ 56 26 70 20, @ hotel@ valloeslotskro.dk, Slotsgade 1), a 200-year-old inn, sits just outside the castle gate. The 11 pleasantly decorated rooms cost from 485/675kr for singles/doubles with shared bath and from 735/825kr with private bath. All rooms have TV and a phone.

The inn's restaurant serves moderately priced Danish country cuisine with a changing menu.

Getting There & Away

Take the train to Vallø station, two stops south of Køge, and from there it's a pleasant 1.25km stroll east down a tree-lined country road to the castle.

By car, take route 209 south from Køge, turn right onto Billesborgvej and then left onto Valløvej, which leads to Slotsgade.

RINGSTED

postcode 4100

Situated at a crossroads in central Zealand, Ringsted was an important market town during the Middle Ages and also served as the site of the *landsting*, a regional governing assembly. The town grew up around the Sankt Bendts Kirke, which was built during the reign of Valdemar I (1157–82). This historic church still marks the town centre and is Ringsted's most interesting sight.

Immediately east of the church is Torvet, the central square, which has a statue of Valdemar I sculpted by Johannes Bjerg in the 1930s, as well as three sitting stones that were used centuries ago by the landsting members.

Information

The friendly Ringsted Turistbureau (☎ 57 61 34 00, fax 57 61 64 50) is at Sankt Bendtsgade 6, at the northern side of Sankt Bendts Kirke. It's open 9 am to 5 pm weekdays year-round, and Saturday 9 am to 2 pm in summer and 10 am to 1 pm in winter.

Blessed Be the Bricks

Shortly after the end of the Viking era, two things happened that had a significant and lasting impact on church architecture in Denmark. First, King Sweyn II (1047–74) found himself deep in a power struggle with the Archbishop of Bremen, the leader of the Danish Church. To weaken the influence of the archbishop, the king divided Denmark into eight separate dioceses, which set the stage for a flurry of new church and cathedral building.

Then, in the 12th century, the art of brick-making was introduced to Denmark from northern Italy and Germany. Before that, most churches were constructed of wood or calcareous tufa and rough stone. The use of bricks allowed for construction on a much larger scale and within a few decades grand churches were being built all around Denmark. A couple of the churches from that era still stand today, including Sankt Bendts Kirke in Ringsted and the Roskilde Domkirke.

Sankt Bendts Kirke

This imposing church, erected in 1170, is a monument to the political intrigue and power struggles of its day. Valdemar I built it partly to serve as a burial sanctuary for his murdered father, Knud Lavard, who had just been canonised by the Pope, and partly as a calculated move to shore up the rule of the Valdemar dynasty and intertwine the influences of the Crown and the Catholic church.

Although Sankt Bendts Kirke was substantially restored in the 1900s, it retains much of its original medieval style and still incorporates travertine blocks from an 11th-century abbey church that had earlier occupied the same site.

The nave is adorned with magnificent frescoes, including a series depicting Erik IV (known as Erik Ploughpenny, for the despised tax he levied on ploughs), which were painted in about 1300 in a failed campaign to get the assassinated king canonised. These frescoes show Queen Agnes, seated on a throne; on her left is a scene of Ploughpenny's murderers stabbing the king with a spear, while the right-hand scene depicts the

ing's corpse being retrieved from the sea
by fishermen.

Sankt Bendts Kirke was a burial place for
the royal family for 150 years. In the aisle
floor beneath the nave (in order from the
front) are flat stones marking the tombs of
Valdemar III and his queen, Eleonora;
Valdemar II, flanked by his queens Dagmar
and Bengærd; Knud VI; Valdemar I,
flanked by his queen, Sofia, and his son
Christoffer; and Knud Lavard. Also buried
in the church is Erik VI (Menved) and
Queen Ingeborg, whose remains lie in an
ornate tomb in the chancel, and King Birger
of Sweden and his queen Margarete, who
occupy the former tomb of Erik Ploughpenny. Some of the tombs, including the
empty one that once held Queen Dagmar,
have been disturbed over the centuries to
make room for later burials. A few of the
grave relics removed from these tombs can
be found in the museum chapel.

The church also has some interesting
carved works, including pews from 1591
(note the dragons on the seats near the
altar), an elaborate altarpiece from 1699
and a pulpit from 1609. The oldest item in
the church is the 12th-century baptismal
font which, despite its historical signifi-
cance, once served a stint as a flower bowl
in a local garden.

The church is open 10 am to noon and 1
to 5 pm daily from May to mid-September,
and 1 to 3 pm the rest of the year. Note that
the church is closed whenever there are
weddings, a particularly common occurrence on Saturdays in spring.

Ringsted Museum

This small museum of local cultural history,
which includes a restored 1814 Dutch windmill, is on the eastern side of town at Køgevej
7, within walking distance of Torvet and the
train station. It's open 11 am to 4 pm Tuesday to Sunday. Admission is 20kr.

Places to Stay

The 78-bed hostel, *Ringsted Vandrerhjem*
(☎ 57 61 15 26, fax 57 61 34 26, Sankt
Bendtsgade 18), has an ideal location opposite Sankt Bendts Kirke. Dorm beds cost

95kr, singles/doubles cost 240/290kr; each
room has its own bathroom. The hostel is
closed 20 December to 10 January.

Staff at the tourist office can book *rooms*
in private homes for 180kr to 250kr per person, including breakfast, plus a 25kr booking fee.

Places to Eat

Raadhuskroen (Sankt Bendtsgade 8), next
to the tourist office, is a pub-style restaurant
that specialises in steaks served with salad
bar, for around 120kr at dinner, a bit less at
lunch. If you take the alley west of Raadhuskroen you'll reach a *Netto* grocery store.

Italy Italy (Torvet 1), at the south-east
side of the church, has good Italian food,
with multicourse meals for around 100kr at
lunch, 200kr at dinner, and cheaper pizza.

Getting There & Around

There are a couple of trains an hour to Ringsted from Copenhagen (59kr, 35 minutes).
Ringsted's town centre is a 10-minute walk
north of the train station. By car, Ringsted
is on route 150 and just off the E20 motorway, 64km from Copenhagen.

TRELLEBORG
History

Of the four Viking ring fortresses discovered in Denmark, two sites, the Trelleborg
fortress in Zealand and the Fyrkat fortress
in Jutland, have been excavated and extensively studied.

These Viking fortresses were constructed
in a ring shape with thick earthen walls and
gates at the four points of the compass.
They were built using the Roman foot
(29.33cm) as a unit of measurement and
were mathematically precise and strikingly
symmetrical. The long wooden stave buildings that once stood inside the walls were
all of an equal measure and were clearly
used as barracks for soldiers – there were no
houses for nobility, as would have been
found inside castle walls.

Although the purpose of these Viking
camps is not entirely understood, it's now
known that all were erected in the early 980s.
The researchers who excavated Trelleborg in

the 1930s originally believed these impressive camps served as staging grounds for the invasion of England by King Sweyn Forkbeard. Current research, however, including the more precise dating (to 981) of the timbers used in the Trelleborg fortress, place the construction time far in advance of the Viking campaign against England in 993. Furthermore, the four base sites were not well located for naval purposes. In the case of Trelleborg, archaeologists believe the marsh streams that connect the camp with the sea probably weren't navigable in Viking times.

A popular current theory suggests that these fortified military camps may have been used by the monarchy to strengthen its domestic position, rather than being involved in Viking forays overseas. The massive earthen walls and moats of the fortresses certainly lend support to that theory, as they suggest a more defensive function than an offensive one.

The Site

Trelleborg, in the countryside 7km west of Slagelse, is the best preserved of the Viking ring fortresses in Denmark and the most accessible from Copenhagen. Despite the passing of a millennium since its construction, this circular earthen mound fortress is amazingly intact.

Naturally the wooden structures that once stood within the fortress have long since decayed, but several Viking-era buildings have been reconstructed using materials and methods authentic to the period. The most impressive is the longhouse, built in Viking stave style, using rough oak timbers erected above mud floors. The inside has benches of the type used by warriors for sleeping and a central hearth with a simple opening in the roof for venting smoke.

Other reconstructions are clustered together to give the sense of a Viking village complete with costumed interpreters doing

Trelleborg's Precise Design

The Trelleborg compound consists of two wards that encompass about seven hectares in all. The inner ward is embraced by a circular earthen rampart which is 6m high and 17m thick at its base. Four gates, one at each point of the compass, cut across the rampart. The gateways are crossed by two streets, one east-west, the other north-south, which has the effect of dividing the inner ward into four symmetrical quadrants. In Viking times, each quadrant contained four long elliptical buildings that surrounded a courtyard. Each of the 16 buildings was exactly 100 Roman feet long and contained a central hall and two smaller rooms.

Following the arc along the exterior of the inner rampart was an 18m-wide ditch; two bridges spanned the ditch, crossing over to the outer ward. This outer ward contained a cemetery with about 150 graves and 15 houses, each of which was 90 feet long and lined up radially with its gable pointing towards the inner rampart. A second earthen ward separated the outer ward from the surrounding countryside.

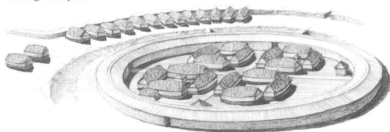

KELLI HAMBLET

chores of the period such as sharpening axes, chopping wood and baking bread. In summer the interpreters also conduct activities for children, such as archery demonstrations and pottery workshops. The site also has a small museum with exhibits of pottery, bronze jewellery, spearheads, human skeletons and other items excavated from the fortress grounds. In addition, there's a 20-minute video on Trelleborg's history.

Still, the highlight at Trelleborg is strolling the grounds. You can walk up onto the grassy circular rampart and readily grasp the geometric design of the fortress. From atop the rampart, Trelleborg appears strikingly symmetrical and precise; cement blocks have been placed to show the outlines of the elliptical house foundations. Grazing sheep wandering in from the surrounding farmland imbue the scene with a timeless aura.

Trelleborg (☎ 58 54 95 06), on Trelleborg Allé, is open 10 am to 5 pm daily from Easter to the last weekend in October, and 1 to 3 pm daily the rest of the year. Admission is 35kr for adults and 20kr for children.

Places to Stay

There are no places to stay in Trelleborg, but there are a number of options in nearby Slagelse.

The Slagelse tourist office (☎ 58 52 22 06) at Løvegade 7, a 10-minute walk south of the train station, can arrange *rooms* in private homes from around 250kr a double and provide details on hotel options.

Slagelse has a hostel, *Slagelse Vandrerhjem* (☎ 58 52 25 28, fax 58 52 25 40, Bjergbygade 78), 2km south of the train station. Dorm beds cost 98kr, singles/doubles cost 210/300kr. The hostel is closed from mid-December to mid-January. You can take bus No 303 (12kr) or a taxi (about 50kr) from the train station.

Places to Eat

Hos Hulda og Hjalmar at the Trelleborg museum is a fun place to eat, with waitstaff dressed in Viking clothes and burlap-covered tables on a sand floor. You can get light dishes at any time, such as hot dogs, burgers, or a baked potato with salad, all

around 35kr. At dinner, from 5.30 pm, they also serve full steak or chicken dinners for around 100kr. Be sure to try the local speciality, a beer-like Viking-era drink called *mjød* (mead). The restaurant is generally open 11.30 am to at least 8 pm daily.

In Slagelse, you can find numerous eating spots clustered around Nytorv, the central commercial square.

Getting There & Around

Trains from Copenhagen run to Slagelse (82kr, 50 minutes), the nearest train station to Trelleborg, a couple of times an hour throughout the day.

From Slagelse, bus No 312 goes to Trelleborg (10kr, 12 minutes) but it's infrequent, typically three to five times a day, and the schedule can vary a bit each year. It's best to call the bus company at ☎ 57 87 27 27 for the current schedule and plan your trip accordingly. Or just take a taxi to the site, which costs around 100kr.

Weather and time permitting, another alternative would be to cycle your way across the rural countryside between Slagelse and Trelleborg. Bicycle rentals can be arranged in Slagelse at HJ Cykler (☎ 58 52 28 57), Løvegade 46, near the tourist office.

To get to Trelleborg from Slagelse, take Strandvejen to its end at the village of Hejninge and then follow the signs to Trelleborg, 1km farther on.

Beyond Zealand

The following three destinations outside the island of Zealand each has something unique to offer.

Odense, the main city on the island of Funen, is easy to reach from Copenhagen and has a variety of sightseeing attractions. The playworld of Legoland, in central Jutland, is Denmark's most visited destination outside Copenhagen and so popular that international flights land at its door. Ribe is more of a sleeper: the oldest and best preserved town in Denmark, it has a solidly historic centre of half-timbered houses and cobbled streets encircling a 12th-century cathedral.

ODENSE
postcode 5000

Odense, which translates as 'Odin's shrine', was named after a powerful Nordic god of war, poetry and wisdom, and the city itself dates back to pre-Viking times.

Odense is now Denmark's third largest city (population 184,000) and the capital and transportation hub of the island of Funen (Fyn).

The city makes much ado about being the birthplace of Hans Christian Andersen though in actuality, after a fairly unhappy childhood, Andersen got out of Odense as fast as he could.

Whatever Andersen's experiences may have been, Odense today is nonetheless an affable university city with lots of bike paths and pedestrian streets, an interesting cathedral and a number of worthy museums. And in an ironic twist, it is the memory of Andersen, relived in his childhood home and in a museum dedicated to his works, that brings flocks of visitors to Odense today.

Information

Tourist Offices The Odense Turistbureau (☎ 66 12 75 20), Rådhuset, is at rådhus (city hall), a 15-minute walk from the train station. In summer, it's open 9 am to 7 pm daily (10 am to 5 pm Sunday); the rest of the year it's open 9 am to 4.30 pm weekdays, 10 am to 1 pm Saturday.

Money Sydbank is at the north end of Kongensgade. Other banks are on Vestergade.

Post & Communications The main post office, north-east of the train station at Dannebrogsgade 2, is open 9 am to 6 pm weekdays and 9 am to 1 pm Saturday. There's also a branch in the city centre at Gråbrødrestræde 1, with similar hours, but it generally has longer queues.

Net Café (☎ 65 91 02 78), Vindegade 43, offers inexpensive Internet access from noon to midnight daily.

Discount Cards Odense has a handy 'adventure pass' that allows free entry into museums and free bus transport; you can buy it at the train station or tourist office for a reasonable 85/125kr for 24/48 hours.

Walking Tour

The following route takes in many of the city's historic sights and museums. Although the walk itself takes only about an hour, if you stop at all the sights along the way you could easily pass the better part of a day. (The major sights listed in this walk are given more detail later in this section.)

Start at **rådhus**, which is predominantly of 1950s vintage, though the west wing dates from the late 19th century.

From rådhus, head east on Vestergade which becomes Overgade and then turn right onto **Nedergade**, a cobblestone street with leaning half-timbered houses and antique shops.

At the end of Nedergade, a left turn onto Frue Kirkestræde will bring you to **Vor Frue Kirke**, erected in the 13th century. It has a rather plain, whitewashed interior, though there's an ornate baroque pulpit that dates from the mid-17th century. It's open 10 am to noon Monday to Saturday.

From the church turn left on Overgade, where you'll soon reach **Møntergården**, the city museum, and then turn right onto Claus Bergs Gade, where you'll pass the city's only casino. Immediately to the north is the **Odense Koncerthus** (Concert Hall) and a museum dedicated to composer Carl Nielsen.

Just past the casino, turn left onto Ramsherred (which quickly changes to Hans Jensens Stræde) to reach **HC Andersens Hus**, the principal museum dedicated to Hans Christian Andersen. The museum is in a pleasant neighbourhood of narrow cobbled streets and old tile-roofed houses. If you desire some green space there's a little **park and duck pond** south of the museum.

Continue down Hans Jensens Stræde, cross Thomas B Thriges Gade and follow Gravene to Slotsgade to reach the **Fyns Kunstmuseum**, Odense's notable fine arts museum. Turn left, then proceed down Jernbanegade to Vestergade. Along the way you'll pass the site of **Gråbrødre Kloster**, a medieval Franciscan monastery that has been converted into a home for the aged.

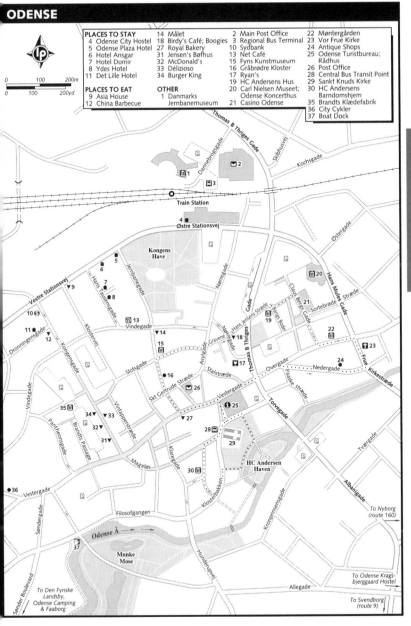

ODENSE

PLACES TO STAY
4 Odense City Hostel
5 Odense Plaza Hotel
6 Hotel Ansgar
7 Hotel Domir
8 Ydes Hotel
11 Det Lille Hotel

PLACES TO EAT
9 Asia House
12 China Barbecue

14 Målet
18 Birdy's Café; Boogies
27 Royal Bakery
31 Jensen's Bøfhus
32 McDonald's
33 Délizioso
34 Burger King

OTHER
1 Danmarks
  Jernbanemuseum

2 Main Post Office
3 Regional Bus Terminal
10 Sydbank
13 Net Café
15 Fyns Kunstmuseum
16 Gråbrødre Kloster
17 Ryan's
19 HC Andersens Hus
20 Carl Nielsen Museet;
   Odense Koncerthus
21 Casino Odense

22 Møntergården
23 Vor Frue Kirke
24 Antique Shops
25 Odense Turistbureau;
   Rådhus
26 Post Office
28 Central Bus Transit Point
29 Sankt Knuds Kirke
30 HC Andersens
   Barndomshjem
35 Brandts Klædefabrik
36 City Cykler
37 Boat Dock

When you reach Vestergade, turn east back to rådhus and then go south to **Sankt Knuds Kirke**, Odense's intriguing cathedral. Opposite the cathedral, turn onto Sankt Knuds Kirkestræde and then go south on Munkemøllestræde, where you'll pass **HC Andersens Barndomshjem**, the writer's childhood home.

Loop back around on Klosterbakken and take the path into the **HC Andersen Haven**, a riverside park with a prominent statue of the author. You can walk north through the park to get back to your starting point at rådhus.

Sankt Knuds Kirke

Odense's 12th-century Gothic cathedral is one of the city's most interesting sights. It boasts an 5m-high ornate gilded altar dating from 1520 that's considered the finest work of the master woodcrafter Claus Berg.

The cathedral's most curious sight, however, lies in the basement where you'll find a glass case containing the 900-year-old skeleton of King Knud II and another displaying the skeleton of his younger brother Benedikt. An inconspicuous set of stairs leads from the right side of the altar down to these basement treasures.

A few metres west of the coffins, steps lead down to the remains of St Alban's church, which stood on this site before the cathedral was built. In 1086 Knud II fled into St Alban's and was killed at the altar by farmers in a tax revolt. Although less than saintly, in 1101 Knud was canonised Knud the Holy by the pope in a move to secure the Catholic church in Denmark. The cathedral is open 9 am to 5 pm Monday to Saturday and noon to 3 pm Sunday; entry is free.

HC Andersens Hus

This museum, on a cobbled pedestrian street at Hans Jensens Stræde 39, depicts Hans Christian Andersen's life story through a barrage of memorabilia. There's a room with slide presentations on Andersen's life, a reconstruction of his Nyhavn (in Copenhagen) study, displays of his fanciful silhouette-style paper cuttings and a voluminous selection of his books, which have been translated into some 80 languages from Azerbaijani to Zulu.

The museum is open 9 am to 7 pm daily from mid-June to August, 10 am to 4 pm Tuesday to Sunday the rest of the year. Admission is 30kr for adults, 15kr for children.

HC Andersens Barndomshjem

In the city centre, at Munkemøllestræde 3, the HC Andersens Barndomshjem has a couple of rooms of exhibits in the small childhood home where Andersen lived from 1807 to 1819.

It's open 10 am to 4 pm daily from mid-June to August, and 11 am to 3 pm Tuesday to Sunday the rest of the year. Admission is 10kr for adults, 5kr for children.

Fyns Kunstmuseum

Fyns Kunstmuseum (Funen Art Museum), in a stately Graeco-Roman building at Jernbanegade 13, contains a quality collection of Danish art, from paintings of the old masters to abstract contemporary works. Among the museum's 2500 works of art are paintings by Jens Juel, PS Krøyer, Asger Jorn and Richard Mortensen. A local highlight is the collection by the Fynboerne (Funen Group), which includes Fritz Syberg, Peter Hansen and Johannes Larsen.

It's open 10 am to 4 pm Tuesday to Sunday. Entry is 25/10kr for adults/children.

Carl Nielsen Museet

This museum, in the concert hall at Claus Bergs Gade 11, details the career of Odense's native son Carl Nielsen, Denmark's best known composer, and displays works by his wife, sculptor Anne Marie Brodersen. It's open 10 am to 4 pm Tuesday to Sunday. Admission is 15kr for adults, 5kr for children.

Møntergården

This city museum, at Overgade 48, has displays of Odense's history dating back to the Viking Age and a couple of 16th- and 17th-century half-timbered houses that you can walk through. There are numerous rooms with period furnishings, medieval exhibits, church carvings and local archaeological finds. It's open 10 am to 4 pm Tuesday to Sunday. Admission is 15kr for adults and 5kr for children.

Den Fynske Landsby

A delightful open-air museum furnished with period buildings, Den Fynske Landsby (The Funen Village) is authentically laid out like a small country hamlet of the mid-19th century, complete with barnyard animals, a duck pond, apple trees and flower gardens. There are about two dozen thatched houses and farm buildings in all, including a windmill, watermill and smithy, which have been gathered from rural areas in Funen. It's open 10 am to 5 pm daily from April to October, until 7 pm in summer. Admission is 35kr for adults and 15kr for children.

The museum is in a green zone 4km south of the city centre via bus No 42. In summer you can take a boat (30kr) from Munke Mose down the river to Erik Bøghs Sti, from where it's a 15-minute woodland walk along the river to Den Fynske Landsby.

Danmarks Jernbanemuseum

Train buffs shouldn't miss the 19th-century locomotives at the Danmarks Jernbanemuseum (Danish Railway Museum), just behind the train station. It has a re-created period station and about two dozen engines and saloon cars, including a royal carriage that once belonged to Christian IX.

It's open 10 am to 4 pm daily. Admission is 30kr for adults, 10kr for children.

Brandts Klædefabrik

This former textile mill on Brandts Passage has been converted into a cultural centre with a photography museum, a modern art gallery and a museum of graphics and printing. Opening hours are 10 am to 5 pm Tuesday to Sunday (daily in July and August). Admission to all three costs 50kr for adults and 10kr for children, or you can buy separate tickets.

Places to Stay

Odense Camping (☎ 66 11 47 02, fax 65 91 73 43, Odensevej 102), open year-round, is a three-star camping ground 3.5km south of the city centre; take bus No 21 or 22.

Staff at the tourist office can book *rooms* in private homes at 175/300kr for singles/doubles, plus a 25kr booking fee.

Odense has two attractive hostels. New 143-bed *Odense City Hostel (☎ 63 11 04 25, fax 63 11 35 20)* is right at the train station in a converted 19th-century hotel, while 168-bed *Odense Kragsbjerggaard (☎ 66 13 04 25, fax 65 91 28 63, Kragsbjergvej 121)* is in a former manor house 2km south-east of the centre via bus No 61 or 62. Both have dorm beds for 100kr and pricier private rooms.

Pension-like *Det Lille Hotel (☎/fax 66 12 28 21, Dronningensgade 5)*, a 10-minute walk west of the train station, has 14 straightforward rooms for 250/380kr for singles/doubles. Good value are the 35-room *Hotel Domir (☎ 66 12 14 27, fax 66 12 14 31, Hans Tausensgade 19)*, which has cheery rooms with TV and private bath for 390/530kr, and its adjacent sister operation *Ydes Hotel*, which has 26 smaller but similarly appointed rooms for 330/450kr. Rates at all three include breakfast.

Hotel Ansgar (☎ 66 11 96 93, fax 66 11 96 75, Østre Stationsvej 32) has a central location and pleasantly renovated rooms with TV, minibar and private bath. Overall the rooms are on par with the city's top-end hotels, but have a relatively reasonable weekend and summer rate of 495/600kr.

The *Odense Plaza Hotel (☎ 66 11 77 45, fax 66 14 41 45, Østre Stationsvej 24)* is a small, period hotel 200m south-east of the train station. A Best Western hotel, it has full amenities and pleasant rooms. The standard rate is 995/1200kr, but there's a special 725kr rate valid at weekends and in summer which covers up to two adults and two children, breakfast included.

Places to Eat

You'll find bakeries and fast-food outlets all around the city. *Royal Bakery*, on Vestergade opposite Jernbanegade, has good pastries and organic ice cream.

There are numerous eateries along Kongensgade. *China Barbecue (Kongensgade 66)* has a 49kr lunch buffet until 3 pm, while *Jensen's Bøfhus (Kongensgade 10)* serves inexpensive steak and chicken lunches. For croissants and baguette sandwiches, there's *Délizioso* on Kongensgade, opposite *McDonald's* and *Burger King*.

EXCURSIONS

The train station has low-priced options including a *bakery*, a *DSB Café*, another *Jensen's Bøfhus*, and a *grocery store* that's open every day until midnight.

Café Biografen at Brandts Klædefabrik is a student haunt selling pastries, coffees, light meals and beer at reasonable prices; it's open 11 am to at least midnight daily. Another popular spot is *Birdy's Café (Nørregade 21)*, which has Mexican dishes for 75kr; it's open 4 pm to around midnight Monday to Saturday.

Målet (Jernbanegade 17), a sports pub and restaurant, features 10 different kinds of schnitzel, all priced at 79kr. It's open until 10 pm for food, to 11 pm for drinks.

Asia House, on the corner of Vestre Stationsvej and Klostervej, serves good authentic Thai food. On Friday and Saturday nights there's a grand buffet spread for 139kr, on other nights a la carte main dishes start around 100kr. It's open from 5 pm nightly.

Entertainment

Ryan's, a friendly Irish pub, is on Nørregade near rådhus. *Boogies (Nørregade 21)*, a dance spot, is popular with students. *Brandts Klædefabrik* has an outdoor amphitheatre that's a venue for free summer weekend concerts. For a quiet evening drink, head for the outdoor cafes on Vintapperstræde.

Getting There & Around

Odense is a 1½-hour, 178kr train ride from Copenhagen, and service is frequent.

Odense is 165km from Copenhagen. If you're arriving by car, Odense is just north of the E20; access from the highway is clearly marked.

Outside rush hour, driving in Odense is not difficult, though many of the central sights are on pedestrian streets, so it's best to park your car and explore on foot.

There are substantial car parks around Brandts Klædefabrik and the Carl Nielsen museum.

For city buses in Odense, board at the back and pay the driver (11kr) when you get off.

Bicycles can be rented for 45kr a day at City Cykler (☎ 66 13 97 83), Vesterbro 27, west of the city centre.

LEGOLAND

Legoland, 1km north of the small inlan town of Billund (postcode 7190), is Den mark's most visited tourist attraction out side of Copenhagen. A 10-hectare them park built from plastic Lego block Legoland has hosted some 30 million vis itors, more than half of them from abroad since it opened in 1968.

Legoland has its own bank, post office tourist office, hotel and restaurants, an even its own airport.

The park's main attraction is a Lilliputian world of 45 million plastic blocks arrange into miniature cities as well as scenes wit Lego pirates and safari animals. Most repl cas are on a scale of 1:20 and includ Amalienborg Slot in Copenhagen and a hand ful of easily recognisable international sight such as Amsterdam and the Acropolis.

At times the park employs as many as 3 'builders' who spend their days snapping to gether the creations. The tallest piece, model of the American Indian chief Sittin Bull, reaches 14m and contains 1.4 millio Lego blocks. The most elaborate piece is th 3.5-million-block Copenhagen Harbour ex hibit, which features electronically controlle ships, trains and cranes.

Legoland also has amusement rides, in cluded in the admission price. Most of th rides are along the lines of merry-go rounds, miniature trains and mechanica boats that are geared for children but ther are a few, such as the water slide, that ca be fun for adults as well.

There's also an antique doll collection; Mindstorms Centre, where visitors ca build programmable robots; and variou theme-park sections such as Legoredo, small Wild West town with a few costume gunslingers and Indians in feather head dresses; Castleland, featuring a train rid through a castle; and Duplo Land, with gen tle rides for the youngest children.

Legoland (☎ 75 33 13 33) is open dail from early April to late October, with th exact dates varying a bit each year. Openin hours are 10 am to 8 pm (until 9 pm from mid-June to late August). Admission cost 145kr for adults and 135kr for children age

Plastic Fantastic

Lego got its start more than 60 years ago when a local carpenter, Ole Kirk Christiansen, tried his hand at making wooden toys to earn income during a Depression-era construction slump. In 1934, after a couple of years of making pull-toys and piggy banks, Ole selected the business name Lego, a contraction of the Danish words *leg godt*, meaning 'play well', and expanded his line to four dozen toy designs.

In the late 1940s, Lego became the first company in Denmark to acquire a plastics injection-moulding machine and began making plastic interlocking blocks called 'binding bricks', the fore-runner of today's Lego blocks. In 1960, when Lego's wooden-toy warehouse went up in flames, the company decided to concentrate solely on plastic toys. By that time Lego blocks had become the most popular children's toys in Europe.

Lego continued to expand. In 1969 it created the Duplo series for younger children, with bricks twice as long and twice as wide as basic Lego blocks. Later, it introduced little vehicles, wooden families and complex theme sets of trains, pirate ships and the like. While there are now advanced kits incorpo-rating motors and fancy gadgets, the basic appeal continues to be the simple interlocking blocks that can be snapped together in endless creative combinations.

CLINT CURÉ

Lego is still a family-run business, today headed by Ole Kirk's grandson, but it's grown into one of Denmark's best-known companies and Europe's largest toy manufacturer. Lego now has 50 branches on six continents. It's estimated that in the past half-century some 300 million children worldwide have at one time or another played with Lego toys.

three to 13. For more information visit the Web site at www.legoland.dk.

Note that the activities and rides usually shut down two hours before Legoland closes. There's no admission charge after the rides stop so even if you arrive late you can still stroll the grounds.

Information

The Billund Turistbureau (☎ 76 50 00 55, fax 75 35 31 79, ℮ info@bgt.dk), Legoland Parken, is situated inside Legoland but has an entrance that faces the road and is open year-round.

During the Legoland season it's open 9 am to 8 pm daily (to 9 pm in July and August). Winter hours are shorter.

The park has a Den Danske Bank branch and a post office that franks mail with a special Legoland stamp.

Places to Stay

In the high season, places to stay near Legoland are often fully booked, so advance reservations are advised. Nonetheless, even then the tourist office can usually find you a hotel, or a *room* in a private home (150kr per person), though sometimes you may have to go 10km to 20km outside town.

Billund FDM Camping (☎ 75 33 15 21, fax 75 35 37 36, ℮ c-billund@fdm.dk, Ellehammer Allé 2), just 400m east of the Legoland gate, is one of Denmark's largest camping grounds, with 550 sites. This three-star facility has a coin laundry, lounges, playgrounds and cabin rentals.

The 228-bed *Billund Vandrerhjem* (☎ 75 33 27 77, fax 75 33 28 77, ℮ billund@danhostel.dk, Ellehammer Allé), a modern five-star hostel, is adjacent to the camping ground. Dorm beds cost 100kr, while family rooms cost from 360kr for one person to 450kr for five people. It's open year-round, and is accessible to wheelchairs.

Opposite Legoland park, but connected by an overhead walkway, is *Hotel Legoland* (☎ 75 33 12 44, fax 75 35 38 10, ℮ hotel@ legoland.dk, Aastvej 10), the area's largest hotel. The staff are helpful and the rooms are comfortable with private bath, TV, phone and minibar. Singles/doubles cost from 925/ 1195kr, breakfast included.

A cheaper option is *Hotel Svanen* (☎ 75 33 28 33, fax 75 35 35 15, Nordmarksvej 8), a motel-style place 600m south-east of Legoland, in the same neighbourhood as the hostel and camping ground. It has 24 modern rooms with phone, TV and private bath starting at 690kr, breakfast included.

Places to Eat

Legoland's many eateries include stands selling popular fast-food items such as hot dogs, burgers and ice cream. Among the sit-down restaurants are the *Grill House*, specialising in grilled steaks and chicken; the *Saloon*, featuring spareribs and draught beer; and the *Cafeteria* which, not surprisingly, has cafeteria fare.

A bit pricier is *Hotel Legoland*, which does lunch and dinner buffet spreads. The hostel has its own *cafe* serving three meals a day.

Getting There & Away

Billund is on route 28, 28km west of Vejle, which has the nearest train service. From Copenhagen the train runs hourly to Vejle, costs 226kr and takes 2½ to three hours; connecting public bus service continues to Legoland (41kr, 40 minutes).

Copenhagen Excursions (☎ 32 54 06 06) offers full-day tours from Copenhagen to Legoland every Thursday and Saturday during the summer. The tours leave Copenhagen at 8 am and are back in the city at 8 pm. Admission to Legoland is included in the tour price of 460kr for adults, 280kr for children.

Billund's airport, literally just outside Legoland's gate, is served by Maersk Air (☎ 70 10 74 74), which has numerous daily flights to Billund from Copenhagen. Maersk Air also provides international service to Billund from Amsterdam, Brussels, Dublin, Frankfurt, London, Paris and Stockholm.

RIBE
postcode 6760

Ribe, the oldest town in Denmark, is chock-full of historic sites. Recent excavations, which unearthed a number of silver coins, indicate that a market town existed on the northern side of the Ribe Å (Ribe River) as far back as AD 700. In 850, Saint Ansgar built the first church in Ribe and the town began to grow. During the Viking era, Ribe, linked to the sea by its river, flourished as a centre of trade between the Frankish empire and the Scandinavian states to the north.

In the 12th century the Valdemar dynasty fortified the town, building a castle and establishing Ribe as one of the king's Jutland residences.

In the late medieval period, as power shifted to eastern Denmark, Ribe's importance declined. A sweeping fire in 1580 destroyed a third of the town and in the century that followed, the incessant wars with Sweden strangled trade and further impoverished Ribe. Meanwhile the river to Ribe silted up, cutting off access to the sea, and the town's population dropped off. With the founding of the port city of Esbjerg in 1868, Ribe was completely bypassed as a trade centre.

Ironically, in terms of preservation, Ribe's economic misfortunes have served to spare its historic buildings from modernisation. As a result the town centre, which surrounds an imposing medieval cathedral, retains a unique centuries-old character. With its crooked cobbled streets and half-timbered 16th-century houses, ambling about Ribe is a bit like stepping into a living history museum.

Indeed, the entire old town is a preservation zone, with more than 100 buildings in the National Trust.

Ribe is a tightly clustered place, easy to explore. Virtually everything, including the train station, is within a 10-minute walk of Torvet, the central square.

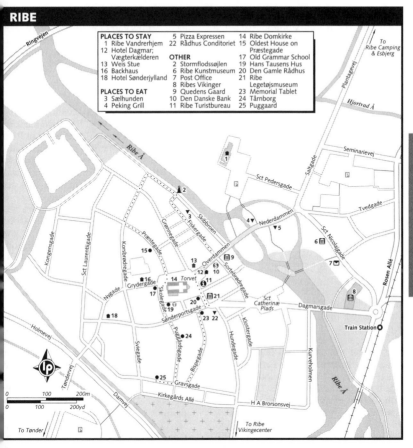

RIBE

PLACES TO STAY
1 Ribe Vandrerhjem
12 Hotel Dagmar;
   Vægterkælderen
13 Weis Stue
16 Backhaus
18 Hotel Sønderjylland

PLACES TO EAT
3 Sælhunden
4 Peking Grill

5 Pizza Expressen
22 Rådhus Conditoriet

OTHER
2 Stormflodssøjlen
6 Ribe Kunstmuseum
7 Post Office
8 Ribes Vikinger
9 Quedens Gaard
10 Den Danske Bank
11 Ribe Turistbureau

14 Ribe Domkirke
15 Oldest House on
   Præstegade
17 Old Grammar School
19 Hans Tausens Hus
20 Den Gamle Rådhus
21 Ribe
   Legetøjsmuseum
23 Memorial Tablet
24 Tårnborg
25 Puggaard

EXCURSIONS

Information

The Ribe Turistbureau (☎ 75 42 15 00, fax 75 42 40 78), Torvet 3, is conveniently located on the central square beside Hotel Dagmar. It's open 9.30 am to 5.30 pm weekdays, 10 am to 5 pm Saturday and 10 am to 2 pm Sunday in July and August. The rest of the year it's open 9 am to at least 4.30 pm weekdays and 10 am to 1 pm Saturday.

The Den Danske Bank on Overdammen, situated just east of Hotel Dagmar, has an outdoor ATM.

The post office is at Sct Nicolajgade 12, 200m north-west of the train station.

Walking Tour

You can make an enjoyable loop route of central Ribe's historic sights in a walk that takes a couple of leisurely hours.

The walk begins at Torvet and follows Overdammen north-east to Fiskergade. On **Fiskergade** you'll see many alleys which lead east to the riverfront.

Notice the 'bumper' stones on the corners of the houses. Because the alleys are so narrow the original residents installed these stones in order to protect their houses from being scraped by the wheels of horse-drawn carriages.

At the intersection of Fiskergade and Skibbroen, you'll find **Stormflodssøjlen**, a flood column marking numerous floods that have swept over Ribe. Note the ring at the top of the column indicating the water's depth (6m above normal!) during the record flood of 1634, which claimed hundreds of lives.

Continue north-west along Skibbroen, which skirts the old medieval quay, now lined with small motorboats. From Skibbroen, turn south on Korsbrødregade and then head south-east on Præstegade. About halfway down on the right, you'll pass this street's **oldest house**, constructed in 1580, as noted by the plaque above the door. Continue back to the **Ribe Domkirke**, skirting around its western side and onto Skolegade.

On the corner of Skolegade and Grydergade is an **old grammar school** that first opened in the early 16th century. On the opposite side of Skolegade is the two-storey **Hans Tausens Hus**, which dates from the early 17th century and is one of Denmark's oldest bishops' residences. A **statue** of Hans Tausen, who helped spark the Danish Reformation, stands opposite in the churchyard.

From Skolegade continue south on Puggårdsgade, a cobbled street lined with older homes. The timber-framed house on the corner of Sønderportsgade and Puggårdsgade dates from 1597. A couple of buildings down on the left there's **Tårnborg**, a 16th-century manor house that now serves as a local government office. On the same side of the street, but a little farther south, is a half-timbered house dating from 1550.

When you reach Gravsgade go right for about 50m and along the northern side of the street you'll come to the brick **Puggaard**, a canon's residence which was constructed around 1500. From there turn around and go east on Gravsgade and then turn north on Bispegade.

On the corner of Bispegade and Sønderportsgade, you'll find a **memorial tablet** to Maren Spliid, who was burned at the stake on 9 November 1641, one of the last victims of Denmark's witch-hunt persecutions.

From that corner continue north past **Den Gamle Rådhus** (the Old Town Hall). Look up at the roof gable to spot a huge round nest made of sticks; each year around the first of April a pair of nesting storks, one of only a handful in all of Denmark, returns to this site to the delight of bird-watching enthusiasts. From there, continue back to your starting point at Torvet.

Ribe Domkirke

The town's dominant landmark, Ribe Cathedral, stands as a fine testament to Ribe's prominent past. The diocese of Ribe was founded in 948, but its original cathedral was a modest wooden building. In 1150, Ribe's Bishop Elias, with the financial backing of the royal family, began work on a more stately stone structure.

The new cathedral was constructed primarily of tufa, a soft porous rock quarried near Cologne and shipped north along the Rhine River. It took a century for the work to reach completion. Although later additions added a number of Gothic features, the core of the cathedral remains decidedly Romanesque, a fine example of medieval Rhineland influences.

One notable feature is the original 'Cat's Head' door at the south portal of the transept, which boasts detailed relief work, including a triangular pediment portraying Valdemar II and Queen Dagmar positioned at the foot of Jesus and Mary. At noon and 3 pm the church bell plays the notes to a folk song about Queen Dagmar's death during childbirth.

The cathedral's interior decor is a hotchpotch of later influences. Among the highlights are an organ with a facade designed by the renowned 17th-century sculptor Jens Olufsen and an ornate altar created in 1597 by Odense sculptor Jens Asmussen. You can find frescoes dating from the 16th century along the northern side of the cathedral, while in the apse are modern-day frescoes, stained-glass windows and seven mosaics created in the 1980s by artist Carl-Henning Pedersen.

In the Renaissance period, arranging for burial inside Ribe Domkirke became trendy among the wealthy. Most of these graves are marked by simple carved stones in the aisles, but there are also more ostentatious memorials and chapels containing the remains of bishops and other distinguished citizens of the day. The highest ranked bones within the confines of the cathedral are those of King Christopher I, who was buried in 1259 directly beneath the great dome in the middle of the sanctuary.

For a towering view of the countryside, climb 27m up the cathedral tower, which dates from 1333. A survey of surrounding marshland makes it easy to understand why the tower once doubled as a lookout station for floods. It's open 10 am to 6 pm from June to August, 10 am to 5 pm in May and September and 11 am to 3 or 4 pm during the rest of the year. On Sunday and holidays throughout the year it opens at noon. The admission of 10kr for adults, 3kr for children, covers both the cathedral and the tower.

Den Gamle Rådhus

This building, opposite the south-eastern corner of the cathedral, dates from 1496, making it the oldest town hall in Denmark. In addition to being the site of council meetings it also houses a small collection of historical artefacts, including some medieval weapons and the executioner's axe. It's open 1 to 3 pm daily in summer, and weekdays only in May and September. Admission is 15kr for adults, 5kr for children.

Quedens Gaard

On the corner of Overdammen and Sorteprødgade, this history museum in is a half-timbered former merchant's house, the oldest wing of which was built in 1583. Part of the house retains merchants' furnishings from the early 17th century; other rooms exhibit furniture and crafts from earlier periods and trade and industry displays of more recent times. It's open 10 am to 5 pm daily from June to August; the rest of the year it's open 11 am to 3 pm (to 1 pm in midwinter) daily except Monday. Admission is 20kr for adults, 5kr for children.

Ribes Vikinger

Ribes Vikinger (Vikings of Ribe), opposite the train station, is a well-presented museum with informative displays on Ribe's Viking and medieval history.

One exhibition hall reproduces a marketplace in AD 800, complete with a cargo-laden Viking ship, while another hall portrays a late-medieval scene of the town centre. There are also many local archaeological finds, including pottery shards, glass and amber beads and an anchor from a Viking ship.

It's open 10 am to 6 pm daily in July and August, except Wednesday when it stays open until 9 pm. During other months it's open 10 am to 4 pm daily, with the exception of November to March when it's closed Monday. Admission is 45kr for adults and 15kr for children.

Ribe Vikingecenter

The Ribe Vikingecenter, 3km south of the town centre at Lustrupvej 4, is affiliated with the Ribes Vikinger museum. This outdoor facility, developed along the lines of a living history museum, has attempted to recreate a slice of life in Viking-era Ribe. It has various reconstructions, including a 34m longhouse, and staff who dress in period clothing, cook over open fires and demonstrate Viking-era crafts such as pottery and leather work. There are also frequent demonstrations in the art of falconry using various birds of prey.

It's open 11 am to 4.30 pm daily in July and August and 11 am to 4 pm weekdays in May, June and September. Admission is 50kr for adults and 20kr for children.

Ribe Kunstmuseum

Housed in a 19th-century villa at Sct Nicolajgade 10, Ribe Kunstmuseum is one of the oldest art museums in Denmark and consequently has acquired a good collection, particularly of the 19th-century Danish Golden Age painters. Exhibits include works by Abildgaard, Juel, Eckersberg, Købke and Lundbye. Among the museum's more notable paintings is Michael Ancher's *Christening in Skagen Church*.

The museum is open 11 am to 5 pm daily from mid-June to 31 August and 1 to 4 pm Tuesday to Sunday throughout the rest of the year. Admission is 30kr for adults and free for children.

Ribe Legetøjsmuseum

This museum, just south-east of the cathedral, has a collection of 19th- and 20th-century antique toys, including porcelain dolls. It's open 10 am to 5 pm daily from June to August, and afternoons only during the rest of the year. Admission is 30kr for adults and 15kr for children.

Guided Walk

Recreating a scene that in centuries past took place each night in towns all across Denmark, a night watchman in period costume makes his rounds through Ribe, carrying a lantern and a spiked wooden staff. As in times past, he sings his way through the old cobbled streets, though these days it's not to reassure townsfolk that he's on patrol, but to delight sightseers who follow Pied Piper-like behind him.

From June to August, the night watchman leaves from Torvet at both 8 and 10 pm. In May and during the first half of September, he makes the rounds just once each night at 10 pm. It's an unabashedly touristy scene that's both fun and free.

Places to Stay

Three-star *Ribe Camping* (☎ 75 41 07 77, fax 75 41 00 01, ℯ ribe@dk-camp.dk, Farupvej 2), 2km north of Ribe centre, is open year-round. It has winter-insulated cabins.

The modern, 140-bed *Ribe Vandrerhjem* (☎ 75 42 06 20, fax 75 42 42 88, ℯ ribed anh@post5.tele.dk, Sct Pedersgade 16) is one of Denmark's most popular hostels, with friendly staff, pleasant rooms and an ideal location. Dorm beds cost 100kr and double rooms 295kr. The tourist office maintains a list of *rooms* in private homes from 175/275kr for singles/doubles.

Three in-town taverns rent second-storey rooms for around 275/500kr with breakfast: *Backhaus* (☎ 75 42 11 01, fax 75 42 52 87, Grydergade 12), *Weis Stue* (☎ 75 42 07 00, Torvet) and *Hotel Sønderjylland* (☎ 75 42 04 66, fax 75 42 21 92, Sønderportsgade 22)

Hotel Dagmar (☎ 75 42 00 33, fax 75 42 36 52, ℯ dagmar@hoteldagmar.dk, Torvet 1), in the centre of Ribe opposite the cathedral, dates from 1581, giving it claim to being the oldest hotel in Denmark. Restored to its period character, it has 50 rooms with full amenities from 745/945kr.

Places to Eat

On Nederdammen, between the hostel and Torvet, there's *Pizza Expressen*, which has long hours and inexpensive pizza by the slice, and *Peking Grill*, which has good-value Chinese food, including 25kr lunch specials. *Rådhus Conditoriet* (Hundegade 2) offers good takeaway and eat-in bakery items, as well as coffee and simple eats.

Sælhunden (Skibbroen 13), opposite the harbour, serves good seafood and steak dishes for around 100kr at dinner, less at lunch. *Vægterkælderen*, an atmospheric basement restaurant in Hotel Dagmar on Torvet, shares a kitchen with the hotel's pricier upstairs restaurant, but its dishes, including a generous spareribs plate, average a reasonable 100kr.

Getting There & Around

To get to Ribe from Copenhagen by train you need to first go to Esbjerg (3¼ hours, 256kr) and then catch a branch line train from Esbjerg to Ribe (37kr, 40 minutes) Both trains run about once an hour.

By car, Ribe is 270km west of Copenhagen, via the E-20 motorway and route 32. There's parking with a two-hour limit near the cathedral, with a three-hour limit at Ribes Vikinger and with no limits at the end of Sct Pedersgade, near the hostel.

Bicycles can be hired from the hostel, at Sct Pedersgade 16, for 50kr a day.

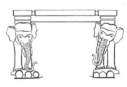

Language

Together with Swedish, Norwegian, Icelandic and Faroese, Danish belongs to the northern branch of the Germanic language group. Consequently, written Danish bears a strong resemblance to all these languages. Spoken Danish, however, has evolved in a different direction, developing sounds and quirks of pronunciation not found elsewhere.

Grammatically, Danish has the same general rules and syntax as the other Germanic languages of Scandinavia. There are two genders: common (or 'non-neuter'), and neuter. Articles ('a/an' and 'the' in English) are suffixed to the noun: -en for common singular nouns and -et for neuter singular nouns.

Danish has both a polite and an informal mode of address (where English uses the universal 'you'); the polite form uses the personal pronouns *De* and *Dem*, the informal, *du* and *dig*. The translations in this chapter are mostly in the informal, except where it's appropriate to use the polite form. In general, use the polite form when speaking to senior citizens and officials, and the informal in all other instances.

Most Danes speak English, and many also speak German. However, any effort to learn even the basics, such as the Danish words for 'Thank you', 'Good-bye', 'Hello' and 'I'm sorry', will be greatly appreciated. With an increased command of the language, you'll be rewarded by gaining a greater insight into the people and their country.

Note that Danish has all of the letters of the English alphabet plus three others, æ, ø and å. These come at the end of the alphabet and we have used this order throughout the book.

Pronunciation

You may find Danish pronunciation difficult. Consonants can be drawled, swallowed and even omitted completely, creating, in conjunction with vowels, the peculiarity of the glottal stop or *stød*. Its sound is rather as a Cockney would say the 'tt' in 'bottle'.

Stress usually falls on the first syllable. As a general rule, the best advice is to listen and learn. Good luck!

Vowels

a	as in 'father'; as in 'act'
e	a short, flat 'e' as in 'met'
e(g)	as the 'i' in 'high'
i	a short, flat 'e' as in 'met'; as the 'i' in 'marine'
o	a short 'o' as in 'pot'; as the 'a' in 'walk'; as the 'oo' in 'zoo'
o(v)	as the 'ow' in 'vow', but shorter
o(r)	as in 'or' but with little emphasis on the 'r'
u	as in 'pull'; as the 'oo' in 'zoo'
u(n)	as the 'a' in 'act'
y	a long, sharp 'u' – purse your lips and say 'ee'
æ	as the 'e' in 'bet'; as the 'a' in 'act'
ø	as the 'er' in 'fern', but shorter
å	as the 'a' in 'walk'

Consonants

Consonants are pronounced as in English with the exception of the following:

b	as in 'box'
c	as in 'cell'
ch	as in 'cheque', but sharper
(o)d	as the 'th' in 'these'
g	before vowels, a hard 'g' as in 'get'
h	as in 'horse'
j	as the 'y' in 'yet'
k	as in 'kit'
ng	as in 'sing'
r	a rolling 'r' abruptly cut short
sj	as the 'sh' in 'ship'
w	as the 'v' in 'Volkswagon'

Greetings & Civilities

Hello.	*Goddag/Hej.* (polite/informal)
Goodbye.	*Farvel.*
Yes.	*Ja.*
No.	*Nej.*

LANGUAGE

Could I please have ...?	*Jeg vil gerne bede om ...*
Please ... (when making a request)	*Vær så venlig at ...*
Please (sit down).	*Værsgo (at sidde ned).*
Thank you.	*Tak.*
That's fine/ You're welcome.	*Det er i orden/Selv tak.*
Excuse me (Sorry).	*Undskyld.*
May I/Do you mind?	*Må jeg/Tillader De?*

Language Difficulties

Do you speak English?	*Taler De engelsk?*
Does anyone speak English?	*Er der nogen, der kan tale engelsk?*
I understand.	*Jeg forstår.*
I don't understand.	*Jeg forstår ikke.*
Could you speak more slowly please?	*Kunne De taler langsommere?*

Small Talk

What's your name?	*Hvad hedder du?*
My name is ...	*Jeg hedder ...*
Where are you from?	*Hvorfra kommer du?*
I'm from ...	*Jeg kommer fra ...*
How old are you?	*Hvor gammel er du?*
I'm ... years old.	*Jeg er ... år gammel.*

Getting Around

What time does the ... leave/arrive?	*Hvornår går/ ankommer ...?*
boat	*båden*
bus (city)	*bussen*
bus (intercity)	*rutebilen*
train	*toget*

Signs

Indgang	**Entrance**
Udgang	**Exit**
Åben	**Open**
Lukket	**Closed**
Forbudt	**Prohibited**
Information	**Information**
Politistation	**Police Station**
Toiletter	**Toilets**
Herrer	**Men**
Damer	**Women**

I'd like (a) ...	*Jeg vil gerne have ...*
one-way ticket	*en enkeltbillet*
return ticket	*en tur-retur billet*
1st class	*første klasse*
2nd class	*anden klasse*

Directions

Where is ...?	*Hvor er ...?*
I want to go to ...	*Jeg vil gerne til ...*
Can you show me (on the map)?	*Kan De vise mig det (på kortet)?*
Go straight ahead.	*Gå ligeud.*
Turn left.	*Drej til venstre.*
Turn right.	*Drej til højre.*
near	*tæt på*
far	*langt væk*

Around Town

I'm looking for ...	*Jeg leder efter ...*
a bank	*en bank*
the city centre	*centrum*
the ... embassy	*den ... ambassade*
my hotel	*mit hotel*
the market	*markedet*
the museum	*museet*
the police	*politiet*
the post office	*postkontoret*
a public toilet	*et offentligt toilet*
the telephone centre	*telefoncentralen*
the tourist office	*turist-informationer*

beach	*strand*
castle	*slot*
cathedral	*katedral/domkirke*
church	*kirke*
main square	*hovedtorv/torvet*
monastery	*kloster*
old city	*den gamle bydel*
palace	*palads*

Accommodation

Where's a cheap hotel?	*Hvor ligger det et billigt hotel?*
What's the address?	*Hvad er adressen?*
Could you write down the address, please?	*Kunne De skrive adressen ned?*
Do you have any rooms available?	*Har I ledige værelser?*

I'd like ... — *Jeg vil gerne have ...*
  a single room — *et enkeltværelse*
  a double room — *et dobbeltværelse*
  a room with a — *et værelse med bad*
  bathroom
  to share a dorm — *plads i en sovesal*
  a bed — *en seng*

How much is it — *Hvor meget koster det*
  per night/ — *per nat/per person?*
  per person?
May I see it? — *Må jeg se værelset?*
Where is the — *Hvor er badeværelset?*
  bathroom?

Shopping
How much is it? — *Hvor meget koster*
  den/ (common)
  det? (neuter)

bookshop — *boghandel*
camera shop — *fotohandel*
clothing store — *tøjforretning*
delicatessen — *delikatesse*
laundry — *vaskeri*
market — *marked*
newsagency — *aviskiosk*
souvenir shop — *souvenirbutik*
stationers — *papirhandel*

Health
Where is the ...? — *Hvor er ...?*
  hospital — *hospitalet*
  chemist — *apotkeket*

I'm ill. — *Jeg er syg.*
My friend is ill. — *Min ven er syg.*

I'm ... — *Jeg er ...*
  asthmatic — *astmatiker*
  diabetic — *diabetiker*
  epileptic — *epileptiker*

I'm allergic to — *Jeg er allergisk over for*
  antibiotics/ — *antibiotika/*
  penicillin. — *penicillin.*

I need medication — *Jeg skal bruge noget*
  for ... — *medicin imod ...*
I have a — *Jeg har en recept.*
  prescription.
I have a toothache. — *Jeg har tandpine.*
I'm pregnant. — *Jeg er gravid.*

antiseptic — *antiseptisk*
aspirin — *aspirin*
condoms — *kondomer*
contraceptive — *præventiv*
dentist — *tandlæge*
diarrhoea — *diarré*
doctor — *læge*
medicine — *medicin*
nausea — *kvalme*
stomachache — *ondt i maven*
soap — *sæbe*
sunblock cream — *solcreme*
tampons — *tamponer*

Time & Dates
What time is it? — *Hvad er klokken?*
It's ... o'clock. — *Klokken er ...*

today — *i dag*
tonight — *i aften/i nat*
tomorrow — *i morgen*
day after tomorrow — *i overmorgen*
next week — *næste uge*
yesterday — *i går*
in the morning — *om morgenen*
in the afternoon — *om eftermiddagen*
in the evening — *om aftenen*
early — *tidlig*

Monday — *mandag*
Tuesday — *tirsdag*
Wednesday — *onsdag*
Thursday — *torsdag*
Friday — *fredag*
Saturday — *lørdag*
Sunday — *søndag*

January — *januar*
February — *februar*
March — *marts*
April — *april*
May — *maj*
June — *juni*
July — *juli*
August — *august*
September — *september*
October — *oktober*
November — *november*
December — *december*

Emergencies

Help!	Hjælp!
Go away!	Forsvind!
It's an emergency!	Det er en nød-situation!
Call a doctor!	Ring efter en læge!
Call the police!	Ring efter politiet!
Call an ambulance!	Ring efter en ambulance!
I want to contact my embassy/ consulate.	Jeg vil kontakte min ambassade/mit konsulat.
I'm lost.	Jeg har gået vild.
Where are the toilets?	Hvor er toiletterne?

Numbers

0	nul
1	en
2	to
3	tre
4	fire
5	fem
6	seks
7	syv
8	otte
9	ni
10	ti
11	elleve
12	tolv
13	tretten
14	fjorten
15	femten
16	seksten
17	sytten
18	atten
19	nitten
20	tyve
21	enogtyve
30	tredive
40	fyrre
50	halvtreds
60	tres
70	halvfjerds
80	firs
90	halvfems
100	hundrede
1000	tusind

one million	en million

FOOD & DRINK

I'd like today's special, please.	Jeg tager dagens ret, tak.
I'm a vegetarian.	Jeg er vegetar.
breakfast	morgenmad
lunch	frokost
dinner	middag
menu	spisekort
set menu	dagens middag
children's menu	børnemenu
daily special	dagens ret
dishes, courses	retter
starters, appetisers	forretter
main dishes	hovedretter
self-serve buffet	tagselvbord

Food Glossary

Note that **æ**, **ø** and **å** come after **z** in the Danish alphabet.

Dishes

engelsk bøf	steak, commonly served with onions
forårsrulle	spring roll, egg roll
gryderet	casserole or stew
karry	curry
oksehaleragout	oxtail stew
parisertoast	toasted ham and cheese sandwich
pommes frites	French fries, chips
smørrebrød	open sandwich
æggekage	scrambled eggs with onions, potatoes and bacon

Soups

gule ærter	split pea soup served with pork
hønsekødsuppe	chicken soup
klar suppe	clear soup
suppe	soup
øllebrød	beer and bread soup

Salads

agurkesalat	sliced cucumber with vinegar dressing
grøn salat	green salad
kartoffelsalat	potato salad

Desserts

chokolade	chocolate, also hot chocolate
fromage	a pudding
ingefærbrød	gingerbread
is	ice cream, ice
kage	cake
kringle	type of Danish pastry
lagkage	layer cake
pandekage	pancake or crepe
ris à l'amande	rice pudding with almonds
tærte	tart
vaffel	waffle
vandmelon	watermelon
vanilleis	vanilla ice cream
wienerbrød	Danish pastry

Meat

dyresteg	roast venison
flæskesteg	roast pork, often served with crackling
frikadelle	fried meatball
fårekød	mutton
hakkebøf	ground-beef burger
haresteg	roast hare
kalvekød	veal
kotelet	cutlet
kød	meat
kødbolle	boiled meatball
kødretter	meat dishes
lamme, lammekød	lamb
lammesteg	roast lamb
lever	liver
leverpostej	liver pâté
oksefilet	tenderloin
oksekød	beef
oksemørbrad,	fillet of beef,
oksesteg	roast beef
pølse	sausage, hot dog
skinke	ham
svinekød	pork
tunge	tongue

Poultry

and, andesteg	duck, roast duck
gås	goose
høns/hønsekød	chicken
hønsebryst	chicken breast
kalkun	turkey
kylling	chicken

Seafood

ansjoser	anchovies
blæksprutte	octopus
fisk	fish
fiskefilet	fish fillet
fiskefrikadelle	fried fishball
fiskeretter	fish dishes
fiskesuppe	fish soup, usually creamy
flynder	flounder
forel	trout
helleflynder	halibut
hummer	lobster
klipfisk	dried, salted cod
krabbe	crab
kryddersild	herring pickled in various marinades
kuller	haddock
laks	salmon
makrel	mackerel
marineret sild	marinated herring
musling	mussel
rejer	shrimp
rødspætte	plaice
røget laks	smoked salmon
røget sild	smoked herring
sild	herring
skaldyr	shellfish
søtunge	sole
torsk	cod
torskerogn	cod roe
tun, tunfisk	tuna
ørred	trout
østers	oyster
ål	eel

Vegetables

agurk	cucumber
asparges	asparagus
bagt kartoffel	baked potato
blomkål	cauliflower
bønner	beans
champignon	mushroom
grøn bønne	green bean
grøntsager	vegetables
gulerødder	carrots
hvidløg	garlic
kartoffel	potato
kartoffelmos	mashed potatoes
kål	cabbage
løg	onion
majs	corn

oliven	olive
porre	leek
rødbeder	beets, commonly served pickled
rødkål	red cabbage
salat	salad, lettuce
selleri	celery
snittebønner	string beans
spinat	spinach
syltede agurker	pickled cucumbers
ærter	peas

Nuts

hasselnød	hazelnut
jordnød	peanut
mandel, mandler	almonds
nødder	nuts
valnød	walnut

Fruit

abrikos	apricot
ananas	pineapple
appelsin	orange
banan	banana
blomme	plum
blåbær	blueberry
brombær	blackberry
citron	lemon
fersken	peach
frugt	fruit
grapefrugt	grapefruit
hindbær	raspberry
jordbær	strawberry
kirsebær	cherry
pære	pear
æble	apple

Eggs

blødkogt æg	soft-boiled egg
flæskeæggekage	scrambled eggs with bacon
hårdkogt æg	hard-boiled egg
røræg	scrambled eggs
spejlæg	fried egg, sunny side up
æg	egg
æggeblomme	egg yolk

Dairy

crème fraîche	sour cream
fløde	cream
flødeost	cream cheese
flødeskum	whipped cream
hytteost	cottage cheese
kærnemælk	buttermilk
letmælk	low-fat milk
mælk	milk
ost	cheese
skummetmælk	skimmed (nonfat) mil‌
smør	butter
sødmælk	whole milk
tykmælk	a pourable yoghurt

Bread

bolle	soft bread roll, also a meatball or fishba‌
brød	bread
flute	type of French bread
kryddere	crispy bread rolls
rugbrød	rye bread
rundstykke	crispy poppy-seed ro‌

Condiments, Herbs & Spices

dild	dill
eddike	vinegar
honning	honey
ingefær	ginger
jordnødsmør	peanut butter
krydderi	spice
peber	pepper
pebermynte	peppermint
peberrod	horseradish
persille	parsley
purløg	chives
remoulade	mayonnaise-based tartar sauce
sennep	mustard
sukker	sugar
syltetøj	jam

Cooking Methods

bagt	baked
dampet	steamed
friturestegt	deep fried
gennemstegt	well-done
grilleret, grillstegt	grilled
kogt	boiled
marineret	marinated
mellemstegt	medium cooked
ovnstegt	roasted
pocheret	poached
ristet	toasted
røget	smoked
stegt	fried

Useful Words

benfri	boneless
frisk	fresh
fyld	stuffing
fyldt	stuffed
glasur	glaze, frosting
hakket	chopped, minced
hjemmebagt	home-baked
hjemmelavet	home-made
hvide	white (as in white potatoes, rice etc)
iskold	ice cold
kold	cold
nudler	noodles
olie	oil
ris	rice
rå	raw
saltet	salted, cured
skive	slice
sky	meat juice (for gravy)
sovs	gravy, sauce
stegeretter	fried dishes
sød	sweet
tilberedt	cooked
varm	warm, hot
vegetar/ vegetarianer	vegetarian
vildt	game

Drinks

alkoholfri	nonalcoholic
appelsinjuice	orange juice
citronvand	lemonade
fadøl	draught (draft) beer
kaffe	coffee
koffeinfri	caffeine-free
mineralvand	mineral water
sodavand	soft drink, carbonated water
te	tea
vand	water
øl	beer

Glossary

Note that the Danish letters æ, ø and å fall at the end of the alphabet.

apotek – pharmacy, chemist

bageri – bakery
bibliotek – library
billetautomat – automated parking-ticket dispenser
bro – bridge
bugt – bay
by – town
børnemenu – children's menu

campingplads – camping ground

dagens ret – special meal of the day
Danmark – Denmark
Dansk – Danish
domkirke – cathedral
DSB – abbreviation and common name for Danske Statsbaner (Danish State Railroad), Denmark's national railway

EU – European Union

Fyn – Funen, both a county and an island
færegehavn – ferry harbour

gade – street
gammel – old
gård – yard, farm

have – garden
havn – harbour
HI – Hostelling International, the main international hostel organisation (formerly IYHF)
hygge – cosy

IC – intercity train
ICLyn – business-class train
IR – inter-regional train

jernbane – train

kirke – church

kirkegård – churchyard, cemetery
klippekort – a type of multiple-use transport ticket
kloster – monastery
konditori – bakery with cafe tables
kro – inn
København – Copenhagen
køreplan – timetable

lur – Bronze Age horn

museet – museum
møntvask – coin laundry

nord – north

plantage – plantation, tree farm, woods
privat vej – private road

røgeri – fish smokehouse
rådhus – town hall, city hall

samling – collection, usually of art
Sjælland – the island of Zealand
skov – forest, woods
slagter – butcher
slot – castle or palace
smørrebrød – open sandwich
strand – beach, shoreline
stykke – piece
sund – sound
syd – south
sø – lake

torv, torvet – square, marketplace
tårn – tower

vandrerhjem – youth and family hostel
vej – street, road
vest – west

ø – island, usually attached as a suffix to the proper name
øl – beer
øst – east

å – river

LONELY PLANET

You already know that Lonely Planet produces more than this one guidebook, but you might not be aware of the other products we have on this region. Here is a selection of titles that you may want to check out as well:

Scandinavian & Baltic Europe
ISBN 1 86450 156 1
US$21.99 • UK£13.99

Scandinavian phrasebook
ISBN 1 86450 225 8
US$7.99 • UK£4.50

Europe on a shoestring
ISBN 1 86450 150 2
US$24.99 • UK£14.99

Read this First: Europe
ISBN 1 86450 136 7
US$14.99 • UK£8.99

Denmark
ISBN 0 86442 609 7
US$17.95 • UK£11.99

Available wherever books are sold

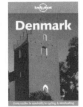

LONELY PLANET

ON THE ROAD

Travel Guides explore cities, regions and countries, and supply information on transport, restaurants and accommodation, covering all budgets. They come with reliable, easy-to-use maps, practical advice, cultural and historical facts and a rundown on attractions both on and off the beaten track. There are over 200 titles in this classic series, covering nearly every country in the world.

 Lonely Planet Upgrades extend the shelf life of existing travel guides by detailing any changes that may affect travel in a region since a book has been published. Upgrades can be downloaded for free from **www.lonelyplanet.com/upgrades**

For travellers with more time than money, **Shoestring** guides offer dependable, first-hand information with hundreds of detailed maps, plus insider tips for stretching money as far as possible. Covering entire continents in most cases, the six-volume shoestring guides are known around the world as 'backpackers bibles'.

For the discerning short-term visitor, **Condensed** guides highlight the best a destination has to offer in a full-colour, pocket-sized format designed for quick access. They include everything from top sights and walking tours to opinionated reviews of where to eat, stay, shop and have fun.

CitySync lets travellers use their Palm™ or Visor™ hand-held computers to guide them through a city with handy tips on transport, history, cultural life, major sights, and shopping and entertainment options. It can also quickly search and sort hundreds of reviews of hotels, restaurants and attractions, and pinpoint their location on scrollable street maps. CitySync can be downloaded from **www.citysync.com**

MAPS & ATLASES

Lonely Planet's **City Maps** feature downtown and metropolitan maps, as well as transit routes and walking tours. The maps come complete with an index of streets, a listing of sights and a plastic coat for extra durability.

Road Atlases are an essential navigation tool for serious travellers. Cross-referenced with the guidebooks, they also feature distance and climate charts and a complete site index.

LONELY PLANET

ESSENTIALS

Read This First books help new travellers to hit the road with confidence. These invaluable predeparture guides give step-by-step advice on preparing for a trip, budgeting, arranging a visa, planning an itinerary and staying safe while still getting off the beaten track.

Healthy Travel pocket guides offer a regional rundown on disease hot spots and practical advice on predeparture health measures, staying well on the road and what to do in emergencies. The guides come with a user-friendly design and helpful diagrams and tables.

Lonely Planet's **Phrasebooks** cover the essential words and phrases travellers need when they're strangers in a strange land. They come in a pocket-sized format with colour tabs for quick reference, extensive vocabulary lists, easy-to-follow pronunciation keys and two-way dictionaries.

Miffed by blurry photos of the Taj Mahal? Tired of the classic 'top of the head cut off' shot? **Travel Photography: A Guide to Taking Better Pictures** will help you turn ordinary holiday snaps into striking images and give you the know-how to capture every scene, from frenetic festivals to peaceful beach sunrises.

Lonely Planet's **Travel Journal** is a lightweight but sturdy travel diary for jotting down all those on-the-road observations and significant travel moments. It comes with a handy time-zone wheel, a world map and useful travel information.

Lonely Planet's eKno is an all-in-one communication service developed especially for travellers. It offers low-cost international calls and free email and voicemail so that you can keep in touch while on the road. Check it out on **www.ekno.lonelyplanet.com**

FOOD & RESTAURANT GUIDES

Lonely Planet's **Out to Eat** guides recommend the brightest and best places to eat and drink in top international cities. These gourmet companions are arranged by neighbourhood, packed with dependable maps, garnished with scene-setting photos and served with quirky features.

For people who live to eat, drink and travel, **World Food** guides explore the culinary culture of each country. Entertaining and adventurous, each guide is packed with detail on staples and specialities, regional cuisine and local markets, as well as sumptuous recipes, comprehensive culinary dictionaries and lavish photos good enough to eat.

OUTDOOR GUIDES

For those who believe the best way to see the world is on foot, Lonely Planet's **Walking Guides** detail everything from family strolls to difficult treks, with 'when to go and how to do it' advice supplemented by reliable maps and essential travel information.

Cycling Guides map a destination's best bike tours, long and short, in day-by-day detail. They contain all the information a cyclist needs, including advice on bike maintenance, places to eat and stay, innovative maps with detailed cues to the rides, and elevation charts.

The **Watching Wildlife** series is perfect for travellers who want authoritative information but don't want to tote a heavy field guide. Packed with advice on where, when and how to view a region's wildlife, each title features photos of over 300 species and contains engaging comments on the local flora and fauna.

With underwater colour photos throughout, **Pisces Books** explore the world's best diving and snorkelling areas. Each book contains listings of diving services and dive resorts, detailed information on depth, visibility and difficulty of dives, and a roundup of the marine life you're likely to see through your mask.

LONELY PLANET

OFF THE ROAD

Journeys, the travel literature series written by renowned travel authors, capture the spirit of a place or illuminate a culture with a journalist's attention to detail and a novelist's flair for words. These are tales to soak up while you're actually on the road or dip into as an at-home armchair indulgence.

The range of lavishly illustrated **Pictorial** books is just the ticket for both travellers and dreamers. Off-beat tales and vivid photographs bring the adventure of travel to your doorstep long before the journey begins and long after it is over.

Lonely Planet **Videos** encourage the same independent, tough-minded approach as the guidebooks. Currently airing throughout the world, this award-winning series features innovative footage and an original soundtrack.

Yes, we know, work is tough, so do a little bit of deskside dreaming with the spiral-bound Lonely Planet **Diary** or a Lonely Planet **Wall Calendar**, filled with great photos from around the world.

TRAVELLERS NETWORK

Lonely Planet Online. Lonely Planet's award-winning Web site has insider information on hundreds of destinations, from Amsterdam to Zimbabwe, complete with interactive maps and relevant links. The site also offers the latest travel news, recent reports from travellers on the road, guidebook upgrades, a travel links site, an online book-buying option and a lively traveller's bulletin board. It can be viewed at **www.lonelyplanet.com** or AOL keyword: lp.

Planet Talk is a quarterly print newsletter, full of gossip, advice, anecdotes and author articles. It provides an antidote to the being-at-home blues and lets you plan and dream for the next trip. Contact the nearest Lonely Planet office for your free copy.

Comet, the free Lonely Planet newsletter, comes via email once a month. It's loaded with travel news, advice, dispatches from authors, travel competitions and letters from readers. To subscribe, click on the Comet subscription link on the front page of the Web site.

LONELY PLANET

Guides by Region

Lonely Planet is known worldwide for publishing practical, reliable and no-nonsense travel information in our guides and on our Web site. The Lonely Planet list covers just about every accessible part of the world. Currently there are 16 series: Travel guides, Shoestring guides, Condensed guides, Phrasebooks, Read This First, Healthy Travel, Walking guides, Cycling guides, Watching Wildlife guides, Pisces Diving & Snorkeling guides, City Maps, Road Atlases, Out to Eat, World Food, Journeys travel literature and Pictorials.

AFRICA Africa on a shoestring • Cairo • Cairo City Map • Cape Town • Cape Town City Map • East Africa • Egypt • Egyptian Arabic phrasebook • Ethiopia, Eritrea & Djibouti • Ethiopian Amharic phrasebook • The Gambia & Senegal • Healthy Travel Africa • Kenya • Malawi • Morocco • Moroccan Arabic phrasebook • Mozambique • Read This First: Africa • South Africa, Lesotho & Swaziland • Southern Africa • Southern Africa Road Atlas • Swahili phrasebook • Tanzania, Zanzibar & Pemba • Trekking in East Africa • Tunisia • Watching Wildlife East Africa • Watching Wildlife Southern Africa • West Africa • World Food Morocco • Zimbabwe, Botswana & Namibia
Travel Literature: Mali Blues: Traveling to an African Beat • The Rainbird: A Central African Journey • Songs to an African Sunset: A Zimbabwean Story

AUSTRALIA & THE PACIFIC Auckland • Australia • Australian phrasebook • Australia Road Atlas • Cycling Australia • Cycling New Zealand • Fiji • Fijian phrasebook • Healthy Travel Australia, NZ & the Pacific • Islands of Australia's Great Barrier Reef • Melbourne • Melbourne City Map • Micronesia • New Caledonia • New South Wales • New Zealand • Northern Territory • Outback Australia • Out to Eat – Melbourne • Out to Eat – Sydney • Papua New Guinea • Pidgin phrasebook • Queensland • Rarotonga & the Cook Islands • Samoa • Solomon Islands • South Australia • South Pacific • South Pacific phrasebook • Sydney • Sydney City Map • Sydney Condensed • Tahiti & French Polynesia • Tasmania • Tonga • Tramping in New Zealand • Vanuatu • Victoria • Walking in Australia • Watching Wildlife Australia • Western Australia
Travel Literature: Islands in the Clouds: Travels in the Highlands of New Guinea • Kiwi Tracks: A New Zealand Journey • Sean & David's Long Drive

CENTRAL AMERICA & THE CARIBBEAN Bahamas, Turks & Caicos • Baja California • Belize, Guatemala & Yucatán • Bermuda • Central America on a shoestring • Costa Rica • Costa Rica Spanish phrasebook • Cuba • Dominican Republic & Haiti • Eastern Caribbean • Guatemala • Havana • Healthy Travel Central & South America • Jamaica • Mexico • Mexico City • Panama • Puerto Rico • Read This First: Central & South America • World Food Mexico • Yucatán
Travel Literature: Green Dreams: Travels in Central America

EUROPE Amsterdam • Amsterdam City Map • Amsterdam Condensed • Andalucía • Austria • Baltic States phrasebook • Barcelona • Barcelona City Map • Belgium & Luxembourg • Berlin • Berlin City Map • Britain • British phrasebook • Brussels, Bruges & Antwerp • Brussels City Map • Budapest • Budapest City Map • Canary Islands • Central Europe • Central Europe phrasebook • Copenhagen • Corfu & the Ionians • Corsica • Crete • Crete Condensed • Croatia • Cycling Britain • Cycling France • Cyprus • Czech & Slovak Republics • Denmark • Dublin • Dublin City Map • Eastern Europe • Eastern Europe phrasebook • Edinburgh • England • Estonia, Latvia & Lithuania • Europe on a shoestring • Europe phrasebook • Finland • Florence • France • Frankfurt Condensed • French phrasebook • Georgia, Armenia & Azerbaijan • Germany • German phrasebook • Greece • Greek Islands • Greek phrasebook • Hungary • Iceland, Greenland & the Faroe Islands • Ireland • Italian phrasebook • Italy • Krakow • Lisbon • The Loire • London • London City Map • London Condensed • Madrid • Malta • Mediterranean Europe • Mediterranean Europe phrasebook • Moscow • Munich • Netherlands • Normandy • Norway • Out to Eat – London • Out to Eat – Paris • Paris • Paris City Map • Paris Condensed • Poland • Polish phrasebook • Portugal • Portuguese phrasebook • Prague • Prague City Map • Provence & the Côte d'Azur • Read This First: Europe • Rhodes & the Dodecanese • Romania & Moldova • Rome • Rome City Map • Russia, Ukraine & Belarus • Russian phrasebook • Scandinavian & Baltic Europe • Scandinavian phrasebook • Scotland • Sicily • Slovenia • South-West France • Spain • Spanish phrasebook • St Petersburg • St Petersburg City Map • Sweden • Switzerland • Tuscany • Ukrainian phrasebook • Venice • Vienna • Walking in Britain • Walking in France • Walking in Ireland • Walking in Italy • Walking in Spain • Walking in Switzerland • Western Europe • World Food France • World Food Ireland • World Food Italy • World Food Spain
Travel Literature: After Yugoslavia • Love and War in the Apennines • The Olive Grove: Travels in Greece • On the Shores of the Mediterranean • Round Ireland in Low Gear • A Small Place in Italy

LONELY PLANET

Mail Order

Lonely Planet products are distributed worldwide. They are also available by mail order from Lonely Planet, so if you have difficulty finding a title please write to us. North and South American residents should write to 150 Linden St, Oakland, CA 94607, USA; European and African residents should write to 10a Spring Place, London NW5 3BH, UK; and residents of other countries to Locked Bag 1, Footscray, Victoria 3011, Australia.

INDIAN SUBCONTINENT & THE INDIAN OCEAN Bangladesh • Bengali phrasebook • Bhutan • Delhi • Goa • Healthy Travel Asia & India • Hindi & Urdu phrasebook • India • Indian Himalaya • Karakoram Highway • Kerala • Madagascar • Maldives • Mauritius, Réunion & Seychelles • Mumbai (Bombay) • Nepal • Nepali phrasebook • Pakistan • Rajasthan • Read This First: Asia & India • South India • Sri Lanka • Sri Lanka phrasebook • Tibet • Tibetan phrasebook • Trekking in the Indian Himalaya • Trekking in the Karakoram & Hindukush • Trekking in the Nepal Himalaya
Travel Literature: The Age of Kali: Indian Travels and Encounters • Hello Goodnight: A Life of Goa • In Rajasthan • Maverick in Madagascar • A Season in Heaven: True Tales from the Road to Kathmandu • Shopping for Buddhas • A Short Walk in the Hindu Kush • Slowly Down the Ganges

MIDDLE EAST & CENTRAL ASIA Bahrain, Kuwait & Qatar • Central Asia • Central Asia phrasebook • Dubai • Farsi (Persian) phrasebook • Hebrew phrasebook • Iran • Israel & the Palestinian Territories • Istanbul • Istanbul City Map • Istanbul to Cairo • Istanbul to Kathmandu • Jerusalem • Jerusalem City Map • Jordan • Lebanon • Middle East • Oman & the United Arab Emirates • Syria • Turkey • Turkish phrasebook • World Food Turkey • Yemen
Travel Literature: Black on Black: Iran Revisited • The Gates of Damascus • Kingdom of the Film Stars: Journey into Jordan

NORTH AMERICA Alaska • Boston • Boston City Map • Boston Condensed • British Columbia • California & Nevada • California Condensed • Canada • Chicago • Chicago City Map • Florida • Great Lakes • Hawaii • Hiking in Alaska • Hiking in the USA • Las Vegas • Los Angeles • Los Angeles City Map • Louisiana & the Deep South • Miami • Miami City Map • Montreal • New England • New Orleans • New York City • New York City City Map • New York City Condensed • New York, New Jersey & Pennsylvania • Oahu • Out to Eat – San Francisco • Pacific Northwest • Rocky Mountains • San Francisco • San Francisco City Map • Seattle • Southwest • Texas • Toronto • USA • USA phrasebook • Vancouver • Virginia & the Capital Region • Washington, DC • Washington, DC City Map • World Food New Orleans
Travel Literature: Caught Inside: A Surfer's Year on the California Coast • Drive Thru America

NORTH-EAST ASIA Beijing • Beijing City Map • Cantonese phrasebook • China • Hiking in Japan • Hong Kong • Hong Kong City Map • Hong Kong Condensed • Hong Kong, Macau & Guangzhou • Japan • Japanese phrasebook • Korea • Korean phrasebook • Kyoto • Mandarin phrasebook • Mongolia • Mongolian phrasebook • Seoul • Shanghai • South-West China • Taiwan • Tokyo • World Food Hong Kong
Travel Literature: In Xanadu: A Quest • Lost Japan

SOUTH AMERICA Argentina, Uruguay & Paraguay • Bolivia • Brazil • Brazilian phrasebook • Buenos Aires • Chile & Easter Island • Colombia • Ecuador & the Galapagos Islands • Healthy Travel Central & South America • Latin American Spanish phrasebook • Peru • Quechua phrasebook • Read This First: Central & South America • Rio de Janeiro • Rio de Janeiro City Map • Santiago de Chile • South America on a shoestring • Trekking in the Patagonian Andes • Venezuela
Travel Literature: Full Circle: A South American Journey

SOUTH-EAST ASIA Bali & Lombok • Bangkok • Bangkok City Map • Burmese phrasebook • Cambodia • Hanoi • Healthy Travel Asia & India • Hill Tribes phrasebook • Ho Chi Minh City • Indonesia • Indonesian phrasebook • Indonesia's Eastern Islands • Java • Lao phrasebook • Laos • Malay phrasebook • Malaysia, Singapore & Brunei • Myanmar (Burma) • Philippines • Pilipino (Tagalog) phrasebook • Read This First: Asia & India • Singapore • Singapore City Map • South-East Asia on a shoestring • South-East Asia phrasebook • Thailand • Thailand's Islands & Beaches • Thailand, Vietnam, Laos & Cambodia Road Atlas • Thai phrasebook • Vietnam • Vietnamese phrasebook • World Food Thailand • World Food Vietnam

ALSO AVAILABLE: Antarctica • The Arctic • The Blue Man: Tales of Travel, Love and Coffee • Brief Encounters: Stories of Love, Sex & Travel • Chasing Rickshaws • The Last Grain Race • Lonely Planet ... On the Edge: Adventurous Escapades from Around the World • Lonely Planet Unpacked • Not the Only Planet: Science Fiction Travel Stories • Sacred India • Travel Photography: A Guide to Taking Better Pictures • Travel with Children

Index

Text

Note that the Danish letters æ, ø and å fall at the end of the alphabet.

Places to Stay

Places to Eat

Boxed Text

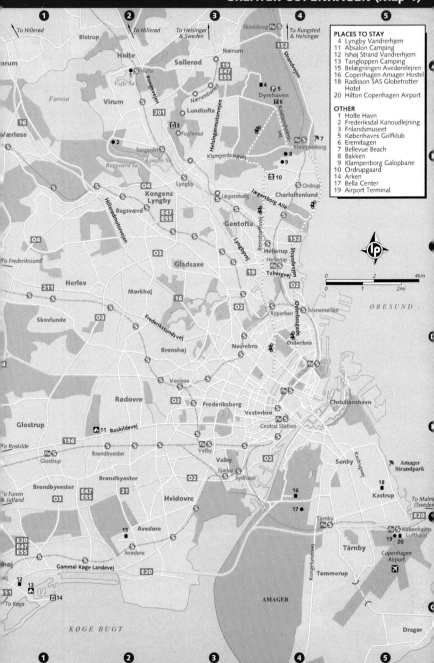

GREATER COPENHAGEN (Map 1)

PLACES TO STAY
4 Lyngby Vandrerhjem
11 Absalon Camping
12 Ishøj Strand Vandrerhjem
13 Tangloppen Camping
15 Belægningen Avedørelejren
16 Copenhagen Amager Hostel
18 Radisson SAS Globetrotter
   Hotel
20 Hilton Copenhagen Airport

OTHER
1 Holte Havn
2 Frederiksdal Kanoudlejning
3 Frilandsmuseet
5 Københavns Golfklub
6 Eremitagen
7 Bellevue Beach
8 Bakken
9 Klampenborg Galopbane
10 Ordrupgaard
14 Arken
17 Bella Center
19 Airport Terminal

Gentofte

Gentofte

MAP 3

Charlottenlund

Charlottenlund

Charlottenlund
Slotspark

152

Bernstorffsvej

Bernstorffsvej

Kildebakke

Vangede

Helsingørmotorvejen

Strandvejen

Vangedevej

Søborg Hovedgade

Hellerup

Dyssegård

Dyssegård

Gladsaxe

Gladsaxevej

Hellerup

152

Ø R E S U N D

O2

Tuborgvej

O2

Emdrup

O2

19

MAP 5

Ryparken

Svanemøllen

MAP 4

Hareskovvej

Bispebjerg
Kirkegård

Tuborgvej

Østerbro

O2

16

Utterslev

Tomsgårdsvej

Frederiksborgvej

Jagtvej

Østerbrogade

211

Bispebjerg

Tagensvej

Nørre Allé

Nordhavn

Frederikssundsvej

Bellahøj

Hulgårdsvej

Borups Allé

Nørrebro

Fælledparken

Kalkbrænderihavnsgade

Bellahøjvej

Nørrebro

Blegdamsvej

O2

Fuglebakken

Nordre Fasanvej

Jagtvej

Nørrebrogade

Assistens
Kirkegård

Østerport

Yderhavnen

Grøndal

Østre
Anlæg

O2

MAP 6

Godthåbsvej

Ågade

MAP 7

Botanisk
Have

Kongens
Have

Nørreport

STRØGET & LATIN QUARTER (Map 8)

Peter
Bangsvej

Falkoner Allé

Frederiksberg

Frederiksberg Have

Vesterport

SLOTSHOLMEN

Roskildevej

Søndre Fasanvej

Pile Allé

Vesterbrogade

Tivoli

Inderhavnen

Christianshavn

Torvegade

Langgade

Søndermarken

Valby

Vesterbro

Central
Station

O2

Kalvebod Brygge

Amagerbrogade

Valby

Enghave

Enghavevej

Dybbølsbro

Amagerfælledvej

Vigerslev Allé